David Hammond, 1928–2008

Reproduction of a page from Edward Bunting's *A General Collection of Ancient Irish Music* (London, 1796). In the bicentenary year of that famous publication, David Hammond's Flying Fox Films funded a replica of the original to be printed in a joint venture with the Linenhall Library, Belfast, and the National Library of Ireland. The page reproduced here contains the score of the tune *The Parting of Friends*. The Preface to Bunting's volume states that '*Scarfuint na G*[c]*ompanach* or the *Parting of Friends*, is considered as very ancient. It is often played by harpers when the audience are about to separate...'

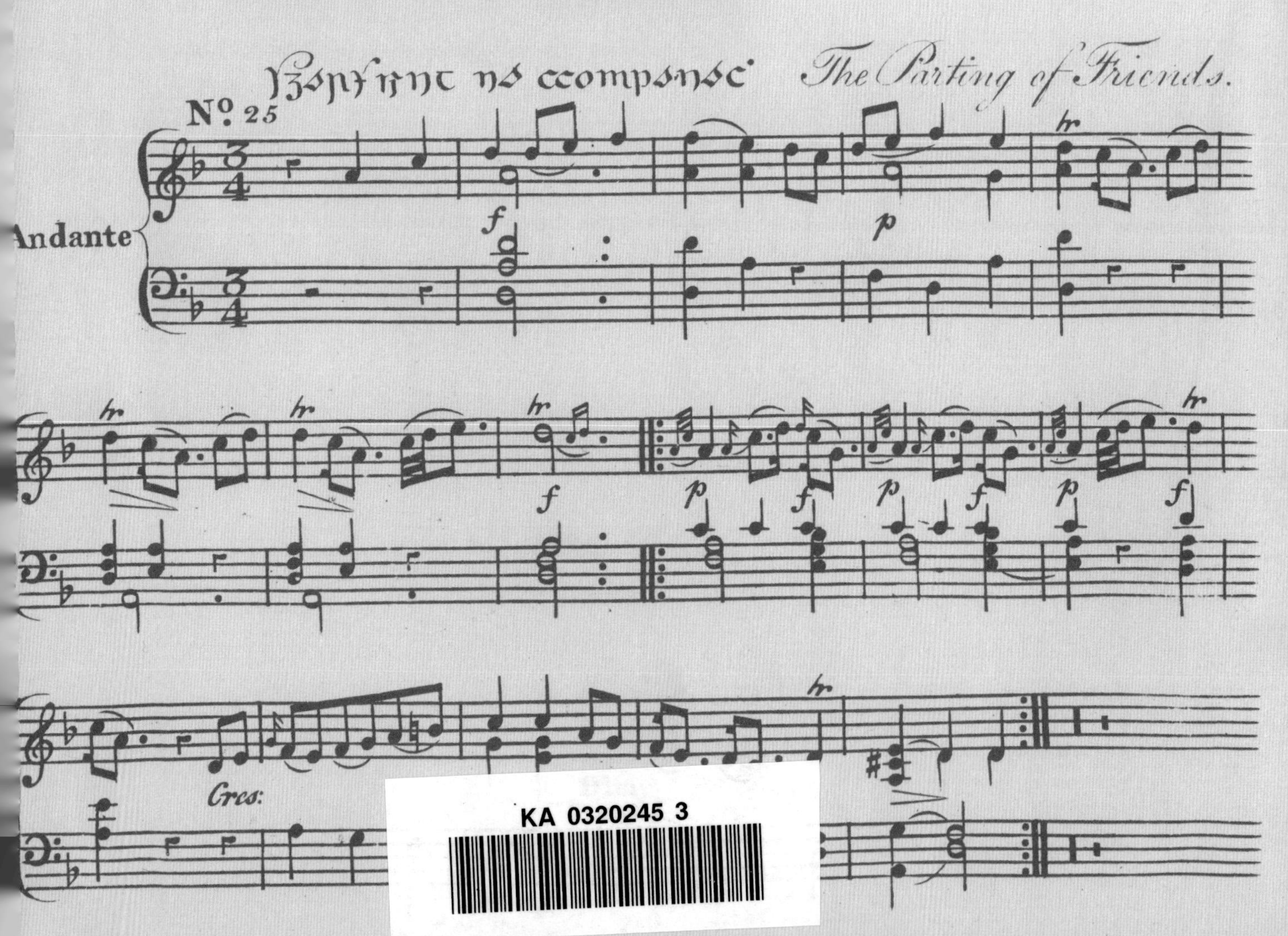

Editors
Seamus Deane
Breandán Mac Suibhne
Ciarán Deane

Assistant to the Editors
Sean Mannion

Copy
Hilary Bell

Design
Red Dog Design Consultants
www.reddog.ie

Fonts
Headlines — Gill Sans 24/28
Body Copy Essays/Reviews — Sabon 9/12

Paper Stock
McNaughton's Challenger Offset

Field Day Review is published annually by Field Day Publications in association with the Keough-Naughton Institute for Irish Studies at the University of Notre Dame.

ISSN 1649-6507
ISBN 978-0-946755-45-5

Field Day Review
Keough-Naughton Institute for Irish Studies
86 St. Stephen's Green
Dublin 2
Ireland

fieldday@nd.edu

www.fielddaybooks.com

FIELD DAY REVIEW
2009

ESSAYS

REVIEWS

ESSAYS

Brian Friel's *Translations*: The Origins of a Cultural Experiment

Ciarán Deane

[To salute Brian Friel on his 80th birthday and to acknowledge the 30th anniversary of his play *Translations*, we are publishing two essays on the play, of which this is the first. The second, by Kevin Whelan, will appear in *Field Day Review* 6.]

'One must not build on the good old things, but on the bad new ones.'

Bertolt Brecht[1]

The original staging of Brian Friel's play *Translations* marked a transitional moment in twentieth-century Irish cultural life, though the nature, extent and value of that transition have been hotly debated. The text of the play deals with concepts of cross-cultural communication, cultural origins and cultural shifts, but it was the first performance — at the Guildhall, Derry, 23 September 1980 — that gave particular intensity to the play's governing concepts and declared the specific public role of art.

1 Brecht, quoted in J. Willett, *Brecht in Context: Comparative Approaches* (London, 1984), 197.

The Field Day Archive, which was donated to the National Library of Ireland in 2008, is both extensive and rich in new information. Some of the earliest documents in the archive are concerned with the creation of the Field Day Theatre Company and with its foundational play *Translations*. They include previously unpublished correspondence between Brian Friel and Stephen Rea (specifically from Friel to Rea), dating to the late 1970s and early 1980s, in which the idea of Field Day is first mooted and then developed. They also include the minutes of the meetings of the board of directors. The archive collates both unexamined documents and other valuable sources of information that are available elsewhere, but in a dispersed fashion, such as press cuttings on individual plays and publications, or the programme notes for each theatrical production. Rea has few written records in this archive, or indeed in the Friel Papers already held in the National Library of Ireland; he chooses instead to express himself largely through interview. However, his opinions are also alluded to through the Friel correspondence. These new sources, and additional correspondence between Friel and Seamus Deane[2] (some of which is not in the archive), one of Field Day's founding directors, whom Friel and Rea invited in 1981 to expand the activities of the company, shed new light on the context out of which *Translations* and the Field Day Theatre Company arose.

Antecedents

> *Translations* is set in a hedge-school in Ballybeg, County Donegal. The year is 1833. The British army is engaged in mapping the whole of Ireland, a process which involves the renaming of every place name in the country. It is a time of great upheaval for the people of Ballybeg; their hedge-school is to be replaced by one of the new national schools; there is a recurring potato blight; they have acquired a new language (English); and because their townland is being renamed, everything that was familiar is becoming strange.[3]

Translations is set at a moment of transition, when the Irish-speaking society of Ballybeg is about to be mapped into a different culture. It continues Friel's long preoccupation with the idea of language as a medium that actively shapes rather than passively records human experience; with how the power of language to shape things is rooted in the process of naming, and how naming is an intrinsic part of private and public self-definition. The implications of this also preoccupied Field Day after it expanded its activities into publishing and criticism. *Translations* was not merely the chronological starting point of Field Day's quest for cultural redefinition in Ireland; it also contained within it the core message of all of the group's subsequent creative endeavours, a message derived from a postcolonial interpretation of Irish history. As Deane declared:

> Field Day's analysis of the [northern] situation derives from the conviction that it is, above all, a colonial one ... [A preoccupation with naming is evident] in the first three pamphlets by Tom Paulin, Seamus Heaney, and myself and evident too in the plays by Brian Friel, Thomas Kilroy, and Tom Paulin ... The naming or renaming of a place, the naming or renaming of a race, a region, a person, is, like all acts of primordial nomination, an act of possession. *The Field Day Anthology* is also an exercise in renaming, the resituation of many texts, well known and scarcely known, in a renovated landscape or context.[4]

Perhaps the first ever self-definition of Field Day to a person outside the organization was delivered by Friel in a letter to Paddy Kilroy, entrepreneur and brother of playwright and later Field Day director Tom Kilroy. In this previously unpublished

2 In the Field Day Archive (hereafter FDA), it is Friel's correspondence with Deane and Rea that is the most revealing. Correspondence with other directors is thinner in quantity and has less to impart.

3 Brian Friel, 'Extracts from a Sporadic Diary', in *Brian Friel: Essays, Diaries, Interviews: 1964–1999*, ed. Christopher Murray (London, 1999), 73.

4 Seamus Deane, 'Introduction', in Terry Eagleton, Fredric Jameson and Edward Said, *Nationalism, Colonialism and Literature*, ed. Seamus Deane (Minneapolis, 1990), 6, 17–18.

letter, written about ten weeks after the first performance of *Translations*, Friel is seeking advice on raising funds for Field Day, and he hesitantly explains Field Day's 'principles' in terms that indicate that he was still primarily concerned with the impact of theatre alone on Irish cultural and political life. These principles reveal his intention to challenge the metropolitan representation of Ireland past and present:

> December 2, 1980
>
> Translations box office returns brought in almost £40,000. The success of the whole venture far exceeded our expectations.
>
> Our next venture, THREE SISTERS, in a new translation by me, is planned for next autumn. Again we will rehearse in Derry and open there. And again our tour will be similar to our first.
>
> At this stage we are hesitant to formulate the 'principles' behind the founding of Field Day. (Of course we hope to do plays of excellence and to do them excellently — but isn't that the stated aim of every theatre company?) Stephen and I are both from the North; that was the first and obvious bond. Another was the shared wish to work together first in the North and then to take our wares on tour around the smaller towns of all Ireland. But — and this is the area I'd prefer not to survey with precision at this stage — we are motivated by deeper interests and concerns which I will touch on only very briefly: a belief that theatre in Ireland can originate outside the metropolis; the sounding of an Irish dramatic voice that is not pitched to be heard outside of this island (if we are overheard — that is fine — in fact we're bringing TRANSLATIONS to Hampstead early next year), the forging of a theatre company that recognises the entire island as its terrain; a sense that in these rapidly changing times in this country the theatre is a unique platform for the exploration of these changes. This list is in no order of priority, nor is it exhaustive. But I hope it gives you some idea of our motivation.[5]

After *Translations*, Field Day quickly expanded beyond its original theatrical ambitions. Within weeks of the play's premiere in Derry, Friel was looking to take more people and ideas on board, and by 1982, the company's three-pronged approach to the cultural redefinition of Ireland had been largely established, comprising theatre, the Field Day pamphlets, and *The Field Day Anthology*.

Translations expressed ideas that emerged from a cultural debate that had been gathering force in the 1970s, and its precursors can be detected in the pages of the journals *Atlantis*, edited by Deane, Derek Mahon and others, and the *Crane Bag*, edited by Richard Kearney and Mark Patrick Hederman. What Field Day shared with these journals was a desire to reinvigorate Irish culture by promoting Irish literary talent and placing it in a new and wider context. The editorial of the first issue of *Atlantis*, published in 1970, heralded Field Day's interventionist stance, declaring a direct link between literature and politics in Ireland:

> In any culture, discussion, informed commentary, a climate of interest, is a necessary hypothesis. It is one to which Ireland pays lip service ... We claim that we will not be, of all things, parochial — nor glossy and cosmopolitan, nor academic — nor bound to any ideological masts. ... The obsessive tedium of so much Irish writing is a reflection on the society which engenders it. We must, therefore, examine that society, and the larger human society of which it forms a minute part, in an attentive and critical spirit. To this extent, *Atlantis* will be a political magazine.[6]

5 FDA: G/D/Friel/Rea/4. Friel provided Rea with a copy of this letter. All FDA citations use the reference system devised by the archivist Cormac Ó Duibhne, who provided the archive to the National Library in summer 2008.

6 *Atlantis*, 1 (March 1970), 5.

Ann Hasson as Sarah and Mick Lally as Manus, *Translations* reheasal, Guildhall, Derry, 1980. Photo: Rod Tuach, © Field Day.

The *Crane Bag*, first published in 1977, developed the idea of the 'fifth province',[7] a province of the mind, which Field Day famously appropriated. This 'unactualized space' was an imaginary meeting place removed from the other four provinces, where differing attitudes to culture and politics could be explored; it was more akin to a 'disposition' than a real position. Like *Atlantis*, the *Crane Bag* 'revealed a new proliferation of ideas based on modern European thought as much as on traditional sources of intellectual life in Ireland'.[8] Some of the 'deeper interests and

7 'Editorial/Endudermis', *Crane Bag*, 1, 1 (Spring 1977), 4. 'Modern Ireland is made up of four provinces. And yet, the Irish word for province is cóiced, which means a "fifth" ... there is disagreement about the identity of the fifth. There are two traditions ... both divide Ireland into four quarters and a "middle", even though they disagree about the location of the middle or "fifth" province ... it was a non-political centre.'

8 R. Welch, ed., *The Oxford Companion to Irish Literature* (Oxford, 1996), 119.

concerns' of Field Day with which Friel and Rea were struggling in December 1980 (as expressed in Friel's letter to Paddy Kilroy, quoted above) were being addressed at a much earlier stage in conversation and in correspondence between Friel, Tom Kilroy, Heaney and Deane, all of whom would later come to join the Field Day board of directors.[9] Field Day gravitated towards the postcolonial critique that was emerging in the 1970s and 1980s, to which it would become a significant contributor in its own right. However, it was also concerned not to tie itself to any 'ideological mast' in proposing solutions. Dismantling stereotypes through art and analysis was its key objective. At the height of Field Day's activities in 1985, its directors stated that they 'could and should contribute to the solution of the present crisis by producing analyses of the established opinions, myths and stereotypes which had become both a symptom and a cause of the current situation',[10] but this was merely redeclaring what they had come to conclude at least a decade earlier. Dismantling stereotypes requires deconstructing the language that creates them. Field Day's task, therefore, was concerned with applying the 'postmodern turn' to its analysis of Irish cultural life, though not in a self-consciously postmodern way. This involved bringing new international and comparative approaches to the stifling and seemingly deadlocked identity conflict in Ireland. On this reading, according to Kearney,

> the postmodern critique of power implies the replacement of absolute sovereignty — theocracy, monarchy, bureaucracy — with 'republican principles' of freedom. ... [It is] a political or ethical community ... where identity is part of a permanent process of narrative retelling, where each citizen is in a 'state of dependency on others'. In such a postmodern republic, the principle of interdependency is seen as a virtue rather than a vice; it serves, in fact, as reminder that every citizen's story is related to every other's. ... The postmodern turn seeks to deconstruct the Official story (which presents itself as official history) into the open plurality of stories that make it up. Modern imperialism and modern nationalism are two sides of the Official story. Genuine internationalism (working at a global level) and critical regionalism (working at a local level) represent the two sides of a postmodern alternative.[11]

Translations introduced the concept of 'narrative retelling' to the mainstream of Irish culture. It concludes with Hugh, the hedge-school master, delivering this key message: 'It is not the literal past, the "facts" of history, that shape us, but images of the past embodied in language ... we must never cease renewing those images; because once we do, we fossilize.'[12] This call for new forms of self-definition is one that Friel made repeatedly and publicly after the play successfully premiered. For example, in a press interview in December 1980, Friel repeats the idea of 'talking to ourselves', which he first made in private correspondence with Paddy Kilroy:

> However, I think that for the first time ... that there is some kind of confidence, some kind of coming together of Irish dramatists who are not concerned with this, who have no interest in the English stage. We are talking to ourselves as we must, and if we are overheard in America, or England, so much better.[13]

What is significant about this interview by Friel, and those he gave subsequently, is that, after *Translations*, the previously reticent playwright is publicly voicing his internal thoughts. Friel's shift is from private exploration to direct public response to the cultural and political crises of late 1970s Ireland, and to the conflict in Northern Ireland in particular. It is his announcement of the fact that the Field Day cultural experiment had formally begun.

9 Deane and Heaney also guest-edited the *Crane Bag*.
10 Richard Kearney, 'Preface' in *Ireland's Field Day* (London, 1985), vii.
11 Richard Kearney, *Postnationalist Ireland: Politics, Culture, Philosophy* (London, 1997), 63. Kearney quotes J. F. Lyotard, *Peregrinations* (New York, 1988), 39.
12 Brian Friel, *Selected Plays*, introduced by Seamus Deane (London, 1984), 445. Hereafter *SP*.
13 'Talking to Ourselves', interview with Paddy Agnew, *Magill* (December 1980), in C. Murray (1999), 60.

The *informal* beginnings of the experiment have earlier roots. A number of letters from Friel to Deane indicate that there already existed a cross-pollination of ideas between Field Day members long before the company was formally inaugurated. In the earliest of these available, dated 13 October 1974, some five years before the completion of *Translations,* and seven years before the formation of the extended Field Day board, we can read that Friel was already sending draft manuscripts to Heaney and Deane for comment and analysis.

> October 13, 1974
>
> Thank you for your report on *Volunteers*: I'm *most* grateful to you for the very detailed & very painstaking analysis. There are very few responses to the play that are important to me & this is one of them. The only other person I've shown the script to is Seamus H. — I mailed a Ms off to him 3 days ago.[14]

In the same letter, Friel reveals that the germ of the Field Day idea already existed at this early stage:

> Seamus [Heaney] told me that you and he and Kilroy had a good night together and that there was some talk of us all getting together — a commune of some sort (?). I like the idea even though I'm not too sure what it means. But it's high time the articles of constitution of literature in this country were redefined, and I think we could forge them. We have each an affinity & an affection & a respect that would make a working party possible.

Redefining 'the articles of constitution' of Irish literature would be the goal that Field Day set itself years later.[15] In October 1974, Friel is stating his belief that cultural change should take place in Ireland ahead of constitutional change, if any form of settlement is to be reached. It was an idea he publicly reiterated six years later in an interview with *In Dublin* magazine: '[Field Day activity] should lead to a cultural state, not a political state. And I think that out of that cultural state, a possibility of a political state follows. That is always the sequence.'[16] In a follow-up letter to Deane, again on the topic of *Volunteers*, we read that long before Field Day was established, Friel had identified some of those whom he regarded to be up to the job of rereading and rewriting Ireland, and that the proposed 'commune' was now scheduled to take place at the home of Tom Kilroy in Portumna, County Galway. This letter is worth quoting at length:

> November 11, 1974
>
> Part 1* was lucid and articulate and honest and generous and *very* welcome and ultimately disturbing which makes it all the more valuable ...
>
> The whole question of my failure once more to dramatize the moment when repudiation stops and the man turns to see or glimpse the source of it ...
>
> I'm as sick of the naturalistic style as I'm sure you are — and I'm talking primarily about language here. But since my trade is theatre, when I talk about language I mean language as *one* of the elements of drama. Maybe this is one of the issues we could examine at the Portumna Think-in, although it's a problem that Irish poets have solved more successfully than Irish dramatists. The only Irish dramatist who faced the difficulty and successfully solved it was Synge ...
>
> It's a problem I haven't solved. And I function with growing impatience in it ... because in theatre it is enormously difficult for naturalistic language to be at ease with its metaphors — one of your strictures. And the dilemma is this. The use of everyday and recognizable melodies and harmonies effects a quick and direct relationship between audience and

14 Letter from Friel to Deane, dated 13 October 1974. Not part of the FDA. Reproduced with permission.

15 Close to ten years later, Deane announced it to be Field Day's intention in his Field Day pamphlet *Heroic Styles: The Tradition of an Idea*: '[E]verything, including our politics and our literature, has to be rewritten — i.e. re-read.' *Heroic Styles: The Tradition of an Idea*, in Deane, ed., *Ireland's Field Day*, 58.

16 FDA: PC/1982/3. 'The Man from God Knows Where', interview with Fintan O'Toole, *In Dublin*, 28 October 1982, 23.

17 Letter from Friel to Deane, dated 11 November 1974. Not part of FDA. Reproduced with permission. *Of Seamus Deane's response to the script of *Volunteers*. **Friel has written 'freudian?' in the margin.
18 Friel, 'Sporadic Diary', 1 June 1979, in Murray, 75.
19 FDA: PC/1982/3. 'The Man from God Knows Where', interview with F. O'Toole, *In Dublin*, 28 October 1982, 23.
20 'Talking to Ourselves', interview with Paddy Agnew in *Magill*, December 1980, in Murray, 85–86.

> stage — that's an attraction and can be valuable. But it's as soon as you establish that relationship — and it's made precisely because the tunes are familiar — that an almost instant communion becomes a trap. Instant recognition — partial deafness. And you panic: you're being taken for what you're not. There are now two potions [*sic*]** open to you: you can introduce discords or at least unfamiliar harmonies which will result in a listening afresh audience but which at the same time will screw up your carefully composed and carefully planted statement-themes. Or you become strident and obvious — as you suggest I do. Maybe you're right. Trust in the metaphor of the play, you say. Of course I do. But if I lose faith I'm trying to explain why I do — when I listen to those 'real' characters speaking a 'naturalistic' language who are my sustenance.[17]

In *Translations*, Friel's language had become more 'strident and obvious' than in previous plays, but he had reservations about the play being read as polemical. During the writing of the play, he recorded in his 'Sporadic Diary' his fear of being taken for what he was not: 'The play has to do with language and only language. And if it becomes overwhelmed by that political element, it is lost.'[18] Later, in a press interview, speaking as a Field Day director, Friel put a public context to these internal struggles with language, as dealt with in *Translations* (and his subsequent Field Day plays, *Three Sisters* and *The Communication Cord*); we can also read here that he is publicly advocating the idea of language as an agent of change:

> I think that is how the political problem of this island is going to be solved. It's going to be solved by language in some kind of way. Not only the language of negotiations across the table. It's going to be solved by the recognition of what language means for us on this island. ... Because we are in fact talking about accommodation or marrying of two cultures here, which are ostensibly speaking the same language but which in fact aren't.[19]

Friel's letter to Deane (11 November 1974) reveals his belief that J. M. Synge was the only Irish dramatist who 'faced the [language] difficulty and successfully solved it'. It is a notion to which he refers a number of times. In another interview, he made a direct connection between *Translations* and Synge, and by extension, implied that Field Day was taking on some of the unfinished business of the Irish Literary Theatre:

> If I can quote from the play, 'We must learn where we live. We must make them [those new names] our own. We must make them our new home.' That is, we must make these English language words distinctive and unique to us. My first concern is with theatre and we certainly have not done this with theatre in Ireland. The only person who did so in this country was Synge ... Nobody since him has pursued this course with any persistence or distinction ... apart from Synge, all our dramatists have pitched their voices for English acceptance and recognition.[20]

Friel's fear was that he would not match Synge's achievement and that his play would be read as political rhetoric. So strong was this fear that his third Field Day play, *The Communication Cord*, would be written as an antidote to the nationalist pieties that others read in *Translations*. Friel's colleagues Deane and Rea argued, however, that his achievement with the earlier play *was* comparable to the work of Yeats and Synge, Deane observing that 'no Irish writer since the early days of this century has so sternly and courageously asserted the role of art in the public world without either yielding to that world's pressures or retreating into art's narcissistic alternatives'.[21] More recently, in a radio interview to mark the twenty-fifth anniversary of *Translations*, Rea professed it to be

> the greatest Irish play since *Playboy of the Western World*. It's really exquisite; it's kind of perfect. It's very humorous, but it also allows people to recall that there is the possibility of a Big Instinct. It was about possibility, and a lot of that possibility has been met.[22]

Such endorsements were clearly important to Friel. During the 1970s, Heaney, Deane, and Tom Kilroy acted as his private critical audience. In the following letter to Deane, he explains what he gains from the critical responses of each of them:

> May 5 [1979]
>
> I don't know what motivates Tom K. or Seamus H. when they show you something they've done. I value Tom's responses because his dramatic instincts and his theatre responses are true and sharp and pertinent. He leaves me behind when he demands what he calls ultimate risks because I think he's converting his peculiar necessity into a virtue and proclaiming a creed he doesn't finally subscribe to; but maybe that's only a question of definition. In the case of Seamus I look for an instinctive response. And because his own instincts about himself are so consciously cultivated and so perfectly harmonised with his surroundings and his profession, I suppose he might be wise for me too. Maybe it's a bit like the bookies touching Phil McLaughlin's* coat on his way home from that famous English treble.
>
> I am always more nervous when I lay something before you because 1. you will see beyond and not be impressed by my theatre-craft competence, as Tom sometimes is, because it is after all only an acquired efficiency and because 2. you don't respond automatically, as I suspect S did to *Volunteers*, to work which trespasses on territory you've already taken an option on. Of the 4 of us, you are the best touch-stone. As a writer you understand the inevitability of failure between aspiration and execution — and that gives you tolerance. And as a critic you have the best informed and most sophisticated equipment, even allowing for political preferences that must insist on its own perfections.
>
> ... I live with a perpetual and persistent sense of failure ... for 20 years I have failed in varying degrees to integrate whatever my emotional experience into a communicable vehicle. And what you have done for me in the past has been to identify with some precision those areas of failure; so that even now, even weighted by a back-log of very flawed work, I may be able to function more truly, with a glimmer of confidence.[23]

Later, as *Aristocrats* was being prepared for the Abbey, Friel sent Tom Kilroy and Deane manuscripts for critical analysis. From a letter accompanying the manuscript sent to Deane, we learn that Friel was planning to make specific changes at Kilroy's prompting:

> September 17 [1978]
>
> This is the play I mentioned to you the other night — due to open at the Abbey next March. The only casting done so far: Casimir will be played by John Kavanagh, Eamon by Stephen Rea.
>
> And, as I told you, Tom K.'s response was very valuable; and because of some things he said about Act III I'm going to have another look at it, primarily to correct the feeling that I've attempted to tie things up in the last few pages (T.K.'s feeling). Anyhow, I'll be anxious to hear what you have to say.[24]

In his earlier letter to Deane of 5 May 1975, Friel had admitted his 'persistent sense of failure'. An understanding of the connection between public and private failure emerges

21 Deane, 'Introduction', *SP*, 22.

22 Interview with Rea, *Arts Extra*, BBC Radio Ulster, 23 September 2005, 25th anniversary of *Translations*.

23 FDA: G/D/Friel/Deane: letter from Friel to Deane, dated 5 May [1975]. *Late brother-in-law of S. Deane; he had recently won a very considerable sum at the Cheltenham race meeting.

24 FDA: G/D/Friel/Deane: letter from Friel to Deane, dated 17 September [1978].

25 Letter from Friel to Deane, dated 3 October [1978] (letter states that *Faith Healer* and *Aristocrats* are in the 'printers' queue'). Not part of FDA. Reproduced with permission.

in his correspondence with Deane three years later. In the following letter, with a certain amount of critical prompting from Deane, Friel is identifying his sense of failure with his Derry background. This realization is crucial to understanding the creative impulse behind *Translations*, and behind Field Day and the significance of the group's Derry origins:

> October 3 [1978]
>
> A lot of what you said surprises me. I suppose it shouldn't. At my time of day I ought to have made many of these abstractions myself and been aware of the overlapping themes in the plays. But I never have. And to be presented persistent themes and obsessions, with a 'Frieldom', a territory I never thought of, is a bit startling and, I suppose if it weren't such a sickly landscape, heartening.
>
> At the first reading of your letter I kept thinking how accurately you were defining (through me) an Irish Catholic, more specifically a Northern Catholic, most specifically a Derry Catholic: the (my) obsession with death; the refusal to subscribe to institutional authority; the inability to establish an alternative personal authority (lapsed Pape); the 'grotesques' who respect the very authority that abuses them (Provos-Church); and the Wessex characters who have always been outside the walls and are on the point of entry (they have, like most Derry people, a residue of Donegal in their metabolism). If this is at all close to what you were saying, then what you have demonstrated to me is that like a true Derry Pape I have structured failure (social, political, cultural) into a half-sustaining philosophy. So be it. It certainly hadn't occurred to me. I wouldn't deny it. And when I wonder why it may be true the only answer I can suggest is that we can never find realization in the Northern state where we are permitted only to be *their* concept of us. And even if the Northern state were to disappear, we would be misfits in the now super-county-council Republic because our concept of ourselves finds no reflection in that shabbiness. So we remain loyal citizens to a state of mind. So in fact we're doomed to political exile — an exile that hasn't even the consolation of certainty because there is still that residue of gombeen in us to haunt us. Derrymen are like Jews: we want to make an out-kingdom of the West Bank.
>
> The alternative to all this, and it's an alternative that some Irish writers have inherited, some cultivate — and I'm thinking primarily of the Northern poets, yourself and one or two others excluded — is to pitch the voice towards England. This, for various reasons, usually evokes a welcoming response. It also provides a home, a warmth, a complete culture — all the consolations of good digs. (As you said to me once before I too am aware that this kind of comment can be contaminated with bitterness and failure. But there is an even greater danger, I think, and it lies in the implication that by renouncing the alternative, one somehow glories in and glorifies this here for God's sake). Anyhow, let's stay as we are. Let's articulate what we have. And if you don't like the dark you can always light a blessed Alliance candle.[25]

The need to dismantle 'structured failure' would emerge in *Translations* as the core message to its Derry audience and, later, to Field Day's wider audience/readership. Deane later pressed the point home by publicizing Friel's sense of failure in his Introduction to Friel's *Selected Plays*, which has *Translations* as its end point, its resolution:

> These factors [Derry's political and economic conditions] have profoundly

> impressed themselves on Friel's writing in which the same blend of disappointment and unyielding pressure is found time and time again to characterize the experience of the protagonists. ... Politics is an ever-present force, but Friel, conscious of the recurrent failures of the political imagination in Ireland, is concerned to discover some consolatory or counterbalancing agency which will offer an alternative. The discovery is never made. But the search for an alternative to and the reasons for failure brings Friel, finally, to the recognition of the peculiar role and function of art, especially the theatrical art, in a broken society ...
>
> Paradoxically, although his theme is failure, linguistic and political, the fact that the play has been written is itself an indication of the success of the imagination in dealing with everything that seems opposed to its survival.[26]

In this context, we can better understand the significance for Friel of George Steiner's declaration in *After Babel* that '[l]anguage is the main instrument of man's refusal to accept the world as it is'.[27] It is an idea that resurfaces in *Translations* when Hugh explains to Yolland the richness of the language of an impoverished and isolated community such as Ballybeg by observing that 'certain cultures expend on their vocabularies and syntax acquisitive energies and ostentations entirely lacking in their material lives ... a syntax opulent with tomorrows. It is our response to mud cabins and a diet of potatoes.'[28] As the conflict between British and Irish cultures develops in the play, language is shown to be both the problem and the solution: Whether it is Ballybeg 1833 or Derry 1980, it is the limitations of language that create intercultural conflict, and yet it is the creative potential of language that also provides the means for cultural synthesis. With 'opulent' syntax, Field Day sought to undermine the existing political reality and to create a new negotiable space.

In his 3 October 1978 letter to Deane, it is again striking how seriously Friel considers the critical response, and in his subsequent musings he raises for the first time the later oft-repeated notion of the northern Catholic being an 'exile', a stateless citizen who remains loyal only to a state of mind. We read here many of Field Day's concerns — the need for self-definition, the need to pitch the voice to an audience other than an English one, and ideas of statelessness, exile, disloyalty, and Derry as a kind of 'out-kingdom' — but this letter was written fully six months before Rea approached Friel with the Field Day idea.

What emerges from these letters, then, is that the inaugural Field Day play *Translations* represents the first public expression of diverse thoughts teased out over a number of years between Friel and others who were invited to join the Field Day board *after* the success of the play. This is not to take credit for the play from Friel and disperse it among his Field Day colleagues. Quite the opposite, it is to confirm the play's excellence — the manner in which it, above all else, gave powerful and coherent expression to new forms of critical thinking as they applied to Ireland in the mid to late 1970s. Friel looked to Synge as the only Irish playwright to have dealt successfully with the problem of language. He felt that the Abbey Theatre had become a dead theatrical space since Synge's time and that what was needed was a physical and theatrical breakaway. Friel's early training with Tyrone Guthrie in Minneapolis gave him an appreciation of the creative potential in bringing professional quality theatre away from the metropolitan centre.[29] In all of this he found a natural ally in Stephen Rea.

Stephen Rea's Proposal

> Proposal by Stephen Rea Regarding the Setting Up of a Theatre Company

26 Deane, 'Introduction', *SP*, 11–12, 22.
27 George Steiner, *After Babel* (Oxford, 1975), 217–18.
28 *SP*, 418.

29 Tyrone Guthrie (1900–71), Anglo-Irish stage director, playwright and writer. At Guthrie's invitation, Friel went to Minneapolis in 1963 to observe the first season at the new Guthrie Theatre.

30 FDA: G/D/Friel/Rea/5.

31 Luke Gibbons and Kevin Whelan, 'In Conversation with Stephen Rea', *Yale Journal of Criticism*, 15, 1 (2002), 5–21 at 5–7. The conversation took place in Yale University on 2 February 2001.

4 April 1979

Brian Friel has agreed to write a play. This play to be worked on by Irish actors, possibly with a preliminary workshop session. Rehearsals and first performances might take place in Derry, followed by performances in theatres and community centres throughout the North — Coleraine, Enniskillen, Belfast.

This obviously would require a high degree of flexibility in both design and performance, given the variety of playing spaces available. The preliminary workshop period would aim to develop a sense of company and a strong attitude among the actors towards the play, something I have never yet experienced in Irish Theatre. It would be stimulating for Friel to be faced with a less traditional rehearsal process than that provided by the Abbey and other companies. The size and composition of the company would obviously be defined by the nature of the play, but one would hope to combine the more interesting of the younger Irish actors with some of our more lively character actors.

It would seem essential to import both lighting and set designers. I know of no-one in Ireland qualified to create the kind of canvas required to produce the clear, uncluttered style of acting which interests me and which I feel Friel's plays demand.

I have no axe to grind with regard to community drama, except that I believe 'knees-ups' and 'come-all-ye's' are often patronising. I believe that the communities are entitled to a fine play by a fine Irish writer performed by the best actors available. The freedom of movement between individual theatres and the more unpredictable community centres should be a liberating experience for the company and therefore for the audiences.[30]

Up to this point, Rea had been based in England. But working for an Irish theatre of ideas, playing to an alternative audience, had always been part of his thinking:

> I was attracted to the Abbey because I was drawn to the theatre of ideas but, as we now know, there were none alive in that place at the time. This was in the late 1960s. They then had no particular strategy about how to be a national theater, which is what they were hoping to be. Everything was moribund really ... So, I hung around for a while and then I went to England ... When I was away in England, I always felt that I was preparing myself to come back. ... [The English National Theatre] is probably the most achieved theater in the world. But I always felt that I was working for someone else. I always felt that I was part of a sub-culture within England. Peter Hall offered me a choice at that time. He said, 'Change your accent and you can do anything you want in this theater' ... I did not change my accent. If I was doing a Russian play, I did not want to pretend to be English in order to pretend to be Russian. It was an absurdity to me.[31]

Rea proposed his new theatre company to Friel at a time when political and cultural life in Ireland was at low ebb. It seemed an inopportune moment to introduce a theatre of ideas, though perhaps its initial success was due to the fact that it emerged at a time when, more than ever, new ideas were needed. Rea denies that he chose his moment:

> I was not exactly sitting in England plotting my moment, but I had a lot of experience by now and either I just remained absorbed in the English theater or did something else ... I went home around 1979, and fortuitously someone in the Arts Council said they had some money ... I went to Brian and asked him to write a play. He instantly said yes and turned out *Translations* ... It

> gave a fantastic lift-off to the company. We did not choose that moment saying 'things are rock bottom, we have to do something about it'. We were going to do a play and it was clear there was a crisis that we were inserting ourselves into. From the beginning there was a political spin put on everything we did, for example, the fact that we went to Derry to open the thing. That wasn't just a political choice. The Abbey was just a dead space. It was a dead theatrical space. There was no live theatrical space in Belfast that I can think of. No traditional theater space had any life, so we went to this place, the Guildhall in Derry, which was not a theater. It was an administrative building, an integral part of the Unionist regime. It was a dead political space. We made it a live theatrical space. That meant that everything we did had a meaning or vibrancy, because of where we did it.[32]

The brevity of Rea's touring theatre proposal is striking, but its impact was immediate. Many of Friel's core concerns are spelled out: the northern focus, the creation of an alternative theatre to the Abbey, and a firm commitment to stage professional plays for a new non-metropolitan audience. Both men had known each other ever since Rea acted in Friel's *Freedom of the City* at the Royal Court in London in 1973 and they got on very well. Rea's proposal marked the beginning of a period of intense engagement between the two men, which would last for the next decade.[33] Rea later recalled these early days:

> It came out of a personal relationship between me and Brian there — and a decision to enter the arena in some way, to have our say in what was going on. ... It was a feeling that we had to go to our audience, saying to the big cities that there is somewhere else. ... It came from a personal feeling, but a feeling also about the place that we lived in and what was happening needs to be heard here. It came from Imelda Foley, who's from Derry. She spoke to me and said that there might be some money from the Arts Council — she worked for the Arts Council. It slowly built so that it seemed right and appropriate that it should be in Derry.[34]

Rea also confirmed the extent of his dialogue with Friel, recalling that during their most creative times, Friel and he would talk every day, by phone if they did not actually meet (several of the letters from Friel to Rea in the archive are headed 'following our phone conversation', or words similar), and he goes on to suggest that some of the play's richness came out of that constant referral:

> I only saw him once between then [*The Freedom of the City* at The Royal Court, London, 1973] and 1979. I decided I'd like to start something in the North, and who better to go to than Brian? ... and I went to him. Everybody has to make a pilgrimage once in their lives, and I made mine, and he gave me the play. ... He hadn't written it at the time and he did say that the fact that he was writing it for this new company may have influenced the outcome in some way. ... We were all changing. ... We had arrived at this crisis in the North. You couldn't not be affected by the collapse of society in the North. Everybody was affected and in some sense maimed by it. You had to have a response and if you were in the business of theatre or writing or acting you had to attempt a principled response.[35]

Things moved swiftly. In May 1979, just one month after Rea's proposal, Friel was recording his thoughts on a new play based on the first Ordnance Survey of Ireland in his 'Sporadic Diary'. By 3 September 1979, the idea of the play, and even its casting, was beginning to take shape. Rea had initially imagined that he would co-direct Friel's play. However, in the following letter, by praising Rea's acting ability, Friel may have been

32 Gibbons and Whelan, 'In Conversation with Stephen Rea', 9.

33 The correspondence in the archive reveals an evident affinity between Friel and Rea. This did not survive Friel's decision not to give his 1990 play *Dancing at Lughnasa* to Field Day, however.

34 Interview with Rea, *Arts Extra*, BBC Radio Ulster, 23 September 2005, 25th anniversary of *Translations*.

35 Interview with Rea, *Rattlebag*, RTÉ, 23 September 2005, 'Field Day Theatre Company Special', marking the 25th anniversary of *Translations* (interviews with Stephen Rea and Kevin Whelan). http://www.rte.ie/arts/2005/0923/rattlebag.html

Translations reheasal, Guildhall, Derry, 1980. Friel sits in foreground, Rea stands at the stage. Photo: Rod Tuach, © Field Day.

36 FDA: G/D/Friel/Rea/5: letter from Friel to Rea, dated 3 September [1979]. *Ken Jamieson of the Arts Council of Northern Ireland.

edging Rea towards taking an acting role.

> Sep 3 [1979]
>
> I'm still very keen (mentally) on the hedge-school/Survey idea. There's nothing on paper. This week I'm going to focus fully and determinedly on it ... the cute thesis is that the subconscious is doing all the work privately.
>
> ... I'm glad you're meeting Ken J.* and that you have some people in mind ...
>
> I saw the revival of ARISTOCRATS. It seemed to be holding together. I thought Liam Neeson had a good, authentic quality. What he lacked — in that part — is either experience or honed skill. (A note from S. Deane this AM; he'd been back to the play; one of his comments was, 'The playing was a little less crisp or harmonised, maybe because the Sun-Rea kid was missing').[36]

In isolation, this reads like a simple act of praise being passed on, but the full context of Friel's thinking emerges in subsequent letters. The following day, Friel wrote to Deane, and in the postscript he spelled out what he saw to be the difference between Rea's and Neeson's respective talents:

> Now back at the desk with Mapping Up, Death By Triangulation, As You Hike It or An Eye on De Mesne Chance, Okay — okay ...
>
> PS. I saw ARISTOCRATS again, too, without Rea. He was a big loss. Neeson, his replacement, had an authentic presence but hadn't the craft to focus and present it — which distinguishes good actors from great actors.[37]

A few weeks later, the first act was written, and Friel's thoughts on the casting were stated to Rea directly:

> September 25, 1979
>
> Here's a version of the first act ... (I've no title as yet. I'm always slow at that). Liam Neeson could play Doalty very well. Keep him in mind when you're reading it.
>
> I'd like you to reconsider your attitude to directing/playing. Of course, direct. But I feel strongly that there is no convincing reason why you shouldn't play *as well*. (Yes, I know all *your reasons*. And finally they don't convince me fully.) And one of the reasons I bring this up now is that I think you'd make an excellent Owen. Keep calm. Yes, I did say he's a P.R. man and that if he had been alive today he could have been a good host of a TV chat show. But –– he is a very interesting and complex character (LOOK OUT FOR EPISODE TWO!!!) and will need subtle and delicate playing. Indeed it seems to me that he becomes more and more central. As the play unfolds he won't cease to be — except for a few brief minutes — the smiling, charming, quick-talking guy; but important and compelling.* And I would very much like you to consider that part. Even now; as an act of faith. Will you? Let me know.
>
> Has Liam Redmond lost his centre? Completely? As you will see, Hugh, the hedgeschool-master, hasn't much of a centre left either, L.R. seems a splendid idea to me. [38]

The development of the characters of Owen and Hugh in the play is echoed in Friel's letters to Rea. Initially, Friel considered the character of Owen to be minor. As we can see in the letter above, this was not the case by the time Act 2 was complete: Owen has become 'important and compelling', while Hugh 'hasn't much of a centre left'. By the time the play is complete, Friel has recognized that both characters are important. The emergence of Owen as the character who is 'more and more central' to the play is fundamental to the play's message; it could even be claimed as a watershed in Friel's *oeuvre*, the point at which he learns how to move beyond the sense of 'failure' that is his Derry inheritance. Owen's moment of recognition at the end of the play, his understanding of how he has betrayed his community, is the transitional moment at the heart of *Translations*; it is also the originating point for subsequent Field Day work — the point from which new forms of Irish identity must be forged. From this moment — that is, the completion of *Translations* — we see the emergence of a theme that would dominate every subsequent Field Day production: the theme of betrayal. The evolution of this idea can be traced in Friel's correspondence with Rea.

In the letter of 25 September 1979, Friel is beginning to realize that Owen must be complex. Hugh, the schoolmaster and Owen's father, is also central, and he makes the pertinent theme statements in the play, but he does so largely in response to the actions of his son. It is to Owen's future that the audience is asked to look. *Translations* is the originating text of Field Day, Owen is the central character, and Friel is therefore concerned that Rea should play that role.

Before he came round to this idea, Friel had written the following in his 'Sporadic Diary', 6 July 1979:

> One of the mistakes of the direction in which the play is presently pulling is the almost wholly *public* concern of the theme: how does the eradication of the Irish language and the substitution of English affect this particular society? How long can a society live without its tongue? Public questions; issues for politicians; and that's what's wrong with

37 FDA: G/D/Friel/Deane: letter from Friel to Deane, dated 4 September 1979.

38 FDA: G/D/Friel/Rea/5: letter from Friel to Rea, dated 25 September [1979]. Friel added a draft cast list to this letter: 'Doalty — Liam Neeson could play this. Hugh — School-master. (No longer a major role.) 60+ Think of Liam Redmond as you read it. Owen — 25+ (the man I described accurately — but in retrospect unhappily — as a TV Host.) Lancey — Brit officer. Not difficult Yolland — I feel this requires a real Englishman (He becomes an instant Hibernophile).' *Margin note: 'for social and historical reasons'.

> the play now. The play must concern itself only with the exploration of the dark and private places of individual souls.[39]

By September, he has worked out that if Owen were to remain a mere television host type, then the 'dark and private places' of his individual soul could not be explored. It is a working out of Yeats's idea that public argument is rhetoric and private argument is poetry. Owen's recognition of his compromised position as someone who has betrayed his community, and his consequent rejection of his British army role, leaves him outside both groups. It is an awkward place to be, but it is also potentially liberating. He develops during the play from a kind of quisling figure to a self-aware, self-questioning representative of a new hybrid identity. It is through Owen, more than any other character, that *Translations* asks its audience to consider shifting its own fixed positions so as to understand what the public implications of private self-reappraisal might be, and vice versa. As Friel said during a press interview:

> [F]or people like ourselves, living close to such a fluid situation, definitions of identity have to be developed and analysed much more frequently. We've got to keep questioning until we find some kind of portmanteau term or until we find some kind of generosity that can embrace the whole island. Of course, there is no better, no more fluid, place to develop and to analyse identity than the theatre, where actors transform themselves every night.[40]

In the following extract from an undated letter, Friel announces that Act 2 is complete, a fact that he records in his 'Sporadic Diary' to have occurred on 9 October 1979.[41] Given that Rea has reported that they were in almost daily contact during this time, and given Friel's stated eagerness for Rea to read the completed script ahead of anyone else, it is safe to assume that this letter was written on or near that date. So, about month after Friel's previous letter, the title of the play is decided and Friel is reiterating his regret that he had first imagined Owen in such a simplistic way.

> Yes, *no* doubt a play — of sorts — will be available towards the end of the next month. Working title: *TRANSLATIONS*.
>
> Maybe a bit 'literary' but it conveys much of the play's content.
>
> Getting worried about Hugh/The master. What would you think of Cyril?* (Doubtful if he'd be available. He's in [Hugh] Leonard's new play** which the Abbey talks of taking to the London Paddy-Parade.) Owen becomes more interesting. I regret the easy tag I gave him when you were here.*** Act 2 written and will require substantial reworking.[42]

Three weeks later, Friel had completed the play and was eager for Rea to read it. The letter that accompanied the script he sent to Rea is enthusiastic, yet the eagerness is tempered by concerns about the potential response of the unionist audience. Friel clearly anticipated hostility. His unease about the 'Belfast burghers', as it turned out, was not without foundation (the opening night in Belfast was the least successful of all shows on the tour, with only 400 of the 1,000 seats at the Grand Opera House taken). At this point, the Guildhall in Derry had not been confirmed as the venue for the premiere. The importance of the role of Hugh is finally established in this letter, and Friel is seeking out an actor on a par with Rea. Ray McAnally is considered the only actor worthy of performing it. Ann Hasson is also proposed for the role of Sarah for the first time because of her 'young-old' face. It is a measure of Friel's reputation that he succeeded in casting each of the actors he proposes.

39 Friel, 'Sporadic Diary', 6 July 1979, in *Essays, Diaries, Interviews: 1964–1999*, ed. Murray, 77.
40 Interview with Friel in *Sunday Independent*, 5 October 1980, quoted in Christopher Morash, *A History of Irish Theatre 1601–2000* (Cambridge, 2002), 241.
41 Friel, 'Sporadic Diary', 9 Ocober 1979, in *Essays, Diaries, Interviews: 1964–1999*, ed. Murray, 77.
42 FDA: G/D/Friel/Rea/5: letter from Friel to Rea, undated (on or near 9 October 1979). *Cyril Cusack. ***A Life*, first production: 4 October 1979. ***The letter is addressed from Muff, County Donegal, Friel's home at the time.

Nov. 1, 1979

TRANSLATIONS enclosed. I'm pleased you're not displeased with the title — when you read the play you'll see that it has other meanings besides the linguistic one.

When you've read the script please get back to me *immediately*. I'm very eager to get your response.

There are two pieces of music required. The first — the reel — is the final track from O'Riada Sa Gaiety, a wild thumpety-thump piece, 'full of the mythologies of fantasy and hope and self-deception'. The second piece is scripted simply as 'guitar music'. And what I want here is a version of Tabhair Dom do Lámh/Give me your Hand. We'll get Arty McGlynn to do it. He's brilliant. (His first record comes out soon. An Omagh man.) And the sound he will produce will be elegant and haunting and courtly -- uniting the two cultures represented by Máire and George. I'll explain this better when we talk. Some of the pupils will be bare-footed. I haven't scripted this because it's something we'd need to talk about. Now that I've read the play again I begin to have some unease about the Belfast burghers — that all they'll see is a play about bloody Irish-speaking Papes being evicted by Our Troops. What do you think? Am I too touchy? Are the Richie McKees still haunting the place?*

The Master is central; and the only name that comes to mind is Ray McAnally. I've worked with him a few times and I've a lot of respect for him. But the idea of traipsing about the North may not appeal to him (although he is on his own now). And he certainly has that hard, mental edge. And the Northern thing. Think about him. And as you read the script, see how you yourself respond to Owen.

... I'll get a copy ... to John Fairleigh** at the beginning of next week. I want you to have it and me to have your response to it *first*.

The Bill Gaskill thing sounds interesting. And as you described it to me it struck me that there were some similarities with this play — a people coming to the end of their cultural seam, even bearing the physical manifestations of that decline (lame, speech defect, drunken, etc. etc.)

[Handwritten postscript] I think Ann Hasson -- depending, of course, on our Manus -- would be a good Sarah. She's from Derry. Strange young-old face. We'll need an Englishman for Yolland.[43]

Rea's response to the script was prompt. We know this because just eleven days later Friel wrote a reply to Rea's reading of the script, expressing his delight that Rea has 'responded so strongly to the play',[44] and reiterating his interest in Ray McAnally, Liam Neeson and Ann Hasson for the roles of Hugh, Doalty and Sarah, respectively.

Once Rea had read the play, Deane was given a copy. The note accompanying the script sent to Deane indicates that his critical input was considered important, but it also confirms that, at this point, he remained formally outside the proposed theatre company. That Friel can refer to the play as 'Colby & Co'[45] indicates that he has already discussed it with Deane; however, it was only at this relatively late stage that Deane learned which role Rea would play and that Arts Council of Northern Ireland money was likely to be made available, though Friel and Rea were clearly determined to proceed whether funding was forthcoming or not. We can also read in this brief note, confirmation that Rea has finally agreed to play Owen, and that an opening night in Belfast rather than Derry was a still a distinct possibility at this time.

43 FDA: G/D/Friel/Rea/5: letter from Friel to Rea, dated 1 November 1979. Hasson's desired attribute can only add to the argument that, through her lost voice, Sarah represents Ireland struck dumb by the shock of modernity and through her young-old appearance, she is both Ireland Past and Future, an embodiment of loss and potential. Elsewhere in the play, the nineteenth-century American vision of Ireland is alluded to by Máire when she addresses Sarah: 'Is that the dress you got from Boston? Green suits you' (*SP*, 438). *Refers to the Sam Thompson play *Over the Bridge* (1957): Ritchie McKee, a prominent unionist and director of the Ulster Group Theatre, stopped rehearsals for the play in May 1959. **John Fairleigh, member of the Arts Council of Northern Ireland.

44 FDA: G/D/Friel/Rea/5: letter from Friel to Rea, dated 12 November [1979].

45 Colonel Thomas Colby, author of one of the source-texts for the play: *Ordnance Survey of the County of Londonderry*, published for HM Government by Hodges and Smith, 1837.

> Nov 21, 1979
>
> This is how Colby and Co. have ended up. When you get a chance to read it let me know what you think. Stephen Rea (he'll play Owen) & I will do it together with Arts Council (NI) money, opening in Belfast some time next year. If they get cold feet, we'll go elsewhere.[46]

After Friel had completed the play, and after Rea had endorsed it and agreed to play Owen, Friel's correspondence turned to the practical matters of attracting funding, incorporating the company, hiring actors and generating publicity. Though intended as a theatre of ideas, Field Day had to make a concession from the outset: to gain the necessary funding, an official body or institution of some sort had to be created. As Friel said in interview: 'They [the Northern Ireland Arts Council] only fund existing establishments so we had to become an establishment.'[47] The Field Day Archive can confirm, for the record, the precise sequence of events leading to the founding of the company as follows. The use of the name Field Day Theatre Company Limited was first approved by the Department of Commerce Companies Register (UK) on 21 May 1980.[48] A certificate of incorporation was signed on 12 August 1980, and received by Paddy Woodworth (company secretary) on 22 August, and the first meeting of the Field Day board of directors, which dealt with matters that were strictly procedural, was held at Friel's home at Ardmore, Muff, County Donegal, on 14 September 1980, shortly before the premiere of *Translations*. In attendance were Friel, Rea and Woodworth. Friel was appointed chairman of the company and Woodworth as company secretary. Having no fixed address at the time, the company was officially registered at the Orchard Gallery, Orchard Street, Derry.[49]

Friel and Rea were largely successful in populating the cast with Ulster actors. This was not just a matter of matching the cast with the geographical setting of the story, but also it came from a feeling that the creative energy of Ireland at that time emanated from the North and from Derry in particular. Christopher Morash highlighted the Ulster focus of the cast:

> Apart from his commanding stage presence, McAnally had another great advantage in playing Hugh: He was born in Moville, just up the banks of Lough Foyle from Derry on the Donegal side. When Friel cast him in *Translations*, McAnally had just finished directing a young Ballymena actor, Liam Neeson, in a Dublin production of John Steinbeck's *Of Mice and Men,* and Neeson followed the older actor to Derry to play Doalty. Selecting a predominantly Ulster cast was a conscious decision, with Brenda Scallon (from Enniskillen) playing Bridget and Ann Hasson as the mute Sarah from Derry. [50]

Hiring an actor of McAnally's stature was a great coup for the play, but it was only agreed at a relatively late stage, as revealed in an undated letter from Friel to Rea describing the publicity event organized to launch the company (which took place 3 June 1980):

> McAnally still not hired ... Hope you like Three Sisters ...
>
> In *all* interviews the question that kept coming up was: What play is Field Day doing next? This, I suspect, because the press release talks of a *first* production being *Translations* ...
>
> So now we're launched boy![51]

As an existing regional company, Field Day was granted £40,000 stg by the Arts Council of Northern Ireland. The Arts Council of Ireland/An Chomhairle Ealaíon awarded the company an additional IR£10,000, and

46 Note from Friel to Deane, dated 21 November 1979. Not part of FDA. Reproduced with permission.
47 Interview with Ciarán Carty, *Irish Times*, 5 October 1980. Quoted in Murray, 81.
48 FDA: G/Meet/1a. Letter to company secretary Paddy Woodworth. Friel stated in an interview with the *Sunday Independent*, 5 October 1980, that the company's name came from a combination of the names Friel and Rea. The publication of Seamus Heaney's *Field Work* in 1979 is also surely relevant.
49 FDA: G/Meet/1a.
50 Morash, *A History of Irish Theatre*, 237.

Derry City Council allocated £13,000 stg towards the building of a lighting rig and constructing a stage at the Guildhall. This choice of venue was of huge importance to the success of the play.

Opening Night

The opening night of *Translations* on 23 September 1980 was, by any standards, a landmark event in the history of Irish theatre. When the cast had first gathered at the Guildhall in Derry on 12 August 1980, it was the first time in almost two centuries that a professional company has rehearsed a play in Derry.[52] This reunification of the city with the dramatic arts was additionally noteworthy because Friel and Rea were men with international reputations; moreover, their, as yet unofficial though open association with Heaney, whose international fame had also been established by 1980, meant that, on that night, Derry became the cultural focus for the whole of Ireland. It was the kind of homecoming that Friel had rehearsed through the character of Frank Hardy in *Faith Healer*, a play that could be read as a metaphor for the Field Day experiment. This was not just a reworking of the notion that a prophet is recognized everywhere but in his own country — although that was certainly an element — it was also an advance comment on the risk involved in Field Day, with Friel and Heaney and Rea now bringing their gift home, to see if it would work there. Robert Hewison, reviewing *Faith Healer* for the *Times Literary Supplement*, was one critic who recognized the link, when he declared that *Faith Healer* seeks to 'convince us that the imagination, willed or unwilled, can be so strong that it is possible to create the conditions under which people can re-create themselves'.[53] The audience for *Translations* had to be convinced in just such a way. The construction of that audience was as important to the play as the script. Marilynn Richtarik quotes theatre director Peter Brook to make this point:

> ... 'the only thing all forms of theatre have in common is the need for an audience'. This makes it, he claims, unique among art forms. The necessity for an audience might be said to be theatre's defining characteristic, and the reaction of audience members at a play constitutes a secondary layer of collaboration.[54]

Field Day was eager to make a statement and the audience was keen to hear it. The sense of collaboration generated as a result was enhanced by the non-confrontational space opened by the text of the play. These factors combined to make the first performance of *Translations* a huge success. As a dramatic statement, it was beautifully crafted, perfectly timed and ideally, if awkwardly, situated. The Guildhall venue was utterly unsuitable for staging plays, even after Derry City Council spent its £13,000 on a new thrust stage, and yet, as the traditional seat of unionist civic power and with its stained glass windows depicting scenes from one narrative of the city's past, it was a powerfully symbolic setting that became part of the wider public drama. Before the actors stepped on stage, there was already a sense of occasion in the city, and the exhilaration that carried the night has tended to conceal the fact that the performances were not particularly good. Only a few commentators were willing to admit this. Mary Holland was one, perhaps feeling freer to say so, a decade after the event:

> Looking back ten years later it seems that the whole concept of Field Day was on display that night, the fifth province of the intellect where questions of culture and identity, art and politics could be explored. But, as Brian Friel has often pointed out, memory plays tricks and reshapes events to meet the demands of subsequent experience. According to those most intimately involved, that first Field Day opening was a lot more haphazard than it now appears.[55]

51 FDA: G/D/Friel/Rea/4. Letter from Friel to Rea, undated. Discusses publicity conference and launch for *Translations* in Derry, which was first reported by the *Londonderry Sentinel* on the subsequent day, 4 June 1980.

52 Morash, *A History of Irish Theatre*, 233.

53 Robert Hewison, 'Forces of Persuasion', *Times Literary Supplement*, 20 March 1981, 310, quoted by C. Murray in 'Friel's Emblems of Adversity and the Yeatsian Example', in A. J. Peacock, ed., *The Achievement of Brian Friel* (Gerrards Cross, 1993), 88. ... The irony is that the faith healer, the artist, finds the mystery of his talent a cross too hard to bear. Beneath the modernism of Friel's exploration of the nature of fiction lies a Catholic symbolism which resolves itself in the faith healer's sense of a necessary sacrifice.' On this reading, Friel's eventual departure from Field Day may also have been heralded by the character of Frank Hardy. Rea speaks of the company's death being 'inbuilt'.

54 Marilynn J. Richtarik, *Acting between the Lines: The Field Day Theatre Company and Irish Cultural Politics 1980–1984* (Oxford, 1994), 50.

55 Mary Holland, 'Field Day's Tenth Birthday', in the programme notes for Heaney's Field Day play *The Cure at Troy*, 1 October 1990.

Guardian critic Ian Hill, though impressed by the play, felt that the performances were no more than adequate. He sensed that the night was carried by a wave of emotion, and that 'the performances weren't stunning, some of the performances were brittle'.[56] Rea himself admitted, 'I had felt the evening to be rather sticky in terms of actual performance.'[57] The stage performance was only part of a wider civic event, however. A number of critics picked up on this. Hill observed that Friel had reduced his first-night audience to a 'state of ecstasy, even before they took their seats'.[58] Paul Wilkins, writing for *Hibernia*, also made this point, but went on to absolve the play from the charge of pandering to its audience:

> I was uneasy that, with the premiere in Derry, this might be an occasion of empathy, local piety, with general civic celebration sliding into self-congratulation. From the start of *Translations*, however, it was evident that what dictated this venue was not sentiment but theme. A play dealing with two disparate cultures could perhaps find no surer test of its impact than with a Derry audience.[59]

Translations was not a crowd-pleaser in the pejorative sense. Critic David McKenna put it well:

> It is difficult, and perhaps wrong, to separate Brian Friel's new play 'Translations' from the occasion of its premiere in Derry City's Guildhall on September 23. ... throughout the evening there was a palpable rapport between the spectators and the performers, an extraordinary sense that the former understood every word, as if, rather than being imposed, the play came out of the audience on to the stage.[60]

Describing the night some twenty-five years later, Rea also recalled that the participation of the audience was unusually intense:

> The audience was extremely alive with something more than a theatrical anticipation. It was a feeling that people were moving out of the darkness. ... I don't want to make too many claims for it, but ... it was celebratory in a sense that something public was going on and it wasn't confrontational.[61]

In another twenty-fifth anniversary interview, he recalled:

> It was a weird mood [in Derry]. People didn't do plays in Derry ... it was kind of a shock and it was very exciting, and Derry was very keen to have this production ... people in the city council were very, very keen on it ... and in some sense it did turn things round. ... It was an unspeakable venue ... there is a way to use it actually.[62]

Field Day turned the limitations of the 'unspeakable' venue to its benefit. The determination to succeed despite the adverse conditions was something that the local audience could appreciate. Had the play opened at a better venue in a larger city such as Dublin, or even in a city like Belfast, which was equally as fractured as Derry, the play would not have had the same impact. As Rea explained to a *Derry Journal* reporter on the opening night:

> If we put it on in a place like Dublin's Abbey Theatre, its energy would be contained within the theatre and its clientele. But its energy is bound to spread much more profoundly through a place like Derry. The Ulster cast, the location close to the fictional Ballybeg fulfilled a need for the '*desiderium nostrorum* — the need for our own'.[63]

Press reports show that Derry's need for its own was met on opening night. In the audience were, among others, John Hume, Seamus Heaney, Seamus Deane, Bishop of Derry Dr. Edward Daly, Eamonn McCann,

56 Interview with Hill, *Arts Extra*, BBC Radio Ulster, 23 September 2005, 25th anniversary of *Translations*.
57 Interview with Rea, *Arts Extra*, BBC Radio Ulster, 23 September 2005, 25th anniversary of *Translations*.
58 FDA: PC/1980/1: *Guardian* review copy undated.
59 FDA: PC/1980/1: Article copy undated, but the author refers to 'last Tuesday', i.e. opening night.
60 FDA: PC/1980/1: *In Dublin*, 3 October 1980.
61 Interview with Rea, *Arts Extra*, BBC Radio Ulster, 23 September 2005, 25th anniversary of *Translations*.
62 Interview with Rea, *Rattlebag*, RTÉ, 23 September 2005, 'Field Day Theatre Company Special', marking 25th anniversary of *Translations* (interviews with Stephen Rea and Kevin Whelan).

Stephen Rea as Owen and Ray Mac Anally as Hugh Mór O'Donnell, *Translations* reheasal, Guildhall, Derry, 1980. Photo: Rod Tuach, © Field Day.

Nell McCafferty, Sinn Féin councillor Martin McGuinness, and Unionist mayor Marlene Jefferson, alongside broadsheet critics from Dublin, Belfast, and London, and an assortment of leading lights of the cultural circuit such as Cyril Cusack, Colm O'Briain and Michael Longley from the two Arts Councils, playwrights Tom Murphy and Tom Kilroy, actress and singer Julie Covington (then a companion of Stephen Rea), theatre director Joe Dowling and film director Jim Sheridan.

Rea recalls the difficulty of constructing the audience for the night:

> Who was going to sit beside each other? In many ways we tried to avoid such things. We didn't invite any churchmen, but then we got a letter from the Catholic bishop saying 'my invitation appears to have been lost in the post', so then we had to invite him, and then we had to invite all the other clergymen as well. ... It [mayor Jefferson's standing ovation] was a huge relief because I had felt the evening to be rather sticky in terms of actual performance.[64]

If the performances were sticky, there were few complaints in the press. The play was almost universally greeted as a triumph. The *Irish Press* dedicated an editorial to it:

> ... hailed by the critics, courageous, a spectacular success ... It was in every sense a unique occasion, with loyalists and nationalists, Unionists and SDLP,

63 *Derry Journal*, 23 September 1980. Rea was quoting the character of Hugh at the end of *Translations*.

> Northerners and Southerners laying aside their differences to join together in applauding a play by a fellow Derryman and one, moreover, with a theme that is uniquely Irish.[65]

David Nowlan in the *Irish Times* described how the excitement of the event extended to the city as a whole.

> It was a night of high excitement and deep emotion in Derry last night when Brian Friel's play *Translations* opened to a packed and glittering audience in the city's Guildhall. Here Derry was on show and the show was for Derry. It was an electric love affair. The hotels were in on it, and the taxi drivers and the people; the town was in on it.[66]

The opening night had developed into something bigger than a play. It was a civic event of historical importance that could not be confined to the happenings on stage. In its most immediate and simplistic sense, it was read as a cultural endorsement of the power-sharing arrangement that had recently been worked out in the city, an explication of why a nationalist city could and should be at that moment represented by a unionist mayor, though it was also, and more importantly, a call for a more complex understanding of how inhibiting those opposing identities are. For London reviewers, the emotional response was something they had never experienced before. Timothy E. O'Grady of the *New Statesman* was a case in point:

> It is a play of extraordinary depth, commitment and intellectual vigour, perhaps in part because it was written for and out of the specific context that the city of Derry and Friel's own company have provided ... [It is] a concise model of contemporary Ireland, with its legacy of conquest and all the attendant grotesqueries — compromised middlemen, star-crossed lovers, dissolute romantics, marauding soldiers and a predicament that has no options but violent resistance. ... The curtain was greeted with the most rapturous and emotional standing ovation I have ever seen.[67]

O'Grady may have overlooked the fact that the play did, in fact, suggest options beyond violent resistance. It is an understandable oversight for a London reviewer, detached from the 'specific context' of the city of Derry to have made, as, by the end of the play, things have gone manifestly wrong for the characters on the stage. The British army raids its way through the locality in reprisal for the assumed murder of the missing Yolland, figuratively performing Ballybeg's imminent cultural ruin, and some of the locals, Owen included, prepare to resist. The play thus ends in the contemporary mode. It explains to the audience how they have inherited a set of problems. Though familiar roles have been assumed, the catharsis of the play is not to be found in the resumption of normality; instead, it is to be found in the recognition of the negotiable space opened up by the play's deconstruction of the imperialist and nationalist narratives. The very fact of the play's performance emphasized the point. The citizens of Derry were aware that their city, which had for so long been a stage set for violent political confrontation before the national and international media, was now the focal point of a more accommodating form of dramatic expression, however briefly. Heaney expressed the public mood as he experienced it on the night:

> It wasn't set out to be a play that trumped one side or the other, and that was recognised. There was a feeling in Derry of some kind of civic event ... and when the mayor of Derry, not only was present ... but ... stood to applaud the play, it wasn't just good personal behaviour, it was good civic behaviour. It said if there is an open space, we'll play in it. We'll all go into it with some kind of

64 Interview with Rea, *Arts Extra*, BBC Radio Ulster, 23 September 2005, 25th anniversary of *Translations*.
65 *Irish Press* editorial, 26 September 1980.
66 David Nowlan, *Irish Times*, 24 September 1980.
67 FDA: PC/1980/1: Timothy E. O'Grady, *New Statesman*, 3 October 1980.

> hope. And that's one of the good things about theatre, it is an open space in this city. ... It doesn't harangue the audience, it suggests things, and they complete them. ... At a psychic level, at a privacy level, it was a tough time for everybody in Northern Ireland ... who wanted to live fully, freely and decently. ... I think there was gratitude that the play wasn't a *j'accuse* ... that it was more a sense of distress, this is what we are left with — how do we negotiate?[68]

If there is a parallel to be drawn in the distinction between the stage and the auditorium — the distinction between fiction and reality — the trend in modern drama is to diminish the difference, to include the audience in the fictional framework. At the Guildhall, the geographical proximity of the fictional events added to this, but so too did the history of the venue and of the disputed territory outside. Rea made this point when recalling the night twenty-five years later:

> It was rough theatre in a very grand building, a rather pompous building. So we took it over and tried to subvert it with a little bit of theatrical immediacy. ... It was a very interesting way to do a play in a way, in a building that wasn't meant to house theatre, but it had a lot of connotations of a previous time in Derry. ... To do a play in Derry is very difficult. There was no infrastructure — there was no costume design, no set builders, there was nothing like that. We had to bring all that with us.[69]

In a society in which violent conflict is the norm, the difference between drama and reality is all the more blurred. Deane argued this point in the specific context of television coverage of violent events in Northern Ireland:

> The violent play is being staged under TV floodlights in front of an audience moved, not only by what they see, but also by the anguish which comes from not knowing the outcome. The death of an individual alters if he died on the side of the heroes, not of the villains. Yet the playwright is the audience. It is imagining what it sees in terms of the outcome which it desires.[70]

Deane's insight here is important. It helps to explain why, even allowing for the aforementioned reasons, a stage play such as *Translations*, lacking in special effects and thrills, should have such an impact in an era when drama is so ubiquitous. Raymond Williams observes that in the current era in the Western world, for the first time,

> a majority of the population has regular and constant access to drama, beyond occasion and season. ... [D]rama ... is built into the rhythms of everyday life. ... [T]he substantial majority of the population [now sees] up to three hours of drama a day, every day. ... What we now have is drama as habitual experience: more in a week, in many cases, than most human beings would have previously seen in a lifetime.[71]

Williams contends that the attraction of drama in contemporary society is that it performs the same purpose as statistics and summaries: it attempts to break down and understand the increasingly complex ways in which we live. That is to say, everyday drama is an expression of the postmodern spirit of questioning, uncertainty, and exploration. Williams goes on to argue that we now live in what he calls a 'dramatized society', in which drama is

> a special kind of use of quite general processes of presentation, representation, signification. The raised place of power — the eminence of the royal platform — was built historically before the raised place of the stage. ... Drama is a precise separation of certain common modes for new and specific ends. It is neither ritual

68 Interview with Heaney, *Arts Extra*, BBC Radio Ulster, 23 September 2005, 25th anniversary of *Translations*.

69 Interview with Rea, *Arts Extra*, BBC Radio Ulster, 23 September 2005, 25th anniversary of *Translations*. Another thing that was lacking in Derry was professional box-office staff. Staff from both the Guildhall and the Orchard Gallery in Derry worked voluntarily at the box office and at the doors on the night. As a result, the final returns remain unclear, but they can be estimated with some precision. The FDA records that there were 246 seats sold, 300 complimentary seats, and 26 unsold. The total attendance for the whole Derry run, 23–27 September inclusive, was estimated at 3,145, or 92 per cent of capacity. Though extremely high, these attendance figures do not match the 100 per cent attendance achieved at other venues: Galway, Tralee, Dublin, Carrickmore, Enniskillen and Armagh.

70 Deane, 'Introduction/ The Longing for Modernity', *Threshold*, 32 (Winter 1982), 3.

71 Raymond Williams, *Writing in Society* (London, 1983), 12.

72 Williams, *Writing in Society*, 15; original italics.
73 Stuart Hall, ed., *Representation: Cultural Representations and Signifying Practices* (London/Thousand Oaks/Delhi, 1997), 5–6.
74 For a good concise discussion of the idea of sense-data, see http://plato.stanford.edu/archives/spr2005/entries/sense-data/

> which discloses to God, nor myth which requires and sustains repetition. It is specific, active, interactive composition: an action not an act; an open practice that has been deliberately abstracted from temporary practical or magical ends; a complex opening of ritual to public and variable action; a moving beyond myth to dramatic *versions* of myth and history. It was this active variable experimental drama — not the closed world of known signs and meanings — that came through in its own right and in its own power.[72]

In other words, drama is an agent for change in contemporary society, because in the modern age it broke from the hierarchical figures and processions of state (though the break was not complete). Postcolonial critics such as Edward Said and Homi Bhabha, to whom Friel and his Field Day colleagues owe a debt, began in the late 1970s to study the controlling power of representation in colonized societies. They focused on the cultural production of colonized and colonizer in order to identify the origins of the modes of representation. They demonstrated that culture underlines the essential role of the symbolic at the heart of social life; that representation of culture occurs through language, which includes the verbal, the visual and the symbolic; and that, in language, signs represent our concepts, ideas and feelings in ways that allow others to read, decode, or interpret their meaning.

Culture is thus conceptualized as 'a primary or "constitutive" process as important as the economic or material base in shaping social subjects and historical events — not merely a reflection of the world after the event'.[73] On this basis, and it is the basis on which Field Day itself operated, the performance of *Translations* did not simply reflect the host society, but it contributed to the way that society represented itself. Williams's argument, and it is one with which Friel would agree, is that, of all the arts, drama is particularly powerful in this regard because it demands interaction and goes straight to the heart of social life.

Audience interaction operates at a near-primal level by engaging with our 'sense-data', a concept explored by Bertrand Russell in *The Problems of Philosophy* (1912).[74] It is part of human nature to interpret sense-data as reality. When we see a table, we see a table. When we think about seeing a table, and think about tables and wonder what is meant by seeing, philosophy begins. Theatre imparts data directly to our senses, and conspires with our natural instinct to skip the philosophy. Since we tend to trust sense-data, we trust and can immerse ourselves immediately in a play. The playwright says, 'This is England in ancient times, this is a king called Lear, over there is a heath, it's morning time ...' and we start automatically and almost unconsciously filling in the missing details. It is part of our genetic inheritance. A playwright not only transports us into a different time, but leaves us in the company of others once we arrive. A novelist has to accompany us. If a playwright declares as unimaginable something that the audience is actually watching, it is more powerful than the novelist's trick of withholding information from a character but giving it to the reader because it is now *knowledge as experience*. In *Translations*, the unimaginable thing is the English language. As the characters express their wonder at the sheer strangeness of the idea of speaking English, the audience is experiencing it. It is not just that it has hindsight and the knowledge of history, but it sees something that is unimaginable being acted out. *Translations* fulfils its own promise/premise.

Shortly after the Derry premiere, Friel wrote to Deane:

> October 3, 1980
>
> Remember — we talked about it in the Teac Ban.* You suggested a Brit. soldier

disappearing. Idea used. 1% of all Cork, Tralee, Carrickmore plus Newry royalties will be forwarded.

Still up to our necks in the TRANSLATIONS business. The modest little enterprise we ventured on has suddenly engulfed us and we're daily bombarded with problems about contracts & fire-insurance & trucking sets & costume bills etc etc. But the freedom to compose the *whole* thing has been an exhilaration and we'd [Friel and Rea] go again. And almost certainly will.

... There was a time when I thought I knew what the play was about but it has been embraced by so many opposing factions that I'm now confused. Ok maybe the thing's about nothing. [75]

It is clear that the success of the play has left Friel with mixed feelings. On the one hand, he is overwhelmed by it: he admits that he and Rea are feeling 'engulfed', 'up to our necks' and 'bombarded'. On the other hand, 'the *whole* thing has been an exhilaration' and he and Rea remain resolved to continue — in fact, we know already from his letter to Rea in June 1980 that he had written Field Day's next play, his adaptation of Chekhov's *Three Sisters*. In this letter to Deane, Friel seems to be preparing the ground for recruiting help. The overwhelming public response to the play has left him and Rea enthused — they will almost certainly 'go again' — yet confused. The success of the play demanded a coherent public strategy, but Friel was still not clear whether he should look beyond the theatre world for support. He took up the issue with Rea straight away. Just one month later, while *Translations* was still on tour and about to visit Cork, Friel put forward the idea of 'extending' the company. He was still thinking in terms of taking on someone from theatre:

November 5 [1980]

Just to wish you well in Cork. My feeling is that it may be a sort of test.

... In case you didn't have a chance to speak to Tom Kilroy he thinks the enterprise is of *great* importance and analysed it with perception and — I felt — wisdom. The defining elements he sees as: a response to Abbey work which only occasionally rises above the mediocre — and of course by extension to all other theatrical work now being done in this country; an articulation of an alternative voice to the metropolitan voice; and an articulation of the Northern vitality — and of course by extension of the dominant and ultimately defining element that is going to shape this island in the years to come. (To any or all of these principles you may assent or demur. But listening to him I felt he had got close to an essence. I told him that the formulation of these kinds of 'principles' — as if we had set out with a clear charter — make me a bit uneasy. To which he responded: What the hell; they're there; and it doesn't matter how or if they're articulated.) He also feels that we need a director who shares those ambitions. Yes, I know, I know. Anyhow, he's solidly enthusiastic. Likes THREE SISTERS idea. He has a very astute sense of what you're about... Says there are no Irish directors we should consider. Etc. etc ...

I've been thinking a lot about 'extending' and although part of me feels that we ought to, the moment a name occurs to me (Kilroy, for example) my next response is 'Why? What for?' Of course, if we had a possible director, I'd have no hesitation. But as for other people I'm not sure. And yet ... and yet ...

... If Cork doesn't embrace you, we'll do a Black-and-Tan job on them.[76]

Kilroy, as we have already seen, had long

75 FDA: G/D/Friel/Deane. Friel to Deane, handwritten addendum to typed letter, dated 3 October 1980. *Pub near Kincasslagh, Co. Donegal.

Liam Neeson as Doalty and Nuala Hayes as Máire, *Translations* reheasal, Guildhall, Derry, 1980. Photo: Rod Tuach, © Field Day.

been a source of inspiration for Friel. He was also at this time adapting Chekhov's *The Seagull* (1981) for the Abbey, and Friel would have been in consultation with him with regard to his own adaptation of *Three Sisters*. Kilroy too has spoken of his involvement with Field Day in the early stages:

> I got involved with Field Day largely out of friendship. I was very close to Brian Friel, and Seamus Heaney, and Seamus Deane, and Stephen Rea. I didn't know Tom Paulin or Davy Hammond as well ... we were constantly in and out of each other's houses so that when Field Day started I was on the sidelines, interrogating, and being told, and arguing what Field Day was ... I was in Derry for the famous first production of *Translations*. And I was up there a lot with Deane, experiencing at first hand the trauma of the North. I was quite surprised when I was asked to join because I had this very clear sense of Field Day as being a northern enterprise ... I think it had partly to do with the fact that both Brian and Stephen felt there should be another playwright involved. Seamus Deane asked me to write a pamphlet but I regret to say that I never got round to producing one.[77]

On the basis of the letters we have read so far, it is safe to conclude that Kilroy was correct — that the desire to maintain a northern focus was what would exclude him, for the time being, from formal membership of Field Day (he joined formally in May 1988). Within a few days of his first letter to Rea about extending the company, Friel had formulated a plan, and where better to imagine it coming together than at another 'think-in', this time at Annaghmakerrig, County Monaghan, formerly the family seat of his mentor Tyrone Guthrie?

> November 8, 1980
>
> ... wondering about our situation: should

76 FDA: G/D/Friel/Rea/4: letter from Friel to Rea, dated 5 November [1980].

77 Gerry Dukes, 'Interview with Thomas Kilroy', in L. Chambers, G. Fitzgibbon and E. Jordan, eds., *Theatre Talk: Voices of Irish Theatre Practitioners* (Dublin, 2001), 247.

> we expand or should we not? And I had a momentary and misleading inspiration: that we should gather together a group of sympathetically-minded people and spend a long week-end in Guthrie's (now Arts Council's) place in Anna[gh] makerrig, County Monaghan, exploring various ideas. The spirit would be there and encouraging. The trouble is that the damn place isn't open yet as far as I know. But the idea of a think-in mightn't be bad. And we could always invoke The Presence. Because what he did in Strat., Ont.,* and in Minneapolis was precisely the kind of thing we stumbled into with Field Day: working *outside* the established centres and gathering together the best possible people and aiming at an artistic excellence. And I believe that we have a strength that he didn't have: this island we want to give voice to is *our* land, not a foreign land.[78]

As it turned out, the 'damn place' was not open, as Friel had feared, but a meeting did eventually take place there two years later. The fact that Friel used the term 'think-in' here indicates that he had decided that he would call upon those with whom he had similar meetings in previous years. It is interesting to note that in November 1980 Friel still considered that he and Rea had 'stumbled' into something, that they had, as yet, no clear idea about what their goals were, even though they had already decided to stage Friel's adaptation of *Three Sisters*. When the selection of a board of directors became necessary in order for Field Day to gain charitable status (and thus avoid tax liability), the idea of 'extending' became a reality. The correspondence between Friel and Rea clearly shows that the directors were invited to join after *Translations* was premiered. However, as if subconsciously endorsing Friel's perennial theme of the unreliability of historical memory, Deane remembers a different sequence of events. He recalls that the extended board formed *before* the play was premiered:

> But before *Translations* inaugurated the company's public activities, Field Day had broadened its scope and its membership. At the invitation of Friel and Rea, four others joined. ... [T]he new directors were brought in because the original idea had grown beyond what could be accomplished by an annual theatrical production. In brief, it was felt that the political crisis in the North and all its reverberations in the Republic had made the necessity of a reappraisal of Ireland's political and cultural situation explicit and urgent.[79]

Deane's alternative sequence of events is instructive, indicating as it does that his involvement with Field Day, and the close involvement of some of the other soon-to-be board members, had been sufficiently thorough and ongoing to make the exact moment when it all began difficult to locate. Certainly, the evidence we have seen would suggest that Deane and Heaney were involved in Field Day before *Translations* to such an extent that they considered themselves part of the enterprise, but the formal invitation to join came later and was only accepted in August 1981, eleven months after the Derry premiere. This can be confirmed by a letter of welcome addressed to all directors, held in the Field Day Archive:

> 4 August 1981
>
> Thank you very much for agreeing to join the advisory panel. We will describe you as directors on our stationery but there is no legal or statutory implications involved as you would be non remunerated directors. There is also no work involved but we would welcome your advice and we would hope that we would all get together ... at least once a year for dinner ... BF and SR.[80]

Rea's recollection of the sequence of events is more reliable: 'The company had to form

78 FDA: G/D/Friel/Rea/4: letter from Friel to Rea, dated 8 November1980. *Refers to Stratford, Ontario, the largest classical repertory theatre in North America. Actor and director Tyrone Guthrie became the first artistic director. The Stratford Shakespearean Festival of Canada was incorporated as a legal entity on 31 October 1952, and work began on a concrete amphitheatre at the centre of which was to be a revolutionary thrust stage created to Guthrie's specifications by internationally renowned theatrical designer Tanya Moiseiwitsch. Also, the Guthrie Theatre in Minneapolis, where Friel worked with Guthrie in 1963.

79 FDA: G/D/Deane/7. Unpublished essay on Field Day by Deane, 1985.

a board of directors because it applied for charitable status. So we decided on people who would challenge us ... who would move the thing on a bit, and not just theatre people.'

Documents in the archive confirm the correct sequence of events:

> Minutes of an extraordinary meeting of the company duly convened and held at 1/3 Clarendon Street, Derry on Monday, 3rd August, 1981 at 3.00 pm.
>
> Present: Brian Friel, Stephen Rea, Seamus Deane, David Hammond and Noel McKenna, Company Secretary.
>
> Mr Friel was in the chair. Mr Friel explained that this extraordinary meeting of members was called so that the company could obtain charitable status and to do this it was necessary to pass a special resolution to change the memorandum and articles as advised by our accountants and the Inland Revenue ...
>
> It was further resolved that the company appoint 4 new directors to advise on the promotion and development of the company. These four new directors who have all agreed to serve on the board shall receive no remuneration whatsoever other than essential out of pocket expenses to attend any board meeting. The 4 new directors, Messrs Seamus Heaney, Seamus Deane, David Hammond and Tom Paulin were duly proposed, seconded and unanimously elected to serve on the board of directors.[81]

As Rea said in interview, Deane and Heaney 'picked themselves'.[82] At the time, Heaney was a poet of international repute and Deane was professor of Modern English and American Literature at University College Dublin and a published poet and critic; the two had been friends since boyhood in Derry. Poet and critic Tom Paulin, from Belfast, was a friend of Rea's, and the late David Hammond was a BBC filmmaker, traditional singer, and long-term friend of Friel's and Heaney's. Unlike Heaney and Deane, Hammond and Paulin were completely new to Field Day. It was felt that they were more or less like-minded and that they could contribute to the opening up of the debate that the others had initiated.

One month later, on 30 September 1981, the first Annual General Meeting of the Field Day Theatre Company Limited took place at the Gresham Hotel, Dublin. Attending were Friel, Rea, Heaney, Hammond, Deane, Paulin and McKenna. Unfortunately, the minutes are perfunctory, simply stating: '... the directors had a long and detailed discussion on future plans for the company. It was not clear what would happen as the exact financial position of the company was not known.'[83] Heaney recalled the sentiment of that first 'long and detailed discussion' with reporter Mary Holland:

> We believed we could create a space in which we would try to redefine what being Irish meant in the context of what had happened in the North, the relationship of Irish nationalism and culture. We were very conscious that we wanted to be quite independent of the British influence exercised through Belfast and the equally strong cultural hegemony of Dublin.[84]

The agenda had also been outlined by Friel in a letter to all directors one week before the meeting:

> Because of the work involved in putting THREE SISTERS together and getting it on the road, Stephen and I haven't had adequate time to discuss the shape and scope of the Sept. 30 meeting. But my instinct — the instinct that brought us together, that animates Field Day, that we now feel may be robust enough for

80 FDA: G/Meet/1b.
81 FDA: G/D/Meet/1b.
82 Interview with Rea, *Arts Extra*, BBC Radio Ulster, 23 September 2005, 25th anniversary of *Translations*.
83 FDA: G/D/Meet/1c. All subsequent Field Day meetings were recorded, usually by Deane, often in verse.
84 Quoted in Mary Holland, 'Field Day's Tenth Birthday', in the programme notes for Heaney's Field Day play *The Cure at Troy*, 1 October 1990.

discussion — is that he will agree to the following (random) thoughts.

We are honoured to have you as board members; and we asked you to join us in Field Day because we believe that you have a sense of what we're attempting (indeed in your own work you have contributed to the climate that bred Field Day) and because we are now at a stage when we need help. Stephen and I also feel that we should take respite from the daily pressures of Field Day and that each of us should return for a time to his own craft. Can the board help us to do this?

The immediate question is: Where do we go from here? — what next?

If a great new Irish play were to land on our desk, of course we would do it — immediately, happily ...

A magazine was mentioned ... a dramatic version of one of our sagas, perhaps the Táin ... of finding some means of celebrating the best of the Northern Protestant tradition ...

The items on the agenda for the meeting were listed thus:

1. First two productions — TRANSLATIONS and THREE SISTERS
2. Funding. Financial situation.
3. Relationship with Arts Councils. Need to apply for funding now. To which committee?
4. Documentaries
5. The future[85]

The absence of minutes for the first three Field Day meetings reflects the group's, specifically Friel's and Rea's, caution about declaring Field Day's aims. But after two years, that is after the success of *Translations*, *Three Sisters* and *The Communication Cord*, things had changed. Having raised many questions with the play in a successfully ecumenical way, Friel and Rea agreed it was time to formulate an agenda. A plan of action of sorts emerged from the fourth meeting, held at Annaghmakerrig in 1982. The deepening crisis in the North, where the hunger strikes at the H-Blocks had taken place in the interim, added extra urgency to the project. The goal of changing the 'articles of constitution' of Irish literature, first suggested by Friel in his letter to Deane in 1974, was from this point on being pursued in earnest. Two days after the meeting, Friel circulated a letter to all directors:

October 26, 1982

Thank you very much for coming to the Annaghmakerrig meeting and for giving Field Day that much of your time and interest and energy. What ought to have been said formally by either Stephen or me at the meeting was how very much we value that interest and your generous investment in the enterprise. I believe that we have the best possible board of directors and that in their various ways they embody the spirit of Field day (whatever that is).

Before we left Annaghmakerrig on Monday morning, David Hammond and I had a chat about the discussions of the previous day. We both felt that (a) they were valuable (b) that any notion of exploring the Reader idea was less than ambitious but good enough — if only as a first step and (c) that the potential of the Pamphlet idea hadn't been fully explored.

We talked about the Pamphlet idea for a time and became excited by it ...[86]

By the end of 1982, the Field Day agenda had to a large extent been set. The pamphlet idea first suggested at Annaghmakerrig was pursued to conclusion, and the 'less than ambitious' reader idea was soon to grow into *The Field Day Anthology of Irish Literature*.

85 FDA: G/D/Friel/4: letter from Friel to Field Day directors, dated 21 September 1981.

86 FDA: G/D/Friel/4: letter from Friel to Field Day directors, dated 26 October 1982.
87 *SP*, 400.
88 Aidan O'Malley in 'In Other Words: Coming to Terms with Irish Identities through Translation: Readings of the Twelve Plays Produced by the Field Day Theatre Company, 1980–1991', PhD thesis in history and civilization, European University Institute, Florence, January 2004. From 'Semiology and Grammatology: Interview with Julia Kristeva', in Jacques Derrida, *Positions*, trans. Alan Bass (London, 1981), 15–36 (20). PhD is held in the FDA.
89 *SP*, 416.
90 *SP*, 418.
91 *SP*, 419.

Betrayal

In the correspondence from Friel to Rea during the period when Friel was writing *Translations*, we read how the character of Owen grew in stature as the play developed. Friel had initially caricatured him as a kind of please-everybody television host. Indeed, even in the completed play, Owen is introduced in this manner by the stage directions: '... a handsome, attractive young man in his twenties. He is dressed smartly — a city man. His manner is easy and charming: everything he does is invested with consideration and enthusiasm.'[87] Friel came to realize the importance of Owen as the character who stood between the two cultures in the play. It became evident that Owen had come to represent Field Day's position and that Rea, therefore, had to play him. Owen's position is characterized by a combination of submission and self-assertion, giving and taking; he discards what is inhibiting in a culture and reclaims what is reaffirming. Owen is an interpreter. A good interpreter must be able to give up a part of his own authorship in order to give the original author his due. The self-obliteration in the act of translation puts into play the relationship between the signifier and the signified. According to Jacques Derrida, it 'practices the difference between signified and signifier'.[88] In the old idiom, there is a strain of 'femininity' in the interpreter, meaning a submission to the creative presence — an interesting point in respect of Owen's relationship with Yolland, and Ireland's relationship with England: Irish with English, female with male.

At the outset, Owen occupies the position of the traitor. He betrays his community by facilitating its demise. He represents the idea of translation as a kind of conversion that is poisonous. Yet his submission contains the potential to be emancipatory; it starts as a betrayal and ends as a discovery. Indeed, all translation involves a betrayal: it implies both a traducing of something and also a revelation or discovery of it. The very idea of translation has betrayal built into it. There is a clear relationship between translating, which involves carrying an idea from one place or polity to another, and betrayal, which involves transporting an idea or person(s) from one authority to another. In the *Translations* setting, one polity is imposed upon another, and some of the natives co-operate. Irish is Englished. The Irish co-operate to make themselves English. Then the question arises, is there some essential Irish or English character involved, or is that really to accept some species of racial destiny or character? In the play, Yolland suspects there *is* an essential racial character. He doubts whether he could ever truly assimilate in Ballybeg, even if he learned Irish: 'I may learn the password but the language of the tribe will always elude me, won't it? The private core will always be ... hermetic, won't it?'[89]

Hugh also raises the question of essential identity: 'We like to think we endure around truths immemorially posited.'[90] Whether Hugh includes himself in the 'we' is left intentionally ambiguous. For romantics like Yolland and Manus, Hugh's statement is 'astute'; Owen, on the other hand, rejects the notion outright: 'Is it astute not to be able to adjust for survival? Enduring around truths immemorially posited — hah!'[91] Neither stance proves to be tenable, however. Manus is (literally) crippled by his convictions, and this leads to his exile. Yolland's romanticism results in his fatal attraction to Máire. A successful outcome to their love affair is just as remote as it is for Jimmy Jack and the goddess Athene. Even Jimmy Jack, who cannot differentiate between myth and reality, recognizes this: '... *exogamein* means to marry outside the tribe. And you don't cross those borders casually — both sides get very angry.'[92] Owen too is compromised, but in his case by his conviction that *all* tradition can be discarded. It is only when he steps back from his certainty and allows 'confusion' to be an acceptable condition, that he is redeemed. *Translations* focused on the ambiguity of the confused *dis*position — on the gap between the two belief systems — as did Field Day.

In his introduction to his Field Day play *Double Cross* (1986), Tom Kilroy argued that 'To base one's identity, exclusively, on a mystical sense of place rather than in personal character where it properly resides seems to me a dangerous absurdity. To dedicate one's life to the systematic betrayal of that ideal seems to me equally absurd.'[93] The play is about the two renegade Irishmen, William Joyce and Brendan Bracken, who exchange their Irish identities for a German and a British one, respectively, and in effect become Germany's and Britain's ministers for propaganda. They are caught in the racial, translation conundrum, with the usual Kilrovian sexual inversions and melodramas. In the finest performance of all his Field Day roles, Rea played both central figures. The outsider role is vital for Rea, since he came from a Belfast Protestant background to embrace a genuine republicanism. Rea has also been drawn to explore sexual inversions and outsider identities in the films of Neil Jordan,[94]as, for example, the Castle spy Ned Broy in *Michael Collins* (1996), or as Fergus, the IRA deserter and third party in a relationship in *The Crying Game* (1992). Rea admits the attraction these roles. In a feature in the *Gazette* (Montreal) in 2000, he indicated a possible link between his role in the latter film and his Field Day activities: 'The whole point of *The Crying Game* is that by an act of imagination, by an act of humanity, you can change things. You can change yourself.'[95] Elsewhere, referring to his role in Les Blair's film *Bad Behaviour* (1993), Rea said:

> Obviously I'm drawn to certain kinds of roles, and someone said I always play the role of an outsider ... Even in a film called *Bad Behaviour*, which was an improvised film — it didn't occur to me, but someone said, 'That guy was an outsider even in his own family', and I suppose it's true.[96]

The idea that betrayal is at the heart of *Translations* and therefore a focal point of Field Day's activities is not new, but it is one that has not been explored to any great degree. The geopolitical significance of Field Day's Derry home underscores the theme. Derry is a historically marginalized border city, divided between two communities, each of which feels isolated from its hinterland; it is also a city that has become a symbolic focal point for the aspirations and grievances of each community in Northern Ireland. Out of this context, Field Day broadcasted its disloyalty. It stood between two jurisdictions in Ireland and pledged allegiance to neither. As Friel himself put it: '... it's located in the North and has its reservations about it, and it works in the South and has its reservations about it.'[97] It stressed its northern identity, but also its Irish identity; it occupied the fifth province of Ireland, a province of the mind, an imaginary place, as we have already seen, borrowed from the *Crane Bag* and described by Friel as a 'place for dissenters, traitors to the prevailing mythologies in the other four provinces'.[98]

Deane argued that play's 'essential preoccupation is with the treachery of the central character Owen who betrays his inherited culture. To put it in the bluntest and most dramatic form, Friel is entranced by the connection between betrayal and freedom.'[99] For Owen, abandoning his allegiance to his community liberates him from a history of bondage, failure and nostalgia, but it also isolates him, making him an outsider to both traditions. His freedom comes from belonging to neither. It is an incomplete freedom, because although he does not fully belong, neither can he fully escape the embrace of each culture. He has repudiated his Irishness, but he never was English. Both cultures view him with suspicion. As Deane stated in a public lecture delivered in Derry in January 1985,

92 *SP*, 446.
93 Thomas Kilroy, 'Author's Note', *Double Cross* (London, 1986), 6–7.
94 Jordan wrote a screenplay for *Translations*, which was never filmed. The manuscript is held in the FDA.
95 Quote taken from www.stephenrea.net. This statement is very similar to Robert Hewison's description of Frank Hardy's role in *Faith Healer*. See footnote 53.
96 Quote taken from www.stephenrea.net, from Carole Zucker, *In the Company of Actors: Reflecting on the Craft of Acting* (London, 1999).
97 *Irish Times*, 14 September 1980.
98 Quoted in John Gray, 'Field Day Five Years On', *Linen Hall Review*, 2, 2 (Summer 1985), 7.

99 FDA: G/D/Deane/7. A short essay by Deane leads to an announcement of plans for *The Field Day Anthology of Irish Writing*, dated March 1985.
100 FDA: G/D/Deane/7. Untitled lecture transcript, p. 23–24. Datable to Jan 1985.
101 *SP*, 420.
102 *SP*, 420–21.
103 *SP*, 421.

> treachery is one of the few available forms of freedom left. ... I don't want to be a Celt. I don't want to be an Anglo. I don't want to be a Protestant. I don't want to be a Catholic. I don't want to be a republican. I don't want to be a unionist. I don't want to gravitate to any one of the magnetic fields in which most of my compatriots live. But the moment you gravitate out of one of them ... you belong, like Derry as a city ... in the twilight zone. It isn't freedom, but it's the nearest available form of freedom that on many occasions either Irish literature or Irish politics has managed to produce.[100]

Owen embraces the standardizing logic of the Ordnance Survey mission; however, he cannot fully escape the gravitational pull of his native tradition. He tries hard; he dismisses the significance of the name of the crossroads called Tobair Vree ('Brian's Well'), yet he alone knows why the place is so named. He claims no romantic attachment to it. He rejects Yolland's feeling that by their renaming activities 'something is being eroded':[101]

> Owen: Do we scrap Tobair Vree altogether and call it — what? — The Cross? Crossroads? Or do we keep piety with a man long dead, long forgotten, his name 'eroded' beyond recognition, whose trivial little story nobody in the parish remembers?
> Yolland: Except you.
> Owen: I've left here.[102]

Owen's defiance seems petulant. He knows that merely declaring that he has left his home-place does not make it true. This would be to deny the apparent logic of the new system he has embraced. Yolland knows it too, and when he insists that the name Tobair Vree stands as it is, he says: 'That's what you want too, Roland'.[103] It is at this point Owen angrily demands in turn that his correct name be used, but in doing so, he loses the argument with Yolland by conceding his own true name and identity are inseparable and that thus, by extension, the Ordnance Survey's renaming enterprise does, in fact, result in an erosion of identity. And yet, this key scene is ambiguous. The same place name also reveals that the notion of things enduring around 'truths immemorially posited' does not hold water. The *tobair*, or 'well', at the crossroads of Tobair Vree has long since dried up. There is no automatic or natural alliance between name and place in the Gaelic tradition either.

Irish historical myths of liberty and freedom, from the Siege of Derry 1688–89, to the United Irishmen rising of 1798 and Robert Emmet's subsequent rising of 1803, to the Easter Rebellion of 1916, all lose their mythic force without the participation of the traitor, the go-between, the ambiguous identity. None of these events would seem so heroic had it not experienced betrayal. The theme was relentlessly pursued by Field Day: in Paulin's *The Riot Act* and Mahon's *High Time*, the connection between authoritarianism and subversive betrayal is the central issue; elsewhere, the character caught between two cultures, the traitor, or the betrayed, occupy centre stage — as Bracken and Joyce in Kilroy's *Double Cross*, as Oscar Wilde in Terry Eagleton's *Saint Oscar*, as Roger Casement in David Rudkin's *Cries from Casement as His Bones are Brought to Dublin*, as Hugh O'Neill in Friel's *Making History*, as Henry Joy McCracken in Stewart Parker's *Northern Star*.

In Parker's play, McCracken, the United Irish leader, cannot find a way to work outside the struggle for power between dogmas, and he is drawn in and destroyed. Field Day was engaged in a similar struggle. It sought to discover a sense of freedom that is not dependent for its sense of belonging to a tradition that is, or was, or is about

Original *Translations* poster, designed by Basil Blackshaw, 1980. © Field Day.

to be betrayed. To do this required the dismantling of stereotypes analytically and performatively. *Translations* did both. It set up its own stereotypes in order to undermine them. As Heaney said: 'The play is subscribing to certain stereotypes, but also subverting them because the characters in the play who seem to represent positive heritage ... Jimmy Jack ... they're also slightly comic.'[104] Owen, who began the play as a sort of quisling, emerges at the end as someone who has rejected both of the stereotypes that try to draw him in, as the personification of the hybrid identity to which contemporary Ireland must look. He has discovered that slavish acceptance of either culture is insufficient and he has learned how to combine local tradition with cosmopolitan ideas. He does not need his father's advice any more.[105] He has learned the new names, he has learned to make them his own, and he has learned where he lives. Of all the characters in the play, he is the best equipped to negotiate the future.

Lionel Pilkington also focuses on how the play rehashes the stereotypes in order to mock them. The implication is that those critics who can only read 'green' nationalism in the play are those who are themselves caught most firmly in the binary trap of the Irish/British, Catholic/Protestant stereotype:

> To consider, as some commentators do, that the nationalist appeal of the first act is an indication of the tendentiousness of *Translations* as a whole is to ignore an extensive irony. Hugh's scorn for English, for example, is spoken in English which the audience, through a dramatic convention, understands as Irish. Thus, while Hugh's teaching is based on the view that Gaelic culture and the classical culture make a 'happier conjugation' ... his actual formulation of this view consists of an etymological pedagogy that demonstrates the opposite: that it is English, not Irish, that has extensive roots in Greek and Latin. It is not the etymology of Irish words that Hugh is constantly asking his pupils to conjugate and recite, but English words ... Hugh may declare that the English language is particularly suited for the purposes of commerce ... and that it makes poetry sound 'plebian' ..., but this is contradicted by his own ostentatious delight in iambic rhythms, alliteration and words that are polysyllabic and latinate.[106]

For most commentators, the fact that *Translations* took place in Derry's Guildhall marked an important shift in Northern Ireland's post-Stormont political order. Consequently, criticism of the play tended to come from those who read the play as being motivated by straightforward anti-state nationalism — as an endorsement of the Romantic nationalist idea of a pre-British Gaelic-speaking utopia. This accusation is inconsistent with the play's central idea, which is that if the political impasse of the present is to be broken, then *both* the nationalist and imperial histories must be reconsidered. *Translations* mocks, for example, the heroic narrative of 1798 through Hugh's admission that his participation in the rising amounted to nothing more than a pub crawl; it undermines the Gaelic idyll by populating Ballybeg with characters who are physically or mentally or addictively impaired; and it even suggests that the modernity that was imposed through empire might also have had benefits for the traditional society (Manus, who is the most hostile to the English soldiers, is the one who benefits most from state incursion into Ballybeg — the state awards him a house, fuel, food, and a salary).[107]

Historian Sean Connolly attacked Friel for exaggerating British military aggression in the play, and for avoiding direct consideration of Irish republicanism. He questioned why Friel chose to arm the military with bayonets when all published accounts, including one of Friel's main

104 Interview with Heaney, *Arts Extra*, BBC Radio Ulster, 23 September 2005, 25th anniversary of *Translations*.
105 *SP*, 444: Hugh: 'We must learn these new names. ... We must learn where we live. We must learn to make them our own. We must make them our new home.'
106 Lionel Pilkington, 'Language and Politics in Brian Friel's Translations', *Irish University Review*, 20, 2 (Autumn 1990), 286.
107 *SP*, 423.

source-texts, *A Paper Landscape* by J. H. Andrews, show the Ordnance Survey to have been an economically motivated project, and he draws our attention to the fact that the soldiers involved in the survey were expressly forbidden to put down any civil disturbances.[108] Unlike Friel, however, Connolly seeks to identify and challenge one narrative only, the nationalist one. He does not investigate how the nationalist and imperial histories are dependent on stereotype, how they are interdependent. It is not sufficient, or even perceptive, to say that soldiers involved in the survey would have been unarmed. Identifying which particular state agency may have been appointed to the fictional task of carrying out reprisals against the people of Ballybeg does not seem to concern him, but that is not the point either. He contends that the most straightforward explanation for the decline of the Irish language in the first half of the nineteenth century 'may be found, not in official policies of cultural imperialism, but in the processes of economic and social change',[109] and he goes on to list the 'benefits' of these changes — increased mobility, improved communications, and greater 'penetration' by the market economy, et cetera. He claims that the idea of cultural imperialism was irrelevant to the government of the day; however, he does not identify the cultural implications of the economic imperialism that he accurately describes but neglects to name. He objects to the way Yolland is stereotyped as being 'culturally as well as socially gauche',[110]and to the crass materialism of the character of Lancey, but he does not recognize that Owen is less gauche than his fellow villagers because of his exposure to metropolitan (that is, Lancey's and Yolland's) culture, nor does he complain about Hugh's drunken verbosity or Doalty's oafishness. With one eye open to his own metropolitan audience and the other eye altogether closed, he has missed the metaphor of the play; he is solely focused on the second part of the two-part test that Friel sets his characters and his audience: 'how to decide between the tender-minded allowance of memory's authentic reinforcements and a tough-minded disallowance of its self-serving deceptions'.[111]

Edna Longley seems to feel that there is a hierarchy of offensiveness, that one form of stereotype is more dangerous than another. She is bothered by the indictment in the play's postcolonial critique. She feels that it amounts to nothing more than a combination of nationalist lament and reassertion. She claims that when Friel suggests that 'out of that cultural state, a possibility of a political state follows',[112] he would be more accurate (or honest) to declare his desire for the reverse to be true: 'The play does not so much examine myths of dispossession as repeat them. ... In a curious way Field Day itself has enacted the process whereby political fixity shuts off imaginative possibility, the ideological tail wags the creative dog.'[113] She contends that Friel's 'misrepresentation' of the Ordnance Survey is a creative device strategically and exclusively employed in the service of Irish nationalism:

> [T]he play criticises his [Hugh's] pandering to colonialist expectations about the drunken, verbalising Irishman, who speaks a 'language ... full of the mythologies of fantasy and hope and self-deception.' Hugh's son Owen, once a literal and metaphorical 'collaborator' in the Ordnance Survey of Ireland (begun in the 1820s), finally rejects his own compromises and his father's 'confusion', when the British soldiers threaten the community. In both these plays* the sense of weak fathers having let down their children makes a political comment on the history of Northern Catholics since 1921. This may be why Friel misrepresents the Ordnance Survey as an imposed Anglicisation, rather than as an effort — supervised by the best Gaelic scholars — to standardise the

108 Sean Connolly, 'Translating History: Brian Friel and the Irish Past', in Peacock, ed., *The Achievement of Brian Friel*, 149–63.
109 Connolly, 'Translating History', 150.
110 Connolly, 'Translating History', 156.
111 Seamus Heaney, 'For Liberation: Brian Friel and the Use of Memory', in Peacock, ed., *The Achievement of Brian Friel*, 231.
112 FDA: PC/1982/3: 'The Man from God Knows Where', interview with F. O'Toole, *In Dublin*, 28 October 1982, 23.
113 Enda Longley, 'Poetry and Politics', *Crane Bag*, 9, 1 (1985), 28–33.

orthography of the best Gaelic place-names. (J. H. Andrews, historian of the Ordnance Survey, has recently castigated 'the credulity shown by serious scholars in swallowing *Translations* as a record of historical truth, or at any rate historical probability').[114]

Longley's assessment is problematic, even when we leave aside her selectivity regarding Andrews's responses to the play, the fact that the military action in the play was undertaken in reprisal for murder rather than in the service of cartography, or the argument that anglicization should be considered imposed, if it arises, as it does in the play, wholly or in part, from economic need, emigration and impending mass starvation. Longley feels herself to be detached from the identity crisis with which Friel is grappling. She does not accept that when Friel urges the audience to move on from the idea of historical imposition, regardless of its veracity, she too is being addressed. To read only 'unreconstructed' green nationalism behind the historical indictment of the play exposes a limited, binary view of the Irish problem that is most evident in her singularly benign view of the Ordnance Survey's application of a standardized orthography to the Irish landscape. Her approach is defined well by Joe McMinn: '[A]rguing for a political analysis of Irish culture which will be sensible, moderate, rational, detached, unemotional, is to take up a political position without naming it. It is an extension of unionist political values in the cultural arena'.[115]

Longley's stance betrays an unwillingness to acknowledge the nature of colonial representation. A 'detached' analysis of Irish nationalism would likely agree with Benedict Anderson's *Imagined Communities* (1991), which demonstrates how nations are heroes of their own national stories, propagated by literature and media — how nations are not primordial, but culturally and socially constructed. But it is neither detached nor rational to read the practice of cartography as being merely a benign exercise in orthographical standardization by the best scholars. The Ordnance Survey in nineteenth-century Ireland, or indeed any mapping process in any era, is best understood as an exercise of power. Anderson defined the nineteenth-century map as one of three institutions (the census and the museum being the other two) that came to shape profoundly 'the way in which the colonial state imagined its dominion — the nature of the human beings it ruled, the geography of its domain, the legitimacy of its ancestry'.[116] He went on to argue that sacred sites were 'incorporated into the map of the colony, and their ancient prestige ... draped around the mappers',[117] and that '[i]t is probably not too surprising that post-independent states, which exhibited marked continuities with their colonial predecessors, inherited this form of political museumizing'.[118] *Translations* queried *all* aspects of this ongoing power play: the legitimacy of the imperial map, the idea of ancient prestige that it appropriated, and the political museumizing that is its legacy. It suggested instead that appropriation should be imagined over historical imposition. This is what Hugh means when he advises: 'We must learn those new names ... We must learn where we live. We must learn to make them our own. We must make them our new home.'[119] It is also a solution proposed by Homi Bhabha,[120]who is concerned specifically with the discourse of colonialism, how its metaphoric and metonymic patterns construct the other as fetish and stereotype in order to reduce, dominate, and discriminate against it. He argues that to attempt to resist the seemingly monolithic, seemingly rational authority of imperialism, it is necessary to work in 'in-betweenness', in strategies tied to fragmentation and displacement.

The most dedicated criticism of the green nationalism of *Translations* came from

114 Edna Longley, *The Living Stream: Literature and Revisionism in Ireland* (Newcastle-upon-Tyne, 1994), 155. *She is referring also to *Aristocrats*.
115 J. McMinn, 'In Defence of Field Day: Talking Among the Ruins', *Fortnight*, 8 September 1985.
116 Benedict Anderson, 'Census, Map, Museum', chapter 10 in his *Imagined Communities* (London, 1991). Web excerpt: www.haussite.net/haus.0/SCRIPT/txt2001/01/a_censu.HTML, 1.
117 Anderson, 'Census, Map, Museum', www.haussite.net/haus.0/SCRIPT/txt2001/01/a_censu.HTML, 7.
118 Anderson, 'Census, Map, Museum', www.haussite.net/haus.0/SCRIPT/txt2001/01/a_censu.HTML, 8.
119 *SP*, 444.
120 Homi K. Bhabha, *The Location of Culture* (London, 1994).

Friel himself in the form of the play *The Communication Cord*. Friel desired that the two plays should be read in tandem. *The Communication Cord*, which premiered at the Guildhall on 21 September 1982, is a farce that pokes fun at traditionalist nationalist pieties that *Translations* enabled. Rea called the play 'a response to the response' to *Translations*,[121] an example of the artist rejecting the fixed position. As Paulin states in the play's programme, 'comic pragmatism redresses or counterbalances some of the more *völkisch* pieties which *Translations* inspired'.[122] Friel's play is a warning against nationalist nostalgia, whatever its hue, as Deane explains:

> In this play, the most sterile of all illusions is exposed — that of a heroic past which has dwindled to a most unheroic present. The belief in a heroic past almost inevitably produces a farcical present because it gives free rein to cheap attitudes, ranging from facile nostalgia to hard-boiled cynicism. Such attitudes beget stereotyped behaviour and when such behaviour is dominant a culture becomes a caricature.[123]

Historian Kevin Whelan has dismissed the idea that *Translations*, or Field Day, was motivated by nationalist sentiment: 'I think the last thing Field Day would have been, or should be seen as, is nationalist. Whether you could say it was republican is another thing, but they certainly had a cosmopolitan view of the situation — were never promoters of "ourselves alone" narrow nationalism.'[124] Whelan may have had Paulin's declaration of Field Day's separatist credentials in mind: 'Like Bostonian patriots, the members of Field Day are separatists, but separatists who also hunger for Europe ... the possibility of a shared *civilitas* and conscience which can be given coherent form.'[125] If republicanism can be identified in *Translations*, it is not militant republicanism, according to Pilkington:

> *Translations* underlines the need for a viable media of political accommodation based on an acceptance of inherited political and cultural identities, and, to this extent, constitutes a rebuttal of republican militancy. It is not at all surprising, however, that the anti-republicanism of Friel's play has been unremarked, whereas *Translations* has been criticized for nursing nationalist grievance. If the play's concluding emphasis on the need for political accommodation is based on an audience's recognition of the universality and permanence of the English language in Ireland and on the play's association of English imperialism with post-Enlightenment modernity, the corollary of this assertion is the plangency of cultural loss. Moreover the play's construction of language difference in terms of ontology rather than semantics necessarily privileges the idea of a lost Irish-speaking essence or 'privacy'. In so far as nationalist Ireland has an identity to be recovered it is an ontological entity, a state of being rather than a state of politics.[126]

Legacy

Field Day was in the anomalous position of not being a national theatre while still in receipt of state funds from two jurisdictions. *Guardian* journalist Michael Billington considered Field Day to have been Ireland's national theatre in the 1980s, though perhaps a more accurate description would be to say that it was *nationwide* rather than *national*. Rea is the person who, as much as Friel, wanted to see Field Day turn into something new and unexpected, and for him it had to be live theatre. He left a career in London in order to commit himself to Field Day and the punishing routine of three months' touring in occasionally squalid conditions and to small audiences for the sake of an idea. He had no regrets; he took pleasure in touring *Translations* throughout Ireland:

121 Interview with Rea, *Rattlebag*, RTÉ, 23 September 2005, 'Field Day Theatre Company Special', marking 25th anniversary of *Translations* (interviews with Stephen Rea and Kevin Whelan). http://www.rte.ie/arts/2005/0923/rattlebag.html

122 Tom Paulin, 'Commencement', programme note for *The Communication Cord*.

123 Seamus Deane, 'In Search of a Story', a brief essay in the programme for *The Communication Cord*.

124 Interview with Whelan, *Rattlebag*, RTÉ, 23 September 2005, 'Field Day Theatre Company Special', marking 25th anniversary of *Translations* (interviews with Stephen Rea and Kevin Whelan). http://www.rte.ie/arts/2005/0923/rattlebag.html

125 Paulin, 'Commencement', programme note for *The Communication Cord*.

126 Lionel Pilkington, *Theatre and the State in Twentieth-Century Ireland: Cultivating the People* (London, 2001), 220.

> It gave me some pleasure to go to towns where people would say 'You're the first professional production we have had since Anew McMaster was here thirty years ago' ... I found it immensely stimulating to go to different towns and feel a different response ... You were proposing things: the play was a proposition that you were offering to an audience and you were getting something back. Because they were mostly plays that had ideas in them, you were disseminating ideas and that seemed to me to be the purpose of theater ...
>
> Field Day was beginning to suggest that we could do something different. It was never particularly insistent on a single model that everyone would have to conform to. But it was very much about opening up new ideas. Whether we were a national theater or not is for other people to say.[127]

For Rea, a theatre without ideas was a theatre without value. He left the Abbey because it lacked ideas, and he left London because he felt that Ireland, and especially Northern Ireland, needed a theatre of ideas that would provide new imaginative outlets. When asked in 2005 about the legacy of *Translations*, Rea replied that it showed that

> a theatre of ideas is possible even in the most difficult of circumstances, that people want to see things discussed, that theatre has a purpose. ... I think we subverted the notion that plays are frivolous confections — that you can do something that's highly entertaining and be saying something at the same time.[128]

For Tom Kilroy, the main legacy of *Translations* is that it transformed the status of the playwright in Ireland, that the play actually delivered what it advocated: the creation of an Irish-English version of what had remained a quintessentially English-language art form in Ireland, thus creating a cultural space for imagining new identities. He made this point shortly after *Translations* was first staged:

> Matters may change now, of course, with the impact of *Faith Healer* and *Translations*. But of the very few living Irish writers of the first rank he, alone, has occupied an ambivalent position in the minds of the critics and academics who write about our literature. In part this is due to the fact that, traditionally, playwrights have not always been accepted as literary artists. Somehow, it is felt that playwrighting isn't writing at all; it hasn't the respectability of poetry, for instance, or even the novel. ... One other difficulty is that we have long lacked a theatre and dramatic criticism in this country which could make the kind of discriminations necessary in viewing the work of an artist like Friel: the point here, as elsewhere, is that Friel succeeded in making drama an Irish art by combining the narrative tradition into it. A case of making it our own.[129]

Christopher Morash, while acknowledging the importance of Field Day in the theatre culture of the 1980s, argues that its aspiration to be a national theatre was outmoded and that even as it toured, 'Irish theatre culture was diversifying, with theatre companies and practitioners opting to explore particular theatrical form or ideas in an Irish context'.[130] Kilroy, on the other hand, has attributed some of the success of Irish theatre since the 1980s to Field Day:

> There is one aspect of the achievement of Field Day which has not yet received due recognition or acknowledgement from theatre historians and that is the fact that Friel and Field Day opened up the London stage for Irish writers ... [where previously there had been] palpable resistance to Irish plays among London managements. I think Field Day did an enormous amount to turn that round,

127 Gibbons and Whelan, 'In Conversation with Stephen Rea', 9.

128 Interview with Rea, *Rattlebag*, RTÉ, 23 September 2005, 'Field Day Theatre Company Special', marking 25th anniversary of *Translations* (interviews with Stephen Rea and Kevin Whelan) http://www.rte.ie/arts/2005/0923/rattlebag.html

129 Tom Kilroy, *Connacht Tribune*, 31 October 1980.

130 Christopher Morash, 'Irish Theatre', in Joe Cleary and Claire Connolly, eds., *The Cambridge Companion to Modern Irish Culture* (Cambridge, 2005), 336.

> particularly with the touring productions of Brian Friel's plays. Field Day unlocked that scene for other writers.[131]

Another impact of *Translations* was that it made the northern crisis part of the southern critical agenda. It might be said that *Translations* presented a discursive template for discussing the northern crisis, and its southern ramifications, for a southern intelligentsia that had been struck dumb by it (in many cases quite literally so, via Section 31 of the Broadcasting Act). As we have already seen, Derry had become the cultural focal point of the island for the opening night. By harnessing the gift and fame of people like Friel, Rea, and Heaney, Field Day was guaranteed an attentive audience in the Irish media. The play was previewed and reviewed extensively at a national level; the *Irish Times* even dedicated a preview editorial to it, describing the 'manner of its presentation across time and territory' as a welcome development.[132] Pilkington has also contended that *Translations* expressed, and perhaps initiated, a new period of Anglo-Irish relations.[133] One document in the Field Day Archive, written by Garret Fitzgerald, one of the most determined advocates of Anglo-Irish détente, gives extra weight to this idea. Speaking as taoiseach at the opening of the Dublin Theatre Festival, Mansion House, Dublin, on 28 September 1981, Fitzgerald made great claims for the power of theatre. In hindsight, and without too much stretching of the imagination, it is now possible to read the entire content of this speech as a comment on what *Translations* had to say the previous year. Fitzgerald identifies the importance of the legacy of the Irish Literary Theatre; the intrinsically political nature of theatre; how theatre directly affects its audiences; how theatre can express the people's aspirations in ways that a political state cannot; and how a theatre of ideas can survive in the most difficult of environments (Derry in 1980). For this reason, it is worth reproducing here in its near-entirety:

> [T]he State, in providing this financial help, is merely paying back a little of what it — and the people it serves — owe to the theatre in Ireland. The full debt is immense, and — unlike some other debts we are looking at in Government — unserviceable.
>
> For there was a theatre in this city to mirror the experience and the hopes of the people before any state existed capable of doing these things. Indeed, when the State was founded here, it owed more than a little of its very existence to theatre and theatre people.
>
> Yeats and Lady Gregory ... established their theatre in a city where no play was to be seen apart from those performed by provincial English touring companies. That cultural impoverishment was a precise reflection of Ireland's political circumstances at the time. Those circumstances began to be changed — and not coincidentally — when Yeats — who first inspired my own father's commitment to the national movement — gave vivid public expression to what he later called 'all that stir of thought' which prepared for that movement.
>
> The patriotic ardour evoked by 'Cathleen Ni Houlihan', and that most classic expression of the tragedy inherent in all violent conflict — Juno's cry: 'Take away our hearts of stone and give us hearts of flesh' — were both alike part of the growing pains of a new national consciousness. Those plays and others were shaping revolutionary ideas. Years later Yeats would wonder did some words of his send out 'certain men the English shot'? Perhaps they did. What is in any case beyond question is that the national movement which swept much of Ireland and changed it in the early part of this century took a good deal of its shape and

131 Dukes, 'Interview with Thomas Kilroy', in Chambers, Fitzgibbon and Jordan, eds., *Theatre Talk*, 248.

132 *Irish Times*, 22 August 1980.

133 Pilkington, *Theatre and the State in Twentieth-Century Ireland*, 210–21.

form from the drama created by Yeats and his collaborators.

So when we pay homage to theatre we are not merely acknowledging a purely cultural resource. We are recognising one of the founding elements of our State. And this is an element which has not said its last word about where our State goes and how it develops. Theatre still has things to tell us, as it told the Abbey audiences in the early years. Theatre in Ireland when it is good — perhaps indeed good theatre everywhere — is intrinsically political. That is, it is engaged with the same conflicts which it is the task of politics to contain and resolve. The abstractions of the politician are given life in the traffic of the stage. Very often, indeed, they are embodied in the drama before they have entered the politician's field of vision. The theatre can tell us what is happening in our society, and where change may occur next, before we have realised these things for ourselves. This can be as true — perhaps even truer — of an old classic revived or adapted as of a new play reflecting yesterday's headlines. And because theatre is an intensely communal form — and because also our community here is still intimate and relatively homogenous — the impact of powerful theatre is felt quickly throughout our society.

I know it is not done to mention individual productions at this stage, and thus to anticipate the judgment of critics and audiences. There may even be superstition about this kind of thing. But I hope it will be understood if I say a word in praise of the Company which has been established in Derry for two years now, and which brings us one of the two keenly-awaited adaptations of Chekhov to be seen at this festival.

... I hope they [Derry people] will allow the rest of us to mingle some amazement with the delight we feel that a city so troubled for so long should have had the resources to produce Field Day, and to let us borrow it for a while.[134]

Whether Fitzgerald was directly influenced by the play or not is ultimately for him to say. Field Day would have considered a political solution such as the Thatcher–Fitzgerald Anglo-Irish Agreement of 1985 to be pointless without some form of cultural fusion first taking place. As Pilkington has pointed out, British–Irish politics in the early 1980s (and since) have sought to resolve conflict by encouraging nationalist Ireland's acceptance of the political status quo in return for recognition of its historical cultural trauma. Despite the rhetoric of reconciliation, this approach does not dismantle stereotypes, nor does it imagine how cultural synthesis can occur. *Translations* suggests that political formulations of identity are fundamentally inadequate because they are always a betrayal of the essential complexity of individual experience. Political formulations encourage fixity of identity; *Translations* advocated that cultural identity be considered as fluid, as an ongoing process, as Hugh puts it at the end of the play, 'it is not the literal past, the "facts" of history, that shape us, but images of the past embodied in language ... we must never cease renewing those images'.[135]

In the 1988 BBC2 *Arena* documentary on Field Day and Friel's *Making History*, Friel was asked what future generations might make of Field Day. He responded: 'History will accommodate Field Day into whatever narrative is appropriate for future people.'[136] *Translations* was read by its Dublin audience in the 1980s as guarantor of a new bourgeois nationalism, albeit an Irish nationalism with a more complex architecture. Having exposed the limitations of ethnic identification, the play was embraced by establishment liberals as a cultural expression of a new inclusive, 'civic' nationalism. This interpretation of the play is insufficient, but it is facilitated by the

134 FDA: G/ACNI/13.
135 *SP*, 445.
136 'History Boys on the Rampage', BBC2 *Arena* documentary on Field Day and Friel's *Making History*, 1988.

fact that there is limit to the play's (Friel's) radicalism. Ultimately, it can be read as a play that seeks to find ways of coming to terms with power, rather than as a play that seeks to question the authority of power. If there is a difference between power and authority, it is that authority comes from the consent of the populace. Power does not require consent. In *Translations*, Friel is seeking to convert power to authority. In his plays, Friel is alert to the injustices arising from the exercise of power, but its source remains unknowable. Instead it is mediated, as a microphone (*Freedom of the City*), a voice box (*Aristocrats*), a ledger (*Living Quarters*), a book (*Making History*), or a map (*Translations*). This absence can be traced back to Friel's main source, Steiner's *After Babel*, a book whose limits have been identified by the postcolonial translation critic Samia Mehrez, who cannot find in it

> precisely the political context and power relations within which language acquisition takes place. Having located his own personal experience within the confines of humanism, Steiner is bound to exclude in his otherwise classic work on translation theory, questions of colonialism and cultural hegemony which many ... postcolonial plurilingual writers, writing in the language of the ex-colonizer, must confront.[137]

Tejaswini Niranjana is even more dismissive of Steiner's position, pointing out a 'blindness' in his work 'to the relations of power implicit in translation',[138] and she detects in it a 'lapse into the classical ahistoricism that Derrida warns against in *Of Grammatology*'.[139] She goes on to declare that Steiner's claim that in translation 'there is ideally exchange without loss' is futile in the colonial context, 'where the "exchange" is far from equal and the "benefaction" highly dubious, where the asymmetry between languages is perpetuated by imperial rule'.[140] Friel too would contest the idea that there can be 'exchange without loss'. This is what makes Yolland feel in *Translations* that because of the Ordnance Survey 'Something is being eroded';[141] it is also what makes us feel uneasy with Yolland and Owen's hasty corruption of Bun na hAbhann to the meaningless Burnfoot.[142] But what Friel fails to establish is that the relationship of the Irish language to authority is a natural alliance, as natural as it is with English, Greek, or Latin. Word and world are only problematic when language is enforced. The play's conclusion that the loss of language is regrettable, but also insuperable, is unsound because it denies the inherent authority of the Irish language.

Field Day targeted the audience for its publications just as precisely as it targeted its theatrical audience. Irish taoisigh were sent copies of the pamphlets, as was the British prime minister. The Field Day Archive includes notes of acknowledgement from 10 Downing Street and from UDA leader Andy Tyrie; letters to Jim Sharkey (Irish ambassador to USA) and Daithí Ó Ceallaigh of the Department of Foreign Affairs about sending pamphlets to US politicians Ted Kennedy, Tip O'Neill, Governor Carey and Senator Moynihan; and correspondence with Mary (later President) McAleese, among others. Even as *Translations* was being written, Friel and Deane were directly addressing a political audience. This is evident in a letter from Friel to Deane: 'I thought you handled yourself adeptly and courageously that night in Ballymanus* with Hume-Donlon.** Donlon, I know, listened intently and heard for the first time a persuasive and articulate alternative to SDLPism.'[143]

Some commentators have recently claimed that there have been *direct* political consequences to *Translations*. Whelan recently claimed that

> [n]ew ways of imagining what it meant to be Irish or British were initiated by

137 Mehrez, quoted in O'Malley, 'In Other Words: Coming to Terms with Irish Identities through Translation', 44. For full text, see Samia Mehrez, 'Translation and the Postcolonial Experience: The Francophone North African', in Lawrence Venuti, ed., *Rethinking Translation: Discourse, Subjectivity, Ideology* (London and New York, 1992), 121.

138 Tejaswini, quoted in O'Malley, 'In Other Words: Coming to Terms with Irish Identities through Translation', 44. For full text, see Tejaswini Niranjana, *Siting Translation: History, Post-Structuralism, and the Colonial Context* (Berkeley and Los Angeles, 1992), 59.

139 Quoted in O'Malley, 'In Other Words: Coming to Terms with Irish Identities through Translation', 44.

140 Quoted in O'Malley, 'In Other Words', 44.

141 *SP*, 420.

142 *SP*, 410.

143 FDA: G/D/Friel/Deane: letter from Friel to Deane, dated 4 September [1979?]
* Friel's holiday home near Kincasslagh, County Donegal.
**John Hume, SDLP leader, and Seán Donlon, Irish ambassador to USA 1978–81.

> *Translations*. ... [a] wider more capacious sense of Irishness. Rethinking the categories by which we defined ourselves offers the potential of creating a new political space. ... In one sense the Field Day process was the beginning of the Peace Process — a way of thinking ourselves out of the cul-de-sac into which we had backed ourselves.[144]

Fintan O'Toole made a similar claim:

> *Translations* undoubtedly remains a political play, but you could say that it is a Peace Process play. ... I think what the play ultimately says is to be found in Hugh's statement that 'Confusion is not an ignoble condition.' That's a line that is not just an expression of his own befuddlement, but that's a line that is actually endorsed in the play. It's a line that says that the pursuit of clarity can be murderous.[145]

Translations suggested to its audience that it should experiment with new modes of self-definition, and to question how existing forms of self-definition had created the situation that existed in 1980: economic and cultural stagnation in the South; complete societal breakdown in the North. It set out to demolish the restrictive terms of the existing political and intellectual debate and to develop a discourse not governed by binary oppositions, but rather a discourse that confronts these and, by doing so, at least weakens them and, at best, leaves them in ruin and disrepute. Since then the oppositions *have* weakened, but they are clearly not in disrepute. Wider ways of imagining what it means to be British and Irish were imagined by the Good Friday Agreement of 1998, which was designed to some extent by the political audience Field Day created for itself. However, the link between the two events is indirect, and the political state promised by the Good Friday Agreement falls far short of the one Field Day had imagined. The Agreement is an effort to replace the legacy of British imperialism's 'difference-as-inferiority' model with a 'difference-in-equality' model, but it is hindered by the identity model of difference, which emphasizes boundaries rather than similarities and loses the potential of the Derridean perception of difference as being 'not an essence or attribute of an object but a position or perspective of signification'.[146] Moreover, the parity of esteem sought by the Agreement implies the undisputed existence of two separate traditions, which in turn pressurizes individuals to conform to a particular group culture.

> Hugh warned at the end of the *Translations* that we must reimagine ourselves, we 'must never cease renewing those images; because once we do, we fossilize'.[147] The lesson *Translations* has for its audience today is that the current clamour for parity of esteem can only result in the fossilization of conflicting identities.

***Translations* itinerary, 1980**

Derry, Guildhall, 23–27 September
Belfast Opera House, 29 September–4 October
Dublin, Gate Theatre, 6–14 October
Newry, County Down, 20 October
Dungannon, County Tyrone, 21 October
Magherafelt, County Derry, 22 October
Carrickmore, County Tyrone, 23 October
Armagh, 24 October
Enniskillen, County Fermanagh, 25 October
Sligo, 27 October
Ballyshannon, County Donegal, 28 October
Coleraine, County Derry, 30 October–1 November
Galway, 3–5 November
Tralee, County Kerry, 6–8 November
Cork Opera House, 10–15 November

144 Interview with Whelan, *Rattlebag*, RTÉ, 23 September 2005, 'Field Day Theatre Company Special', marking 25th anniversary of *Translations* (interviews with Stephen Rea and Kevin Whelan).
145 Interview with O'Toole, *Arts Extra*, BBC Radio Ulster, 23 September 2005, 25th anniversary of *Translations*.
146 Máiréad Nic Craith, *Culture and Identity Politics in Northern Ireland* (London, 2003), 11–12.
147 *SP*, 445.

Portrait of Irish writer Sean O'Faolain (1900–91), born John Francis Whelan, as he smokes on a park bench with a open newspaper in his hands, 1964. Photo: Bernard Gotfryd/Getty Images.

Distress Signals: Sean O'Faolain and the Fate of Twentieth-Century Irish Literature

Joe Cleary

I

Like Seán Lemass or T. K. Whitaker, Sean O'Faolain can be considered one of the major architects of the modernizing programme that was consolidated in the 1960s and 1970s and that has reshaped Irish society over the last half century. He supported de Valera's refusal to accept the Anglo-Irish Treaty of 1921, and his abandonment of the military struggle against the Free State to enter parliamentary politics. But once de Valera came to power in 1932, O'Faolain became increasingly disenchanted with him. In a furious polemic titled 'The Gaelic Cult,' published in 1944 in *The Bell*, the journal he had founded in 1940 to challenge the cultural dispensation taking shape after independence, O'Faolain accused de Valera of being enslaved to an antique notion of a Gaelic culture that had no solid basis in reality, and, in passing, identified Lemass as someone less in thrall to such dogmas and delusions. In O'Faolain's view, only when the Irish political establishment had abandoned de Valera's mystique of the Gael, a cult which was 'the opponent of all modernisations and improvisations', could a new and more dynamic Irish culture ever hope to emerge. The Irish education system developed under de Valera, and supported by the Gaelic League and by public intellectuals such as Daniel Corkery was, O'Faolain argued, damagingly backward-looking and anti-modern: 'Can we seriously hope to develop', he asked, 'a dynamic industrial future with a system of education which is based on an uncritical adoration for Finn MacCool (or Thomas Davis) and which has no interest in encouraging, let alone in producing, young technicians?' The cult of the Gael, O'Faolain claimed, had conditioned a national politics that was 'shiveringly isolationist' but, he asked, again rhetorically, had Irish politics or Irish industry any other option than to look outwards 'seeing that we can have no large commercial future unless we look to the wide world as our market?'[1]

The modernizing vision of Irish society that O'Faolain was already attempting to articulate in his essays and editorials in *The Bell* and elsewhere in the early 1940s would eventually gain momentum with the First Programme for Economic Expansion developed in 1958 by Lemass and Whitaker. But whereas Lemass and Whitaker tend to be revered today as founding fathers of the new Ireland that has emerged since that initiative was launched, O'Faolain's own contribution to that modernizing agenda seems to be largely forgotten; his reputation has certainly fallen into relative neglect. Once regarded as one of the country's leading writers and still widely acknowledged as one of twentieth-century Ireland's most formidable public intellectuals, O'Faolain has now only a very limited readership. His novels and short stories are mostly out of print and are only rarely to be seen on the shelves of Dublin's leading bookshops in contrast with the works of his contemporaries, such as Elizabeth Bowen, Frank O'Connor or Liam O'Flaherty. O'Faolain's extensive and arguably much more influential critical writings have never even been collected or edited. As one would expect, he still features prominently in cultural histories of modern Ireland, but even there he tends to appear in a somewhat flattened version of things: as a secular liberal critic of clericalism and censorship, as an early revisionist who challenged 'romantic' versions of Irish nationalist history, or as a Counter-Revivalist who tried to work out new directions for Irish literature once the energies of the Literary Revival had run down. These cameos all contain versions of the truth of course, but since O'Faolain had been intellectually formed in the world of the Gaelic League and had come of age during the War of Independence and the Civil War his relationship to Catholicism, to liberalism and secularism, and to nationalism, republicanism and modernization was complex, much more so than the stereotype (partly self-fashioned) of the progressive cosmopolitan artist-intellectual incarcerated in a hopelessly backward time and place would indicate.

But perhaps O'Faolain's faded presence in the post-1958 Ireland that he helped to create is not all that difficult to explain. For all its censoriousness, 'de Valera's Ireland' arguably attributed greater importance to notions of cultural renewal than did the 'Lemassian Ireland' that came afterwards. In their different ways, Yeats and the Literary Revival, the Gaelic League, the Catholic church, and the early post-independence governments all attached a fundamental importance to ideas of cultural decolonization and, by extension,

1 'The Gaelic Cult', *The Bell*, 9, 3 (December 1944), 185–96, 193.

to drives for national cultural and spiritual regeneration, whereas the new Lemass and Whitaker modernizing programme gave cultural initiatives a much more junior role. By the same token, in the increasingly differentiated or specialized, technocratic and media-saturated society and 'knowledge economy' eventually created by the post-1958 modernizing drive, the role of the amateur 'general intellectual' of the sort that O'Faolain had created for himself in *The Bell* was much more difficult to sustain. Indeed, in an essay titled 'The Parnellism of Seán O'Faoláin,' published in *Irish Writing* in 1948, and reprinted in *Maria Cross* (1954), Conor Cruise O'Brien was already arguing that O'Faolain's novels remained fatally attached to the romantic nationalist world of the writer's youth. Only if he managed to drop 'the idolatries of "parnellism"' — meaning the idea that there was 'a firm connection between the separate ideas of national, spiritual and sexual emancipation' — would O'Faolain, in Cruise O'Brien's view, ever have 'a chance to turn his energies to something of more than local significance'.[2] This verdict suggested that for a younger critic such as Cruise O'Brien, O'Faolain appeared even in the late 1940s as someone imaginatively shackled to the national revivalist mentality that he was contesting in *The Bell*. It is striking that the two most internationally-distinguished Irish men of letters to emerge immediately after O'Faolain, namely Cruise O'Brien and Denis Donoghue, never devoted their energies to worrying over the general fate of an 'Irish national literature' in the way that Yeats, Corkery and O'Faolain had all done, such concerns only returning strongly to the fore again in Irish cultural criticism perhaps in the work of Field Day and Seamus Deane in the 1980s.[3] Like Sherlock Holmes and Professor Moriarty, then, O'Faolain and 'de Valera's Ireland' can to some extent be regarded as mutually dependent antagonists, the one bound eventually to disappear into oblivion with the other.

But this is not the whole story. O'Faolain may no longer be greatly regarded in the new Ireland that he helped to create because the values he championed are now thoroughly naturalized and thus no longer controversial or newsworthy. Yet it is also the case that his reputation, and that of his own mid-century generation of writers, has suffered in no small measure at his own hand. Like Daniel Corkery, the repudiated mentor against whom so much of O'Faolain's critical writing is directed, O'Faolain remained surprisingly sceptical across his career about the achievements and likely development of an Irish national literature in English. That new literature, he averred, had been established by the Young Irelanders in the nineteenth century and had experienced an extraordinary burst of creativity during the high-tide of the Revival, but succeeding generations had never managed to advance much beyond the Revival, and therefore the prospects for a vibrant Irish national literature remained, in his view, radically uncertain. Thus, whereas O'Faolain's criticisms of clericalism, censorship and 'shivering isolationism' may currently be so integral to the normative value-world of Irish Studies as to be no longer noticeable, his concerns about the development, or rather the arrested development, of Irish national literature are now largely uncongenial, maybe even heretical, to a society convinced that its progress beyond the world of 'de Valera's Ireland' has been universal across all spheres and is as readily apparent in the field of literature and the arts as in all others. However, in O'Faolain's view, the failure of Irish literature to flourish and progress in new directions after the Revival remained an anxious and abiding concern, and it is this more neglected dimension of his work that this essay will attempt to reconstruct and to evaluate.

II

In a series of essays written between the

2 Donat O'Donnell [Conor Cruise O'Brien], 'The Parnellism of Seán O'Faoláin,' *Irish Writing* 5 (July 1948), 59–67; reprinted in O'Donnell, *Maria Cross: Imaginative Patterns in a Group of Modern Catholic Writers* (London, 1954), 95–115, 103, 114.

3 See, for example, Seamus Deane, ed., *The Field Day Anthology of Irish Writing*, 3 vols. (Derry, 1991).

Sean O'Faolain (centre) with RTÉ cameraman Godfrey Graham (left) and an unidentified member of the production crew of 'We, the Irish', during the filming of that programme in 1971. © RTÉ Stills Library.

1930s and the 1960s, some published in American and English journals and others in *The Bell* or *Studies*, O'Faolain habitually presents himself to the reader as a spokesperson for a generation whose sense of the world differs from that of its Revivalist predecessors, most notably Daniel Corkery and W. B. Yeats. That older generation, he contends, were revolutionaries and romantics who thought of art and society exclusively in terms of politics and nation and who, consequently, could never adapt themselves to the post-revolutionary world or to the post-revolutionary tasks that O'Faolain and his peers had inherited. O'Faolain conceives of his own generation as more worldly and tougher-minded than its predecessor because it had not only fought to realize a national dream but had also lived to outgrow that phase of its life. Nevertheless, even though he recurrently strikes the pose of its most cosmopolitan intellectual representative, O'Faolain never writes as a 'booster' for his own generation or as an enthusiast for its achievements. He does, of course, readily defend it when Catholic nationalist critics accuse it of dealing only with the sordid and seamy side of Irish life and of damaging national morale,[4] but his assessments of his own achievements and those of his peers become in time increasingly severe and the verdict on the development of modern Irish literature ever more wistful and gloomy. Thus, in 'The Emancipation of Irish Writers'

4 Examples of O'Faolain's repudiations of such criticism include 'Our Nasty Novelists', *The Bell*, 2, 5 (August 1941), 5–12, 'The Bishop of Galway and *The Bell*', *The Bell*, 17, 6 (September 1951), 15–17.

published in 1934,[5] O'Faolain defends his own generation from Corkery's critique in *Synge and Anglo-Irish Literature*,[6] on the basis that Corkery cannot understand a later generation of writers for whom the national revolution was a formative but now completed phase. But in 'Fifty Years of Irish Writing', published twenty-eight years later in *Studies* in 1962,[7] O'Faolain himself divides twentieth-century Irish literature into two phases — one of growth and achievement up to 1921, one of decline thereafter. Although they would certainly have disagreed on the causes of the decline, and while Corkery was a little more optimistic about Irish-language writing, they were in agreement, strangely, that an incipiently major literature had been halted in its development and was now becoming minor.

The distinctions between 'romance' and 'realism' that had governed O'Faolain's largely negative conception of Gaelic literature in works such as *King of the Beggars: A Life of Daniel O'Connell* (1938) or in *The Great O'Neill* (1943)[8] continued to mould his conception of twentieth-century Irish literature in English also. For all its many and impressive achievements, the literature created by the Yeats–Corkery generation was, he contended, a 'romantic literature' and what it lacked, what the new post-independent Ireland now urgently needed, was real intelligence. The governing premise here is that the Irish people, and Irish writers, are particularly addicted to 'romance' — that term encompassing a number of interrelated debilities, ranging from a loss of touch with reality to an unwillingness to confront 'hard conflicts' to anti-intellectualism. At times this proclivity to romance is attributed simply to an ethnic essentialism. O'Faolain argues that intelligence is not an Irish quality, 'the Irish mind being too undisciplined and imaginative'.[9] In other instances, the deficiency is said to be either a consequence of nineteenth-century European nationalism, mediated locally through Young Ireland, or to be the product of a 'curious condition of visual obliquity [that] can become chronic among people who have been too long subject to prolonged colonial rule'.[10] The extraordinary influence of Yeats on twentieth-century Irish writing provides another frequently cited and more proximate explanation. But, whatever the cause, O'Faolain always returns to the fact that '[i]n the most creative fifty years of Anglo-Irish literature ... (from about 1890 to about 1940) the writers saw Irish life, in the main, romantically' and that it was 'as a poetic people that they first introduced themselves to the world, and it is as a poetic people that we are still mainly known abroad'.[11] In this vocabulary, 'romance' and 'poetry' have an especially intimate affinity and always point toward an imaginative high-minded idealism, which, however attractive or commendable it may be, will eventually intoxicate and entrap a society in its own illusions and therefore requires a ruthlessly tough-minded 'realism' as its antidote. To supply this antidote was, in O'Faolain's view, the task that his generation had inherited as its distinctive vocation. But, with the passing years, his confidence in its capacity to live up to that vocation diminished.

However, the apparently simple dichotomy between 'romance' and 'realism' is complicated by the fact that what O'Faolain really aspires to is not so much 'realism' in any of the standard twentieth-century modes as some sort of higher 'poetic realism'. Or, to put it another way, what his criticism pursued was not a 'realism' that was simply the opposite of 'romance' but rather one that has somehow merged with and assimilated 'romance' into itself. Even in the 1930s essays, this search for a particular version of realism is evident. In his 'Plea for a New Type of Novel' (1934),[12] English realism is criticized for its excessive materialism and homocentrism; O'Faolain at this stage hopes for something better from peripheries like Ireland or Russia, which are still enlivened, in his view, by

5 'The Emancipation of Irish Writers', *Yale Review*, 23, 3 (March 1934), 485–503.
6 Daniel Corkery, *Synge and Anglo-Irish Literature: A Study* (Cork, 1931).
7 'Fifty Years of Irish Writing', *Studies*, 51, 201 (Spring 1962), 93–105.
8 Sean O'Faolain, *King of the Beggars: A Life of Daniel O'Connell* (London, 1938) and *The Great O'Neill: A Biography of Hugh O'Neill, Earl of Tyrone, 1550–1616* (London and New York, 1942).
9 'Ah, Wisha! The Irish Novel', *Virginia Quarterly Review*, 17, 2 (Spring 1941), 265–74, 266.
10 *The Irish* (West Drayton, 1947; rev. edn. Harmondsworth, 1969), 127. The chapter on 'The Writers' is considerably expanded in the revised 1969 Penguin edition of *The Irish* and contains a good deal of new material on Joyce and Yeats not present in the earlier versions. All references in this essay, unless otherwise stated, are to this later revised edition.
11 *The Irish*, 142–43.
12 'Plea for a New Type of Novel', *Virginia Quarterly Review*, 10, 2 (April 1934), 189–99.

less secular conceptions of history. Striking a similar note in 'The Modern Novel: A Catholic Point of View' (1935), he had warned that '[n]o art can flourish ... hating what it recreates';[13] this lack of enthusiasm or relish for the world it depicted was, for him, the real weakness of naturalism, and the quality that distinguished the works of even the greatest naturalists from earlier classical realists such as Dickens. In 'It No Longer Matters' (1935) he revisits the same theme, arguing there that the subjectivism of the Flaubertian novel, and of the modern psychological novel that it had generated, had proved a poor substitute for the classical realism it had overthrown, while the naturalism and objectivism of Émile Zola had proved only the sour 'crabtree fruit' of a modern literary orchard that needed 'new plantings'. The works of both Joyce and D. H. Lawrence are offered as examples of the dead end to which naturalism has brought the modern novel: 'The young men like Joyce and Lawrence are already sitting back from life, shrugging their shoulders, or with a last brutal despairing effort objectivising with a grand courage what they so hate. It is only a matter of a few years before the novelists is to find himself isolated in the universe by his disbelief.'[14] Were there to be any hope of 'new plantings', it must come, he argued, from 'the heart of the writer whose outlook on life is of a spiritual and transcendental kind', but the difficulty was that if the secular writer overvalued the material world at the expense of the spiritual, the religious writer did exactly the reverse. '[U]ntil this antinomy is resolved', he concluded, 'it is futile to expect great literature from either Catholic or Protestant, futile to hope to see again the like of that great corpus of literature which is bounded by the overlap of the last century'.[15]

'Realism', then, is a term that connotes for O'Faolain the opposite of the woolly-minded romantic imagination or transcendental high idealism, but in its impoverished modern forms it had also become associated with a secularism that led either to a negation of the higher or more spiritual things altogether or to a kind of crude naturalism that had crippled the imagination. 'Romance', by the same token, is a negative term when it connotes an idealism or a spiritualism so otherworldly that it wants to avert its face from the material world altogether, but it also incorporates qualities of elevated poetic imagination and warm spiritual sensibility that the modern world and modern literature still need and sorely lack. Associated as it is with the French and English literary traditions, 'realism' carries essentially 'secular' or 'Protestant' connotations in O'Faolain's criticism, whereas 'romance' is usually associated with non-modern (and thus more 'spiritual') societies like Russia or Ireland. By seeking for some sort of reconciliation between these terms — the modern and the non-modern, the spiritual and the secular, the Catholic and the Protestant, poetry and the novel — he was effectively seeking to heal what was for him a deep historical split that had fissured the modern Western world generally and Ireland in particular.

Not surprisingly, it was always easier for O'Faolain to expatiate upon the defective modes of realism that he wished Irish writers to avoid than to identify or to celebrate versions of the 'poetic realism' towards which he aspired. Emily Brontë was one example of a writer who had been able to marry mimesis and imagination ('Compare Charlotte Brontë, who rarely soared, with Emily Brontë and you will see what I mean'[16]); he also claimed that 'Hardy is on the Celtic fringe' and that his 'Jude suffers from "Russian longings"'.[17] In the early 1940s, he expressed 'an almost uncritical admiration for Graham Greene'[18] (though this had obviously cooled considerably by the time he published *The Vanishing Hero* in 1956).[19] But, consistent with the wider geo-cultural value-scheme at work here, the two most exemplary figures were inevitably Irish and Russian. Of all the writers he admires, O'Faolain writes:

13 'The Modern Novel: A Catholic Point of View', *Virginia Quarterly Review*, 11 (July 1935), 339–51, 346.
14 'It No Longer Matters, or, The Death of the English Novel', *Criterion*, 15, 58 (October 1935), 49–56, 56, 51.
15 'It No Longer Matters', 54.
16 'The Emancipation of Irish Writers', 501.
17 'Ah, Wisha!', 274.
18 'Ah, Wisha!', 268.
19 *The Vanishing Hero: Studies in Novelists of the Twenties* (London, 1956).

20 'Ah, Wisha!', 268.
21 'Ah, Wisha!', 266–67.
22 'Ah, Wisha!', 267.
23 'Ah, Wisha!', 267.
24 'Ah, Wisha!', 267.

> we would sacrifice every single one of these were we left only with Chekov ... That is, I feel, because he repeats, in the manner of a prose-writer, the Synge recipe of poetry and realism, mood and consideration, laughter and opinion, brutality (which we must always have) and tenderness (which is essential to us), and all sunk in a thick atmosphere. If Irish prose fiction ever does develop a distinctive quality, it will be as much by virtue of this influence of the Russians as Yeats developed his distinctive quality under the influence of the Symbolists and Pre-Raphaelites.[20]

In one crucial sense, twentieth-century Irish literature had comically scrambled O'Faolain's whole conceptual schema, since the country's greatest poet and exemplar of the 'romantic' imagination was the Protestant Yeats, while its greatest exponent of the novel and of 'realism' was the Catholic Joyce. However, one way to read O'Faolain would be to say that for him Yeats and Joyce each exemplified the modern 'romantic' and 'realist' tendencies at their extremes — the art of the former was too detached from the mimetic impulse altogether and too imaginatively high-flown and idealist and anti-intellectual; that of the latter too deeply rooted in naturalism and/or aesthetic subjectivism and thus too coldly objective and clinically cerebral or too narcissistic and self-obsessed — and that what 'Chekhov' signifies therefore is really a kind of symptomatic absence in the Irish canon; what his name registers is a felt need on O'Faolain's part for some missing 'third way' figure who would combine the virtues of Joyce and Yeats ('the Synge recipe of poetry and realism') yet without toppling over into the excesses of either.

But why had the Irish novel never produced some kind of Chekhovian or Syngean 'poetic realism'? O'Faolain's essays offer not one but many explanations and they fluctuate with the years. In 'Ah, Wisha! The Irish Novel' (1941), he argues that Yeats had a well-developed doctrine of poetry and had thus offered a lead that subsequent Irish poets could follow. But Yeats's prose, by contrast, 'is almost impossible to read' and the Irish novelist, unlike the poet, 'cannot work with the symbolic language of the Rosy Cross, characterless characters like Michael Robartes or Ossian, [or] shadowy scenery of the mind'; the novelist requires, rather, 'direct and precise language, real people, muddy fields, streets with trams'. Hence 'Irish prose has no such line' to follow as Yeats had bequeathed to the poets, and novelists had no option 'but to turn towards more extrovert models'.[21] Like their counterparts elsewhere, the Irish novelist could take a lead from Flaubert. But since it was 'in [the Irish writer's] nature — which makes him both rich and poor — to hanker after that renounced symbolism and those regretted worlds of the mind', he would always seek something more poetic, even though '[e]vidently there are no established models in prose for this kind of thing'.[22] George Moore had attempted something along such lines in *The Lake* (1905), but this was a one-off and Moore otherwise oscillated between 'a crude naturalism' and a rarefied aestheticism. Joyce had done something wonderful in *A Portrait of the Artist as a Young Man* (1916), but had he been 'less subjective and preoccupied he might have given Irish prose a model as Gogol gave one to Russia with "The Cloak"'. James Stephens's *The Charwoman's Daughter* (1912) was also to be admired, but neither Joyce nor Stephens, O'Faolain surmises, 'faces the problem squarely enough' and 'the later history of both writers was dismaying'.[23] The upshot was that none of these leading novelists had established a generative model and '[a] model which does not repeat itself is hardly a fructifying example'.[24] The arguments here may not be very persuasive, but what is clear is that as O'Faolain surveys the 'crude naturalism' of the early Moore or Stephens, the aestheticism of the later Moore or early Joyce, or the avant-garde experimentalism or high fantasy and whimsy of the mature Joyce and Stephens, he finds them all deficient. None represents a satisfying model for the kind of realism he is after.

When he returns to this theme much later in his revised chapter on 'The Writers' for a new edition of *The Irish* in the late 1960s, O'Faolain appears much more critical of Yeats and much less so of Joyce, but the weight of responsibility this time falls less on the founders for not having provided generative models and more on his own generation for its inability to learn from Joyce. In that piece, Yeats's great powers are fully acknowledged, but he is described as man of the transcendental imagination who 'did not have an observing eye'[25] or the mimetic powers a novelist needs, and who also was not an intellectual — a deficiency that had exercised a negative influence on subsequent Irish writing. Joyce, in contrast to Yeats, 'was far less imaginative. He was concrete, dry, cold-eyed, clear-headed and, though utterly rebellious against all the gods, all-accepting towards man ... to a degree as far beyond the powers as it was beyond the desires of his great romantic contemporary'.[26] These qualities made Joyce, 'with his feet planted on the ground', Ireland's 'one great realist' writer, the foil to Yeats.[27] In this account, Joyce is no longer sidelined as a naturalist, aesthete, or as a writer whose later career is dismaying. Now the question is why his lead was not better emulated. The blame falls on O'Faolain's own peers — 'the 1920–1950 generation' — who were all formatively 'soaked in romantic Yeats',[28] whereas the vagaries of history had meant that they missed out on Joyce, because *Portrait* had appeared during the high excitement of 1916, and *Ulysses* (1922) had appeared just on the verge of the horrors of the Civil War. Thus, by the time his generation had properly read Joyce, in the sense of digesting him, it was too late: 'we were already set. Too old to be influenced by him.'[29] But whether the fault lay with the founders for not providing better models for a later generation to follow, or with the later generation for having missed the 'one great realist' when he did present himself, the net result was still the same: 'However they might think of themselves, and many thought themselves tough realists, ruthless satirists, or even (Heaven help us!) keen intellectuals, Irish writers remained *au fond* incurably local and romantic.'[30] To get beyond 'a merely descriptive local naturalism'[31] and 'the incurably local and romantic' remained even then in O'Faolain's estimate the perennial dilemma.

Despite such strictures, O'Faolain's writings tend more often to attribute the failures of modern Irish literature to Irish society rather than to Irish writers as such. Although he had claimed in an early essay such as 'The Modern Novel' (1935) that any hope for the renewal of twentieth-century prose would come from Russian Communism or from Irish Catholicism, no such expectations were fulfilled and by mid-career O'Faolain was habitually critical of both Ireland and the Soviet Union. Far from proving a potential fructifying resource for the imagination, Irish Catholicism had served as one of the greatest impediments to Irish writing, both through the state censorship laws and through the Church's general anti-intellectualism. This was a theme to which he returned repeatedly through *The Bell* years, often in editorials. In his more searching articles on this theme, such as 'The Priest in Politics' (1947), he traced the roots of this anti-intellectual conservatism back to the nineteenth century. A misfortunate merger in a seriously underfunded, demoralized Maynooth between an austere French Jansenism or 'rigorism' and Irish peasant patriotism had, he argued, nurtured a clerical culture that was temperamentally timorous, nervy and defensive. John Henry Newman had tried to cultivate a more sophisticated, better-educated Catholicism in the mid-nineteenth century on the grounds that an intellectually sophisticated laity was the only solid long-term defence against the threats

25 *The Irish*, 138.
26 *The Irish*, 139.
27 *The Irish*, 139, 131.
28 *The Irish*, 140.
29 *The Irish*, 141.
30 *The Irish*, 141.
31 *The Irish*, 130.

of atheism and agnosticism. But Rome had denounced Newman as an exponent of Catholic liberalism and it was Archbishop Cullen, suspicious of the laity and stressing clerical authority, who had prevailed over Newman's teaching church. After the Famine, writers and priests ought to have been 'on the one side fighting the vulgarity that fills the vacuum left by the collapse of traditional culture', but the Catholic Church, taking its lead from Cullen, had preferred 'the easy way of authority' and reliance on the state to enforce its teachings. The loss to writers and to clergy, O'Faolain suggested, 'is mutual', and the consequence was that there was 'not in Ireland to-day a single layman's Catholic periodical to which one could apply the adjective "enquiring", or even "intelligent"',[32] and the country now met Newman's description: 'A population of peasants ruled over by a patriotic priesthood, patriarchally'.[33] Elsewhere in Europe, such as Italy, he ventured in 'Religious Art' (1951), the Roman Church was kept mentally on its toes by the Communist challenge, but because Ireland lacked such a challenge, the real danger domestically was complacency. We in Ireland, he concluded, 'export boys and girls with minds quite unprepared: and those we retain are insulated, isolated, and smug', whereas in Italy 'the pressure of the world outside, and of the world inside through various relentlessly-challenging groups leaves no room for smugness'.[34] The cultural consequences were ominous — the ground had been tilled to produce not an Irish Dante but an anti-Dante: 'I do not know whether the Catholicity of Ireland is pure enough, or powerful enough, or cultured enough, to produce its Dante, though it has certainly produced its Joyce', he wrote in 1934.[35] Looking backwards in *The Irish* in 1969 to an age that was now passing, he wrote, 'it is probable that, between 1929 and, say, 1955, a greater proportion of native writers were [*sic*] banned in Ireland than in Russia'.[36] In both instances, then, Europe's outer peripheries had failed to realize a potential to make good through their literatures the deficiencies of the modern metropolitan world; both had delivered only state authoritarianism and a dogmatic anti-intellectualism.

There is an obvious connection between the disappointed promises of the Russian and Irish revolutions and O'Faolain's increasing impatience with backward 'provincialism' and his cultivation of a worldly 'cosmopolitanism', something that became more pronounced than ever in his writings after the Second World War.[37] However, it would be a mistake to conclude that it was the calamities of the Irish or Russian revolutions or his bitter experience of Irish clerical authoritarianism that persuaded him to embrace European cosmopolitanism as an alternative. After all, even in the writings of the 1930s, when he still looked for the seeds of cultural renewal in Ireland and Russia, it was not to a more revolutionary republicanism or to a more democratic socialism that he turned for hope but to the Catholic heritage of the one country and the Orthodox spirituality (and to a lesser extent the Communist sense of history as universal drama) of the other. In fact, a distinct suspicion of the popular and even of the democratic runs throughout O'Faolain's criticism and propels him from the start in the direction of a cosmopolitanism that is distinctly élitist in temper. In 'The Emancipation of Irish Writers', for instance, he suggests that the impairment of Irish writing owes something to the fact that writers

> have been too caught up by the emotion of the mob. It is another day of the rabblement. What has the mob to do with us that we should weep for them? Yet into our books they creep, so many types of the life that harass us, and there we waste our spirit on them as one might belabour a furze bush to expel one's rage.[38]

In 'Fifty Years of Irish Literature' (1942) he observed that the revolution that Yeats's

32 'The Priest in Politics', *The Bell*, 13, 4 (January 1947), 4–24, 23–24.
33 'The Priest in Politics', 24.
34 'Religious Art', *The Bell*, 16. 4 (January 1951), 39–42, 41.
35 'Emancipation of Irish Writers', 500.
36 *The Irish*, 143.
37 For a useful overview of contemporary debates about the varieties and uses of cosmopolitanism, see Daniele Archibugi, ed., *Debating Cosmopolitics* (London and New York, 2003). O'Faolain's advocacy of a broad cosmopolitan outlook as opposed to the inward-looking provincialism he attributed to Irish culture generally is often accepted on its own terms. But obviously these are loaded terms and it is the character, scope, limits and uses of O'Faolain's version of cosmopolitanism that calls for more careful examination and contextualization.
38 'The Emancipation of Irish Writers', 498.

generation had supported had rebounded on literature, since it had inaugurated a shift from the creative imagination to the 'aridly critical' orthodoxy 'approved by literary theologians' of the post-independence period — he has in mind Catholic and Gaelic League cultural critics — and he wonders if Yeats was not after all correct in his suspicion of democracy:

> Yeats lived to see the first portents of that devastating stage [of the new literary orthodoxy], and it must have been his bitter thought as well as the bitter thought of many Irish writers of his generation, that he and they had done as much as any men to bring about the social and political revolution that made it possible. How did this calamity occur? Was there something inherent in the Familiar that made it inevitable for it to decline into the Vulgar? Was it the sight of what was happening that made [Yeats], in his later poems, insist more and more on the aristocracy of poetry, and on his own descent from the aristocrats of Ireland's eighteenth century?[39]

O'Faolain's own generation, he says, had resented this in Yeats:

> We believed in that democracy which O'Connell created and which was a keener memory to us than his 'ancient memory'. But he was within his rights. He had been consistent. He had equally nourished 'the distinguished' and 'the familiar'. And if we had gone the way of realism, 'the people', Democracy, Kate and Theigue, then the problem was up to us. It still is.[40]

The matter is rhetorically posed here, but what O'Faolain is suggesting is that popular democracy as a social philosophy and realism as a literary mode both tend to fetishize the local and the mundane ('the Familiar') in ways that may inevitably incline to 'the Vulgar' in life and in art. O'Faolain's particular wrath was often directed in this regard at what he calls 'the Irish peasantry', and he repeatedly attributes the poverty of Irish political and intellectual life to that class. In *The Irish*, for example, he writes:

> The reason why, apart from the land-war, Irish Nationalism in the nineteenth and early twentieth century was lacking in social content is simple. The backbone of all nationalist politics since Daniel O'Connell (1775–1847) was a semi-educated peasantry, led by a comparatively few men and women of the middle classes and lower middle classes mostly urbanized but also rarely more than a generation or two removed from the land. The immediate result was that our Nationalism, having no proletarian-industrial class in this mainly pastoral island to inject a social content into it, developed almost wholly as a mystique. Politics as the technology or blueprint of a new way of life, was beyond it. Davitt or Connolly apart, we produced no Bazarovs.[41]

The condescension towards the 'semi-educated peasantry' here inverts Corkery's idealization of that class in his elaboration of the national-popular. The reference to the lack of a 'proletarian-industrial class in this mainly pastoral island', one which might have injected 'social content' into nationalism, presumes that working classes are automatically more enlightened than peasant ones, conveniently overlooking the fact that in Ulster, where there was a concentrated industrial working class, its politics were of a sectarian unionist kind hardly in advance of that of the 'semi-educated peasantry' to the south. O'Faolain's scepticism concerning Corkery's appeal to the national-popular is not unwarranted, and his sense that literature should not concede to popular opinion is also well-founded. But O'Faolain's own assessment of Irish culture as backward

39 'Fifty Years of Irish Literature', *The Bell*, 3, 5 (February 1942), 327–34, 333.
40 'Fifty Years of Irish Literature', 334.
41 *The Irish*, 148.

Liam O' Flaherty, 1925. Photo: E. O. Hoppe/Mansell/Time Life Pictures/Getty Images.

and provincial often compounds a Yeatsian disdain for the middle classes and their easy-going but vulgar democracy with a Joycean intellectual disdain for the uneducated 'mob' or 'rabblement' and a 'high cultural' disdain for the supposed vulgarities of an emergent 'mass culture' shared by mid-twentieth-century intellectuals on all sides, from the Catholic Church to the Frankfurt School.

The arguments on Irish literary development, serially elaborated during the 1930s and 1940s, received their most synthetic and accomplished elaboration in two wide-ranging survey articles written at the height of O'Faolain's career, 'The Dilemma of Irish Letters', published in the English Jesuit journal *Month*, in 1949,[42] and 'Fifty Years of Irish Writing' published for the fiftieth-anniversary of the Irish Jesuit journal *Studies* in Spring 1962. 'The Dilemma of Irish Letters' opens in

42 'The Dilemma of Irish Letters', *Month*, 2, 6 (December 1949), 366–79. Hereafter, 'The Dilemma'.

what had by then already become a fairly typical retrospective mode. Yeats and Shaw, O'Faolain recalls, had founded the Irish Academy of Letters in 1932, but that Academy 'had hardly been well founded before it began to founder'.[43] At the time of writing in 1949, O'Faolain continues, the average age of its members is between sixty and sixty-five, and over half the total membership when last counted lived in exile, while the Academy itself 'has no money'.[44] Most academies, O'Faolain allows, tend to smack of ancient museums, and thus it might be unfair to read the Irish Academy's fortunes as indicative of those of the current state of Irish writing. But, he insists, the particular deliquescence of the Irish Academy is signalled by the fact that many of those who had become members 'when still in their thirties — Frank O'Connor, Francis Stuart, myself, Peadar O'Donnell, Elizabeth Bowen' — were now 'all in our middle years, and are still moderately prolific', yet none 'except perhaps Miss Bowen, has arrived at the stage of consolidated achievement'. 'None, certainly', O'Faolain asserted, 'is in the unassailable position of such founder-members as Yeats, AE, James Stephens or Shaw'.[45] No national literature will ever be wholly comprised of 'writers of the first order', he added, yet one does expect any thriving one 'to include a few large figures'. But '[t]o-day we have nobody in Ireland of the stature of Joyce, Moore, Synge or Yeats'.[46] Even looking beyond the Academy, O'Faolain concludes, 'it is difficult to see any budding grove to alter the impression that the two outstanding marks of Irish literature to-day are exile and lack of originality'.[47] 'When AE died, and George Moore, and Yeats, and Lady Gregory, and Joyce, a period came to an end.' Irish writing now, O'Faolain surmises ruefully, 'still carries an honourable prestige; but nobody would care to say it has as much prestige as it had in 1915'.[48]

Contemplating the causes of this decline, O'Faolain begins with the 1929 Censorship Act, which had aggravated the already well-established phenomenon of expatriation in Irish letters. Yet neither censorship nor expatriation is the prime cause of Ireland's literary problems; these are only indices of a deeper domestic dilemma. As far back as the early medieval Celtic diaspora, O'Faolain surmises, Irish writers had always displayed a tendency towards exile, and their peregrinations had not always been motivated by material want so much as by a craving for wider horizons: 'They have always gone, by the tens of thousands, for sheer devilment — or for sheer sanctity.'[49] Still, the very fact that Irish intellectuals were so frequently drawn away over the centuries by the lure of excitement, or by some necessity to serve their vocation abroad, points, he argues, to some inadequacy in Irish life deeper than the censorship or the lack of domestic financial reward to which literary exile is usually attributed.

What is this domestic inadequacy? To explain it, O'Faolain turns to Henry James's study of the life and work of Nathaniel Hawthorne.[50] James's view of Hawthorne's America is, he concedes, that of an exile but what matters is not whether James is in every respect objectively correct but that this is how things should have appeared to be to the 'restless heart' of the literary exile. For James, Hawthorne was one of only 'three or four beautiful talents' to have emerged in nineteenth-century America, thus confirming James's convictions that: 'the flower of art blooms only where the soil is deep, that it takes a great deal of history to produce a little literature, and that it needs a complex social machinery to set a writer in motion'. The history of the United States 'was so thin and impalpable a deposit', James believed, that the writer there very soon touched 'the hard substratum of nature, and Nature herself in the Western world has the peculiarity of seeming rather crude and immature'.[51] Unable, in other words, to draw on the resources of a rich national history or an advanced society, the writer was compelled

43 'The Dilemma', 366.
44 'The Dilemma', 366.
45 'The Dilemma', 366–67.
46 'The Dilemma', 367.
47 'The Dilemma', 367.
48 'The Dilemma', 367.
49 'The Dilemma', 368.
50 See Henry James, *Hawthorne* (New York, 1887).
51 The quotations from James cited here and below are taken directly from O'Faolain, 'The Dilemma', 369–70.

Henry James (1843–1916) in his study, 1900. Photo: Hulton Archive/Getty Images.

to draw instead on those of landscape or nature, but in the USA even landscape itself might appear 'crude and immature'. Difficulties of this order were compounded for Hawthorne by what James described as the 'social dreariness of a small New England community' and by the fact that in such an unintellectual atmosphere the writer must always feel a solitary, alienated oddity.[52] For James, O'Faolain avers, all of these deficiencies were summed up 'under the word provincialism' and the list of wants connoted by that word could easily be transposed onto twentieth-century Ireland. In James's estimation, the tell-tale signs of American 'provincialism' were:

> No State in the European sense of the word, and indeed barely a specific national name. No sovereign, no court, no personal loyalty, no aristocracy, no church, no clergy, no army, no diplomatic service, no country gentlemen, no palaces, nor castles, nor manors, nor old country houses, nor thatched cottages nor ivied ruins; no cathedrals, nor abbeys, nor little Norman churches; no great universities nor public schools — no Oxford, nor Eton, nor Harrow; no literature, no novels, no museums, no pictures, no political society, no sporting class — no Epsom, nor Ascot. ... The natural remark in the almost lurid light of such an indictment would be that if these things are left out everything is left out.[53]

Even if James is writing as much here of the terrors that had motivated his own exile as about Hawthorne's actual circumstances, this, O'Faolain insists, does not alter the veracity of the perception. Even allowing for James's exilic emotion, the fact that Hawthorne was poor, solitary and had 'to devote himself to literature in a community in which the interest in literature was as yet of the smallest' was not in doubt.[54] 'We understand that very well in this Ireland', O'Faolain concludes, adding that even if the analogy was not exact in all particulars, any

52 James quoted in 'The Dilemma', 370.
53 James quoted in 'The Dilemma', 372.
54 James quoted in 'The Dilemma', 370.
55 'The Dilemma', 370.
56 'The Dilemma', 372.
57 'The Dilemma', 375–76.

contemporary Irish writer would recognize the fundamentals of James's description of nineteenth-century New England in his own mid-twentieth-century native land.[55]

Anticipating objections to this analysis, O'Faolain engages with several possible counter-arguments. For example, even if the case for the impediments to literary achievement in such an unpropitious environment were allowed, Hawthorne had nonetheless triumphed over adversity and had even been acclaimed by a domestic American public. This was certainly true, and James had acknowledged as much, but he had also held that writers work best when surrounded by colleagues working in the same line; solitary individuals, therefore, might indeed sometimes triumph over adverse circumstance, but, lacking intelligent company and established conventions, they would do so only at the cost of many 'awkward experiments'. To James's question as to 'What remains?' to the list of things the US lacked, his countryman William Dean Howells had responded with an indignant 'Why, simply the whole of life', and the patriotic Irishman would, O'Faolain remarked, inevitably cheer Howells and respond similarly.[56] But, he countered, when one looked at the meagre, and often clumsily experimental, prose works that twentieth-century Ireland had yielded, one had to conclude that James's scepticism about 'the limits set by "the thinly-composed society"' was well founded. 'No! William Dean Howells is not right', O'Faolain insists:

> The 'whole of life' does not remain when social conventions and social institutions are simple, few, or in flux. In such an unshaped society there are many subjects for little pieces, that is for the short-story writer; [but] the novelist or dramatist loses himself in the general amorphism, unthinkingness, brainlessness, egalitarianism, and general unsophistication.[57]

A third objection that might be raised to James's analysis was that even if it was right about nineteenth-century America, hadn't twentieth-century American literature gone on to greater things anyway in the works of Ernest Hemingway, Theodore Dreiser, William Saroyan, Eugene O'Neill, Willa Cather and scores of others? This was indeed the case, O'Faolain contended, but far from disproving James, this demonstrated rather that American society had to be transformed first for literary change to follow and for a secure national literature to emerge. 'When society "thickened" letters could grow thicker. Not before', O'Faolain asserted. 'At the earlier period too much had been missing, as James's list insisted, for literature to flourish.'[58]

Having established this Jamesian frame, O'Faolain's essay then proceeds to elaborate its local application. Energized by the excitement of the national revolution, he argues, Irish literature had thrived in the early twentieth century, and that excitement had continued to be generative even for a time after the revolution itself had ended. Gradually, however, once the revolution had passed, 'literature began to feel the water getting colder and colder',[59] and by the time Joyce and Yeats had died its most fertile moment had clearly ended. The paradox was that the very revolution — one that had even been led by poets — that had inspired and stimulated Irish writing in the shorter term had in the longer term also created 'the circumstances in which Irish writing would begin to wilt'.[60] Why had the revolution had such negative long-term effects? Because, O'Faolain answered, that revolution had actually swept away whatever social complexity there had been in Ireland and had replaced it by a socially-much-simpler republican society that was non-conducive to high literary production. Lacking a complex, stratified society, which the revolution had abolished, the Irish writer, like his American counterpart a century earlier, had no recourse but to turn to landscape and nature to fill the social void. O'Faolain's description of this

58 'The Dilemma', 373.
59 'The Dilemma', 367.
60 'The Dilemma', 367.
61 'The Dilemma', 373.

62 'Fifty Years of Irish Writing', 103.

transformation was heated and is worth citing at some length:

> We see this [condition] very clearly in Ireland to-day where the stratified, and fairly complex social life which a writer of 1915, say, could have known in Dublin has given way to a far more simple and uncomplex, a much 'thinner' social life. The life now known, or knowable, to any modern Irish writer is the traditional, entirely simple life of the farm (simple, intellectually speaking); or the groping, ambiguous, rather artless urban life of these same farmers' sons and daughters who have, this last twenty-five years, been taking over the towns and cities from the Anglo-Irish. They have done it, so to speak, by rule of thumb, empirically, with little skill. Their conventions are embryonic; their social patterns are indistinct. True, the 'whole of life' remains. But at what level of intelligence and sensibility? True, we do possess many of the things James missed in Hawthorne's America; but they are largely inherited by us, not made by us. They are not marks or measurements of us. Their quondam significance, of that order, is lost in a jelly-like mass of friendly egalitarianism which is as comfortable as it is indeterminate and where ideas are so few or so elementary as to suggest a quite unperplexed and uninquisitive communal mind.[61]

The Tocquevillian, and indeed Yeatsian, timbre of phrases such as 'jelly-like mass of friendly egalitarianism' here is unmistakable. When looked at closely, the real deficiency of nineteenth-century New England in James's account is essentially that it is not Old England — that it lacks Oxfords and Etons, Derbys and Ascots, royal courts and gentlemanly manors and ivied rustic cottages — and O'Faolain's endorsement of James's analysis seems by extension to accept that modern Ireland's problem too is that it is not England, or not enough like James's version of England at least.

But if 1940s Ireland resembles 1840s America, the general thrust of O'Faolain's larger argument seems to be that the histories of these two regions have actually been moving in opposite directions. After all, in the US at least the general curve of historical development had been from the simple and uncultured republic, of the kind Hawthorne had had to survive, to a complex and advanced industrial society where a high national literature could finally prosper. But in the case of Ireland the curve of historical development had apparently been the reverse of this, because in this instance there had in the nineteenth-century been some kind of complex society — that of the Anglo-Irish Ascendancy — but the national revolution between 1916 and 1922 had demolished this, establishing in its place not a complex industrial society such as that of twentieth-century America, but only a simple farming republic closer in its social composition to that of nineteenth-century America. It was because it had abolished an older kind of aristocratic, stratified society, without creating any kind of newer industrial equivalent, therefore, that the national revolution could be said to have had stimulated the national literature only temporarily, while ultimately creating the conditions that guaranteed its long-term retardation.

Lest it be missed, this point was again repeated in 'Fifty Years of Irish Writing':

> the change-over from a stratified society — ranging from aristocrat to outcast — to a one-class society, where there are no native aristocrats and no outcasts (except the writers?), and where the hard, traditional core is a farming population, rarely induces a fertile awareness either among people or writers.[62]

Because it had once had a complex society, before the national revolution had eliminated it, Ireland did 'possess many of the things James missed in Hawthorne's

America' — O'Faolain may be referring here to an ancient Gaelic culture as well as to the abolished Ascendancy, of course, — but this historical heritage was only an already-made bequest from the past ('largely inherited by us, not made by us') and thus not something that modern Ireland had by itself created in its own image. As such, it was merely an alienated inheritance, one the society could neither legitimately claim for itself nor even put to creative use.

In this diagnostic, the problems of twentieth-century Irish letters ultimately find their roots in republicanism, or in the Irish variety of republicanism at least. '[I]n theory', O'Faolain writes in 'The Dilemma of Irish Letters (1949), 'we struggled, up to 1922, for Liberty. In practice, as we now see, Liberty was a very secondary goal'. 'Liberty', he continued, 'is an English ideal' and is 'expressed in terms of personal rights, often hard won, usually embodied in class and convention'.[63] However:

> In republican countries, like France, America or Ireland (or must I add 'Southern' to Ireland?) this idea of Liberty is constantly struggling with the idea of Equality, and so far as I can observe from the course of events in modern Ireland, if there were a toss-up between the two ideas Equality would always be much more likely to win. We are a friendly, sociable, light-hearted and easy-going people, and we do not, so far at any rate, take kindly to the notion that we must protect our liberties, that is our rights, from our neighbours. ... From the point of view of the *homme moyen sensuel* this may, or may not, according to his taste or upbringing, sound delightful. In many ways it *is* delightful. (I find it so.) But from the point of view of the novelist it is a total disaster. The novel is a social document; it is what Trollope wrote and what Balzac wrote; it does not deal with amorphous crowds but with a closely organized and stratified society; it deals with the play of personality on personality; with accepted or debated values and conventions; with the clashes between the aberrants and the tradition.[64]

Irish republicanism, in short, has had a levelling, egalitarian effect on Irish society, and such levelling expresses itself pleasantly enough in social terms — as evidenced by 'the free-and-easy atmosphere of an Irish race-course'[65] — but it has been fatal to any kind of literary endeavour that required a strong sense of personal liberty or 'a closely organized and stratified society'. In passages such as this, O'Faolain seems to have repudiated not only Corkery's version of the national-popular, but also his own early republicanism. The theory of literature and society espoused here is, in any event, one with a strongly-pronounced aristocratic colouration.

How exactly had Ireland's development into a rural republic affected its literary development? Because the country remained, O'Faolain argued, such a raw, easy-going 'unshaped society', where people gave formal deference to the Church but were largely indifferent to conscience or morality in any more personal, individualized sense, '[a] Mauriac novel is unthinkable here' since '[o]ur sins are tawdry, our virtues childlike, our revolts desultory, and our brief submissions formal and frequent'.[66] The Abbey Theatre had fed for years on the stuff of Irish rural life — 'mixed marriages, land-hunger, peasant greed, religious fervour, political passion, small-town intrigue, family feuds'[67] — but the farces and melodrama this yielded were ultimately thin stuff for national drama, 'and to tell the plain truth plainly we are rather bored with them'.[68] In the case of the novel, the costs of the 'thinly-composed society' were even more severe: the country's best realist novelists — Elizabeth Bowen, George Moore, Somerville and Ross, Lennox Robinson, Daniel Corkery and James Joyce — 'all got one novel each out of the social picture in Ireland, and no

63 'The Dilemma', 374.
64 'The Dilemma', 374.
65 'The Dilemma', 374.
66 'The Dilemma', 375.
67 'The Dilemma', 375.
68 'The Dilemma', 375.

69 'The Dilemma', 375.
70 'The Dilemma', 376–77.
71 'The Dilemma', 375.
72 'The Dilemma', 378, 377.
73 'The Dilemma', 378.
74 'The Dilemma', 378.
75 'The Dilemma', 378.
76 'The Dilemma', 379.
77 'Fifty Years of Irish Writing', 94–95 (hereafter 'Fifty Years').

more'.[69] 'The realist, content to describe, without comment, the local life he knows intimately, will get one powerful book out of its surges and thrustings and gropings. After that he will have to repeat himself endlessly, or stop.'[70] Others, such as Lord Dunsany, Austin Clarke or James Stephens, had wisely worked in more fantastical modes, but even there it was evident that the contemporary moment was 'a period in which the stage is set for prose' and not poetry, but that 'prose is starving for something to write about'.[71] The 'two dissolvents of this earthly material' had always been humour and poetry, and these were to be welcomed because they lifted the Irish novel out of its dreary homespun naturalism. But even poetry, O'Faolain opined, was ebbing and 'cannot be brought back into literature by an act of will'. In such circumstances, the kind of crude trial-and-error literary experiments, relieved by occasional, intermittent successes, that James had deemed to be the fate of provincial societies that lacked strong nurturing social supports and established literary conventions, seemed set to be Ireland's lot for some considerable time to come.

'The Dilemma of Irish Letters' concludes by widening out but not relieving the Irish problem. 'There is nothing like being gloomy when one is being gloomy', O'Faolain remarks, arguing that the Irish dilemma is really only a variation of that of 'all regionalist or provincial writers'.[72] Jane Austen, William Wordsworth, the Brontës, Thomas Hardy had all found ways to overcome provincial limitations, and Elizabeth Bowen, who could at least have recourse to the life of the Big House, might yet succeed in doing so in modern Ireland. In France, Flaubert had not overcome such circumstances: 'he got the usual one book out of the provinces, and that was not a solution but a *tour de force*'.[73] However, O'Faolain surmised, the twentieth-century provincial writer's dilemma might be even worse than his nineteenth-century counterpart's had been. 'One adultery had sufficed for a Hardy novel. A hundred would not make a modern novel.'[74] What had exacerbated matters with the passage of time was that even though the novel continued to be disabled in 'unshaped' provincial societies like Ireland by the absence of a complex, stratified society and developed literary conventions, the metropolitan countries had, for their own reasons, now also outgrown those same conventions and there too literature had also become increasingly aimless, without rudder. 'On the one hand [in provincial societies] values are not established and codified; on the other [in advanced metropolitan ones] they have become disestablished and disintegrated.'[75] By the time any order had returned to the wider international situation, O'Faolain concluded, Ireland might well have fallen so far behind the times as never to recover 'and so we shall never resolve our literary problems at all'.[76]

'Fifty Years of Irish Writing' elaborates the same fundamental analysis as 'The Dilemma of Irish Letters', but offers a more detailed conspectus of the perceived contour of decline in the disciplines of theatre, novel and poetry. Reiterating the earlier essay, 'Fifty Years' begins with the assertion that the decline it diagnoses 'began to operate immediately after the Free State was founded, in 1921', even though that decline had been held at bay for a time by 'the continuing momentum of nationalist excitement persisting after the revolution was over'.[77] Superficially, the riots provoked by O'Casey's *Plough and the Stars* in 1926 might seem to have recalled those occasioned by Synge's *Playboy* in 1907, both suggesting that literature continued to be vital and socially challenging. However, the crucial difference between the two was that the Catholic middle classes that had protested Synge's work had been without political power, while those that protested O'Casey's had already come to power. It might be objected that this downplayed the degree to which those who protested O'Casey's *Plough* were actually disaffected anti-Treaty republicans who had just lost the Civil War, but for O'Faolain the larger social transformation was what mattered. In the period between the Synge and the O'Casey riots, the Catholic Church and the Catholic middle class had taken control of state power, and 'centuries of depression (*sic*) had bred in both [the Catholic Church and the native government] not only a passionate desire for liberty — each with its own interpretation and its own aims — but the antithesis of that natural desire. It had induced a nervy, sensitive, touchy, defensive-aggressive, on-guard mentality as a result of which patriotism became infected by chauvinism and true religious feeling by what most Irish writers after 1921 tended to call "puritanism"'.[78] In the earlier period, 'an élite had been in the saddle' and Yeats's view of art, in keeping with that older world, had been 'aristocratic though nationalist, ... both European and Irish, as excited by the *Axel* of Villiers de l'Isle-Adam as by the peasant folktales of Biddy Early'.[79] In the later period, in contrast, the new ruling class was a petit bourgeois middle class, which had 'had very little education and could have only a slight interest in the intellectuals' fight for liberty of expression'.[80] The upshot was 'an alliance between the Church, the new businessmen, and the politicians, all three nationalist-isolationist for, respectively, moral reasons, commercial reasons, and politico-patriotic reasons, in themselves all perfectly sound reasons'. However valid these reasons might have been in themselves, they had been fatal for literature and for intellectuals, the latter combating the culturally depressing new climate, but also absorbing it and becoming 'infected by the atmosphere around them'.[81]

The political effect of this change could be detected, O'Faolain opined, in all of the arts. Twenty years earlier in his 'Fifty Years of Irish Literature' (1942), published in *The Bell*, O'Faolain had already proposed that the Abbey Theatre represented in one sense Yeats's greatest triumph but in another his greatest failure, because it had become famous precisely for the kind of realism and naturalism Yeats had always abhorred. Returning to this subject again in his *Studies* article, O'Faolain now explained that change as one that stemmed from a wider passage from a conception of art that was aristocratic and expansive to one that was petit bourgeois and narrow. Yeats, he argues, 'had loved all art that was remote and uncommon, 'distinguished and lonely'. He had seen the element of nobility in the simplest people but he had never permitted his affection for familiar life to be confused with a preoccupation with the common or the popular'.[82] This attitude had conditioned his dislike of realism, a low mimetic form that valued character and moral and social problems over personality, which is what preoccupies drama when its concerns are with higher and more spiritual things. Thus, after control of the theatre passed from Yeats's hands, O'Faolain detected a 'lowering of intellectual standards',[83] and this was explained by the fact that 'our new, ambitious, hardfaced democracy understood none of this aristocratic concept. It understood only "realistic plays", political plays, representationalism, characterization, explanations, social comedies and tragedies'.[84] As a long-time advocate of realism, O'Faolain might have been expected to welcome such a transition, but the Abbey mode was clearly not the kind of realism he wanted. The new audiences, he explained, really only wanted realism in a lower or '*ersatz* form: plays that merely gave the illusion of being political, realistic, social, critical, and so on. They were ready to laugh at plays dealing with the surface of things'.[85] An old aristocratic view of art had disappeared, and what had succeeded it was not the higher realism O'Faolain had once hoped for, but only an inferior, low-grade anti-intellectual naturalism.

Turning from theatre to the novel, O'Faolain again detected decline, and drew

78 'Fifty Years', 95–96.
79 'Fifty Years', 95.
80 'Fifty Years', 97.
81 'Fifty Years', 97.
82 'Fifty Years', 99.
83 'Fifty Years', 99.
84 'Fifty Years', 100.
85 'Fifty Years', 100.

86 'Fifty Years', 101.
87 'Fifty Years', 101.
88 'Fifty Years', 101.
89 'Fifty Years', 101.
90 'Fifty Years', 102.
91 'Fifty Years', 104.
92 'Fifty Years', 104.
93 'Fifty Years', 104.
94 'Fifty Years', 104.

on the arguments of *The Vanishing Hero* to explain it. The dilemma for the Irish novel was in one sense that of the novel everywhere: to achieve high art '[a]n artist must, in some fashion, love his material, and his material must, in some fashion, co-operate with him. It is not enough for the artist to be clinically interested in life: he must take fire from it'.[86] The difficulty was that for thirty years or more now, Irish novelists, like those everywhere, had found it difficult to love the materials they wrestled with because 'writers everywhere feel that life no longer has any sense of Pattern or Destination' to lend their materials meaning. Hence the modern novel everywhere was aimless: 'The argosies set out. They forget why.'[87] 'The result is', O'Faolain mourned, 'that men of genius have been writing as the matador kills bulls, by virtuosity or by savagery'[88] — Joyce being the exemplar of technical virtuosity, Hemingway of savagery — or by wilfully imposing pattern and destiny — as François Mauriac or Graham Greene did by means of their Catholicism or the later O'Casey did by way of his Communism.

This account seems to depart from 'The Dilemma of Irish Letters' because the problems of the Irish novelist in this version of things appear to be at least coeval with those of writers elsewhere, but, as though reluctant to acknowledge as much, O'Faolain's survey returns in the end to the idea that the Irish were actually labouring under conditions well behind those of more advanced societies. 'The novel elsewhere', he wrote, 'may be frustrated by the certainties of men lost; here it is frustrated by the certainties of men saved'.[89] There had thus been plenty of honourable efforts in the Irish novel, including O'Faolain's own novels, but if one 'were to exclude Joyce — which is like saying if one were to exclude Everest — and Liam O'Flaherty how little is left!'.[90] The conclusion to be drawn was that in Ireland, despite its retarded complacency, the modern novel too survived, as it did elsewhere, only by dint of technical virtuosity (Joyce) or primal savagery (O'Flaherty).

O'Faolain's survey of Irish poetry is characteristically more perfunctory than that of the other literary forms. Irish poetry after Yeats demonstrated, he asserted, no lack of technical skills — 'if anything a far greater verbal sophistication has arrived in Irish poetry over the last thirty years than existed previously' — and likewise 'there is no decline in receptiveness'.[91] The later work of Austin Clarke, Patrick Kavanagh, Thomas Kinsella, Padraic Fallon, Valentin Iremonger and others 'show poetry just as much on tiptoe, ready for flight, as it ever was'.[92] In Gaelic poetry too there were new voices, Máire Mhac an tSaoi, Tomás Tóibín, and especially Seán Ó Riordáin, who had escaped the now threadbare idiom of the Literary Revival. All that Irish poetry in either language wanted, therefore, was 'width of personal vision' and 'a modern idiom, a modern speech' to rise above the local and the national.[93] Since most writers in all modes had 'by the grace of God and the savagery of Oliver Cromwell' the English language at their disposal, and thus access to a wider world in which 'the periodicals and publishers of Britain and America are waiting for them with open arms and purses', Irish artists generally had no reason to feel sorry for themselves. The worst enemies they had to overcome, he concluded, 'were impalpable and insinuating; self-pity, bitterness, sentimentality, cynicism, their own unsophistication, barren rage, even their love of country, their love of friends'.[94]

The concluding section of 'Fifty Years of Irish Writing' strikes a briskly determined tone and O'Faolain strives to end on an up-tempo, can-do mood absent from many of his survey essays. But that ending, with its image of metropolitan publishers waiting with open arms and purses for the writers who had the talent and the temperament to overcome the usual pitfalls of a small and slack society, is nevertheless rather forced and temperamentally out of kilter with the deeper currents of the essay's arguments,

Daniel Corkery (1878–1964), O'Faolain's mentor.

which had suggested that Irish literature, like twentieth century literature generally, had somehow lost its bearings and its sense of purpose. Signing off here, O'Faolain seems to suggest that for those with enough grit and ability the literary world was waiting to be conquered; over several decades, however, the stronger thrust of his criticism is that the local conditions of Irish society specifically, combined with the circumstances of the twentieth century period more generally, were unpropitious and would therefore probably conspire to make literary achievements of a level with those of Joyce and Yeats, for the foreseeable future at least, quite unlikely. Revisiting the same subject of national literary development again in the revised chapter on 'The Writers' in *The Irish*, he struck again a more familiar mordant note. Joyce, Yeats, Synge and O'Casey, he claimed, 'did what, in different ways, Georg Brandes, Ibsen, Björnson and Strindberg did for their capitals. They made Dublin into a European literary centre.' 'But whether we are thinking of poetry, of drama, or

95 *The Irish*, 143.

of the novel, Irish literature without [this] Big Four', he surmised, 'would now be regarded throughout the world as no more and no less than an interesting regionalist literature.'[95] And in the period that followed the departure of 'the Big Four' — his analysis suggested — it was to the level of 'an interesting regionalist literature' that Irish writing had essentially reverted.

III

It is one of the ironies of O'Faolain's career as a critic that he should have become the severest assessor of the historical moment or generation of which he himself was one of the most distinguished literary representatives. The critical idiom that underpins essays such as those just discussed, and that sustains O'Faolain's overall conception of twentieth-century Irish literary history, has by now obviously fallen into disuse in Irish literary studies, but some elements of the overarching structure of his vision, or his manner of conceptually organizing modern Irish literary history, remain deeply embedded in Irish cultural history nonetheless. The perception of the mid-century period — that between, say, 1930 or 1940 and 1960 or 1970 — as a creative valley between what are commonly believed to be the higher crests of the Revivalist and modernist period on one side and, on the other, a new surge of creativity that came after the opening up of 'de Valera's Ireland' to the outside world in the 1960s or that was whetted by the Northern conflict and the women's movement from the 1970s onwards, remains largely unchallenged. That perception of things has indeed been consolidated in many ways by the term 'Counter-Revival' (not one used by O'Faolain himself), which defines that whole interim period largely as a reaction against the Revival, and that commonly enough takes it as read that the period was one of salutary reassessment but lesser achievement. Damned by its own, or by O'Faolain's, hand, as it were, the period remains something of a byword for the frustration of art in the Free State, that frustration now commonly attributed — usually in a manner much more simplistic than O'Faolain's own version of things — mainly to censorship, poverty and isolationism.

However, one does not have to be a kind of cheerleader for mid-century Irish writing or to be invested in producing some radical counter-version of this period to notice that O'Faolain's vision of things (to use one of his own metaphors) is a very particular one. Even on an empirical level his surveys of the mid-century decades habitually take in only a very narrow spectrum of Irish writing, and the writers that inform his sense of things tend in the main to be southerners, novelists and realists. O'Faolain's criticism, in other words, repeatedly measures the heroic generation of Joyce and Yeats against a later and lesser one coming into maturity in the 1940s and in which the key figures are O'Faolain himself, O'Connor, O'Flaherty, Bowen, the later O'Casey, and then a few others who are usually roll-called only. In his recurrent round-ups of writers to elucidate this sense of generational change several writers are — to contemporary twenty-first-century perceptions at least — conspicuously absent. Among the more notable absentees are what we might now call 'late modernist' figures, most obviously Samuel Beckett, but also Flann O'Brien and Máirtín Ó Cadhain, none of whom ever even feature in O'Faolain's lists, and also Francis Stuart, whose attempt to produce the kind of high or visionary realism towards which O'Faolain's own criticism seems to reach might have earned him more than the merely passing mention which is all he ever receives. Such absences are partially explained by the fact that the organization of his criticism in terms of an agon between Revivalist 'romance' and his own generation's 'realism' blinds O'Faolain to anything that we might now call 'late modernism' and in so doing causes him repeatedly to miss or sidestep these figures.

As we have already seen, this critical agon had always rendered even Joyce a highly problematical figure for O'Faolain, leading him in the 1930s to dismiss his work in then-conventional terms as a subjectivist cul-de-sac, viewing him respectfully but still critically in the 1950s in *The Vanishing Hero* as an intellectual Lucifer who had rejected too much in his rebellion against Ireland and Catholicism ('He could record a revolt but he could never go farther than the revolt. There could be no sequel to those first two books. He had, by his too total rejection, walked himself into an impasse. ... In the splendid effort to cast away everything old to create something utterly new he left himself with only one thing to write of, himself, child of Adam'[96]). He then adopts him, rather belatedly, in the revised version of *The Irish* in 1969 as a tutelary 'realist' whose lessons had unfortunately been missed by a Yeats-besotted generation. For all his modernizing drive, O'Faolain's own literary tastes remained in many ways that of a nineteenth-century classical realist; his work rarely reaches with sustained approval beyond Chekhov and seems instinctively sceptical of high modernism. However, the increasingly 'aristocratic' and anti-republican tendency of O'Faolain's critical worldview may also be a factor here: Ó Cadhain and Stuart in particular would almost certainly have seemed to him to be republican extremists and thus automatically suspect 'romantics'. Both Corkery and O'Faolain shared a dislike of comic-satire, though the grounds for their dislike differed — the one disliking it for its tendency to blaspheme against national-popular pieties; the other suspecting it as a vehicle of catharsis that allowed writers, especially Irish writers, to laugh off social ills instead of intellectually confronting or probing their deeper causes. These factors may have sharpened O'Faolain's tendency, or maybe even his resolve, to keep his distance from writers such as Beckett, Behan and O'Brien.

The other significant absences — again to contemporary eyes at least — are women writers, and especially women realist novelists. Bowen repeatedly figures largely and honourably in O'Faolain's assessments, of course, but from such a doughty champion of realism one might have expected to hear more of figures such as Kate O'Brien, Mary Lavin, or M. J. Farrell. It is unlikely that any of these would have troubled O'Faolain's view that the post-Revivalist generation had failed to realize the 'consolidated achievement' that he allowed only to the earlier generation and partially to Bowen. But it is telling nonetheless that the kind of realism that does catch O'Faolain's attention is the latter's Big House and more English-affiliated version, and here again O'Faolain's 'aristocratism' surely conditions his assessment. Whether this or a more conventional masculinist bias be the pertinent explanation, his lack of attention to women's realist fiction undoubtedly vitiates his assessments of the history of Irish realism and bypasses the obvious, if still largely unexplored, connections between gender and genre where this mode of fiction is concerned. When other notable figures, such as Louis MacNeice for example, are added to the list of writers missing from O'Faolain's post-Yeats generation, it becomes even more apparent that even by a crudely empirical measure his conception of the mid-century literary decline is really a reflex conditioned by his disappointment that Irish writing had 'failed' to produce the — always elusive — kind of realism he aspired to, rather than a comprehensive assessment of the various modes of writing that had emerged after the foundation of the new state order and the partition of the island.

In the end, though, O'Faolain's mode of analysis is more vulnerable on a conceptual than on an empirical level. The demarcation of twentieth-century Irish literary history in terms of 'generations' is at best a weak mode of historicism, and the orchestration of that

96 *The Vanishing Hero*, 220–21.

97 Alexis de Tocqueville, *Democracy in America*, 2 vols. (New York, 1972), vol. 2, 70.

generational divide in terms of an agon between 'romance' and 'realism' compounds matters because it is terminologically too narrow-gauge to deal adequately with a literary field that was always more complex and diverse than such terms can cater for. It is not just that O'Faolain lacks an adequate critical vocabulary to deal with literary modes that might better be described as 'modernist' or 'late modernist' or that he fails to discriminate sufficiently between different varieties of twentieth-century 'realism' (psychological realism, the more modernist-inflected versions, naturalism, et cetera) or 'romanticism' (fantasy, gothic, the marvellous). It is also that any stronger mode of historical criticism would need to deal not just with individual 'authors' or 'generations' but also with the fortunes of different literary forms and genres. In the case of literary forms, for example, even if we accept O'Faolain's case that the Irish novel could not advance on Joyce and struggled to rise above a kind of sour 'local naturalism', it does not follow that all the arts suffered similar or equal crises or declines in lockstep. Likewise, a mode of criticism that assessed Irish fiction in terms of its more common modes or genres — the *bildungsroman*, the Big House novel, the historical novel, the romance-across-the-divide, the fantastical or satirical novel, to name but a few — might well yield a graph of literary fortunes quite different to the kind that O'Faolain's work suggests.

However, the aspect of O'Faolain's work that is ultimately the most interesting and the most controversial is not his assessment of the standard of mid-century Irish writing but his wider diagnosis of post-independence culture and society. The thesis that it was the Irish national revolution that initially produced the voltage that charged the accomplishments of the Revival, and that made possible the achievements of Yeats and Joyce, but which simultaneously created the 'thin' and 'unshaped society' that disabled high literary production, or that retarded the novel at least, over the longer term is fundamental to O'Faolain's whole conception of post-independence Ireland. A thesis of this kind is likely to have little appeal to nationalist, republican or even liberal-democratic-minded critics, but the question remains as to whether it might nonetheless be persuasive. The Tocquevillian idea that aristocratic societies tend to be more culturally refined than democratic ones — ('Taken as a whole, literature in democratic ages can never present, as it does in the periods of aristocracy, an aspect of order, regularity, science, and art; its form will, on the contrary, ordinarily be slighted, sometimes despised. Style will frequently be fantastic, incorrect, overburdened, and loose, — almost always vehement and bold. Authors will aim at rapidity of execution, more than perfection of detail')[97] — is of course an aesthetic ideology that need not command assent; Oscar Wilde, for one, repudiated it when he declared himself a republican on the grounds that republics were more hospitable for art. But one does not even have to become immersed in this long-standing debate to discern that there is something decidedly odd about O'Faolain's argument that the post-independent Irish Free State or Republic prized values of equality above personal liberty to the extent that this had ultimately created a 'jelly-like mass of friendly egalitarianism' that was socially pleasant but culturally disastrous (or disastrous for the novel at least, which seems for O'Faolain to be more or less the same thing). To describe the society that emerged at any stage since 1922 in terms of a 'change-over from a stratified society — ranging from aristocrat to outcast — to a one-class society' is frankly astonishing; it ignores the real social inequality and class stratification, not to mention gender oppression, that have remained consistent and conspicuous features of modern Irish society at every stage of its development. It is unlikely that rural and urban workers emigrating from Ireland in their tens of thousands to England and to the US would have felt that a republican tendency to prize equality over personal liberty was one of twentieth-century Ireland's graver ills. That one of post-independent Ireland's most distinguished and combative dissident critics could even indulge the idea that Ireland had become a 'one-class society' is an index of the degree to which even the apparently more reform-minded versions of Irish cultural criticism remained in hock to conservative aristocratic and anti-republican value-systems handed down from previous centuries; in O'Faolain's case at least the transmission of such values was derived in part at least, as observed earlier, via Henry James, though the influence of Yeats and to some extent Joyce are also evident in this respect.

It must be allowed, of course, that O'Faolain, in *The Bell* and elsewhere, was nonetheless a critic of, and not an apologist for, the post-independence Irish establishment, and that he was often much more sympathetic to the plight of those oppressed by the various post-independence regimes than were the literary patriots and cultural nationalists who would have taken umbrage at his ideas about Irish backwardness and 'provincialism'. But this does nothing to alter the fact that the value-system that informs O'Faolain's cultural criticism, and that enables such extraordinary judgements on his part, is ultimately far closer to the right- rather than the left-wing of the political spectrum: the proposition that there is an inevitable conflict between social equality and individual liberty and fullness of self-expression is a fundamental tenet of right-wing social thought, whereas, for the left, social equality is a necessary precondition for any genuine flowering of individual liberty and expression. For all his dissidence, therefore, O'Faolain's worldview is actually philosophically quite close in this key respect at least to that of the Cumann na nGaedheal or Fianna Fáil establishments he opposed.

Might one reject O'Faolain's characterization of post-independence Irish society as a flat-class society that prized egalitarianism over liberty, but still find persuasive his thesis that anti-colonial revolutions typically bring less educated classes to power than the more cosmopolitan and culturally sophisticated classes they displace? This is always a possibility, of course, and the history of anti-colonial revolutions is not wanting in instances where the newly incumbent regimes were more culturally doctrinaire, repressive or plain philistine than the old colonial ones they ousted. Since a revolution by its very definition is an accelerated structural transformation of a society that involves the replacement of historically privileged classes by ones less privileged (and hence likely to be less well-travelled, cultured or cosmopolitan in the more elite sense of that word), a period of post-revolutionary cultural stagnation or retardation would seem one of the inevitable risks of any revolutionary situation. But even on cultural grounds alone such risks must be measured against the social and cultural and intellectual energies released by rapid structural transformation and by the coming to power of new classes. And it is also the case that when new classes do come to power they can be expected to acquire cultural capital, along with their other new opportunities and privileges, over time. Thus O'Faolain's thesis that the Irish national revolution was good for literature in the short term but seriously detrimental to it in the longer term is itself at best a short-term view of things, at worst a conservatively snobbish nostalgia for the kind of 'complex' (meaning highly class-stratified) society that had supposedly enabled nineteenth-century English and European fiction. It might well be the case — as the Frankfurt School critics have argued, for example — that the development of twentieth-century advanced or consumer capitalism would eventually create a cultural climate inhospitable to all kinds of high culture, including the kinds of nineteenth-century classical realism that O'Faolain approved of, as well as the kinds of high or late modernism with which he was by disposition never very comfortable. But since O'Faolain's cultural criticism lacks any theory of capital as such, and since he was in any case an advocate of modernization, which in practical terms meant developing Ireland in conventional capitalist terms, to accept as much would be to acknowledge that O'Faolain as social critic endorsed the very modes of development that created the cultural consequences and dilemmas his literary criticism lamented. In other words, as a champion of modernization O'Faolain effectively endorsed the idea that the only way for Ireland to become an economically prosperous and socially progressive and culturally sophisticated society was to accommodate itself to international capitalism, but at same time his literary criticism never really had the conceptual resources or reach that would allow him seriously to diagnose the ways in which advanced capitalism re-conditioned cultural production generally or even the novel or realism more particularly. Indeed, as this essay has shown, there is a serious conceptual dissonance in O'Faolain's work between, on the one hand, its frank endorsement of capitalist modernization and its attendant critique of Irish fetishizations of tradition, and, on the other, its Jamesian-inflected cultural aristocratism, which led him to take such a dim view of a rough-and-ready adolescent republic lacking in mature English-style old-world graces and refinements. No accomplished republican-minded literary criticism could develop from these strangely contradictory conceptual affiliations.

Does this mean that O'Faolain's anxieties about the capacity of Irish literature to develop are simply of his time — the outlook of a late revivalist preoccupied, despite himself, with the 'national thing' — and ought no longer to trouble critics now? For the reasons adduced above, any critic pondering the fate of national literatures in conditions of twenty-first-century advanced global capitalism is unlikely to find O'Faolain's work a strong resource. Even so, the fact that so many of Ireland's more passionately intelligent and engaged critical intellectuals were troubled by the direction of Irish letters once the energies of the Revival had abated is itself a historical curiosity of some note and not something that ought to be too easily brushed aside. Yeats, Corkery and O'Faolain all felt that Irish literature had achieved great things between the 1890s and the establishment of the Free State, but all were troubled by the fear that the achievements might be temporary and that the long-term prospects for Irish literature remained dubious. Given their contrasting temperaments and political allegiances, their diagnoses of the prospects for a strong national literature naturally differed significantly. Yeats as critic became increasingly aristocratic-minded and in his later career especially was horrified by modern heterogeneity — 'All out of shape from toe to top' — as something inimical to grace and form and thus to high literary expression; Corkery feared that post-independence Irish writers remained too dependent on colonially-inherited literary moulds and on foreign audiences and critics to create a robust and accomplished national-popular literature in English; O'Faolain, as we have seen, combined commitments to capitalist modernization with a kind of Yeatsian- or Jamesian-inflected disdain for Ireland's unsophisticated peasant republic. In a later moment, Seamus Deane in *Celtic Revivals* (1985) would argue that Irish literature after independence was vitiated by the lack of any strong indigenous socialist culture and by variants of aesthetic aristocratism transmitted through both the Yeatsian and Joycean literary inheritances. Critics who have relinquished the idea that the category of 'national literature' as such retains any value or who have abandoned the conviction that national literatures can perform any strong social function in our contemporary world will obviously find these preoccupations archaic. For those who do not hold such views, these critical diagnoses of Irish literary development still merit careful consideration.

Houses on Eccles Street, Dublin. Photo: Curran Collection, University College Dublin Library, by kind permission of Prof. Helen Solterer. Digital images reproduced by kind permission of the Irish Virtual Research Library and Archive.

Family and Form in *Ulysses*

Barry McCrea

I

It is a fairly common presumption that the idea of narrative is linked on a deep level to ideas of family, kinship and ancestry.[1] This connection is especially clear in certain periods and genres: nineteenth-century novels of bloodlines and bequests, for example, or the marriage and paternity plots of comic theatre, take the rhythms and mechanisms of genealogical family life as the natural framework for telling stories. But what vision of family underpins modernist or experimental narrative forms? If family provides one of the chief metaphorical foundations for conceiving of narrative, then radical experiments in narrative form ought to imply a radically different understanding of what the family is and how it is sustained.

Since family and plot are so associated with one another in

1 See for example, Patricia D. Tobin, *Time and the Novel: The Genealogical Imperative* (Princeton, 1978).

the nineteenth-century novel, the assumption has sometimes been made that the 'plotless' modernist novel rejects the idea of family itself, that it involves a turn away from connection and kinship toward fragmentation and alienation.[2] Using *Ulysses* as a case-study, this article argues the opposite: that the eschewing of traditional narrative forms does indeed imply the eschewing of traditional models of family, but that modernist writers do not turn away from the idea of family altogether. On the contrary, while Joyce and other modernists reject genealogy as the fundamental frame of narrative, they look to alternative models of kinship, to 'queer' networks of community and solidarity, as a source of narrative coherence and continuity.

The family is central to the action, structure and meaning of *Ulysses*, even on the most superficial reckoning. Each of the principal *dramatis personae* in the novel is chiefly identified in terms of a family role: Stephen the son, Bloom the father and husband, Molly the mother and wife. Many of the novel's chief concerns, explicit and implicit, are expressed as questions of family life: paternity, maternal love, conjugality, filial piety, adultery, orphanhood.[3] Structurally, moreover, the plots that shape the content of *Ulysses* are versions of two classic family plots: the day-long marriage plot of the Blooms, and the 'spiritual' paternity plot between Stephen and Bloom. The work's narrative progress is measured and controlled by these two family reunions, each of them delayed, deferred and anticipated from the beginning through to the end; the three major actors in these plots eventually gather under the same roof for a grand family finale in 7 Eccles Street.

What a reader takes from *Ulysses* hinges to a great degree on how he or she understands these plots. The family dramas of *Ulysses* have been at the centre of critical debate on that novel. Its earliest critics viewed the reunification of Bloom and Molly at home as a reassertion of the conjugal unit and of a natural order against the temptations and perversions of the modern metropolis, and the meeting between Bloom and Stephen as the culmination of a quest for 'spiritual' paternity, a kind of mythic version of family values.[4] For many later critics, on the other hand, the family plots are ironic structures, offered in a spirit of mockery, set in place in order to fail.[5] Fredric Jameson, for example, believes that *Ulysses* dramatizes the atomization of human relationships in capitalism. He sees the meeting between Bloom and Stephen as a 'miserable failure', and suggests that the 'impoverished interpersonal schemas drawn from the nuclear family [in *Ulysses*]... are to be read as break-down products and defence mechanisms against the loss of the knowable community'.[6]

Queer theory has opened up exciting avenues of exploration into *Ulysses*,[7] but has tended to avoid the question of its governing family plots, focusing instead on moments of hidden or repressed desire, on ambiguity, secrecy or indeterminacy, uncovering queer local moments within the novel's teeming content, while tacitly accepting that the family structure in the novel is a fundamentally 'straight' one.[8] The major challenge for queer theory, of course, is that there is so little overt homosexuality in *Ulysses*. Richard Brown declares that 'Joyce did not apparently wish to make a special case for "inversion" or homosexuality ... in Joyce [it] is peripheral',[9] and David Norris[10] writes that homosexuality in Joyce is 'an occasional external threat introduced in the margins of heterosexual order'.[11] Where queer theorists *have* argued for a structural role for queerness and deviance in *Ulysses*, the emphasis is on gaps, errors, or slips, on what is hidden, repressed or excluded by the novel's family plots. These readings enrich our understanding of Joyce's text, but do not concern themselves with the question of the novel's more basic

2 See for example Anny Sadrin, *Parentage and Inheritance in the Novels of Charles Dickens* (Cambridge, 1994), 24–25.

3 Robert Caserio goes so far as to say that 'there is nothing *but* family life in *Ulysses*'; see Caserio, *Plot, Story and the Novel* (Princeton, 1979), 240. Andras Ungar writes that '*Ulysses* proceeds to unravel Irish political concerns through the family concerns of its dramatis personae'; see Ungar, *Joyce's Ulysses as National Epic: Epic Mimesis and the Political History of the Nation State* (Gainesville, 2002), 7.

4 Eliot '*Ulysses*, Order and Myth', *The Dial*, 75 (November 1923).

5 See Franco Moretti, *Signs Taken for Wonders: Essays in the Sociology of Literary Forms* (London, 1988), or Umberto Eco, *Le Poetiche di Joyce* (Milan, 1982).

6 Jameson, Fredric. 'Ulysses in History', in Margot Norris, ed., *A Companion to James Joyce's Ulysses: Case Studies in Contemporary Criticism* (Boston, 1998), 149–50.

7 See Joseph Valente, *Quare Joyce* (Ann Arbor, 1998). It is striking how few of the essays in Valente's seminal volume deal with *Ulysses*, given its dominance in Joyce studies generally.

8 For an eloquent account of the different waves of queer theory, see Joseph Valente, '*Ulysses* and Queer Theory: A Continuing History', in Michael Patrick Gillespie and

Martello Tower, Sandycove, County Dublin. Photo: Bill St Leger. © RTÉ Stills Library.

A. Nicholas Fargnoli, eds., Ulysses *in Critical Perspective* (Gainesville, 2006), 88–116.

9 Richard Brown, *James Joyce and Sexuality* (Cambridge, 1985), 84.

10 David Norris, 'The "Unhappy Mania" and Mr. Bloom's Cigar: Homosexuality in the Works of James Joyce', *James Joyce Quarterly*, 31, 3 (1994), 357–74.

11 Even if, as Tanner notes, 'perversion is the usual mode of procedure' in the novel; see Tony Tanner, *Adultery in the Novel: Contract and Transgression* (Baltimore, 1979), 13.

12 See especially Colleen Lamos, *Deviant Modernism: Sexual and Textual Errancy in T. S. Eliot, James Joyce, and Marcel Proust* (Cambridge, 1998) and Colin MacCabe, *James Joyce and the Revolution of the Word* (London, 1978).

narrative structures, its 'story'.

The evident similarity between this story and the family plots of the nineteenth century, or even the romance, seems to be something of an embarrassment for those making claims for the queerness of *Ulysses*.[12] For the queer theorist Leo Bersani, this obvious similarity is one of the elements which leads him to conclude that *Ulysses* is ultimately a conservative work, as far as 'the field of human relations' is concerned. In Bersani's view, the *dénouements* in Eccles Street are an assertion of the traditional family unit as a form of redemption, and a reinscription, however disguised by formal pyrotechnics, of regressive Dickensian sentimentality about the family.[13] For most queer theorists (however much they may find other sources of queerness in *Ulysses*), the assumption, at least tacitly, is that the family structures of *Ulysses*, and the nineteenth-century plots they echo, are fundamentally hostile to queerness.

Yet there is an important claim to be made for structural queerness in *Ulysses*, and, perhaps surprisingly, this queerness is to be found in the affinities, rather than the differences, between Joyce's novel and the family dramas of Dickens. Far from suggesting a shared conservatism about the family, the correspondences between Joyce and Dickens strikingly highlight the ways in which *Ulysses* is constructed upon a queer rewriting of family structures.

This conflicts with a long history of claims made for the modernism of *Ulysses* touting its supposed rejection of the Victorian novel (T. S. Eliot assured Virginia Woolf that Joyce's novel would be a landmark because it 'destroy[ed] the whole of the nineteenth century.'[14]) In fact, however, the clearest source of *Ulysses*'s queer reimagination of kinship is to be found in those alternative communities in Dickens (such as Fagin's den) which rival the family for control of novelistic form and of the destiny of protagonists.[15] To view Joyce's Dickens as the crass sentimentalist pastiched in 'Oxen of the Sun' is not only to miss the complex currents of queerness and modernity that run through Dickens's novels,[16] but also to risk misunderstanding the nature and origins of *Ulysses*'s modernism.[17]

In *Beginnings*, Edward Said discusses modernism's relationship to the family plot, noting that a key feature of modernist fiction, as opposed to nineteenth-century novels, is the shifting of the organizing paradigm of social relationships from what he calls 'filiation' and hierarchy to 'affiliation' and adjacency. Despite his family-inflected terminology, Said does not deal with the question of alternatives to the family itself — which looms so large in Victorian fiction — or how the representation of such alternatives might lead to a fundamental reorientation of narrative form.

The purpose of this essay is to make a queer narratological case for *Ulysses* on the basis of its vision of the family. Queerness here is not by any means co-terminous with homosexuality or sexual deviance. The argument instead is that *Ulysses* is a novel in which the *idea* of homosexuality — what homosexuality *represents* in terms of narrative — is foundational to its form, to the communal, and collective realities that provide the framework and scaffolding of the novel. *Ulysses* is neither a rediscovery nor a wreckage of Victorian family values, but a work and a world structured by an alternative ideology of kinship, a queer family epic.[18]

II

Oliver Twist is given his surname by the beadle of the workhouse in which he is born, not by his dying mother or anonymous father. From the moment of his birth, a slow but single-minded genealogical plot is devoted to de-Twisting Oliver, to bringing him back to the bosom of his forgotten natural family. In the meantime, as he adventures through life as Twist, alone and unparented, the chaotic streets of London offer Oliver a set of connections, a network of community and solidarity to replace this lost kin. A random encounter with another orphan, the Artful Dodger, leads him to an alternative family with Fagin's band of pickpockets and prostitutes. Two chronological impulses and two competing models of social and personal formation thus compete throughout the novel. The forward passage of the years shows Oliver growing up into Oliver Twist the pickpocket, a social being who

13 Leo Bersani, *The Culture of Redemption* (Cambridge, Mass., 1990).

14 Virginia Woolf, *A Writer's Diary* (London, 2003 [1953]), 57.

15 My claims here for a queer *Ulysses* are in keeping with a critical tendency to revisit the continuities rather than the ruptures between Dickens and Joyce. See for example, M. Bolton, 'Joycean Dickens/ Dickensian Joyce', *Dickens Quarterly*, 23, 14 (2006), 243–52; or T. Schwarze, *Joyce and the Victorians* (Gainesville, 2002).

16 For ersatz families and deviant sexuality in Dickens, see: Holly Furneaux 'Charles Dickens' Families of Choice: Elective Affinities, Sibling Substitution, and Homoerotic Desire', *Nineteenth Century Literature*, 62.2 (2007), 153–92; Sally Ledger, *Dickens and the Popular Radical Imagination* (Cambridge, 2007), especially 99–105; Helena Michie, 'From Blood to Law: The Embarrassments of Family in Dickens', in *Palgrave Advances in Charles Dickens Studies*, ed. John Bowen and Robert L. Patten (Basingstoke, 2006).

17 There is evidence, beyond the many allusions to him in *Ulysses* and *Finnegans Wake*, that Joyce had a broad and careful knowledge of Dickens, despite Stanislaus's claim that his brother 'didn't much like' him. Clayton points out, for example, that there are more allusions to

is hammered into profession and shape by his adventures and encounters in London with his adoptive criminal family. At the same time, the novel gradually reaches backwards in time, towards the recovery of his forgotten genealogical relatives, and the unearthing of a lost, authentic identity.

Oliver is restored, in every sense, to his 'in-laws'; the illegitimate 'family' is literally rendered as a band of outlaws. As it straightens out the line of hereditary succession, the novel's plot straightens out Oliver too, removing him from the adopted, illegitimate name 'Twist' and from the criminal identity associated with it, restoring him both to his lost, legitimate patronymic and to his law-abiding, real family. This mechanism is implicit in the word *dénouement*, literally, un-knotting (even un-twisting). The tying up of loose ends at the end of the novel is also a process of untying, of removing the protagonist from contaminating, contingent connections, and placing him back among his rightful, natural family. As the denouement reveals some meetings, but not others, to have a retrospective, genealogical meaning, it undoes the illegitimate bonds formed by purely 'random' encounters. All of the possibilities of non-genealogical connection, formation and community unleashed by Oliver's encounter with the Dodger are ultimately undone by 'coincidences' that lead him to Brownlow and to his lost genealogical connections.

Even if Oliver's destiny is ultimately decided by the force of his genealogical attachments, however, it is the characters and vivid reality of Fagin's den which provide the novel's colour and adventure. We could even go so far as to say that where family provides the form, anti-families provide the content. By *Bleak House* (1852–53), published fifteen years later, the sheer volume of this content, the range and complexity of London's extra-familial networks threaten to overwhelm the family form. A powerful allegory for the creaking mechanism of the family plot lies at the heart of this novel in the shape of Jarndyce and Jarndyce, a mammoth court case, which, as it winds its way slowly through the legal system, touches almost every character in the novel in one way or another. The suit is charged with the settlement of an estate on the rightful heirs, who must be identified from among a morass of competing claimants and documents. Jarndyce and Jarndyce is thus concerned, in the most literal sense, with legitimacy, transmission and family.[19] The morbid, obsessive *waiting* for this inheritance to come through, on the part not only of the presumptive heir, Richard Carstone, who is destroyed by it, but also by his cousin Ada, John Jarndyce, Miss Flite, and a host of other characters who accumulate and cluster around the suit, is a savage satire on the passive waiting of Oliver Twist, a scathing indictment of the automatic inheritances of the genealogical family plot.

Great Expectations (1861) opens in a family graveyard, and is littered with aborted genealogical plots which try and fail to control the novel's form. In the end, however, the only bond which comes to have the force of structure is between Pip and an outlawed stranger. Pip's random encounter with Magwitch is a criminal tie that ultimately gives shape to the novel's chronological and symbolic structure. (In this particular sense, of how in nineteenth- and twentieth-century novels the family and its rivals compete for narrative form, we might consider *Great Expectations* to be an anticipation of the modernist novel). The fierce competition between genealogy and queerness for control of the protagonist, which generates the suspense and action of *Oliver Twist*, *Bleak House* and *Great Expectations*, is a struggle between the family and its rivals for *form*. This is the key point of continuity between Dickens and Joyce, and the crucial missing background to what is perhaps the most discussed subject in *Ulysses* scholarship,

Dickens in *Ulysses* than to Defoe and Sterne combined; see J. Clayton, 'Londublin', *Novel: a Forum on Fiction*, 28, 3 (1995), 327–28.

18 Although he does not deal with Dickens, a somewhat parallel account of alternative families in Balzac, can be found in Michael Lucey's *The Misfit of the Family: Balzac and the Social Forms of Sexuality* (Durham, 2003).

19 See D. A. Miller, *The Novel and the Police* (Berkeley, 1989), 98–100.

the question of paternity.[20]

When viewed in the light of Dickens's family plots, the earliest origins of *Ulysses* ought to arouse interest in the queer eye. Joyce's novel began its life as a planned extra story for *Dubliners*, in which Alfred Hunter, a middle-aged Dubliner with an unfaithful wife, would stumble across a young literary man caught up in a drunken brawl, rescue him and take him home.[21] The sprawling, multivocal novel that *Ulysses* became seems to have little in common on the surface with this account of small-time heroism which Joyce was planning in 1904. But in terms of family and how it relates to narrative structure, this autobiographical kernel remains fundamental to *Ulysses*'s final form, to its style, shape and vision. The narrative device of a chance encounter between two strangers in an urban public space connects *Ulysses* to the family dynamics of Dickens's London, and to their central question: what can a random encounter in the city streets mean or produce?

In *Oliver Twist*, only those meetings which turn out to have a secret genealogical subtext are permitted to be generative: Fagin, the Dodger and Nancy are all severed from Oliver and transported to the gallows, colonies or the grave. In the final reckoning of *Oliver Twist*, only when you coincidentally run into your natural family, unbeknownst to yourself, do unplanned streetside meetings have any lasting significance. The nature of the encounter which is the 'story' of *Ulysses* places Stephen in the role of Oliver or Pip, and Bloom in the role of Fagin or Magwitch. The portrayal of Stephen as a dispossessed, unparented youth[22] and of the older, Jewish Bloom as an urban wanderer in search (as his original name, Hunter, implies) of a new attachment in the city,[23] is deeply connected to the formal ambitions of *Ulysses*. The search for alternative forms of structure and connectedness is part of the novel's general interrogation of systems of continuity and connection (including nationalist ones).[24] Like Oliver, Esther and Pip, Stephen is gripped not only by a longing to belong to some other family, but also, more powerfully, with a sense that he should and could be part of some entirely different structure of kinship altogether.

In *Ulysses*, the Bloom plot (whether ironic or not) corresponds to an ideal, expressed persistently throughout the novel, of 'apostolic succession' — that is, non-biological kinship — and the Dedaluses to a system of paralysing genealogical determinism. In *Ulysses*, however much it may fail in the eyes of Jameson or Franco Moretti as an actual father–son dyad, the encounter between Stephen and Bloom undeniably wins out *narratively*, insofar as it gives structure to the novel's progress, and gives the novel its sense of coherently related beginning, middle and end — something only genealogy was permitted to do in *Oliver Twist*. The meeting between Stephen and Bloom hosts and arranges the unruly gallery of styles in the novel, and gives coherent shape to its sprawling depiction of Dublin life, to literary history and social reality. In other words, if we compare the narrative *outcome* of *Ulysses* to the Dickensian family plots to which it is indebted, we find that the illegitimate criminal encounter, undone by the genealogical *dénouement* in *Oliver Twist* but tentatively allowed to win out in *Great Expectations*, becomes in *Ulysses* the very centre of narrative legitimacy, endowed with form-giving properties.

It is for this reason that, in 'Eumaeus', the two men's final departure towards Eccles Street, for which we have waited so long, is described as a marriage: 'The driver never said a word, good, bad or indifferent, but merely watched the two figures, *as he sat on his lowbacked car*, both black, one full, one lean, walk towards the railway bridge, *to be married by Father Maher*.'[25] Surprisingly little has been made by queer criticism of the fact

20 See for example, Karen Lawrence, 'Paternity as Legal Fiction in *Ulysses*', in Bernard Benstock, ed., *James Joyce: The Augmented Ninth* (Syracuse, 1988), 233–43.

21 For information about the real-life Alfred Hunter, see Peter Costello, *James Joyce: the Years of Growth 1882–1915* (London, 1992), 231; 265–66, and Terence Killeen, 'The Case of Alfred H. Hunter', *Dublin James Joyce Journal, 1* (Dublin, 2008), 47–53.

22 Ann Martin argues that the 'haunted figure of Stephen ... make[s] overt Joyce's emphasis on "Cinderella" as a text that has tremendous resonance in the context of modern consumer culture'; see Ann Martin, *Red Riding Hood and the Wolf in Bed: Modernism's Fairy Tales* (Toronto, 2006), 62.

23 The fact that Magwitch and Bloom have both lost a child — Estella and Rudy — perhaps leaves them with a desire for a new young attachment.

24 See MacCabe, *James Joyce and the Revolution of the Word*, 5.

25 James Joyce, *Ulysses*, ed. Hans Walter Gabler (New York, 1986), chapter 16, lines 1885–88. Hereafter cited as *U* plus episode and line number(s)

that the plot — central to the construction and interpretation of the whole novel — is here, at the very moment of its resolution, the key turning-point of the novel, rendered as a gay marriage. Marriage traditionally has a central structural function in narrative, retrospectively bestowing order and legitimacy on the chaos or strife that precedes it, and implicitly guaranteeing a fruitful and intelligible world to come after it; it generates legitimacy and order.[26] The reference at the end of 'Eumaeus' to the 'marriage' of Stephen and Bloom is an explicit recognition that this is the narrative purpose of their delayed and foreshadowed meeting. This is underscored by the fact that the whole of 'Eumaeus', which opens the climax of *Ulysses*, is full of homoerotic allusions.[27] These puzzling references to homosexuality throughout this episode are not there to suggest that there is a sexual subtext to the meeting between the two men, but rather that the structural function of their union displaces the marriage and family plot as the generator of order, continuity and coherence.

Narratology turns out to be a key to the variety of homosexual references throughout *Ulysses* (neither as numerous as queer theorists might hope nor as peripheral as Norris or Brown believe). The novel opens in a fairly queer world, the all-male anti-family of the Martello tower, presided over by Buck Mulligan, who flirts with Stephen and alludes to Wilde.[28] D. B. Murphy, the sexually ambiguous sailor at the centre of the action in 'Eumaeus', is connected to Mulligan not only by virtue of the letters of his name (B. Mu);[29] his profession links him to Mulligan's talking up of Dublin Bay to Stephen as Homer's 'winedark sea' and his exhortation to Stephen to read 'the Greeks'. Moreover, Murphy, according to his own account at least, has sailed to Greece, and he gets Stephen and Bloom to look at a tattoo on his arm, given to him, he claims, by a Greek.[30] In 'Telemachus', Mulligan had told Stephen to become a sort of Greek sailor, to embark on Hellenic voyages away from Dublin and his family (imaginatively at least). Mulligan, like Murphy, is an energetic and evocative raconteur, and there is something seductive about his ideas. The difference is that while both men tell tall tales, the Greek adventures Mulligan recounts are rooted in the future, whereas Murphy's yarns are all in the past, all entirely retrospective, and his body, with its tattoos and scars, is marked, like Magwitch's, with the signs of engagement and interaction with the world. In Joyce's schema for *Ulysses*, 'Eumaeus' is twinned with 'Telemachus'; the fact that the chapter that opens the *Telemachiad* — and thus opens the novel — and the one that opens the *nostos* — its closing— are both deliberately infused with homoerotic elements suggests in itself a structural role for homosexuality in *Ulysses*. The narrator of 'Eumaeus' is not implying real erotic involvement between any of the participants (with the possible exception of Murphy and Antonio), but is emphasizing the fact that the union of Stephen and Bloom is usurping the narrative function of marriage. Their biologically barren conjunction is generative and legitimizing, it is a beginning and an end in itself.

Homosexual assignations obviously cannot end in biological reproduction, nor in its symbolic 'home' of marriage. Since a gay couple cannot replicate the family set-up in which the lovers grew up, homosexual couplings imply, *ipso facto*, a different model of chronological continuity; the gap between the 'birth family' of childhood and the conjugal family of maturity, is more clearly delineated.[31] In its inability to repeat or reproduce the structures of its forebears, to be reassimilated into familiar forms, the homosexual encounter encapsulates certain basic ideas underpinning the project of modernism itself.

It is in this narratological light that the muted but definite references to

26 See Northrop Frye, *Anatomy of Criticism* (Princeton, 1957).
27 The full extent of the episode's homoerotic content is elegantly and irrefutably laid out by Jennifer Levine in 'James Joyce, Tattoo Artist: Tracing the Outlines of Homosocial Desire' in Joseph Valente, ed., *Quare Joyce* (Michigan, 1998), 101–20.
28 See David Weir, 'A Womb of His Own: Joyce's Sexual Aesthetics', *James Joyce Quarterly*, 31, 3 (1994), 207–31.
29 Some critics, partly on the basis of a typist's error in the first edition which rendered him 'W. B. Murphy', see the character of Murphy as an allusion to Yeats. See for example, Damian Love, 'Sailing to Ithaca: Remaking Yeats in *Ulysses*', *Cambridge Quarterly*, 36, 1 (2007), 1–10.
30 For an exhaustive and brilliant reading of this tattoo, and its extraordinary web of resonances, see Levine.
31 See Lee Edelman, 'The Future Is Kid Stuff: Queer Theory, Disidentification, and the Death Drive', *Narrative* 6, 1 (1998), 18–30.

homosexuality throughout *Ulysses* should be read. Frank Budgen tells us that Joyce agreed with his assessment that there was an 'undercurrent of homosexuality' in Bloom.[32] Buck Mulligan certainly thinks so: when Bloom passes him and Stephen in the entrance of the National Library, Mulligan sneers: 'Did you see his eye? He looked upon you to lust after you. I fear thee, ancient mariner. O, Kinch, thou art in peril. Get thee a breechpad.'[33]

According to all the (ample) evidence given to us in the book, this accusation (not the only one of its kind to be levelled against Bloom) is a false one.[34] But in *Ulysses*, as we know, Mulligan's flippant jokes and parodic songs, whether he knows it or not, usually point in the right direction. In the context of family and narrative form, the whiff of homosexuality that seems to follow Bloom is a by-product of the novel's passionate interest in alternative systems of relationality, in models of connection and continuity not subtended by natural, automatic or pre-approved systems such as the family.

The accusations of homosexuality thrown against Bloom may be read in the same light as the anti-Semitic gossip of which he is the object.[35] The Jewishness that Bloom and Fagin share[36] is also in some respects a symbolic consequence of their role as alternative modernist fathers, as agents from a secret underworld. The more or less lurid fantasies about Bloom's hidden associations that recur in *Ulysses* — that he is a Mason, that he has access to confidential information about horse races, that he has hidden stores of wealth — emphasize his narrative role as an agent of an alternative system of connection.

The narrative suspense of *Ulysses* is based around the question of whether this alternative system will fail or succeed. In essence, the novel plays on the same doubt that keeps us turning the pages of *Oliver Twist*: will Stephen fulfil his own queer dreams (as fuzzily elaborated in 'Proteus'), and move in with Leopold and Molly, setting up an alternative household to replace his genealogical family's oppressive 'house of decay'?[37] For all its cherished nineteenth-century-style realism, however what is at issue in *Ulysses* is not Stephen's literal destiny, in the way Oliver 'ends up' living with his in-laws the Maylies rather than with Fagin and the gang. *Ulysses* takes place on a single day, and we know nothing of the afterlife of its characters, not even where Stephen spends the night after refusing Bloom's offer of hospitality. In the end, in terms of pure diegetic realism, Stephen does not move in, certainly not for the time being, and we suspect that when he leaves Eccles Street he goes back neither to his father nor to Sandycove.[38] But when considered in retrospective terms, the outcome is different: the shape and focus and form of *Ulysses* derive from the fact that Bloom, the randomly encountered alternative Jewish father, the Fagin of the situation, definitively trumps the ties and claims of genealogy. First, in the simple fact that, as the novel ends, Stephen is last seen in his company — it is the relationship that, for Stephen, ends his narrative life. Second, in that Stephen has consciously rejected his identity as a natural father's son, in favour, at least momentarily, as far as the so-called 'spiritual' quest for paternity goes, for the possibilities released by his encounter with Bloom. But more important than these concerns of character and story is the fact that *Ulysses* itself, the most formalist of novels, whose vision far exceeds its simple plot in its narrative structure and rhythm, in its own strange forms, in the angle from which it views historical and social realities, and in the way it chooses to depict and deliver these realities to the reader, is produced by their meeting. The entire novel is finally an extrapolation of the principles of queer, non-genealogical paternity which the meeting represents.

32 Frank Budgen, *James Joyce and the Making of Ulysses* (London, 1934), 146.

33 *U* 9.1211. Lamos traces all of the homoerotic allusions in the relationship between Stephen and Bloom in 'Signatures of the Invisible: Homosexual Secrecy and Knowledge in *Ulysses*', *James Joyce Quarterly*, 31, 3 (1994), 337–55. She writes, for example, that 'Stephen's panicked references to homosocial and homosexual relations have the horror of an open secret whose knowledge he admits and suppresses' (340).

34 False in that we are given frank and apparently unfettered access to Bloom's sexual thoughts and fantasies during the day, and homoerotic desires never feature here.

35 In his essay on *Ulysses*, Nabokov suggests at some length that Bloom's perverse sexuality is a major failing in the novel; see Vladimir Nabokov, '*Ulysses*', in *Lectures on Literature* (London, 1980), 285–365.

36 And which Proust's Swann will, for the same reasons, share too. See Marcel Proust, *Du Côté de Chez Swann* (Paris, 1915), 14–20. Bloom's model, Alfred Hunter was not Jewish, but a Northern Ireland Presbyterian who had converted to Catholicism (Costello, 228). Joyce's decision to make Bloom a Jew may partly be connected to this literary lineage, as well as to the cosmopolitan Jewish community he encountered in Trieste.

III

The sense, at the heart of *Ulysses*, that the unforeseen encounters hosted by the city streets are powerful enough to rival to other, more predictable human connections, is a vital (and under-appreciated) link with Dickens. In Dickens, as in parts of *Ulysses*, the spontaneous life of the streets is associated with criminality or sexual deviance (Bloom and Stephen get together in a brothel, after all). Joyce's Dublin is a far cry, however, from Dickens' imperial metropolis. *Ulysses*'s embrace of queer narrative alternatives to the family plot can be connected to aspects of the socio-historical situation of bourgeois Dublin in 1904.[39] It is in part the idea that citizens were 'at home' in shared public spaces that leads Declan Kiberd to see *Ulysses* as an elegy to late nineteenth- and early twentieth-century civic bourgeois culture. In the Dublin of the time, Kiberd writes:

> the streets were ... places which people felt that they owned, whereas seldom did they own their own houses, which Leopold Bloom likens to coffins. For him and for them, it was the public zone which was warm, nurturing and affirmative. It was there that the random encounters which propel *Ulysses* kept on happening, before the rise of the shopping mall put a brake on such unexpected meetings and an end to the idea of a neighbourhood.[40]

On one level, then, it is as though the outcome of the genealogical *dénouement* in *Oliver Twist* is simply reversed in *Ulysses* — queer networks win out over blood family ties in the competition to give shape to content. In this most simple sense, *Ulysses* is a queer family epic. At the same time, however, the novel is deeply wary of the implications of a simplistic replacement of the private by the public, of the 'natural' by the 'cultural', or the 'straight' by the 'queer'. Fagin's den, after all, may be colourful and exciting, full of unexpected connections and intimate links with the world at large, but it is nonetheless a dark and brutal place. The fate of Nancy, who is murdered for her collaboration with agents of Oliver's genealogical family, starkly highlights the fact, by which *Ulysses* is constantly troubled, that alternatives to the family — be it mystical apostolic succession, Freemasonry, or the criminal underworld — are often predicated on the obliteration of the female. And, as Kiberd points out, the in other respects attractive civic culture of Dublin in 1904 was also segregated along the lines of gender, with men in the streets and public houses, and women often sequestered in the home. *Ulysses* is aware of the risk that its radical queer vision will simply favour one side of the public/domestic binary over the other, romanticizing groups of men talking and drinking in public spaces, while repressing the reality of their wives and children, imprisoned in a domestic offstage. The quick-fix escapism of homosociality was a major part of the 'paralysis' diagnosed in the stories of *Dubliners*, many of which are built around a doomed attempt to seek freedom from the debilitating force of the family in just such places from which women are excluded.

Before they can come together, then, our queer heroes, Stephen and Bloom, the keyless couple, must negotiate and escape from a perilous series of easy homosocial temptations. First of all Mulligan's 'Hellenic' cult in the Martello tower, when Stephen resolves to throw off the shackles of his genealogical inheritance but not to fall in with Mulligan and his friends; then the all-boys school in 'Nestor', and especially the chauvinist intellectual solidarity offered by Mr. Deasy; the 'omnium gatherum' of journalists in 'Aeolus'; the *ad hoc* salon in the back-rooms of the National Library in 'Scylla and Charybdis', where fantasies of female betrayal are threaded through the men's conversations about paternity and

See John McCourt *The Years of Bloom: James Joyce in Trieste, 1904–1920* (Madison, 2001), 218–19.

37 *U* 3.105.

38 The various possibilities as to where Stephen might plausibly spend the night, based on textual evidence, are clearly laid out in John Gordon, *Almosting It: Joyce's Realism* (Dublin, 2004).

39 McCourt shows how the public culture of the street, café and piazza in Joyce's Trieste may also have influenced his emphasis on this aspect of Dublin life.

40 Declan Kiberd, *Ulysses and Us* (London, 2009), 24–25.

Shakespeare; the sing-song at the Ormonde Bar in 'Sirens', with Stephen's natural father, Simon Dedalus, where thoughts of female adultery also haunt the male refuge, and where the only women present (Miss Kennedy and Miss Douce) are servants and objectified fantasies of generalized male desire; Barney Kiernan's pub in 'Cyclops', which mixes, as Mr. Deasy did, misogyny and anti-Semitism.

Finally, 'Oxen of the Sun' can be read as Joyce's most critical expression of the dangers inherent in exalting a simplistic model of public fraternizing as an alternative to the tyranny of genealogy. The fact that this is troubling for Joyce and for *Ulysses* may well be the reason for the deliberate stylistic and intellectual excesses of 'Oxen of the Sun', a grotesque depiction of pure form, without a connection to the material, lived world. The chapter presents an ironic view of the grand idea of apostolic succession and non-biological paternity as a group of drink-sodden wits bantering at a party, while in the next room, ignored by them, a woman gives birth. The almost absurd irony of the situation is underscored by the delivery of men's beery verbiage to the reader as series of pastiches, which supposedly mimics the gestation of the foetus in the womb. 'Oxen' is the key moment in the 'plot' of *Ulysses*, when the long-awaited 'match'[41] between Stephen and Bloom finally occurs; as this queer closure approaches, the meeting is almost hidden under the obfuscatory, pointedly male layers of imitation and pastiche.[42]

The conviviality and ease of these homosocial anti-families is immediately appealing not only to characters in *Ulysses* in search of an alternative to genealogy as a framework for their position in the world, but also to the novel itself, which is capable of being seduced by the wit and literacy of Dublin pub conversation as a haven from the complicating realities of women and of family, and which is attracted by the possibilities of a wholly cultural, and wholly male, system of kinship and ancestry.[43] The long odyssey of *Ulysses* is an account of the contingencies that lead to Stephen and Bloom finding each other outside of these homosocial contexts, but also a struggle within the novel itself to leave the pub, to 'marry', as it were, the spheres of the domestic and the social, to house them under the same roof — which is what happens in 'Eumaeus', 'Ithaca' and 'Penelope', when Bloom invites Stephen out of the brothel and into his home, causing the two family plots, and the realms of the public and the private, to collide in 7 Eccles Street.[44]

'Ithaca', as its Homeric title suggests, is the 'promised land' of *Ulysses*, the place where the meaning of the novel's plots is revealed, or at least located. For Bersani, the 'tedious', pseudoscientific description of facts and phenomena is showy bluster designed to disguise the fact that under all the supposed modernism, the human relationships within the narrative are unexamined Victorian sentimentalisms.[45] For the Marxists, the cold, clinical nature of the narrative eye is a ruthless ironizing of the narrative climax we have been foolish enough to pin such hopes on, an unstinting mockery of the possibilities of connection and redemption in a late capitalist world.

From the point of view of the queer family, however, the form of 'Ithaca', and its fixation with apparently irrelevant facts and phenomena of the physical universe, is an exposition of queer genealogical principles applied to the world, the retrospective offspring of the marriage between Stephen and Bloom.

The concluding episodes of *Ulysses* are a vision of the shared (male) civic space of the streets with its unpredictable queer encounters, and the (female) family home, as fully interpenetrating spheres of life. The catechism of 'Ithaca' is a lens through which to view the preceding chaos of the narrative. In this sense, it performs the ordering function of traditional family plots, but without relying on

41 For the meaning of the word 'match' in relation to Bloom and Stephen, and how it illuminates a connection between Joyce and Dickens see Robert Spoo 'Teleology, Monocausality, and Marriage in *Ulysses*', *ELH*, 56, 2, 439–62.

42 See Sherry B. Ortner, 'Is Female to Male as Nature is to Culture?', *Feminist Studies*, 1, 2 (1972), 5–31.

43 For Jean Kimball, the threat to Stephen is one of 'homosexuality as a life pattern'; see 'Freud, Leonardo, and Joyce: The Dimensions of a Childhood Memory', *James Joyce Quarterly*, 17 (1982), 165–82.

44 Ralph W. Rader suggests that the entirety of *Ulysses* can be read as an odyssey from homosexuality to homosociality; see Rader, 'Mulligan and Molly: The Beginning and the End', in Morris Beja and David Norris, eds., *Joyce in the Hibernian Metropolis: Essays* (Columbus, 1996), 270–78. I will be arguing here that, quite to the contrary, the novel is an odyssey away from homosocial traps towards a more fully articulated queer version of the family.

genealogy, biology, or on futurity. Unlike a genealogical resolution, 'Ithaca' does not rely on a providential moment in the future when all will be rendered meaningful — this meaning is already located in the past, and the project of generativeness will be a retrospective reframing of this past. The connection with the homosexual marriage that leads into the chapter is clear: what is involved here is the build-up of time and experience without promise of issue, without the possibility of deferring the problem of meaning, through biological offspring, to the future.[46] The streetside 'marriage' of Stephen and Bloom is not fertile in any sense that it will produce a joint issue into the future, but in 'Ithaca' it generates a retrospective rearrangement of the past framed through their encounter. Its joint issue is in the past — or rather, its joint issue *is* a certain framing of the past.

This function of their union, in fact, goes some way to explaining the narrative style of 'Eumaeus', which has attracted a great deal of critical comment and controversy. Linguistically, the entire episode is stitched together out of clichés, commonplaces, stock phrases, middlebrow Latin tags, the journalese of provincial newspapers, and so on. Just as the 'marriage' of Stephen and Bloom locates its generative possibilities in the rearrangement of what has gone before, so does the narrator of 'Eumaeus' reanimate the second-hand linguistic debris in order to narrate the chapter of their meeting.[47]

The Blooms' house as we find it in 'Ithaca' is characterized as one that is not reproductive, even though it used to be. This is spelt out most explicitly by the candid account of the Blooms' sex life: 'there remained a period of 10 years, 5 months and 18 days during which carnal intercourse had been incomplete, without ejaculation of semen within the natural female organ'.[48] Whatever hope the text offers that this situation might change, in some notional future beyond the text, the *narrative* function of this marriage plot is not to promise or guarantee a fertile future, but to give shape to, to house, a collective vision of the protagonists' individual pasts.

A common plot in the nineteenth-century novel revolves around a once-central branch of the family that finds itself suddenly left to one side of the line of succession, cut loose — *dénoué* — from the genealogical centre of action. This is the fate, for example, of the Miss Dashwoods in *Sense and Sensibility*, forced to leave the ancestral home for a cottage at the edge of another family's estate, consigned to watch the action from the genealogical wings. Heroines in Austen, like the Dashwoods, who find themselves left to one side of a genealogical line must battle to marry themselves back into the centre (a dramatized version of the lot of all women in patrilineal genealogical systems). In *Oliver Twist*, all the realities to one side of the single line of genealogy are violently erased. The point of genealogy, after all, is to excise lateral realities by isolating a single, legitimate line of succession. What is beside is discarded in favour of what comes next or what came directly before. The key queer technique that 'Ithaca' showcases is *lateralism*, a parenthetical vision in which any given account of reality is constantly revised and expanded to house ever more adjacent elements that have been occluded or excised. It is this process, the retrospective expansion of the past, which replaces the genealogical promise of reproduction — instead of promising to generate new realities in the future, it accommodates more and more of those that are excluded from any one version of the past.

This lateralism of 'Ithaca' is in keeping with Edward Said's suggestion in *Beginnings* that modernism shifts the organizing principle of relations from filiation and hierarchy to affiliation and adjacency. But Said's analysis does not draw the connection between this aspect of the transition from the Victorians to modernism

45 Bersani, *The Culture of Redemption*, 177.

46 Critics differ on this: Ungar, for example, sees Milly as a symbol of 'procreative increase', and suggests that she is crucial to the novel's meaning. Ungar crunches the numbers from the details in the text about Milly's menarche and birthday to show that 16 June 1904 is the first day on which Milly could theoretically have given birth to a full-term child; Ungar, *Joyce's Ulysses as National Epic*, 76–80.

47 An indication of this is given by the fact that, as Lawrence points out, the text refers obsessively to the anus and, especially, to human excrement. She lists a huge array of examples ('Lot's wife's arse', 'Butt bridge', the 'three smoking globes of turds' which the horse 'let[s] drop', etc.), suggesting that in the episode 'what is viewed as waste ... produces meaning', and that what is at stake is 'a connection ... outside the classical economy of *reproduction*'. Lawrence, 'Paternity as Legal Fiction in *Ulysses*', 370.

48 *U* 17.2279–84 For a different take on the Blooms' marriage and an optimistic view of a reconciliation between Bloom and Molly, see S. A. Henke and E. Unkeless, *Women in Joyce* (Urbana, 1982).

and the question of the family, and the ways in which so many nineteenth-century novels are built around a struggle between a straight, genealogical filiation and queer, adjacent, affiliations. What 'Ithaca' shows is that the shift in narrative perspective from hierarchy to adjacency, the parenthetical mode of 'Ithaca', is connected to a queer redrawing of family relationships, and cannot but be associated, to some degree, with the idea of homosexuality.

But heterosexuality is not excluded or repressed in this vision: marriage, ancestry and blood kinship are part of the variegated portrait of the world and its relationships painted by 'Ithaca'. It is this episode, after all, that provides us with most of the information we get concerning the protagonists' seed breed and generation, filling in gaps in our knowledge about Molly's father, Major Tweedy, the Virags, Higginses, and of course the Blooms' daughter Milly (hence the question: 'What, the enclosures of reticence removed, were their respective parentages?').[49] Family ties are included in 'Ithaca's vision, but they are expressed through a queer framework; the family itself is not the containing form of forms. Genealogy, like many other subjects, is of interest to the catechist of 'Ithaca', but it is not given a monopoly or special privilege as the arbiter of human or temporal interconnection.

The household we are presented with at the end of 'Ithaca' is produced by the encounter of Stephen and Bloom, and by a series of other non-reproductive encounters, marital as well as extra- or anti-marital: Molly's adulterous adventures, Bloom's random run-ins in streets, pubs and at funerals, the cabman's shelter, and so on.[50] Number 7 Eccles Street *retrouvé* is built not upon reproduction, futurity or regulated genealogical syntax, but on the alternative principles of hospitality and 'retrospective arrangement'. The home at the end of the novel, the fulfilment of its promises, is not a springboard for the future, as the happily-ever-after newly-wed homestead is in a romance or comedy, but an open space, like the public street, in which connections can be made. Just as the language and narrative tactics of the chapter that houses 'Ithaca' force us to make incongruous links and create unexpected patterns as we read, so is the homestead it describes one that is constructed around unpredictable and 'unnatural' traffic.

The first question of the catechism in 'Ithaca' — 'What parallel courses did Bloom and Stephen follow returning?' — gives us a sign of what the queer marriage plots of *Ulysses* are about: after the marriage comes the triumphant homecoming. Here Stephen and Bloom are indeed proceeding towards home, but the fact that they are following 'parallel courses' already implies a non-teleological meaning to their union: instead of a culminating big bang, providing a reproductive impulse towards the future, their meeting remains in permanent negotiation. The chief characteristic of 'Ithaca', indeed, is its fondness for parallels and series. A parallel, as opposed to a fusion, suggests a consistent pattern of relationship that can be construed across different times, but has no claims to monopoly — any number of parallels can be postulated, and each one will produce a different, but equally consistent arrangement of relationships.

The parallel between Stephen and Bloom allows for extensive extrapolations that move and stretch backwards and forwards across the generations, through time. Their coming together is used, through analogies, parallels and juxtapositions, to create a series of retrospective 'genealogies' that, while always clearly engendered by the meeting between the two men, becomes a vehicle to elucidate and fill in aspects of the whole novel, and to describe wider social, historical and physical realities. For example, Stephen (and the catechist) construct an imaginary 'lineage' leading from the moment in which Bloom lights the fire in front of him:[51]

49 *U* 17.532–33.
50 Brown writes that even if Molly's adulterous adventures are not as wide-ranging as the list in 'Ithaca' suggests, 'Joyce made this adulterousness or pseudo-adulterousness a persistent and structurally significant element in his novel'. *James Joyce and Sexuality*, 21.

James Joyce with his wife Nora, son Giorgio and daughter Lucia, 1924. Photo: Curran Collection, University College Dublin Library, by kind permission of Prof. Helen Solterer. Digital images reproduced by kind permission of the Irish Virtual Research Library and Archive.

> Of what similar apparitions did Stephen think?
>
> Of others elsewhere in other times who, kneeling on one knee or on two, had kindled fires for him, of Brother Michael in the infirmary of the college of the Society of Jesus at Clongowes Wood, Sallins, in the county of Kildare: of his father, Simon Dedalus, in an unfurnished room of his first residence in Dublin, number thirteen Fitzgibbon street: of his godmother Miss Kate Morkan in the house of her dying sister Miss Julia Morkan at 15 Usher's Island: of his aunt Sara, wife of Richie (Richard) Goulding, in the kitchen of their lodgings at 62 Clanbrassil street: of his mother Mary, wife of Simon Dedalus, in the kitchen of number twelve North Richmond street on the morning of the feast of Saint Francis Xavier 1898: of the dean of studies, Father Butt, in the physics' theatre of university College, 16 Stephen's Green, north: of his sister Dilly (Delia) in his father's house in Cabra.[52]

In place of reproduction, a joint issue into the future, a series of retrospective relationships is constructed starting from the point of view of 'Stephen plus Bloom'. Almost all of the lists and series in 'Ithaca' have as their starting point, in one way or another, the encounter between the two men. Their encounter becomes the window on the past, expanded and extrapolated to include Irish, European and international politics, local gossip, revolutions and science. The 'marriage' here does not push towards the future, or promise distant returns, but proceeds according to a careful, ever-shifting system of retrospective arrangements.

In another moment, it is Bloom who constructs a lineage for himself by analogy with an aspect of this evening with Stephen. Here, the names of streets are listed like a genealogical table,[53] but among the actual random encounters enumerated is one which would not be out of place in a Jane Austen novel — the visits to Matthew Dillon's house, during the course of which Bloom meets his future wife and father-in-law. The queer family of *Ulysses* is an open house where all encounters may occur, including traditional heterosexual courtship:

> Had Bloom discussed similar subjects during nocturnal perambulations in the past?
>
> In 1884 with Owen Goldberg and Cecil Turnbull at night on public thoroughfares between Longwood avenue and Leonard's corner and Leonard's corner and Synge street and Synge street and Bloomfield avenue. In 1885 with Percy Apjohn in the evenings, reclined against the wall between Gibraltar villa and Bloomfield house in Crumlin, barony of Uppercross. In 1886 occasionally with casual acquaintances and prospective purchasers on doorsteps, in front parlours, in third class railway carriages of suburban lines. In 1888 frequently with major Brian Tweedy and his daughter Miss Marion Tweedy, together and separately on the lounge in Matthew Dillon's house in Roundtown. Once in 1892 and once in 1893 with Julius (Juda) Mastiansky, on both occasions in the parlour of his (Bloom's) house in Lombard street, west.[54]

'Ithaca' neither mocks nor glorifies the meeting between Stephen and Bloom, it *employs* it. It is important not for what it is or what it means, but for what it generates, what relationship to existing, concrete reality it produces. The long lists of 'Ithaca' do not serve to mock or obscure the supposedly mythical meeting of father and son, as so much criticism suggests. For the characters, the meaning of their meeting remains undisclosed, a matter finally for the reader's own sensibility; whether the meeting fails or succeeds, whether it is a spiritual revelation or an absurd

51 Mark Osteen, *The Economy of Ulysses: Making Both Ends Meet* (Syracuse, 1995), 398, points out that earlier kindlings Stephen recalls as he watches Bloom here were all 'performed by actual or surrogate parents', and that the words 'pyre,' 'crosslaid,' and 'Abram's coal' suggest a 'sacrificial consecration of ... familial ties'.

52 *U* 17.134–47.

53 Anticipated in 'Circe': 'Leopoldi autem generatio. Moses begat Noah and Noah begat Eunuch and Eunuch begat O'Halloran and O'Halloran begat Guggenheim ... and Jasperstone begat Vingteunieme and Vingteunieme begat Szombathely and Szombathely begat Virag and Virag begat Bloom et vocabitur nomen eius Emmanuel.' *U* 15.1855–69.

54 *U* 17.46–59

failure is an open question, a variable. But for *Ulysses* itself, a sprawling, unruly work, what matters is not the encounter's spiritual function, but its narrative one: it is this meeting that produces and structures the particular account of reality the novel gives us.

The chapter jokingly acknowledges the limits of this system in its exposition of the ratio of their ages, creating a consistent relationship between the two men, which spans the period from '81,396 B.C.' to '3072 A.D.'. This passage mocks the logic of 'Stephen plus Bloom' as a framework for the whole of history, by pushing it to its logical and absurd conclusion:

> What relation existed between their ages?
>
> 16 years before in 1888 when Bloom was of Stephen's present age Stephen was 6. 16 years after in 1920 when Stephen would be of Bloom's present age Bloom would be 54. In 1936 when Bloom would be 70 and Stephen 54 their ages initially in the ratio of 16 to 0 would be as 17½ to 13½, the proportion increasing and the disparity diminishing according as arbitrary future years were added, for if the proportion existing in 1883 had continued immutable, conceiving that to be possible, till then 1904 when Stephen was 22 Bloom would be 374 and in 1920 when Stephen would be 38, as Bloom then was, Bloom would be 646 while in 1952 when Stephen would have attained the maximum postdiluvian age of 70 Bloom, being 1190 years alive having been born in the year 714, would have surpassed by 221 years the maximum antediluvian age, that of Methusalah [SIC - bmcc], 969 years, while, if Stephen would continue to live until he would attain that age in the year 3072 A.D., Bloom would have been obliged to have been alive 83,300 years, having been obliged to have been born in the year 81,396 B.C.[55]

As P. A. McCarthy and others have shown, the maths in the passage above are 'either confused or flat wrong'.[56] But if the errors are deliberate, they may slightly undermine the otherwise mocking thrust of the passage, suggesting that the point of the mockery is not that the 'fusion' between Stephen and Bloom is a failure. The calculations demonstrate mathematically how the meeting of Bloom and Stephen could theoretically be a point of view for all of human history; but *Ulysses* as a whole does not push it this far, and the passage is designed to highlight that it does, indeed, keep the idea within certain limits. The mistaken calculations serve as a reminder that this is a novel, and that no account of the relationship between Bloom and Stephen, or of reality itself, is sufficient, universal or precise. This is the key recognition about genealogy — that it is but one mode among many of structuring time and relations — and it applies equally well to all and any queer alternatives to it.

The Linati organ of 'Ithaca' is the skeleton, and the chapter, a portrait of a family, brings together two kinds of metaphorical skeletons relevant for a queer family epic: an architectonic metaphor of structure and articulation, as well as the proverbial skeletons in cupboards, the secrets hidden inside closets. Instead of uncovering just same-sex erotic desires, however, 'Ithaca' flings open all kinds of doors, covers and cupboards. The 'pseudoscientific' eye of the catechist, which scrutinizes physics, biology, geology, astronomy and mathematics, turns its attention to the personal and the domestic. Just as the house is opened to the street to admit Stephen (and Boylan), so are its closets opened for the readers, as the indefatigably curious catechist goes rummaging through the house, throwing open its drawers and dressers, prising off its lids and corks, enumerating hidden contents. The queer secrets of the household, previously hidden, are not

55 *U* 17.446–61.

56 P. A. McCarthy, 'Joyce's Unreliable Catechist: Mathematics and the Narration of "Ithaca"', *ELH*, 51, 3 (1984), 605–18. Unlike the majority of critics who ascribe the mistakes to Joyce's distraction and haste, McCarthy adduces some convincing and engaging explanations for the mathematical errors in 'Ithaca', including an adherence to a principle of 'indeterminacy'.

only 'outed' but become the 'official', legitimating centre of the narrative.

More than any signs of the future, what we find in 7 Eccles Street, thanks to the catechist's enquiries, is sign after sign of the past. As the narrative seeks out and interrogates these signs, the indelible, adulterating traces of many arrivals, departures and passings-through, the husks of long-gone moments, by-products of a life, 'Ithaca' fulfils the promise uttered by Stephen at the opening of the novel, when seeking out his future: 'Signatures of all things I am here to read, seaspawn and seawrack, the nearing tide, that rusty boot.'[57] The collection of debris, the flotsam that has accumulated in the house, is constantly transformed and rearranged to accommodate new realities. The pickpocket's den, with its unpredictable collection of members, and ragbag collection of stolen scraps of the city, has taken over the gentleman's house as the home of narrative bookending.

Among the first items catalogued from the contents of the drawer are 'diagram drawings ... marked Papli', drawn by Milly Bloom, graphic depictions of the genetic relationship between Bloom and Milly. Milly is referred to at the very beginning of the novel in the opening pages of 'Telemachus', in the snot-green waters of biological paternity:

> --Is the brother with you, Malachi?
> --Down in Westmeath. With the Bannons.
> --Still there? I got a card from Bannon. Says he found a sweet young thing down there. Photo girl he calls her.
> --Snapshot, eh? Brief exposure.[58]

Not that brief: the 'sweet young thing' is Milly on her apprenticeship with Bannon in Mullingar, a connection, hinted to in 'Calypso' (4.407) but which only becomes fully clear now. Just as the *dénouement* of a traditional paternity narrative uncovers hidden genealogical connections, here Stephen's arrival reveals a sort of non-genetic lineage for Milly, an alternative link between Milly and Bloom, routed not through marriage and genes but via the streetside encounter between her father and Stephen: Milly–Bannon–Mulligan–Stephen–Leopold (the connection between the names 'Milly', 'Mulligan' and 'Mullingar' also gives her another, purely textual, lineage). Such a retrospective arrangement, which the reader is in a position to make at the end of the novel, accounts for lived reality, and gives a coherence to identities and relationships as much as genealogy does. The point is that humans exist in many series and alignments and juxtapositions, any of which can be placed at the centre.

As Bloom enters his marital bed, the catechist creates for him another alternative genealogy, connected, this time, to Molly. It concerns the possible encounters (real or imagined) the bed has hosted in his absence, a version of the word he pondered at the opening of the day now ending, 'metempsychosis', or better still, Molly's own phonetic transformation of this word, 'met him pike hoses', the first two words of which point to the encounter as an agent of transformation and movement. The meeting here, the juxtaposing encounter that engenders the genealogical table, is Molly's with Blazes Boylan:

> If he had smiled why would he have smiled?
>
> To reflect that each one who enters imagines himself to be the first to enter whereas he is always the last term of a preceding series even if the first term of a succeeding one, each imagining himself to be first, last, only and alone whereas he is neither first nor last nor only nor alone in a series originating in and repeated to infinity.
>
> What preceding series?

57 *U* 3.2–3.
58 *U* 1.682–86.
59 *U* 17.2126–42.

Assuming Mulvey to be the first term of his series, Penrose, Bartell d'Arcy, professor Goodwin, Julius Mastiansky, John Henry Menton, Father Bernard Corrigan, a farmer at the Royal Dublin Society's Horse Show, Maggot O'Reilly, Matthew Dillon, Valentine Blake Dillon (Lord Mayor of Dublin), Christopher Callinan, Lenehan, an Italian organgrinder, an unknown gentleman in the Gaiety Theatre, Benjamin Dollard, Simon Dedalus, Andrew (Pisser) Burke, Joseph Cuffe, Wisdom Hely, Alderman John Hooper, Dr Francis Brady, Father Sebastian of Mount Argus, a bootblack at the General Post Office, Hugh E. (Blazes) Boylan and so each and so on to no last term.[59]

IV

Ulysses deals with the needs of the present and the realities of the past, refusing a promise of duplication and future in favour of retrospective arrangements and the accommodation of parenthetical realities. But the principal 'accommodation' offered at the end, an 'extemporised cubicle' which Bloom suggests making up for Stephen to spend the night, is refused. Whatever the success of the encounter between Stephen and Bloom in narrative, formal terms, within the imagined reality of the novel it is partly a disappointment.

> What proposal did Bloom, diambulist, father of Milly, somnambulist, make to Stephen, noctambulist?
> To pass in repose the hours intervening between Thursday (proper) and Friday (normal) on an extemporised cubicle in the apartment immediately above the kitchen and immediately adjacent to the sleeping apartment of his host and hostess.
> [...]
> Was the proposal of asylum accepted?
> Promptly, inexplicably, with amicability, gratefully it was declined.

And it is in the aftermath of this disappointment, after Stephen has turned down the offer of a bed for the night, that the men's conversation does turn to the future, in search of a redemptive salve for the failures of the past, as they plan between them a variety of collaborative projects between Stephen and the Blooms:

> What counterproposals were alternately advanced, accepted, modified, declined, restated in other terms, reaccepted, ratified, reconfirmed?
> To inaugurate a prearranged course of Italian instruction, place the residence of the instructed. To inaugurate a course of vocal instruction, place the residence of the instructress. To inaugurate a series of static, semistatic and peripatetic intellectual dialogues, places the residence of both speakers (if both speakers were resident in the same place), the Ship hotel and tavern, 6 Lower Abbey street (W. and E. Connery, proprietors), the National Library of Ireland, 10 Kildare street, the National Maternity Hospital, 29, 30 and 31 Holles street, a public garden, the vicinity of a place of worship, a conjunction of two or more public thoroughfares, the point of bisection of a right line drawn between their residences (if both speakers were resident in different places).[60]

Bloom (like many readers) remains ruefully unconvinced that these plans will ever come to fruition. In support of his pessimism about the possibility of a future of intimate fellowship between Stephen and himself and Molly, Bloom mentally adduces two examples from his own past:

> What rendered problematic for Bloom the realisation of these mutually selfexcluding propositions?
> The irreparability of the past: once at a performance of Albert Hengler's circus

60 *U* 17.1301–02.

> in the Rotunda, Rutland square, Dublin, an intuitive particoloured clown in quest of paternity had penetrated from the ring to a place in the auditorium where Bloom, solitary, was seated and had publicly declared to an exhilarated audience that he (Bloom) was his (the clown's) papa. The imprevidibility of the future: once in the summer of 1898 he (Bloom) had marked a florin (2s.) with three notches on the milled edge and tendered it in payment of an account due to and received by J. and T. Davy, family grocers, 1 Charlemont Mall, Grand Canal, for circulation on the waters of civic finance, for possible, circuitous or direct, return.
>
> Was the clown Bloom's son?
> No.
>
> Had Bloom's coin returned?
> Never.[61]

In this melancholy series of questions and answers, *Ulysses* is reflecting on its own limits as a fictional contrivance, made consistent and pleasing through imposed forms, and on the existence of the raw, uncrafted future as something that exceeds this closed and ordered arrangement; it is considering, with some sorrow, the price, as it were, of its queer, retrospective model. The language of the passage — 'for circulation on the waters of civic finance, for possible, circuitous or direct, return' — brings us back to Mulligan's fanciful evocations of Homeric voyage in 'Telemachus', his future-oriented fantasy of escape on the water, and his utopian transformation of Dublin Bay from restrictive womb to expanse of Greek adventure. That moment in 'Telemachus' was only the first of many invocations of water as a symbolic means of circulation and return. *Ulysses* succeeds, of course, where Mulligan fails, transforming the streets of Dublin into a sea that can host an Odyssey, and finding alternative circuits to those of genealogy. What we learn from the family reunions of 'Ithaca' is that within the confined waters of this novel, returns, whether 'circuitous or direct', are guaranteed: Bloom will get back home, Stephen and Molly will show up again at the end of the novel. But we don't even know where Stephen spends the night: the queer, retrospective system of *Ulysses* is closed to the future, to the cold open seas of reality that lie beyond it, where there are no such guarantees.

The contingent parallels and lineages of Joyce's novel, queer versions of genealogies, unlike 'straight' ones, are in theory infinitely inclusive in the past, capable of being indefinitely enlarged and open to being retrospectively added to. But retrospective genealogies cannot be expanded into the future; this is the limit to their inclusiveness. 'Had Bloom's coin returned?' receives the answer 'Never'. In an essay on prophecies in *Ulysses*, Paul Saint-Amour questions this answer.[62] While it might be grammatically correct, Saint-Amour writes, that 'the coin has *never* — that is, *not ever* — returned ... in a temporal sense, that "never" is hyperbolic, is not strictly true; it would be more accurate to say "not yet"'.

Although Saint-Amour poses this question in a different context, his observation is illuminating for our purposes. For a start, the question is in the pluperfect, not the preterite, because the only knowledge the novel has ends on 16 June 1904; the answer to the question the catechist does not ask here, '*Did* Bloom's coin ever return?', or '*Will* Bloom's coin ever return?' lies in our own world, the world that continued on, without Molly or Bloom or Stephen or Milly or Nosey Flynn, after the 16th of June 1904. In this sense, the florin is given to us, a debt acknowledged and paid to our reality, to the unforeseeable times and generations to come. The symbolic partner of Bloom's notched florin is the one that was reluctantly handed over by Buck Mulligan to the milkwoman in

61 *U* 17.973–87.

62 Paul K. Saint-Amour, 'On Joycean Prophecy', paper delivered at the 21st International James Joyce Symposium, Tours, June 2008.

63 *U* 1.399.
64 *U* 17.1788; 18.1563; 18.1601.

'Telemachus'. That was a debt owed by Mulligan to the world outside his tower ('old and secret she had entered from a morning world'[63]), which he did not want to acknowledge. Bloom's florin here is the acknowledgement due to the reality beyond the closed world of the novel, a recognition of the debt owed to our world, to the future, which is not within the novel's sphere of attention but which is the home of its readers, beyond even the generous reach of its retrospective parenthetical system.

Another kind of prophecy ends the novel, as Molly's thoughts perform a vast retrospective sweep across her life and across Europe, through all the vagaries and vicissitudes that have gone into the construction of the present moment. She reassesses and reassizes her past in terms of a series of encounters, moving so quickly between them all that it is hard to tell whom she means when she says 'as well him as another'. It is Bloom, and it is a proposal of marriage: the end of *Ulysses* does invoke the closure of a marriage plot, and all of the visions of natural fruitfulness in Molly's last lines ('flowers ... springing up even out of the ditches primroses and violets' or 'the rosegardens and the jessamine and geraniums and cactuses'), its promise of fertility and the future. But the novel does not end with a reproductive promise for the future. Molly's *yes* displaces the future-oriented *yes* which implicitly ends a traditional marriage plot. Like the 'sealed prophecy (never unsealed)', written by Bloom, which the catechist finds in the drawer, Molly's parting words, 'I said yes I will Yes',[64] are a prophecy in the past, a retrospective rearrangement encoding its own contingency, one always capable of readjustment, an open parenthesis on the past, ready to accommodate whatever queer things might retrospectively bloom from the next encounter.

The French in Killala Bay, 1798,
William Sadler II (c. 1782–1839).

'Our Separate Rooms': Bishop Stock's Narrative of the French Invasion of Mayo, 1798

Catríona Kennedy

In Thomas Flanagan's best-selling historical novel *The Year of the French* (1979), one of the central characters and narrators is the Rev. Arthur Vincent Broome, the slightly priggish but well-meaning Church of Ireland minister to the parish of Killala, unexpectedly caught up in the upheaval triggered by the French landing in Mayo in August 1798. English-born and Oxford-educated, Broome initially believes that his outsider status and enlightened education will allow him to navigate with greater clarity and penetration the conflicted society in which he has settled and to chronicle the United Irish rebellion with 'strict impartiality'. Yet, as the rebellion progresses, this position of detached objectivity comes under pressure and Broome is forced to acknowledge that his aspiration to be 'the Gibbon of Mayo', deliberating with the cool judgement of the historian on the events he has witnessed, is impossible, and his own account necessarily 'partial and fragmentary'.[1] The idea of multiple, competing perspectives, none of which can fully capture the densely packed layers of meaning and experience generated by the Connacht rebellion, is a central theme in Flanagan's novel, which is narrated through a series of supposedly authentic testimonies written by various eyewitnesses.[2] Within this 'polyphonic structure', the voice of Broome, Tom Paulin suggests, 'speaks for the powerless centre of Irish politics'.[3] According to Flanagan, he is a 'loyalist, upon both nature and principle, but he is also a man of warm human sympathies, and he grieves for the sufferings endured by them all'.[4]

The Rev. Arthur Broome is partly based on Joseph Stock, the bishop of Killala and Achonry at the time of the rebellion. Because of an Irish postal strike, Flanagan was unable to read Stock's *Narrative of What Passed at Killala ... during the French Invasion in the Summer of 1798* until after the character had been substantially developed, but there are, nonetheless, significant parallels between the fictional Broome and the Church of Ireland bishop.[5] Unlike Broome, Stock was born in Dublin and educated at Trinity College, but he too was a recent arrival in Mayo at the time of the French landing, having only been appointed to the diocese in January 1798. An accomplished classical scholar and linguist, and author of the first biography of Bishop George Berkeley, Stock was holding his first episcopal visitation when the French landed in Killala Bay.[6] He was captured and the episcopal palace commandeered as a military headquarters, and his experiences during this period are detailed in his account, which describes the surprisingly amicable relationship that developed between Stock and the invading forces. First published anonymously in 1800, the bishop's *Narrative* eventually achieved at least six editions in Dublin, Limerick, London and Bath between 1800 and 1809. In the Preface, Stock explained his decision to present his version of events to the public:

> As I know that inaccurate accounts of remarkable events must at length be taken for true, and be adopted by the historian, if he is not supplied with better, I feel myself drawn against my liking by the very imperfect narratives I have yet seen of what passed at Killala, while foreign and domestic enemies possessed that town in the summer of 1798, to state to you as much as fell under my consideration at that critical period.[7]

Stock's aspiration to provide the authoritative account of the Mayo rebellion would prove successful and his narrative has long been the standard source for the history of the French landing. Recently, it has been situated within the politically charged historiography of 1798, Kevin Whelan identifying Stock's narrative as one of a corpus of liberal Protestant histories that sought to counterbalance partisan depictions of the rebellion as a sectarian-motivated popish jacquerie.[8] Indeed, as Guy Beiner observes in his study of the vernacular historiography of the 'Year of the French', an overreliance on Stock's narrative and similar sources written at a remove from the experience of the local population has limited the investigation of the broader social and cultural significance of the Connacht rebellion.[9] Yet despite its status as the most authoritative and oft-cited account of what transpired at Killala, there are grounds for revisiting this familiar text. Not only is it written with an unusual literary sensibility and an eye for the telling detail or revealing vignette, it also complicates the conventions of the invasion narrative and suggests how a contact zone might emerge within a zone of conflict.

1 Stock's ability to write against the grain of contemporary invasion narratives, and to draw out the humanity of his captors, partly legitimates this reading of his narrative. Yet this interpretation necessarily elides some of the complexities of his account, and the questions it raises about the limits of sympathetic engagement, the 'separate rooms' that continued to confine and divide the Church of Ireland prelate and his Catholic neighbour.

2 Thomas Flanagan, *The Year of the French* (New York, 2005 [1979]), 26, 496.
On the novel's structure, see Shaun O'Connell, 'Imagining Eire: History as Fiction in the Novels of Tom Flanagan', *MELUS*, 18, 1 (1993), 21–29; Seamus Deane 'Introduction', in Flanagan, *Year of the French*, x.

3 Tom Paulin, 'Review of *The Year of the French*', *Encounter* (January 1980), 62.

4 Thomas Flanagan, 'My Scholarly and Sagacious Friend', in Richard English and Joseph Morrison Shelley, eds., *Ideas Matter: Essays in Honour of Conor Cruise O'Brien* (Lanham, MD, 2000), 77.

5 Michael Garvey, 'Re-creating 1798', in Grattan Freyer, ed., *Bishop Stock's 'Narrative' of the Year of the French: 1798* (Ballina, 1982), vii.

6 James Kelly, 'Joseph Stock (1740–1813)', in *Oxford Dictionary of National Biography* (hereafter *ODNB*).

7 Anon. [Joseph Stock], *A*

Narrative, in the County of Mayo, and the Parts Adjacent during the French Invasion in the Summer of 1798. By an Eyewitness (Dublin, 1800), 1. An earlier, more immediate and less guarded, account of Stock's experiences had been published in 1799 in the form of a series of letters by the bishop to his brother Stephen in Dublin, entitled *Proceedings at Killala during the French Invasion, and the Subsequent Rebellion, from August 22 to October 27, 1798: In Letters from the Right Reverend Joseph Lord Bishop of Killala to his Brother, Mr Stephen Stock, of Dame-Street Dublin, and Others* (Bath, 1799).

8 Kevin Whelan, ''98 after '98: The Politics of Memory', in his *The Tree of Liberty: Radicalism, Catholicism and the Construction of Irish Identity, 1760–1830* (Cork, 1996), 145–46.

9 Guy Beiner, *Remembering the Year of the French: Irish Folk History and Social Memory* (Madison, 2007), 140.

10 [Robert Jephson], *The Confessions of James Baptiste Couteau. Citizen of France. Written by Himself and Translated from the Original French by Robert Jephson Esq.*, 2 vols. (London, 1794), I. 168.

11 Martha McTier, Belfast, n.d. [1798] in Jean Agnew, ed., *Drennan–McTier Letters*, 3 vols. (Dublin, 1999), 2. 388.

12 [William Cobbett], *A Warning to Britons against French Perfidy*

Moreover, as will be shown, it is a text that has transcended its origins in the 'war of words' that followed the 1798 rebellion to become an unlikely reference point and source of inspiration for more recent discussions of Irish conflicts and concerns.

French invasions

The distinctiveness of Bishop Stock's narrative of the French landing is best illuminated by locating it within the broader context of contemporary imaginings and representations of a French invasion. While the army of the French republic pressed into Holland, Germany and Italy, carrying war and revolutionary upheaval to millions of continental Europeans, for much of the 1790s the British and Irish experience of invasion was confined to the public and personal imaginary. Conservatives' fears of a French invasion were fuelled by a steady stream of imaginary invasion scenarios that sought to depict the nightmarish consequences of a cross-channel assault and to dispel any illusion that the French would come as liberators rather than rapacious conquerors. In Ireland, the gathering force of United Irish radicalism and the alliance between the Irish republican leadership and the French revolutionary regime, which had led to the first failed expedition to Bantry Bay in 1796, made loyalist fears even more acute. Anxieties were stoked by publications such as the fictitious memoirs of James Baptiste Couteau, a French envoy to the United Irishmen, who fantazises about cutting the throat of the 'Dublin ladies' in the event of a successful invasion.[10] Imagined invasion scenarios were supplemented by supposedly 'authentic' reports of the French occupation of continental Europe. In 1798, a conservative acquaintance presented the Belfast radical Martha McTier with an account of French depredations in southern Germany in the hope that it might modify her republican sympathies. McTier remained unmoved by the pamphlet, dryly commenting: 'What a scene of ravishings the good lady has sent me'.[11]

The pamphlet in question was William Cobbet's *Warning to Britons against French Perfidy and Cruelty*, one of the most widely circulated pieces of atrocity literature during this period, a graphic, and at times pornographic, account of the republican army's incursions into Swabia in 1796. As McTier noted, this work paraded a seemingly endless scene of ravishings, in which no woman, young, old, sick or pregnant, was spared from the 'brutal lust' of these 'depraved wretches'. It catalogued in lurid detail the horrors a French invasion would involve: the desecration of all religious sites, outrages against ecclesiastics of every sect, merciless plundering by the 'privileged locusts' of the revolutionary army, and the complete destruction of domestic and familial security.[12]

The imagined horror of a mass French invasion ultimately materialized in the less terrifying form of a small-scale landing by republican troops on the Pembrokeshire coast in February 1797. Although the French outnumbered local troops by two to one, the expedition, assisted by the discovery of large quantities of Portuguese wine that had been shipwrecked off the coast the previous month, soon descended into chaos and disorder. Within less than three days, they had surrendered. Described by Gwyn A. Williams as a 'comic opera landing', the French invasion of Wales is often viewed as more akin to a farce than the tragedy prophesied in loyalist propaganda.[13] Yet despite its brevity and chaotic execution, contemporary and retrospective narratives of the landing tended to echo and reproduce many elements of the imaginary and 'authentic' invasion scenarios published during the 1790s. In this way, events in Pembrokeshire appeared to enact on a miniature scale the more apocalyptic vision of a French assault that Britons had been roused to expect. The republican soldiery's notorious hostility to religion was supposedly borne out in reports of the desecration and looting of the small church near to where they landed. The image of the French republicans as rapacious locusts stripping the countryside bare with their insatiable appetite for plunder also figured in several narratives. Following this narrative pattern, many accounts turned to the ill-treatment of women at the hands of the French. At least one told how the soldiers had shot and then raped a woman, an echo of the gruesome scenes of female violation described in *A Warning to Britons*.[14] This is not to say that there was no foundation to these reports, but the details that narrators tended to focus on were those that reinforced and conformed to well-established 'invasion scripts'.

The Fishguard episode seemed to present a straightforward encounter between a hostile invading force and a loyal and unanimous populace. The bitter aftermath of the landing, however, suggests a more complicated version of events, as the invasion brought to the surface underlying tensions and antagonisms within Pembrokeshire society. In the 'recriminatory mood' that, according to a recent account, was a leading characteristic of Pembrokeshire life after the invasion, several local inhabitants were brought to trial, charged with having been in collusion with the French.[15] Rather than uniting local inhabitants in the face of external threat, the French landing seems to have exacerbated underlying frictions and animosities, highlighting, in particular, the abrasive relationships that existed between the Anglican gentry and local Methodist and Baptist communities. These complexities, however, could not be accommodated within the rigid framework of the invasion narrative, a reductive interpretation of the Fishguard landing that persists in some recent histories.[16]

In certain respects, the French landing in the west of Ireland in August 1798 did not differ dramatically from the previous year's expedition to Wales. The French force was roughly the same size, consisting of around a thousand soldiers, and the landing occurred in a similarly remote and isolated region. However, there were also crucial differences. While there may have been a minority sympathetic to the French in Pembrokeshire, in Ireland the revolutionary army was joined by a local insurgency involving thousands, despite the fact that Connacht was an area in which United Irish organization was relatively weak. Led by General Humbert, the French forces that landed in Ireland were of superior quality to the troops that had been dispatched to Wales, described by Wolfe Tone as 'blackguards' and 'desperadoes', and were much more effectively disciplined and organized.[17] With the support of Irish auxiliaries, they were able to make sustained progress through the country. Within five days of the landing, they had secured a victory over a much larger force at Castlebar. A 'Republic of Connacht' was declared and the French army and its Irish recruits marched through Mayo and into the adjoining counties. On 8 September their progress was halted by a decisive defeat at the hands of General Lake's forces at Ballinamuck and two weeks later the French and rebel insurgents remaining at Killala were overwhelmed. The French surrendered and were recognized as prisoners of war, while their rebel allies were massacred.[18]

The French invasion of Connacht lasted little over a month but it exposed, in a dramatic fashion, acute sectarian, ethnic and political tensions in what had been considered a relatively tranquil province. The unstable mixtures of amity and enmity made it impossible to narrate the landing as a straightforward encounter between invaders and invaded. Bishop Stock's encounter with the French began the day after the landing, when, following a brief show of resistance from the local yeomanry, Killala Castle, the bishop's seat, was commandeered by General Humbert. Crucial to Stock's experience of the invasion was the fact that he spoke fluent French. This allowed him to act as an interpreter

and Cruelty (London, 1798).

13 Gwyn A. Williams, 'Beginnings of Radicalism', in T. Herbert and G. E. Jones, eds., *The Remaking of Wales in the Eighteenth Century* (Cardiff, 1988), 126.

14 [H.P. Williams], *An Authentic Account of the Invasion by the French Troops, on Carrig Gwastad Point, near Fishguard* (Haverfordwest, 1842), 16; Richard Fenton, *A Historical Tour through Pembrokeshire* (London, 1811), 9. J. E. Thomas, *Britain's Last Invasion: Fishguard 1797* (Stroud, 2007), 67–114.

15 Thomas, *Britain's Last Invasion*, 125.

16 Linda Colley, for instance, draws on the episode to affirm her argument that a British patriotic unanimity crystallized in opposition to the French 'other' in this period. Linda Colley, *Britons: Forging the Nation, 1707–1837* (London, 1996 [1992]), 271.

17 Theobald Wolfe Tone, *Life of Theobald Wolfe Tone*, ed. Thomas Bartlett (Dublin, 1998), 645, 647–48.

18 For a military history of the expedition, see Harman Murtagh, 'General Humbert's Futile Campaign', in Thomas Bartlett et al. eds., *1798: A Bicentenary Perspective* (Dublin, 2003), 174–88.

for, and mediator between, the soldiers and local inhabitants. Once the French had secured Killala, Humbert requested an interview with the bishop and assured him that he and his family would be treated with respectful attention for the duration of their captivity. At this point, Humbert even offered Stock a position in the Connacht Directory, which he politely declined. This tone of mutual respect and military *politesse* would characterize much of the bishop's interactions with the French, even after two of his sons had been taken hostage. Though the episcopal palace was soon filled with nearly three hundred soldiers and their baggage, Stock readily conceded the excellent discipline and order that prevailed amongst the French troops, a discipline that he contrasted with the disorder of their Irish recruits. 'It would have been ridiculous', the Bishop claimed, 'not to prefer the Gallic troops in every respect before their new allies. Intelligence, activity, temperance, patience, to a surprising degree, appeared to be combined in the soldiery that came over with Humbert'.[19]

In this respect, Stock's account of the French was not so different from that of other Irish loyalist commentators. The comparison between the discipline of the French troops and the disorderly Irish rabble that had joined their standard was a common theme in conservative histories of the Connacht rebellion and many were quick to note the contempt in which the Irish rebel forces were held by their supposed French allies. For loyalist Protestants, fearful that the sectarian atrocities that had accompanied the rebellion in Wexford earlier that summer would be re-enacted in Mayo, the French invaders could be perceived as a protective rather than a destructive force.

This fear of local Catholics partly explains the largely sympathetic account of the French in Stock's narrative. But he goes much further, to the extent that his account almost becomes an apology for the republican forces, one which consciously challenges the lurid depiction of the French 'other' in loyalist propaganda. While contemporary invasion literature portrayed the revolutionary soldiery as gluttonous hordes with extravagant appetites, Stock stressed their modest tastes and simple requirements, noting that they seemed perfectly content to live on bread or potatoes. According to Stock, the troops quartered in the castle showed the utmost respect for his property, 'despite many temptations to plunder'.[20] One conscientious soldier even removed the bishop's valuable dining set to the safety of the pantry, away from the prying hands of his less honourable comrades. Instead of the aggressive hostility to religion imputed to the soldiers of the French Revolution, they showed the utmost respect for their captives' religious devotions, taking pains to ensure that the castle was protected from any noise or disturbance on Sundays. And, finally, the bishop emphasized the 'scrupulous delicacy' with which the women of the household were treated.[21]

The 'castle family'

The complex relationship between insiders and outsiders, invaders and protectors, that structures Stock's narrative emerges most clearly in his account of the transgression and defence of domestic space during the invasion. As has been frequently noted, representations of the violation of the domestic sphere and the spectre of the French invader bringing war, destruction and desolation to the cottage, or in this case, the castle, was a key conceit through which loyalist propaganda sought to yoke together personal, familial and national security.[22] Yet in Stock's narrative the relationship between external threats and domestic security becomes increasingly complex. At the centre of his narrative is an account of three weeks following the departure of General Humbert, during which he and his family were confined to Killala Castle with a guard of three French

19 Stock, *Narrative of What Passed at Killala*, 33 (hereafter *Narrative*).
20 *Narrative*, 16.
21 *Narrative*, 17.
22 See, for example, John Barrell, *The Spirit of Despotism: Invasions of Privacy in the 1790s* (Oxford, 2006), 220–42.

Bishop Stock c. 1788–98, artist unknown. Christ Church, Delgany, Co. Wicklow. Courtesy of Patrick Comerford

officers. Thrown together by the vagaries of war, a strange intimacy developed between the bishop's family and the French. Rather than disrupting familial bonds and domestic order, the French were, according to Stock's account, incorporated into an expanded domesticity, becoming for the duration of the invasion part of what he called the 'castle family'.[23] They dined, drank and spent long evenings conversing together, the bishop's wife even playing cards with the commandant. The affectionate portraits and sentimental histories of the three French officers, which Stock included in his narrative, clearly show the bonds that this daily intimacy produced. The commandant, Lieutenant Colonel Charost, tearfully confided to the bishop that, having lost all

23 *Narrative*, 77.

24 *Narrative*, 62–68.
25 *Narrative*, 12–13, 91–93.
26 *Narrative*, 89–90.
27 *Narrative*, 90.
28 *Narrative*, 157.

his property in the slave rebellions in Saint-Domingue, he had been forced to enlist in the French army and had not seen his family in over six years. Boudet, his second-in-command, meanwhile, though seemingly distant and taciturn, possessed 'more than a common share of feeling' and shared with Stock painful stories of military life during the French campaigns in Flanders and the Rhine. Completing the trio, was Ponson, a committed atheist and, according to the bishop, a 'comic, low bred monkey', but who, nonetheless, kept the spirits of the 'castle family' buoyant with his incessant prattle.[24]

The blurring of the distinctions between insider and outsider, friend and foe, narrated by Stock was partly a product of the close quarters in which the bishop's family and their captors were forced to live, but it should be noted that the episcopal palace also housed many others during the invasion. Local Protestants had flocked to the bishop's residence seeking refuge and were accommodated along with his family in the cramped rooms of the castle attic, while a local rebel captain, Ferdinand (Ferdy) O'Donnell, also claimed a room in the castle. A small farmer from Erris, O'Donnell had replaced the drunken Matthew Bellew, a French-speaking former officer in the Russian army, as the effective commander of the insurgents in Killala. Stock paid grudging tribute to O'Donnell's role in sheltering a loyalist fugitive from Killala in his Erris farmhouse and his later efforts to maintain order in Killala town.[25] Significantly, however, while the French, the bishop and the loyalist refugees participated in a shared domesticity within the castle, O'Donnell was firmly excluded from these intimate gatherings. According to Stock, referring to himself in the third person:

> The airs the young jackanapes gave himself became every day more troublesome. On pretence that he must have a bed at the castle to take the orders of the commandant in case of any disturbance at night, he took to himself one of the bed-chambers of the middle floor, from which it was not possible afterwards to dislodge him; and this apartment he was pleased to distinguish by the name of *his* room. His next attempt was to be admitted to mess with the family; but here he failed of success. The bishop, disgusted with his forwardness and vulgar manners, avoided as much as he could all intercourse with him ...[26]

Stung by this rejection, O'Donnell, who claimed with some justification that it was he and not the French who was responsible for protecting the castle from rebel depredations, spent his evenings locked in his room drinking with his comrades and muttering darkly about the bishop's ingratitude. Insofar as spatial segregation within the castle demarcated the division between insider and outsider, O'Donnell and the Catholic rebels were placed firmly outside, while the French officers emerged as the devoted guardians of a shared, familial privacy. At one point Stock related how a heavily armed rebel thrust himself upon the 'castle family' while they were at dinner in order to deliver a message to the commandant and was angrily rebuked by the French officer for alarming the ladies and disturbing their domestic harmony.[27] This familial intimacy was sustained right up to the invasion's closing moments. When the government forces entered Killala on 23 September, they were accompanied by the bishop's son Arthur, who had joined the local yeomanry and fought against the insurgent army at Castlebar. Although their appearance heralded the inevitable defeat of the expedition, Stock noted that Charost 'expressed as much joy at seeing Arthur safe, as if he had himself been one of the family'.[28]

While Stock is generally understood as providing a sympathetic commentary on the Catholic rebels, in his narrative they lurk menacingly at the threshold of the castle asylum and are only kept at bay by the French deliverers and protectors, a situation he likened to that of 'travellers in a desert surrounded by wild beasts'.[29] Yet in a revealing moment, he also hints at an emerging awareness of the restricted compass of his sympathies and the gulf in understanding that lay between the castle and the cabin. As the king's forces progressed towards Killala, the rebels led the local loyalists to a nearby hill to witness the destruction they left in their wake. Stock observed how:

> A train of fire too clearly distinguished their line of march, flaming up from the houses of unfortunate peasants. 'They are only a few cabins,' remarked the bishop; and he had scarcely uttered the words when he felt the imprudence of them. 'A poor man's cabin', answered one of the rebels, 'is to him as valuable as a palace'.[30]

The arrival of the British militia forces in Killala towards the end of the invasion would add a further layer of complexity to the already intricate configurations of affinity and exclusion that had developed within the castle walls. When, in the aftermath of the invasion, their French protectors were replaced by the officers of the Prince of Wales Fencibles, who were quartered in Killala Castle, the bishop expressed much more irritation at this imposition than he had ever directed at the French. Instead of the easy sociability and peaceful domesticity that he seems to have found with Humbert's officers, the arrival of the British involved 'the labour and weariness of living in a manner in public' and the 'annoyance of continual public dinners'.[31] In this instance, it is the government officers who are the unwelcome guests, the invaders of domesticity, and Stock was bitterly critical of the brutal and disorderly conduct of the loyalist forces who had been charged with pacifying the region. Their rapacity, he wrote, 'differed in no respect from that of the rebels, except that they seized upon things with somewhat less ceremony or excuse and ... were incomparably superior to the Irish traitors in dexterity at stealing'.[32]

An impartial narrator?

By refusing to reproduce a straightforward dichotomy between friend and foe, invaded and invader, Bishop Stock's narrative seems to problematize contemporary imaginings and depictions of a French invasion. It was his willingness to acknowledge the ambiguities of the Killala Protestants' experience of the invasion that supposedly reinforced Stock's claim to be an 'impartial narrator' of the events he had witnessed. Yet, by his own account, there were several points during the invasion when Stock's impartiality could have been interpreted as a more active collusion with the French. As he candidly admitted, during his captivity he had enjoyed the fine food and excellent wine that the French had requisitioned from the cellars and larders of his loyal neighbours. And when the French sought a financial contribution from the Killala inhabitants to finance the defence of the region, the bishop voluntarily donated fifty guineas. Approached by local loyalists anxious that their co-operation with the French might be interpreted as treasonous, Stock counselled them that in such a situation the 'great law of self-preservation' superseded all other laws. Noting that there were some who, in the wake of the landing, 'muttered against this doctrine', Stock nonetheless maintained this Hobbesian justification for his conduct, arguing that: 'To submit to a king *de facto* ... provided by so doing you do not preclude yourself from returning under the government of a king *de jure*, is a practice sanctioned by the authority of our most equitable English law'.[33]

As the mutterings against Stock suggest, there were some suspicions regarding the rectitude of his conduct during the

29 Stock, *Proceedings at Killala during the French Invasion*, 78.
30 *Narrative*, 135.
31 *Narrative*, 171.
32 *Narrative*, 163.
33 *Narrative*, 57.

invasion. Combined with the avowed 'impartiality' of his narrative, this may have led to the blocking of his advancement, as he was left to languish in his west-coast diocese until elevated to the bishopric of Waterford and Lismore in 1810. According to a nineteenth-century history, this was due to Stock's flattering portrait of the French troops, which had caused much offence to the government.[34] Whelan, however, suggests that it was the narrative's sympathetic treatment of the Killala rebels and its pro-Union message, whereby the cause of the rebellion was attributed to the misgovernment of the Protestant Ascendancy, that provoked conservative loyalists and blighted his career.[35] Yet contemporary reviews did not necessarily read Stock's narrative as an apology for the Connacht Catholics. Instead, the conclusion that many drew from it was that, as the *Gentleman's Magazine* noted, 'the natives under whatever influence (most probably that of ignorant and bigoted Catholic priests) were the most formidable enemies to the peace of the sufferers, as well as to the true interest of the nation'.[36] Indeed, the complexity of the bishop's account seems to have allowed it to be read and appropriated in various ways. Both the liberal divine the Rev. James Bentley Gordon and the loyalist polemicist Sir Richard Musgrave would draw on Stock's narrative in their histories of the rebellion, the latter praising the bishop's 'laudable fortitude' during the landing.[37]

This persistent uncertainty about how to interpret the bishop's narrative is strikingly illustrated in the response of Thomas de Quincey. As a young man, de Quincey had travelled to Ireland shortly after the rebellion and in 1834 he published a series of articles in *Tait's Magazine* on the Mayo rebellion, which drew heavily on Stock's narrative and wrote admiringly of the bishop's moderation and impartiality. When he republished the essay as part of his *Autobiographical Sketches* in 1853, however, he included an astonishing footnote, claiming that his younger self had been 'duped' by the bishop and that he had failed to see the 'insidious colouring' that Stock had placed on events. Pinpointing what he saw as a fundamental contradiction in Stock's narrative, he observed that whenever it wished to present the English army and the English government in a negative light, the Irish peasantry were presented as paragons of moderation and self-control. Yet, as the bishop's own account attested, it was only through the intercession of the French that the inhabitants of Killala Castle were protected from the rebellious hordes. This reversal in de Quincey's opinion of Stock can be partly attributed to the mature repudiation of his youthful liberal leanings, but it also rests upon a more fundamental scepticism about the possibility of an impartial narrative of Irish affairs. Stock, according to de Quincey, was subject to the 'spirit of fiery misrepresentation' that had always prevailed in Ireland, which made it 'impossible to seek for anything resembling truth'. 'If', he wrote, 'in any quarter you found candour and liberty *that* was because no interest existed in anything Irish, and consequently no real information'.[38] According to de Quincey, to know Ireland, or to have experience of Irish life, was inevitably to be partisan; a position of informed impartiality was impossible.

Curiously, the most extended challenge to Bishop Stock's narrative was written by a fellow Church of Ireland clergyman, James Little, the rector of Lacken in the Killala diocese, who had found refuge in the palace during the invasion. While Little's account is generally bracketed with Stock's as an example of the moderate loyalist interpretation of events, it also challenged the bishop's claim to be an 'impartial' or authoritative narrator of events in Mayo. According to Little, 'it would require sketches by many pencils ... to form from the whole a compleat likeness of the dreadful picture'.[39] Throughout, he stressed the very different ordeal that those situated in the countryside outside

34 John Thomas Gilbert, *A History of the City of Dublin*, 3 vols (Dublin, 1859), 2. 308.
35 Whelan, ''98 after '98', 146.
36 *Gentleman's Magazine* (August 1800), 758–59.
37 According to Gordon, Bishop Stock's narrative was 'extremely honourable to the writer since it evinces a genuine goodness of heart, and a mind, so cultivated, so candid, so elevated above vulgar prejudices, and the servile fear of party, as to discern and publicly acknowledge the virtue of an enemy'. James Bentley Gordon, *History of the Rebellion in Ireland in the Year 1798 &c. Containing an Impartial Account of the Proceedings of the Irish Revolutionists* (London, 1803), 305; Richard Musgrave, *Memoirs of the Different Rebellions in Ireland from the Arrival of the English ...* 2 vols (Dublin, 1802), 2. 133.
38 Thomas de Quincey, 'Autobiographic Sketches [Volume I]', in Daniel Sanjiv Roberts, ed., *The Works of Thomas de Quincey* (London, 2003), 170–71.
39 'Rev. James Little's diary of the French landing in 1798' (hereafter *Little's diary*), Royal Irish Academy, 3.B.51, f. 2.

Killala town had endured, and his very different perception of the French. As Little observed in the Preface to his narrative, while the bishop's residence may have remained a protected sanctuary throughout the landing, at the time of writing he was confined to the only habitable apartment of his almost demolished house. Whereas the bishop's fluency in French had eased relations with the foreign invaders, in Little's first encounter with the French he was forced to communicate with them in his stilted schoolboy Latin. The encounter was awkward but not violent; nonetheless, it ensured that the French remained a fundamentally alien presence. To a much greater degree than Stock, Little was alert to the linguistic barriers that divided the anglophone community from their Gaelic-speaking neighbours, recognizing that without knowledge of Irish 'no one can know the country'.[40]

Striving to exculpate the Irish insurgents of responsibility for the rebellion, Little was adamant that the system of destruction that prevailed during the landing had 'been imported, completely fabricated in all its parts by the French'.[41] Embedded in his account was an implicit critique of the bishop's failure to extend the same sympathy and imaginative understanding to the Irish rebels that he had so evidently shown the French. It was not the French, the rector claimed, but the rebel captain O'Donnell, whom Stock had so assiduously shunned during their residence together at Killala Castle, who had been the chief protector of the Killala Protestants. Challenging Stock's efforts to humanize and individualize these armed representatives of the French republic, Little advanced a Burkean analysis of the French Revolution and a Burkean solution to the perennial conflicts and divisions within Irish society. The French who had landed in Killala were 'machines, inanimate and inflexible to every human sentiment and actuated by no spring but the French Revolution'.[42] The benevolent universalism that shaped the bishop's encounter with the French would be more properly directed towards his Catholic neighbours. According to Little, only through free and familiar intercourse between the two nations could the entrenched antagonisms between Catholic and Protestant Ireland be replaced with a unity of sentiment:

> It is not identity of Territory, or race or language, or constitution, or government that in the real nature of things constitutes the unity of a nation; but the identity of its will ... This unity of will ... arises from that unity of sentiment in men, which results from familiar intercourse in moral & civilized society, influencing & forming people's education habits & character; & the more confidential such intercourse is, the more readily do men yield to the impression of the sentiments of their acquaintance, acquiring thus a similarity of manners & character ... which is the basis of friendship & affection.[43]

In other words, the Catholics too had to be allowed to sit at the dining-room table.

'Prisons within prisons'

As the events of 1798 became one of the dominant themes of Irish historical fiction, the dramatic potential of the scenes that unfolded within Killala Castle was recognized by various authors. Bishop Stock would feature in several fictional accounts of the Connacht rebellion, including Charles Lever's adventure story, *Maurice Tiernay* (1852), and J. Percy Groves's *The Duke's Own; or, The Adventures of Peter Daly* (1890), a work of juvenile fiction in the style of G. H. Henty. The suggestion that the patterns of inclusion and exclusion produced within Killala Castle during the invasion could in some sense be paradigmatic of Irish relations, however, would be taken up in two later literary reworkings of the French invasion:

40 *Little's diary*, f. 13.
41 *Little's diary*, f. 42.
42 *Little's diary*, f. 52.
43 *Little's diary*, f. 99.

A scene from the RTÉ/FR3 television drama 'The Year of the French', during filming on 26 June 1981. © RTÉ Stills Library

Emily Lawless and Shan F. Bullock's, *The Race of Castlebar* (1913), and Thomas Flanagan's *Year of the French*. Both works engage, in different ways, with the idea of Killala Castle as a space in which Irish conflicts are reproduced and potentially transcended. In so doing, they appear to draw on the long-standing metaphor in Irish literary and political discourse in which the home, or household, is figured as a site of contestation. It is a trope employed most famously perhaps in W. B. Yeats and Lady Gregory's *Cathleen ni Houlihan* (1902), set in Killala during the 1798 rebellion, in which the title character laments the 'strangers in the house' who have set her wandering.[44] While images of the unwelcome invasion of domestic space are usually taken to represent the irreconcilable antagonisms resulting from Ireland's history of conquest and colonization, the possibility, implicit in Stock's narrative, that the unwanted house guest could become an intimate, and that enforced cohabitation could become peaceful coexistence, offered an alternative model for imagining relationships within the nation.

One of many fictional accounts of 1798 published in the decades following the 1898 centenary, *The Race of Castlebar* is narrated by a fictional Englishman, Charles Bunbury, staying at the bishop's residence during the landing, and large parts of it are drawn directly from Stock's narrative. As Eileen Reilly notes in an analysis of the historical fictions of '98, *The Race of Castlebar* is emphatically unionist in tone, and this unionist perspective is arguably

44 For a recent discussion of the political symbolism of the household in Irish culture, see Maria-Elena Doyle, 'Strangers in Her House: Staging a Living Space for Northern Ireland', *New Hibernia Review/Iris Éireannach Nua*, 7, 3 (2003), 106–26; and Csilla Bertha, 'The House Image in Three Contemporary Irish Plays', *New Hibernia Review/Iris Éireannach Nua*, 8, 2 (2004), 64–84.

reflected in the account of relationships between the captors, captives and refugees confined in the castle prison.[45] In the novel, the inhabitants of the episcopal palace function as a microcosm of Irish society. There is McVittie, the militant northern loyalist, Bellew, the rebel captain, Stock, the Church of Ireland bishop, as well as those implicated in Irish affairs - the French represented by three republican officers, and the English in the form of Bunbury. While these various elements coexist uneasily within the castle walls, the novel suggests how Stock's benign and impartial mediation prevents these differences from spilling over into outright conflict:

> Between Catholics and Atheists, Catholics and Protestants, French and Irish, between England herself and her enemies, between his own people and their foes, the Bishop stood out; the friend, the servant of them all, mediator, counsellor, consoler, interpreter, trusted by Humbert, trusted by McVittie, trusted even by Bellew.[46]

It is possible to read this reimagining of Killala Castle during the rebellion as an allegory of the Union, and of an imperial government, which cannot dissolve intractable enmities, but which can at least, like Stock, manage and contain them.

Thomas Flanagan's *Year of the French* employs the idea of a contact zone within a zone of conflict in quite a different way. Early in the novel, the Rev. Arthur Broome, reflecting on the fundamental breach in intersubjectivity that separates the Killala Protestants from their Catholic countrymen, observes: 'How little we will ever know of these people, locked as we are in our separate rooms'.[47] Contained within this architectural metaphor is the possibility that the chaos and upheaval of the rebellion might jolt both communities out of this state of mutual incomprehension, forcing them to emerge from their separate rooms. Like Stock, Broome finds his home designated the headquarters of the rebel army and is compelled to see out the invasion in close confinement with the insurgent forces. In Flanagan's reimagining of this scenario, however, the French are completely absent and the central encounter is reduced to that between the Protestant cleric and the Irish rebel captain, Ferdy O'Donnell. While Stock, as discussed, recoiled from contact with the actual O'Donnell, in this literary reworking their month-long confinement together produces exactly the same strange intimacy that the bishop, in his narrative, had described as emerging between him and the French officers. Rather than the vulgar 'jackanapes' described by Stock, Broome identifies O'Donnell as a 'superior instance of his race and class', possessed of an 'air of polite deference which was so attractive an aspect of his being'.[48] While the French had related tales of the hardship and miseries wrought by war, during their long conversations together, the rebel captain illuminates for his Protestant interlocutor the sorrows and joys of the Irish Catholic peasantry, and in the process establishes the grounds for a greater degree of mutual understanding. In the aftermath of the invasion, as Broome looks back on his experiences, it is this encounter that stands out most forcibly in his recollections:

> When I seek to recall those days and nights in which we were all locked together in Killala, prisons within prisons, it seems strange that I remember most vividly evenings spent in talk with O'Donnell. Imagine us if you will, a clergyman past middle years, balding but with a ludicrous aureole of greying hair falling to the collar's edge, plump and soft after a half-century of sedentary life ... And a large-boned young peasant, a face firm yet puzzled, skin coarse and reddish of hue, great murderous pistol thrust into his belt. As we leaned towards each other across the table, we leaned from two worlds which had no knowledge the one of the other. Perhaps my face, like

45 Eileen Reilly, 'Who Fears to Speak of '98? The Rebellion in Historical Novels, 1880–1914', *Eighteenth-Century Life*, 22, 3 (1998), 118–27, 123.

46 Emily Lawless and Shan F. Bullock, *The Race of Castlebar* (London, 1913), 211.

47 Flanagan, *Year of the French*, 21.

48 Flanagan, *Year of the French*, 304.

his, bore the marks of puzzlement, as I strained to understand him.[49]

Writing in the 1970s, Flanagan clearly had the conflict in Northern Ireland in mind and in this version the castle prison becomes the setting for a dialogue, a meaningful engagement between Catholic and Protestant Ireland.

Towards the end of Flanagan's novel, as Rev. Broome sets to work compiling his *Impartial Narrative of What Passed at Killala in the Summer of 1798* he recalls a conversation with a 'scholarly and sagacious friend', in which he posed the question '"Does man learn from history?"' His friend's response, delivered after some deliberation, is '"No, I believe we do not. But it is possible to learn from historians."'[50] This assessment appears particularly apt when applied to Bishop Stock's narrative. Exceeding the author's original modest intention to provide an 'impartial' record of events during that fateful summer, it has become in some sense an exemplary text, a model of ethical conduct in the midst of conflict and a source of optimism when reflecting on seemingly intractable Irish enmities.

The impulse to draw from Stock's history a moral message that can be applied to issues and problems in modern Irish life may be seen most clearly in the establishment of the 'Bishop Stock Address' at the General Humbert Summer School, held annually in Mayo since 1987.[51] In this lecture, delivered from Bishop Stock's pulpit in St. Patrick's Cathedral, Killala, from which Bishop Stock preached, public figures are invited to use his narrative as a springboard for discussing topical national and international concerns. It is a brief that can lead to quite strained connections. In 2006, Dr. Diarmuid Martin, archbishop of Dublin, addressed the 'crusading secularisation' afflicting modern Ireland and proposed that the forced encounter between the bishop and the French illustrated how '[i]nvaders and invading ideas can be positive if what emerges is a genuine engagement in mutual respect and mutual enrichment of culture'.[52] In 2008, Cardinal Seán Brady, archbishop of Armagh, used the lecture to discuss the 'loss of Christian memory and values in Europe', extracting from Stock's account a lesson in 'respect for the inherent human dignity of the other'.[53] At the core of the Bishop Stock Address are the twin themes of peace and reconciliation, and, translated into the post-Good Friday Agreement language of dialogue, engagement and parity of esteem, the bishop's narrative appears to yield multiple lessons for the peace process in Northern Ireland. As John Hume observed in the 2007 address: 'Bishop Stock is a prelate who still speaks to us over two centuries later, at a time when we are constructing a permanent peace in the North, based on the respect of diversity of whatever tradition'.[54]

49 Flanagan, *Year of the French*, 312–13.

50 Flanagan, *Year of the French*, 495. Flanagan would subsequently reveal that this exchange was reproduced almost verbatim from a conversation he once had with Conor Cruise O'Brien. Flanagan, 'My Scholarly and Sagacious Friend', 78.

51 See Beiner, *Remembering the Year of the French*, 328–29.

52 General Humbert Summer School, 'The Bishop Stock Address', 20 August 2006. http://www.dublindiocese.ie/index2.php (accessed 4 May2009).

53 'The Bishop Stock Address', 24 August 2008. http://www.irishtimes.com/focus/2008/brady/index.pdf (accessed 20 July 2009).

54 'Brady Pulls No Punches in Knock', *Western People*, 29 August 2007. http://archives.tcm.ie/westernpeople/2007/07/29/story37954.asp (accessed 4 May 2009).

IN THE ZOO DUBLIN 6097 W L

Enclosure housing camels, c. 1880–1914. More than half a century after they opened, the gardens had changed very little. Enclosures were still very small and wooden huts had been replaced with slightly larger brick houses. From the Lawrence Photographic Collection, National Library of Ireland, Royal 6099. Reproduced courtesy of the National Library of Ireland.

Animal Knowledge: Zoology and Class-ification in Nineteenth-Century Dublin

Juliana Adelman

> Mulgrave went to have a lark,
> At the '*Gardens*' in the Park,
> (Where, confined in iron cages,
> Beasts and birds — all sorts and ages,
> Russian bears, and wolves from Siam,
> Are much better fed than I am.)
> As the Countess and her *suite*,
> With a few of the *elite*,
> Also went to see the fun,
> I determined to make one
> Of the party ...[1]

In a lengthy poem introducing the 10 June 1835 issue of *Paddy Kelly's Budget*, the eponymous correspondent poked fun at the Dublin Zoological Gardens and a recent fund-raising fête. A similar event two years prior had also merited a mocking 'rigmarole'.[2] Although intended primarily to provoke a laugh, Paddy Kelly's complaints are relevant to the historical interpretation of the gardens and their role in Dublin city during the nineteenth century. Paddy found the animal spectacle somewhat disappointing:

> A Puma, very like a cat —
> Some Rein Deer, very large and fat —
> Two Polecats, sent in as a present,
> Whose smell was any thing but pleasant.[3]

On the other hand, the possibility for social observation was considerable: 'a whole group of Castle-hacks enjoying / The awkward figures of the cockney *slobs*'.[4] Paddy's biggest gripe, however, was the lack of alcohol at either gathering, which made the gardens compare unfavourably with the raucous Donnybrook Fair.

The Dublin Zoological Gardens was among the most popular attractions in Dublin during the nineteenth century. Attendance averaged between 80,000 and 100,000 per year, and upwards of 5,000 people were often admitted on a summer Sunday when the weather was favourable.[5] In 1841, the population of Dublin, including its suburbs, was estimated at 281,206 persons.[6] In the same year 81,404 people were admitted at the price of one penny to the gardens.[7] If half of these people were either repeat visitors or visitors from outside Dublin, the figure suggests that almost 15 per cent of the city's population visited the zoo[8] in that year. Even in the midst of the Great Famine, Dublin zoo averaged 60,000 visitors per year.[9] The London Zoological Gardens, drawing from a much larger population, had an average of 200,000 visitors per year in its first five years (1828–33). Figures declined thereafter.[10] Similar numbers visited the famous Donnybrook Fair every year, in a single two-week period: observers estimated that it attracted 20,000 visitors per day in 1859 and a more modest 2,500 in 1862.[11]

The modern zoological garden, of which the London zoo was arguably the first, was an invention of the nineteenth century.[12] The new zoos were established at the intersection of popular leisure, science and urban culture. As zoos continue to be among the most visited sites in modern cities, they have attracted substantial scholarly attention. Assessments of the zoo have tended to see it as symbolic of a number of human impulses and desires, from imperialism and conquest to voyeurism.[13] Geographers have taken a particular interest in the zoo environment.[14] Kaye Anderson's study of the Adelaide Zoo in Australia argues that the zoo was an important location for negotiating the opposing ideas of human versus animal and reason versus nature.[15] Anderson claims the zoo as an example of Tony Bennett's 'exhibitionary complex', a location for the popularization of power and discipline, where the visitors were complicit in observing and controlling one another and the animals on display.[16] For Anderson, the zoo embodies and idealizes the triumph of the rational mind over the animal body in Western culture, especially in Western science. While drawing on the perspective of Anderson and others to address how the Dublin Zoological Gardens enacted class hierarchies, this essay also points to the ways in which social control was contested and resisted within them.

The display of power, and the relationship between science and power, has been a common theme among historians' interpretations of the zoo. Harriet Ritvo has convincingly demonstrated that the London Zoological Gardens was a place for popularizing imperialist narratives.[17] Many of the zoo's specimens were the spoils of empire and their presence in a scientific space allied science to colonialism. As a place of public leisure, the zoo also speaks to domestic social hierarchies. In particular, the zoological garden was one of many new spaces in nineteenth-century cities that were run by and for the middle classes and can be interpreted as displays of middle-class power.[18] It was also a location for promoting rational recreation to the working classes.

What role science, and particularly zoology, played in demarcating class boundaries deserves consideration. The Dublin Zoological Gardens offers a case study of that role in the development of

1 'The Vice-Regal Visit to the Zoological Gardens', *Paddy Kelly's Budget*, 3 (10 June 1835), 154.
2 'The Grand Fête in the Zoological Gardens!!!', *Paddy Kelly's Budget*, 1 (17 July 1833), 193–94.
3 'The Vice-Regal Visit', 154.
4 'The Grand Fête', 193.
5 D. J. Cunningham, *The Origin and Early History of the Royal Zoological Society of Ireland* (Dublin, 1901); see, for example, 8, 22, 58, 93, 114.
6 M. E. Daly, *Dublin: The Deposed Capital, a Social and Economic History, 1860–1914* (Cork, 1984), 3 (quoting figures from the census).
7 Cunningham, *Royal Zoological Society of Ireland*, 8.
8 The term 'zoo' did not come into popular usage until the 1870s. For the sake of brevity, I will use it throughout the essay.
9 Cunningham, *Royal Zoological Society of Ireland*, 58.
10 W. Blunt, *The Ark in the Park: The Zoo in the Nineteenth Century* (London, 1976), 35.
11 F. D'Arcy, 'The Decline and Fall of Donnybrook Fair: Moral Reform and Social Control in Nineteenth-Century Dublin', *Saothar: Journal of the Irish Labour History Society*, 13 (1988), 7–21.
12 E. Baratay and E. Hardouin-Fugier, *Zoo: A History of Zoological Gardens in the West* (London, 2002), 80–85.
13 See, for example J. Berger, 'Why look at animals?', in L. Kalof and A. Fitzgerald, eds., *The Animals Reader: The Essential Classic and Contemporary Writings* (Oxford,

Figure 1
The original gatehouse at the Dublin Zoological Gardens. From P. D. Hardy, *A Visit to the Zoological Gardens, Phoenix Park, Dublin* (Dublin, 1838). Reproduced courtesy of the National Library of Ireland.

popular leisure in the Victorian city and its implications for social class. The rise of rational recreation, which aimed to replace traditional amusements with controlled leisure, is easily observed in the Dublin zoo.[19] The zoo sought to draw working-class visitors away from public houses and events like the notorious Donnybrook Fair and to expose them to scientific spectacle and fresh air. While the zoo itself was extremely popular, its explicit project of civilizing and classifying was never as successful as its supporters claimed. Visitors and exhibits alike found ways to thwart its purpose.

Despite being one of the oldest zoological gardens in Europe, the Dublin zoo has not attracted much scholarly inquiry.[20] In a considered analysis of the zoo and its historical role, Eve Patten argues that the gardens and the Society provide an instance of 'civic science' in which the science was reserved for an élite group but was used to justify the provision of entertainment for the masses, and to enhance the image of Dublin as a European metropolis.[21] As she points out, Dublin zoo aimed for parity with London and Paris. While accepting Patten's conclusions, this essay links the scientific with the social and asks what the role of animals was in an agenda of social control. Most zoo visitors did not participate in scientific research and probably barely engaged with the limited scientific information available. However, the scientific views of its patrons influenced the gardens' social agenda.

'Reader! Have you ever visited the Zoological Gardens in the Phoenix Park?'[22]

The Royal Zoological Society of Ireland was founded in 1830, and its gardens were opened the following year. The founders were inspired by the example of the London Zoological Gardens, which had been opened in 1828, and the earlier Jardin des Plantes in Paris (1794). The duke of Northumberland, then lord lieutenant, granted a site in Phoenix Park adjacent to the viceregal lodge and the gardens were stocked with gifts. The king, William IV, donated a leopard, hyena and wolf from the Tower Menagerie and the Zoological Society of London gave exotic deer and birds. The new society's founders

2007), 249–61; H. Ritvo, *The Animal Estate: The English and Other Creatures in the Victorian Age* (Cambridge, 1987).
14 C. Philo and C. Wilbert, eds., *Animal Spaces, Beastly Places: New Geographies of Human–Animal Relations* (London, 2000).
15 K. Anderson, 'Culture and Nature at the Adelaide Zoo: At the Frontiers of Human Geography', *Transactions of the Institute of British Geographers*, 20 (1995), 275–94.
16 T. Bennett, 'The Exhibitionary Complex', *New Formations*, 4 (1988), 73–102.
17 Ritvo, *The Animal Estate*, 217–26.
18 N. Rothfels, *Savages and Beasts: The Birth of the Modern Zoo* (Baltimore, 2002), 32–34.
19 P. Bailey, *Leisure and Class in Victorian England: Rational Recreation and the Contest for Control, 1830–1885* (London, 1978), esp. 35–55.
20 A. E. J. Went, 'The Dublin Zoo', *Dublin Historical Record*, 24 (1971), 101–11. Also E. Patten, 'Isaac Butt, Zoology and Civilization', a paper given at Collins Barracks, Dublin, in

Figure 2
The gardens were built to encircle the lake as an aesthetic focal point. From Hardy, *A Visit to the Zoological Gardens*. Reproduced courtesy of the National Library of Ireland.

and well-wishers also donated animals, including an alligator and four zebu. Advice on laying out the gardens was provided by the architect of the London gardens, Decimus Burton. Over 36,000 people visited the new gardens within the first twelve months of opening.[23]

Before examining how the Dublin Zoological Gardens sought to introduce social aims through science, it is worth considering exactly what type of spectacle greeted visitors. The gardens developed slowly, through a mixture of donations and purchases and a building programme that was frequently in debt and behind schedule. Philip Dixon Hardy's numerous articles on the zoo and its collection in his *Dublin Penny Journal* offer some insight into the early appearance of the gardens. Figure 1 shows the original entrance gate and lodge. Figure 2 is a view that includes the keeper's house, which also housed the Society's council meeting rooms. The lake in the foreground was among the most noted features of the gardens, in terms of its aesthetic appeal. In the early years, animals were enclosed behind basic wire fences and their indoor accommodation consisted of wooden sheds (see Figure 3). Different species were often mixed together in one enclosure. Visitors had ready access to the animals and often fed them. Enclosures displayed very limited information about the animals, often no more than their common and Latin names. Much later in the century, the zoo had changed very little, although it had acquired more permanent, and warmer, brick houses for some of the animals. Figure 4 (*c.* 1890s) shows a camel in a very similar enclosure to the llama's pen dating from the 1830s.

Visitors to the gardens entered at the gate-lodge. Members had their name checked against the membership list before entry and non-members paid the admission fee. The initial entrance fee of one shilling, which limited the zoo's audience to the middle classes, was later reduced to sixpence. In 1836 the Society's council decided to offer a threepenny admission on Sundays to encourage working-class visitors. The discounted admission was reduced to a penny in 1840 and extended to weekday evenings after 6 p.m.[24] Visitors were free to follow one of many paths that wove between the animal pens and circled the

2005. Dr Patten kindly provided me with a manuscript version of this paper. Two books are forthcoming on the subject, although both take a different perspective from the present essay: Catherine De Courcy is preparing a brief history for a wide audience and geographer and historian Gordon Herries Davies is completing a detailed study of the Zoological Society.

21 Patten, 'Isaac Butt, Zoology and Civilization'.

22 P. D. Hardy, *A Visit to the Zoological Gardens, Phoenix Park, Dublin* (Dublin, 1838), 2.

23 Royal Zoological Society of Ireland, Rough minutes 1830–40, 19 November 1832 (10608/2/1) Trinity College Dublin [TCD], Manuscripts Department; (hereafter, RZSI Rough minutes 1830–40).

24 RZSI Rough minutes 1830–40, see 12 August 1836, 9 September 1836 and 25 April 1840.

Figure 3
The original enclosures were simple wire fences, which allowed visitors to get very close to the animals and even to feed them. During the winter, most animals were crowded into small wooden huts, as seen in the background of this image. From Hardy, *A Visit to the Zoological Gardens*. Reproduced courtesy of the National Library of Ireland.

central feature of the lake. The paths were ornamented by plantings, intended both to enhance the visual appeal of the gardens and separate and screen the exhibits, in order 'to present a succession of objects to please by variety'.[25] Favourite attractions included the refreshment stand, the elephant enclosure, the bear pit ... and the other visitors. For the last, Sunday was best, when 'material for studying the peculiarities of the *genus Homo*' were 'considerably more abundant'.[26]

The gardens were by no means the only place where a Dubliner could examine foreign and exotic animals. Travelling menageries from England frequently passed through the city's fair at Donnybrook.[27] After Donnybrook was suppressed, the menageries found other spaces, often theatres or circuses. Performing animals also appeared in theatres, such as Mademoiselle d'Jeck, the elephant which starred in *The Elephant of Siam and the Fire Fiend* at Dublin's Theatre Royal in 1830.[28] Van Amburgh, the nineteenth-century's most famous animal tamer, also toured Ireland with his lions and tigers.[29] Collections of animals were added to the attractions of private gardens used for promenades, such as those in Portobello and Kingstown. With so many other animal spectacles available for their consumption, visitors to the Dublin Zoological Gardens were probably not easily astonished or impressed by exotic creatures alone. The Dublin zoo differentiated itself from these other spectacles by claiming a scientific motive for the exhibits and educational benefits for visitors.

'Exciting a greater interest in the study of natural history'[30]

Although the Society's council members acknowledged that they were providing a popular amusement, they also claimed scientific aims for the gardens. The display of animals in the gardens was intended to popularize the sciences of zoology and natural history. The founders felt that the study of these subjects had received proportionally less attention in Dublin than in comparable European centres of scientific thought. The Society regarded the mere existence of the gardens as scientific progress, but it also saw them as a means of teaching

25 RZSI Rough minutes 1830–40, 19 November 1832.
26 'Sunday at the Zoological Gardens', *Irish Times*, 24 July 1873.
27 S. Ó Maitiú, *The Humours of Donnybrook: Dublin's Famous Fair and its Suppression* (Dublin, 1995).
28 'Theatre Royal', *Freeman's Journal*, 5 May 1830.
29 'Theatre Royal', *Freeman's Journal*, 14 May 1839.
30 RZSI Rough minutes 1830–40, 22 April 1837.

'rational' observation. This emphasis on cultivating rational observation, as opposed to gaping, was one of the ways in which the Society sought to distinguish the zoo from competing animal spectacles.

When observation was directed towards a purpose, the display of exotic animals could be justified on the grounds of scientific interest. The first guidebook to the gardens, *A Descriptive Catalogue of the Animals in the collection of the Zoological Society of Dublin, With Preliminary Observations upon the Natural Groups of the Mammalia and Birds*, was published in 1833. Written by William Tighe Hamilton, a member of the Society, the book was not a souvenir, but an introductory text on natural history. The guide, he claimed, aimed to encourage in its readers the transition from 'superficial curiosity' to the more scientific 'taste for studying the intrinsic properties of different animals'.[31] The Society had the cages of the animals numbered in accordance with the numbers in Hamilton's guide, so that visitors could more easily use the book to enhance their knowledge of the animals.[32] Hamilton's entries described aspects of the animals' habits and diet, and gave details of the regions whence they came. He focused on the animals in the gardens as representatives of a natural order, each species displaying the characteristics of a particular group, and his book tied these groups together into a system of classificatory relationships. The scientific gaze encouraged visitors to view the animals not as unique individuals, but as type specimens, and the gardens as a kind of animated museum.

Hardy's 1838 guide to the gardens was intended for a wider audience, but it also focused on the educational benefits that could be derived from observing animals. It combined articles that he had published in the *Dublin Penny Journal* with scientific material lifted from Hamilton's guide, and its aim was to help readers become 'acquainted with the localities of the place, and the history and properties of the various animals'.[33] The introduction claimed that only a scientifically ordered space could convert the frivolous curiosity that humans feel towards 'rare and living animals' into rational contemplation.[34] Despite its rhetoric regarding education, Hardy's guide catered to perceived popular tastes. Much of the information was provided in such a way as to generate a simple curiosity about the animals rather than engender a deeper scientific interest: statistics about the size of an elephant's ear, for example, were paired with a romantic tale of an elephant hunt. Hardy, also a publisher of proselytizing religious tracts, added overtones of Christian morality and reverence.

The theme of self-improvement through rational observation was also taken up by the *Dublin University Magazine*. In an article endorsing the zoological project, the journal claimed that 'a knowledge of animated nature can never be acquired perfectly through any medium but the eye'; observation of animals was necessary before one could make use of lectures or textbooks.[35] A visit to the zoological gardens was a prerequisite for understanding natural history; and the article went further, claiming: 'It is impossible to examine the works of nature, without being made better by the enquiry'.[36] Self-improvement had both scientific and religious benefits: knowledge was acquired, while reverence for God was reinforced.

The focus on animal observation in the gardens was mirrored by a similar interest in observing visitors. Observing animals could remind the visitor of the ways in which rationality and science made mankind superior to the beasts. A zoological lecture on instinct, delivered by one of the Society's members (and reprinted in Hardy's guide), encouraged visitors to compare the 'expressions of destruction in the beast of prey' to 'the countenance, eye, gestures and manners of an infuriated man'.[37] Many similarities would be evident, but man had the ability to control urges towards violence and to channel them into nobler causes. The difference between animals and

31 W. T. Hamilton, *A Descriptive Catalogue of the Animals in the Collection of the Zoological Society of Dublin, With Preliminary Observations upon the Natural Groups of the Mammalia and Birds* (Dublin, 1833), vi.
32 RZSI Rough minutes 1830–40, 2 August 1833.
33 Hardy, *A Visit*, 2.
34 Hardy, *A Visit*, i.
35 J. Scouler, 'Zoology in Dublin', *Dublin University Magazine*, 10 (1837), 666–71, 666.
36 Scouler, 'Zoology in Dublin', 671.
37 Hardy, *A Visit*, v.

man, therefore, was the capacity for self-control and for 'the cultivation of the higher faculties', which enabled such control.[38] By extension, those people who exercised control over animal-like passions were superior to those who could not. Thus, the observation of natural order in the gardens was easily transposed to the natural order of the human world.

'A specimen in political zoology'[39]

The Society was founded a year after Catholic emancipation was won in 1829. As Patten and Went have pointed out, the founders represented a mixture of urban professionals, landed gentry, politicians and civic officials.[40] They also included people of different religious backgrounds. As such, the society was similar to other scientific societies in Britain and Ireland.[41] Speakers at the foundational meeting were frank about their project's relationship to the recent achievement of Catholic emancipation, claiming it as an attempt to begin reconciliation and growth after a period of rancour, with Richard Lalor Sheil commenting hopefully:

> now that the subject of animosity has been past away [sic], the obstacle that stood in the way of national improvement is removed, and a field is thrown open to the intelligence and the exercise of the high mental attributes of Ireland.[42]

Sheil expected the proposed zoological gardens to be one of many new projects that would flourish now that political disagreements could be set aside. Although the idea of the scientific space as a neutral space was by no means unique to the zoological gardens, here the neutrality was linked to a very specific time, place and function. The new Society and its gardens would heal the fissures between the élite of Dublin, who, if they did not share political views, shared a sense of pride in their city and of their own importance as cultural and intellectual leaders.

Emancipation was no doubt accompanied by fears of how it might alter Dublin's and Ireland's social structure and particularly how it might challenge the governing role assumed by élite Protestants. With its patronage by powerful individuals on both sides of the emancipation question, the zoological gardens enabled the adjustment and refining of Dublin's class structures in the aftermath of the passing of the Act, and can be interpreted as an attempt to consolidate an agreed social hierarchy through the provision of 'scientific' public leisure. It is true that the growth of Dublin's suburbs in the second half of the nineteenth century tended to further separate Catholic and Protestant, rich and poor, as Mary Daly has shown.[43] Social classes were relatively stable and linked with religious persuasion; upward mobility was infrequent.[44] Nevertheless, Catholic emancipation opened higher level government appointments to the Catholic middle classes and allowed for a specific type of social advancement.

While offering access to a wide range of persons, the zoo maintained social hierarchies, as Paddy Kelly had noticed during his attendance of the 1835 fête. Accompanying guidebooks and literature indicate how the interpretation of zoology itself could enforce these boundaries and demarcations, encouraging visitors to 'know their place'. Hamilton's guidebook aided readers in 'reflecting upon the relation which each [animal] bears to the circumstances in which it is placed, and to the rest of animated nature',[45] and his classification systems assigned to nature God-given, unchangeable, characteristics. Zoology in this case was not only influenced by the culture in which it developed, but it could be used to reinforce and maintain human differences. A natural order or higher power placed Dublin's different classes in their respective situations; their relations with one another were fixed.

The links between comparative anatomy, zoology and social theory are many. Lamarckian evolution, which posited a

38 Hardy, *A Visit*, viii.
39 From the speech of Richard Lalor Sheil, as reported in 'Zoological Society', *Freeman's Journal*, 11 May 1830.
40 Patten, 'Isaac Butt, Zoology and Civilization'; Went, 'The Dublin Zoo'.
41 J. Adelman, 'Communities of Science: The Queen's Colleges and Scientific Culture in Provincial Ireland, 1845–75', PhD thesis, National University of Ireland, Galway, 2006, 55–60; E. Neswald, 'Science and Sociability in Nineteenth-Century Provincial Ireland: The Galway Mechanics' Institute', *British Journal for the History of Science*, 39 (2006), 503–34.
42 'Zoological Society', *Freeman's Journal*, 11 May 1830.
43 Daly, *Dublin*, Chapter 5.
44 Daly, *Dublin*, 145.
45 Hamilton, *A Descriptive Catalogue*, vi.

Figure 4
This style of wire-fronted cage was common to zoos and travelling menageries throughout the nineteenth century. Lions and tigers remained in small dens after a failed effort to interest them in a large 'deambulatorium' in 1838. From the Lawrence Royal Photographic Collection, National Library of Ireland, Royal 6373. Reproduced courtesy of the National Library of Ireland.

mutable and progressive idea of species, was promoted by working-class radicals in early nineteenth-century London.[46] Comparative anatomy could be used to support evolutionary ideas and social change. By contrast, Richard Owen's anatomical concept of unchanging 'archetypes' argued for the stability of an existing hierarchy in nature and society. Dublin of the 1830s was an important centre for medical education and research, of which comparative anatomy comprised a part. Members of the 'Dublin School' pioneered new surgical techniques, as well advocating the physical diagnosis of disease pathology by post-mortem examination.[47] Post-mortems were often conducted on animals from the zoo and medical education through comparative anatomy was cited as a reason for maintaining the gardens.[48] The lessons of anatomical examinations were almost invariably related to the perfection of animal forms and their God-given adaptations for life. Samuel Haughton, professor of geology at Trinity College, performed extensive investigations of animal mechanics during the 1860s, using deceased zoo specimens. His studies confirmed for him that structure and musculature were perfectly designed in order to minimize any waste of energy. Deviations from the expected anatomy were often attributed to disease or deformity.[49] The fixity of form and species, which the animals in the zoological gardens were thought to demonstrate, was linked to a message of social harmony maintained through hierarchy and stasis. This link was not obscure: the *Dublin Penny Journal* ran an article on comparative anatomy in 1836, which noted the science's capacity to elucidate 'fixed and invariable principles' in the form of natural laws written by God.[50]

Although ostensibly open to all, the zoological gardens effectively separated middle-class and working-class visitors by admission policies. Visitors were differentiated into groups which almost never encountered one another within the gardens. Members paid at least £1 per annum, with a ten shilling supplement for the privilege of bringing guests.[51] Members could visit for free on any day the gardens were open, but they almost never visited on Sundays, when the penny admission rate was in operation. For example, of almost 3,000 visitors on a Sunday in September of 1850, only 3 were admitted free as members.[52] A further

46 A. Desmond, 'Artisan Resistance and Evolution in Britain, 1819–1848', *Osiris*, 3 (1987), 77–110.
47 E. O'Brien, *Conscience and Conflict: A Biography of Sir Dominic Corrigan, 1802–1880* (Dublin, 1983), 140–55.
48 D. Houston, 'Extract from a Paper Read by Dr. Houston, at a Meeting of the Zoological Society of Dublin, on the Diseases of the Animals which died in Their Collection', *Dublin Journal of Medical and Chemical Science*, 5 (1834), 285–88.
49 Many of these are collected together in S. Haughton, *Notes on Animal Mechanics* (Dublin, 1866).
50 'On the Structure of Animals', *Dublin Penny Journal*, 4, 199 (1836), 337–38, 337.
51 RZSI Rough minutes, 1830–40, 15 May 1833.
52 See Royal Zoological Society of Ireland, 12 September 1850, Weekly Returns book I, May 1847 to June 1852 (10608/16/1) TCD; (hereafter, RZSI Weekly Returns book I).

Figure 5
Bear pit, Dublin Zoological gardens, c. 1880–1914. Lawrence Photographic Collection, National Library of Ireland, Royal 6371. Reproduced courtesy of the National Library of Ireland.

gradation accommodated those who chose to pay the full price of admission, sixpence, in order to attend on a day other than Sunday. Members rarely visited the gardens at all and when they did it was for a special occasion or on a Saturday, which coincided with the Society's weekly meeting. A fund-raising fête in 1850, for example, was held on a Wednesday and attracted 467 members, as well as further 226 persons paying 2s. 6d.[53] Dominic Corrigan, a president of the Society, later remarked: 'I very rarely visit the gardens, except on Saturday morning, for the transaction of business; and occasionally on Sunday, when, being the neighbourhood of the gardens, I go in to see how the people are behaving themselves'.[54] This remark highlights the importance the society attached to the surveillance of working-class visitors.

Middle-class visitors were believed to have the greatest scientific interest in the contents of the gardens. Hamilton's guidebook, for example, was relatively expensive and required significant background knowledge to use. In addition, the Society introduced public zoological lectures, payable by subscription, intended to supplement knowledge acquired in the gardens. The first series was given in 1838 at the Royal Dublin Society at a cost of £1 for five lectures,[55] an amount that would almost certainly have excluded the attendance of working-class people. Although well attended, the impact of the lectures on the experience of visiting the gardens may have been minimal. The fact that they were given in the rooms of a scientific society, rather than at the gardens themselves, separated the scientific work of zoology from the spectacle of the gardens. This practice mirrors the distinction made by scientific members of the Zoological Society between animals as spectacles for public consumption, rarely if ever used for scientific study, and their carcasses, as anatomical specimens for dissection.

For Dublin's middle classes, the zoo was an important site for socializing and

53 RZSI Weekly Returns book I, 2 May 1850.
54 *Report on the Scientific Institutions of Dublin*, House of Commons (1864), Minutes of evidence, 22.
55 RZSI Rough minutes 1830–40, 11 January 1838.

it soon became one of many possible leisure outings in the city. Its public nature allowed for the titillating possibility of encountering unknown, and potentially unsuitable, persons. However, the cost of admission on days other than Sunday tended to limit the audience. For example, the diaries of a Dublin medical family in the 1830s record numerous visits to the zoo. The son, in particular, visited the gardens unaccompanied, in order to rendezvous with friends and in the hope of catching sight of an attractive young woman. His visits were sandwiched between attendance at the theatre, scientific lectures at the Royal Dublin Society, and visits to the Royal Hibernian Academy.[56] His sister, whose social rounds were dependent on her parents, fitted in a visit to the zoo before an inspection of the lunatic asylum with her father.[57] She also attended one of the zoo's fund-raising fêtes with her father, when the rain prevented them from doing anything other than staying in the tent to eat, drink and dance.[58] Neither sibling remarked on the animals in the gardens. By contrast, their visits to other types of animal spectacles are recorded in more detail. For example, the young man saw 'wild beasts' at Donnybrook Fair, recording: 'Tiger — superb — alone worth the trouble not to mention a fine lioness'.[59] His sister saw 'Toby the sapient pig', an exhibit that merited not only an extensive entry in her diary but a second visit with friends.[60] These two examples, albeit from the same family, offer an indication that the careful observation of animals was perhaps one of the least significant attractions of the zoological gardens. Audiences were lured, as Paddy Kelly put it, by 'bipeds to be seen', and the society frequently invited the lord lieutenant, military bands and foreign dignitaries to visit the gardens in order to draw larger crowds.[61]

A number of pieces in the *Dublin Penny Journal* perhaps reveal the manner in which visitors viewed the animals. In his first article on the zoological gardens, Hardy's imaginary spectators were more interested in making unfavourable comparisons between humans and the animals. The emu was 'some overgrown *gommagh* of a fellow', who spends his time 'thrusting his long Paul Pry neck into every body's business'.[62] The owl was a hypocrite, who behaved well in public, but 'amidst the shades of night was abroad pursuing things vile and atrocious'.[63] Hardy used these imaginary conversations to impart a great deal of factual information on the size and habits of the animals, mixed with moral lessons that particularly reflected his views on the source of Irish problems. For example, the bear reminded a visitor of the story of two Irish émigrés who decide to become bear hunters, looking for easy money over hard work. Receiving an advance, they spend most of it on alcohol and set out without enough gunpowder, only to be mauled by the bear.[64] Thus the observation of animals in the gardens was, for Hardy, not simply a lesson in natural history but a homily on human nature as well.

Hardy was not the only author to suggest that visitors in the zoological gardens failed to observe animals in a solely scientific manner. *Paddy Kelly's Budget* repeatedly depicted visitors as ignorant and mocked the idea of scientific observation as the dull amusement of teetotallers. 'Darby Dunn', the *Budget*'s correspondent, visited the gardens with his wife, who begged him to part with his shillings for their entrance fee. Once inside, Dunn was astonished at the misinformation that visitors were imparting to their companions. Despite his offer to provide Mrs. Dunn with an 'explanation of the manners and habits of the different animals, and a geographical description of the countries from which they came', she appeared to prefer the invented stories of another man who told anecdotes of 'the wild man of the woods' (an orang-utan).[65]

Dunn's ignorant visitor was not an artisan, but 'genteel-looking'. Hardy's visitors were also middle class and educated. Middle-class visitors, they implied, did not always present the example of self-improvement that the promoters of rational

56 See entries for January through April of 1834, 'Diary of a young man living in Dublin, 1834–37', MS 32,633, National Library of Ireland; (hereafter 'Diary, 1834–37'). Despite its title, the manuscript consists of two volumes, one clearly written by a woman, covering the period 1836–37.

57 'Diary, 1834–37', 16 May 1837.

58 'Diary, 1834–37', 29 May 1837.

59 'Diary, 1834–37', 28 August 1834.

60 'Diary, 1834–37', 1 and 3 April 1837.

61 'The Vice-Regal Visit to the Zoological Gardens', *Paddy Kelly's Budget*, 3 (10 June 1835), 154–55. See, for example, RZSI Rough minutes 1830–40, 12, 19 and 25 August 1837.

62 P. D. Hardy, 'A Visit to the Gardens of the Zoological Society of Dublin', *Dublin Penny Journal*, 1, 1 (1832), 4–6, 4.

63 Hardy, 'A Visit to the Gardens', 5.

64 Hardy, 'A Visit to the Gardens', 5.

65 D. Dunn, 'A Visit to the Zoological Garden', *Paddy Kelly's Budget*, 1 (1833), 143–44, 144.

Figure 6
Two women and a child at the zebra enclosure, 1880–1914. Lawrence Photographic Collection, National Library of Ireland, Royal 6101. Reproduced courtesy of the National Library of Ireland.

recreation had hoped the working classes would emulate. Instead, they engaged in frivolous conversation and socializing, the animals merely serving as an interesting backdrop. So-called respectable visitors also violently attacked animals in the gardens. Campaigners against animal cruelty noted recurrent incidents, including the whipping of a pelican and the feeding of 'pepper nuts' to the monkeys.[66] On one occasion a seal was stoned to death. Several boys were found guilty of the crime, and on pronouncing the sentence, the judge remarked that 'the poorer classes always conducted themselves most creditably, and when mischief was done, it was generally done by persons of the better classes'.[67] He therefore chose to punish the boys severely in order to set an example and imposed a fine of £5 each.

Although it was the middle-class visitors who repeatedly misbehaved in the gardens, it was the reform of working-class visitors that most interested the Zoological Society. The penny admission days were intended to provide an alternative to entertainments like the public house and Donnybrook Fair. Working-class visitors were singled out for special observation in the garden, particularly on Sundays, when most members stayed away. Council members were appointed as inspectors by the society, each on a weekly or monthly basis. The inspector visited the gardens with the aim of observing the inhabitants — both human and non-human.[68] While reporting on the state of the collection, inspectors frequently noted the behaviour of visitors. The self-control and comportment of the humans was a point of pride. One inspector reported that 'a stranger would be struck on paying a Sunday visit to these gardens by the absence of rudeness, the good-thought and civility that one sees in the crowded houses'.[69] Inspectors recorded the impressions of foreign visitors, eager for evidence that the crowds in the zoological gardens were dispelling images of the Irish as ignorant and rowdy.

The Zoological Society applied itself enthusiastically to the task of civilizing the working classes. The reduction in the price of admission had been originally mooted as early as 1836, 'with the view to create a diversion from the dissipations of Donnybrook Fair'.[70] After the first year of penny admissions on Sundays and evenings, the Society congratulated itself on providing

66 H. Madden, 'Correspondence', *Irish Times*, 3 October 1864, and A Friend to Animals, 'Correspondence', *Irish Times*, 15 May 1861.
67 'Outrage in the Zoological Gardens', *Irish Times*, 5 November 1874.
68 A visitors' book was started in 1837, see RZSI Rough minutes 1830–40, 4 March 1837. Unfortunately this book is not extant.
69 Royal Zoological Society of Ireland Visitors' notebook, 7 July 1861 (MS 10608/8/1), TCD; (hereafter, RZSI Visitors' notebook).
70 RZSI Rough minutes 1830–40, 12 August 1836.

'a powerful aid to the confirming of the people in their improved habits'.[71] The open admission policy of the gardens also carried out 'the great principle of the Society, the spread of useful information',[72] the Society's council and supporters repeatedly confirming that the working classes were the true patrons of the gardens. Social reformers claimed that working people were improving as a result of their attendance at the zoological gardens and other sites of rational recreation. One writer in the *Irish Penny Journal* opined in 1840 that 'a most decided improvement in the habits and feelings of the humbler classes of the community has really taken place in the last few years'.[73] Visitors, according to the author, had learned how to behave and how to observe. Spaces like the zoo encouraged the working classes to refine their skills of observation, 'to draw out the latent talent in those who, having eyes, yet see not'.

Despite the praise of working-class behaviour, the Society felt the need to employ a police officer on Sundays. Police presence helped to discourage 'ragged boys' from entering the gardens by climbing over barriers instead of paying the entrance fee, and to deter the many pickpockets, who were rife in the gardens.[74] Prosecutions for pickpocketing at the gardens were routine. Even one constable on duty in the gardens was not immune.[75] Deviant behaviour was in fact more frequent on a Sunday than the Society's proprietors were often willing to admit. Intoxication and theft were the most common problems. The Society discharged one of its own keepers, found drunk, demanding that he take a temperance pledge in order to return to work.[76] Orders were given to the gatekeepers to turn away intoxicated visitors and to prevent the sale of alcohol near the zoo's entrance.[77] Occasionally, visitors stole the animals. Two boys, for example, were arrested in 1849 for the theft of several exotic birds, which they later sold in Patrick Street. The unfortunate young thieves were offered the choice of fines of £2 each or two months' imprisonment with hard labour.[78] Usually, however, visitors stole from other spectators.

Deviance from the Society's vision of an Eden of rational recreation was not limited to humans. Animals, too, might resist the Society's efforts at control. Animal smells intruded upon the atmosphere of the zoo and were a frequent cause of complaint. Animals were crowded into very small rooms during the winter months. Protection from the weather was important to prevent deaths, and the Society could not afford larger structures. However, the lack of capacity for housing the animals did not prevent it from acquiring more specimens. Overcrowding, leading to filth and odour, was a common problem. One visitor described a room 20 feet by 25 feet that contained a leopard, a leopardess, a hyena, several monkeys, a squirrel, an ichneumon, a pelican, several macaws and parrots, a kestrel hawk, two herons, birds and tortoises.[79] Not only did this overcrowding impede their visibility to visitors, but the droppings of so many animals in such a small space must certainly have generated an awful stench. Animal waste was a constant problem, even when the waste was removed from the cages. In 1859, one of the Society's own inspecting visitors reported that the pile of manure was so high 'as to be visible from the Park'.[80] The visitors' notebook also recorded the foul smells emitted by rotting vegetation in ponds and the carrion accumulated for the carnivores.[81] As late as 1873, the *Irish Times* complained of 'the stench pervading several departments of the menagerie', as well as the foul odour of rotting meat coming from many of the cages.[82] Problems were exacerbated on warm days when the gardens were crowded with visitors as well as residents. Instead of a healthy, open place of rational recreation, the gardens could resemble the crowded and pungent menageries visiting Donnybrook Fair.

Animals also occasionally thwarted efforts to exhibit them. In 1838 the Society created a 'deambulatorium' for exercising the carnivores. The new, larger cage was

71 Cunningham, *Royal Zoological Society of Ireland*, 7.
72 Cunningham, *Royal Zoological Society of Ireland*, 7.
73 B., 'Improper Conduct in Public Places', *Irish Penny Journal*, 1 (1840), 95–96, 95.
74 Arrests for picking pockets at the gardens were routine. See, for example, 'Police intelligence', *Irish Times*, 4 June 1859.
75 'Capel Street police office — yesterday', *Freeman's Journal*, 27 September 1864.
76 Royal Zoological Society of Ireland Transaction book for May 1836 to December 1841, 21 July 1836, f 24 (MS 10608/9/1), TCD; (hereafter, RZSI Transaction book).
77 RZSI Transaction book, 11 August 1836, f 30.
78 'Dublin police — yesterday', *Freeman's Journal*, 2 January 1849.
79 I.D.M., 'The Dublin Zoological Gardens', *Dublin Penny Journal*, 1, 23 (1832), 181–82, 181.
80 RZSI Visitors' notebook, 23 February 1859.
81 RZSI Visitors' notebook, 2 July 1864 and 18 June 1861.
82 'Sunday at the Zoological Gardens', *Irish Times*, 24 July 1873.

intended to allow the carnivores greater freedom of movement and was presented as an effort to improve their health. In reality, however, the expanded cage was an attempt to make the animals more visible to the visitors and to encourage them to exhibit characteristics, such as power and ferocity, impossible to discern in a cramped den. As the *Freeman's Journal* remarked, the 'exhibition of this fine animal [a tigress] in a situation where she can display her powers, promises much entertainment during the ensuing week'.[83] The animals' release into the new cage was scheduled in consultation with the lord lieutenant, whose attendance at the event would ensure a numerous audience. Military bands were hired and a special song gave voice to the supposed emotions of the soon-to-be-roaming beasts: 'now we bound from thraldom freed, and frisk with joy and glee, large is the space allotted us, Oh! Glorious liberty'.[84] The accompanying song sheet depicted leaping carnivores, displaying hunting behaviour. Unfortunately, the tigress that was offered the deambulatorium refused to demonstrate her gratitude for her new environment. The *Freeman's Journal* reported that 'instead of being desirous to avail herself of the liberty offered here, the animal seemed determined to remain in her den, and it required the exertion of several persons to force her from it'.[85] The reaction of the animal, and the disappointment expressed at her reticence to oblige the audience, further demonstrates that the deambulatorium was designed primarily for gratifying human interest. The simultaneous appearance of Van Amburgh's trained animals in a Dublin theatre suggests that the deambulatorium was partly conceived of as a means of competing with travelling showmen.[86] The tigress was never won over by the new enclosure and eventually it was broken up to make cages for the polar bears.

Conclusion

The Dublin zoo was seen to represent a microcosm of an Irish working class made up of orderly and productive citizens with the middle classes as their capable overseers. A park full of 'wild' animals was an apt location for demonstrating how Ireland might be tamed: the rational Irishman, visitor to the zoo, contrasted with the bestial Irishman, slave to his passions, who was frequently depicted in the British press.[87] Irish passion and animality were associated with resistance to British rule and thus the Dublin zoo made a political statement. The techniques of zoological science — observing, classifying, ordering — could be applied to the management of people. The provision of sufficient food and water and limited 'freedoms' would keep the captives tame.

Studies of the zoo have allocated social agendas to the collection and exhibition of animals, but have tended to diminish the importance of resistance to these agendas. In fact, deviance from desired behaviour was routine by both visitors and animals. 'Misbehaviour' reminds us that the impact of social control measures was not always as substantial as its promoters would have wished to achieve. Much in the same way as the zoo was about the display of animal forms and did not offer insight into the animals' 'natural' habits, public leisure was about the display of suitable behaviour. Visitors might appear to conform to the expectations of rational recreation by attending the zoological gardens, but they could also choose to use the gardens as a site for drinking, courting and picking pockets.

83 'Enlargement of the Tigress at the Zoological Gardens', *Freeman's Journal*, 27 August 1838.
84 Royal Zoological Society of Ireland Ephemera volume, item 108 (MS 10608/24/1), TCD.
85 'Enlargement of the Tigress at the Zoological Gardens', *Freeman's Journal*, 27 August 1838.
86 'Astley's Amphitheatre', *Freeman's Journal*, 31 August 1838.
87 For an example of this in the context of political cartoons, see L. Perry Curtis, *Apes and Angels: The Irishman in Victorian Caricature* (London, 1997).

Giovanni Arrighi, 2006.
Courtesy of Beverly Silver

Up for Grabs

Giovanni Arrighi in conversation with Joe Cleary

Giovanni Arrighi was one of the most innovative scholars in world systems theory. Born in Milan in 1937, he received a PhD in Economics from the University of Milan in 1960, and in 1963 moved to Africa to teach at the University College of Rhodesia and Nyasaland. There, he studied the proletarianization of African labour and the dynamics of labour resistance. Jailed and deported by the Rhodesian government in 1966, Arrighi spent time in Tanzania, returning in 1969 to Italy, where he co-founded the Gruppo Gramsci in 1971. He moved in 1979 to SUNY Binghamton, working with Immanuel Wallerstein and Terence Hopkins at the Fernand Braudel Center for the Study of Economies, Historical Systems and Civilizations. During a long and extremely productive career he wrote many widely translated books on the dynamics of global capitalism and anti-systemic movements. His late works,

The Long Twentieth Century (1994) and *Adam Smith in Beijing* (2007), are particularly brilliant reinterpretations of the development of capitalism, offering cogent and daring accounts of the transformation of the world system in the early twenty-first century. Arrighi was a guest of the Irish Seminar at the Keough Naughton Notre Dame Centre, Dublin, in June 2008, where he discussed his recent work with Joe Cleary and other seminar participants. Diagnosed with cancer later that summer, Arrighi died in June 2009, having lived to see the beginnings of the global capitalist crisis that *The Long Twentieth Century* had predicted more than a decade earlier.

JOE CLEARY: *The Long Twentieth Century: Money, Power and the Origins of Our Times* [1994] and *Adam Smith in Beijing: Lineages of the Twenty-First Century* [2007] might be read as independent books or as part of a longer, continuous study of modern capitalism and imperialism. One of the things I admire about *The Long Twentieth Century* is that it wasn't only a history of capitalist accumulation or finance capital, nor of state-building and territorial expansion, nor of war machines and war-making, not even of hegemony and consensus. The construction of modern empires has regularly been addressed in terms of one or other of these things, but *The Long Twentieth Century* sustains the dialectic between these different aspects of power in an extraordinarily dynamic way. I know it's a very broad question to begin with, but is it possible to summarize how you see that dialectic working?

GIOVANNI ARRIGHI: The dialectic between capitalism and imperialism and war-making and state-making — well, let me say as a premise that it was not my intention to write *The Long Twentieth Century* in the way I did, and even less to write two other volumes that now basically form a trilogy with it, the other two volumes being *Chaos and Governance in the Modern World System* [1999], co-authored with Beverly Silver, and now *Adam Smith in Beijing*. My original project in *The Long Twentieth Century* was really a comparison of three crises of capitalism. My thinking on the project goes back to the 1970s, a period when global capitalism was obviously in crisis and when there was widespread discussion of the origins and nature of that crisis. So, in the original project I was comparing three depressions, or systemic crises, one that took place in the late nineteenth century, one in the 1930s, and one that was coming to a head in the years when I was writing *The Long Twentieth Century*. I was in Binghamton University, New York, at that time and I was encouraged by Immanuel Wallerstein not only to read Fernand Braudel but to take from him the idea of the *longue durée*. The *longue durée* is an analytical concept that defines the lifetime of a system or structure — in this case, capitalism. So this is a problem posed by Braudel — how to apprehend what the lifetime of this structure is, if you want to understand its processes. The first step was my discovery in Braudel's work that what in the late nineteenth century was considered by Marxists to be the highest stage of capitalism — finance capital — and what in the 1980s and 1990s was considered to be a new phase of capitalism — namely, globalization, capital moving across the globe, and states competing with one another to attract it — were in fact neither of them very new.

So the first thing I had to do was to define the time frame that would allow me to understand this thing called 'capitalism'. And following Braudel's work, I took as my time frame the period when we can observe the phenomenon called finance capital and financialization, which, as Braudel put it, was not a novelty of the nineteenth, let alone of the twentieth century, but was in fact the oldest form of capital, and a recurrent one at that. Braudel observed that the Italian city-states and the Italian capitalists were the first to experience the phenomenon of finance capital, and that sent me back to the period of the Italian Renaissance. I noted, with Braudel's help, that there has been a recurring tendency for capital, at certain cyclical moments, to move out of production or manufacture and trade and to go into financial speculation. In fact, if one takes the lifetime of capitalism defined in this way — a period of over 500 –600 years —one realizes that capitalism has been for the most part involved in financial speculation and only exceptionally involved in the expansion of trade and production.

Now, coming to your question: Braudel looks at these financial expansions as the defining characteristics of capital, but he doesn't quite realize what other historians were pointing out — that there were periods when the units and the agencies of these capitalist processes underwent major transformation. For him, financial expansion seems to be a constant, something that never changes, from the fourteenth and fifteenth centuries to the twentieth. What he misses, therefore, is that periods of financial expansion do not simply return or repeat themselves; such periods are always historical moments of great transformation. And these moments of great transformation in finance are also periods of war-making and state-making, and so on. Thus, once we take this long view, and we look at the agencies that were involved in the financial expansions, we also realize that state-making and war-making have been a constant in this process and that the obsession with nation-states in much of the literature on modern history is totally misplaced. In fact, the nation-state, as theorized in Western social science, plays almost no role in the wider development of modern capitalism, because the driving agencies are not now and never have been nation-states.

Italian city-states such as Venice and Genoa are often conflated, but Genoa was a very pathetic city-state compared to Venice, which was a very powerful one. The power of Genoese capital was never based on the city itself; it was based on a diaspora that was operating out of Antwerp, out of Lyon, out of various places. Genoese capitalists operated like a transnational organization. Later, Holland, or the United Provinces as it was then called, was a proto-nation-state — something in between the city-state and the nation-state, but certainly not a modern nation-state in the sense we now know it. The next major centre of finance capital was Britain, and Britain was not a conventional nation-state. It was a state comprised of four nations, including Ireland. It was thus a multinational state and, at the same time, a globe-encompassing empire. The British conquered an empire, its colonization of India was obviously a crucial moment, and that empire provided the material foundation of much of the power of Britain in its heyday. And then after Britain ceased to be the world's greatest superpower, we have the United States — a continental-sized state.

The nation-state, then, has never been the centre of the modern world system; the idea that it has been is in fact a fiction. Once you observe the longer history of capitalist development, you see that the state-form changes across this history; if one looks at capitalist development in a particular country and in a particular place, one inevitably misses its most important feature, which is the fact that, through war-making and state-making, the containers of capitalist power have expanded over the centuries from tiny city-states to proto-nation-states to multinational states to a continental-sized state, and the US had ambitions to become a world state from the beginning. State-making, war-making and capital accumulation, then, have to be looked at as jumping from one place to another, because jumping is one of the main characteristics of capitalism. Capitalism jumps, and if you want to understand its dynamic, you have to jump with it from one place to another and try to identify the places that are important. Most studies in social science or economic history, however, have focused on the development of capitalism in terms of the history of one, supposedly exemplary, national or nation-state development, particularly Britain and France. Hence, state-centred studies of this kind miss the most important characteristic of the animal they aim to investigate.

'Le Peril Jaune', c. 1910. One of set of 6 postcards showing six grave dangers facing France. This one is the Yellow Peril: the rise of China. Europeans are devoured by a Chinese monster. The artist, T. Bianco, was one of the leading satirical illustrators of the era. © Science and Society Picture Library, London.

Could I ask you to say a bit about the period in the early twentieth century when British world hegemony was challenged by Germany and the United States. You make the point in *The Long Twentieth Century* that when Britain emerged as the leading centre of modern capitalism in the nineteenth century, it owed its power to the Industrial Revolution and to the development of the factory system, obviously, but also to its capacity to be the clearing house of finance capital, and to its world naval supremacy, and to its articulation of the ideology of free trade. These were the combined elements that made Britain the hegemonic centre of the modern capitalist system, and you say as well that one of the paradoxes of that system was that, despite having entered into a conservative Holy Alliance to defeat the French Revolution, Britain could nevertheless also operate as a guarantor of democracy, at least in Britain itself and in America and in some parts of Europe, and yet still be the most powerful world hegemonic power that had ever emerged until then. Thus, in your view, the British state can serve these dual and apparently contradictory functions — acting as a guarantor of democracy in some regions and as an instrument of world capitalist hegemony that was anything but democratic in other parts of the world. Could you talk to us a little bit about that dynamic, and maybe say something as well about what brought about the eventual decline of Britain's global position, given that it had for long enjoyed such unprecedented levels of global power and hegemony?

The interesting thing about these systemic cycles of accumulation that I have derived from Braudel is that they show that all periods of expansion, precisely because they are embedded in a particular state structure or container, are bound to come to an end. And the more successful they are, the more quickly they come to an end, because the very logic of the systemic cycle is a logic of over-accumulation. Over-accumulation means that capital accumulates so fast and so successfully that it cannot find a profitable investment in production and trade within the container that created it in the first instance and that, in turn, is why capital then goes into speculation. The whole process is driven by a simple business logic and that is why the US, which in its heyday was even more powerful than Britain, has also experienced this same kind of phenomenon.

Now, turning to your question and going back to Britain — the logic of over-accumulation is the same for all cycles, but the fact that the expansions are contained in institutional, physical containers means that at some point this institutional container acts as a brake on further expansion and brings down the rate of profit. At the same time one must note that there is not just an expansion on the level of scale — the point made earlier about a shift in modern capitalism from city-states to proto-nation-states to multinational states with an empire, and so on — but also a social and global deepening of the whole process as the agencies involved internalize more and more functions. The Genoese were probably the purest capitalists in world history because they externalized all functions; they even externalized protection by letting the Spanish and the Portuguese do all the dirty work of discovering new territories to expand into and fighting wars of conquest and inter-imperial rivalry, while the Genoese themselves specialized strictly in money-making. The Dutch later internalized the protection function or, put another way, the business of war-making was internalized by the Dutch in a way that it had not been done by the Genoese. Coming later still, the British went even further. They were not just a capitalist power like the Genoese or the Dutch, nor were they merely self-sufficient from the point of view of protection like the Dutch, they were also a territorialist imperialist power. By this I mean that the heyday of British industrial and financial power was coterminous with the establishment of a territorial empire in India, a region of the globe that was almost the size of Western Europe in terms of population and resources. This empire provided all kinds of military and financial manpower. Thus, imperial Britain fought its wars very cheaply because it fought them throughout what Karl Polyani has called the 'Hundred Years Peace'. However, the Hundred Years Peace was strictly a European phenomenon; throughout this period Britain was constantly at war elsewhere in the world, as the United States would later be during its own period of global hegemony.

For both hegemons, then, it was a case of peace at home, war overseas. However, one of the big differences between the United Kingdom and the United States was that the British wars were fought with the help of Indian troops. More precisely, the British wars in Africa and Asia were fought with the help of Indian troops and they were paid for by Indian taxpayers. The British Empire was started here in Ireland, but then the thing was reproduced on a huge scale in the Indian subcontinent. The empire, of course, was sustained for so long because the other distinguishing characteristic was that Britain was not just the financial entrepôt of the expanding economic system but also the manufacturing workshop of the world. Whatever industrial development there had been in Holland was built on its commercial supremacy, whereas in the case of Britain, commercial supremacy was reproduced on a large scale by development through the Industrial Revolution. And so Britain became the hub, not just of world finance, but also of industrial production, with raw material coming into Britain to be transformed into products that were then sold to the rest of the world — so that it became an industrial, financial and commercial entrepôt.

But when competition in the area of industrial goods started in earnest with competing industrial powers, most notably Germany and the US, Britain retreated more and more to its financial functions. However, it was not just that Britain's rivals followed in its footsteps and created competition in industrial production; they also followed Britain by taking up empire-building. Thus, India was profitable as a basis of British world hegemony only as long as there was no serious competition. But as soon as there was competition with the escalation of the armaments race, and when the cost of the protection of the empire soared, Britain was simply incapable of sustaining its position as global hegemon. The First and Second World Wars were the turning points that transformed India from an asset into a liability. It cost too much to protect. In sum, it was a combination of increasing competition in industrial production and imperial protection that undermined Britain's role as workshop of the world. And then the financial strains created by the world wars left Britain increasingly indebted to the United States. And that, in turn, allowed the US to become the next world hegemon.

Can I move us on to the contemporary moment? Two elements of your work are especially controversial. Firstly, many are arguing now that the United States has had its belle époque and that it is now suffering its crisis of hegemony, but you argue that its period as hegemonic superpower is already long over and that its role is now one of domination without hegemony. Secondly, and maybe even more controversially, you argue that China will be the dominant superpower of the twenty-first century and you take a relatively benign view of this in *Adam Smith in Beijing*. People may increasingly accept that China will be the economic and political powerhouse of the future, but many commentators tend to see this as a rather malign prospect. People on both the right and the left of the political spectrum will argue that Chinese world leadership presages a version of capitalism that may well be more red in tooth and claw than the American version, in the sense that, under its regime, labour will have even fewer protections and fewer rights, and also that China will oversee an international system even more authoritarian and neo-liberalist than the US-dominated one we now have. *Adam Smith in Beijing* takes issues with such views and offers quite a different prospect. Can you say more about that?

Yes. First, I think that the period of US and also national global hegemony is actually over and the Chinese probably know this is the case. In other words, the succession of hegemonies that I traced in *The Long Twentieth Century* is ending now with the US. The US tried to lengthen its term as global leader-state by having another American century and it failed miserably to do so. The Chinese, I think, are perfectly aware of the fact that there is no possibility that any single state will rule the world, even temporarily, by itself, as the British did in the nineteenth century and the US did in the second half of the twentieth century. So, the first point is that China is unlikely to become hegemonic in the sense that Britain or the US once were in the past.

Because it doesn't have the capacity to be so or because it doesn't have the will and has a different kind of historical memory and social vision?

The will? I don't believe in will, or the will may be there, but it's just that it's a question of pragmatism or realism. The Chinese ruling class is very pragmatic and realistic. It knows that it already has a hard time ruling China with its 1.3 billion people — the last thing it wants to do is to rule the world. This indeed reflects the path of Chinese history for centuries. Historically, the European states came into being through a long process of war-making. The history of the Chinese state is a totally different one. It may be the case that the Chinese state was brought into being by war-making two or three thousand years ago — I don't know, I don't know enough of Chinese history of that period to know exactly how the Chinese state originally came into being. But what has been true over the last two thousand years is that Chinese state-making was not driven by war but developed as a result of rebellions from inside and invasions from outside. For a very long time what the Chinese ruling élites feared was the steppes and the safeguarding of their frontiers. Invasions by external forces,

Two men overlooking the city of Peking (Beijing) as they stand on the Drum Tower. H. G. Ponting in Asia 1900–06. Photo: Popperfoto/Getty Images.

combined with rebellions from within, were the two big pressures that constituted the central governance problem for the Chinese state. And then, of course, the advances in navigation and armaments by the Europeans, as William McNeill put it, turned Eurasia upside down. Thereafter, with the arrival of the Europeans, the state frontier was replaced by the sea frontier — that's where the new barbarians were now coming from, the sea, and they were a far greater threat to China than the barbarians of the steppes.

So the Chinese problem has always been one of preventing the rebellions from inside and the invaders from outside from reducing China to a mess of warring states. Indeed, putting together all the periods of breakdown, some Chinese historians say that 'in the history of China there is one thousand years of chaos'. Today, the same concerns govern the Chinese outlook on the world. And that experience has important implications; it affects how the Chinese relate to the outside world. On the other hand, partly related to this, China has well-regulated relations with the other states of East Asia. In fact, a proper, well-developed interstate system in East Asia is in place, one that is much older that the European interstate system. The idea, or myth, that the nation-state was invented in Europe is ridiculous. Long before there was a single nation-state in Europe, Japan, Korea, China, Vietnam, Laos, Cambodia were all national states and they were also organized in an interstate system, with China at the centre. Compared to the European system, to the extent that it existed at all, this Asian interstate system was a peaceful one. Polanyi may say that the Hundred Years Peace in Europe was 'an unheard of phenomenon in the annals of European history', but he doesn't say that when the European great powers were at peace in Europe, they were at the same time constantly at war and conquering the world beyond Europe.

The East Asian system was different. Wars were very much less frequent. Indeed, were one to define things by the same standards that allow Polanyi to speak of a Hundred Years Peace in Europe, then one would have to say that Asia enjoyed a Three Hundred Years Peace, extending from the Japanese invasion of Korea in the 1590s to the Japanese invasion of Korea in the 1890s. And as far as China is concerned, by the same quantitative criteria that Polyani uses, one would have to say that it experienced a Five Hundred Years Peace. This is not, of course, because the Chinese are innately more peaceful, but paradoxically because the Chinese masses are anything but peaceful — they are indeed very rebellious. The point I'm making is that, structurally, the Chinese state was self-centred, and since it was constantly contending with the twin problems of invaders from the steppes and internal rebellion from its own peoples, it was obliged to manage international relations through an elaborate tribute system. This system simply consisted of emissaries coming to Beijing to pay their respects to the Emperor, although they frequently left with more gifts than they brought. Thus, the Chinese centre in effect bribed vassals to accept its dominance; it was a kind of cultural/economic hegemonic exercise. Contemporary China evolved, from the Ming to the Qing period, through this tradition.

The Western world system has come to resemble, on a much larger scale, what the East Asian interstate system once was, and now some kind of hybrid form is emerging and it is not yet clear what its eventual outcome is going to be. Now to your question: will it be democratic?

Some people would argue that what China portends for the future is simply neo-liberalism with a Chinese face ...

That has simply no foundation at all. What do we mean by 'neo-liberal'? If we mean the kind of doctrine that was born in Britain with Thatcher — the doctrine that there is no alternative to capitalist shock therapies and that everyone must compete against everybody else to attract capital — then this has simply not been taken up in China, as Joseph Stiglitz and others have argued. The Chinese have not adopted the shock therapies that were typical of the Washington Consensus and that were adopted in many Latin American states. The Chinese embrace of capitalism has been very gradual. They were very gradual in opening up their market, and, as I pointed out in *Adam Smith in Beijing*, they started to do so in the rural areas. Foreign capital came late — it jumped on a boat that was already moving and has come in on conditions that have been set by the Chinese. So there is very little evidence for the kind of neo-liberalist reading of recent Chinese development that has been put forward by some people. Indeed, analysts point out that the reforms that have succeeded in China failed in the former Soviet Union because Russia in the nineties took the shock therapy route ...

So what you contend is that, far from being a Chinese version of what has already happened either in Eastern Europe or indeed in South America, the Chinese policy since the 1980s has been to develop capitalism in a very controlled, gradualist manner?

Yes. That's not my argument, though, that's Joseph Stiglitz's thesis, one with which I entirely agree. But I go further. My case is not that had others followed the same gradualist policies of the Chinese then they too would have had the same success. Gradualism was a necessary condition for Chinese success, and gradualism was, among other things, what Adam Smith had advocated in his work. Adam Smith would have been appalled by the present Washington Consensus and by the neo-liberal doctrine of these shock therapies — they would have been totally alien to him. But the success of the Chinese is not just due to the fact that they did not follow the prescriptions of the Washington Consensus but because they built on two traditions. One was the Chinese revolutionary tradition. If one looks statistically at whatever data we have, China's big advances in terms of basic welfare indices — life expectancy, adult literacy, and all the basic welfare indicators — were won before the reforms of the 1980s. Thus, we can say that the reforms really only built on the welfare successes of the revolutionary tradition. The revolutionary tradition itself was, from certain points of view, both a negation and also a continuation of an even older Chinese relation, which is the tradition of the welfare state.

Adam Smith claimed that the Chinese national market equalled the combined national markets of all the European countries. The Chinese possessed a very advanced market system, but it was not a capitalist system in the sense that we know it in the West; in China the capitalists were kept subordinate to the welfare needs and purposes of the state. They were kept subordinate precisely because of the things I said earlier — namely, that in order to hold that kind of state together, threatened as it was by a rebellious domestic population and by invaders always ready to overwhelm it, the Chinese leadership had to regulate the capitalists very carefully. To shore up its legitimacy, the Qing, who were invaders themselves, redistributed land to the peasantry. So the redistribution of land to the peasantry by the Communists in the last century had already a precedent under the Qing in the eighteenth century. The Chinese had also perfected a granary system, whereby they were able to alleviate the shortages of certain periods with the abundance of others. With this system, they were able to move grain around the empire to keep prices under control. Thus, eighteenth-century China became a model for a faction of the European intelligentsia — Leibniz, Voltaire, Kant and others took China as a model because it was peaceful, it was a kind of a welfare state, though it was autocratic and not a democracy.

Can I return to the question of class and democracy here again because you've mentioned the rebelliousness of the Chinese peasantry several times. Some leftist critics would argue that your work struggles to accommodate class struggle. Some would argue that this is true of world systems theory generally, as well as of your own work more particularly; they would say that *The Long Twentieth Century* is an account of the competitive rivalries and the periods of succession when control of the world system passes between the great hegemonic states, but that these states are the only real actors in your work and that class struggles are assigned remarkably little historical agency. How do you respond to such critics? More precisely, what do you say, firstly, to the question of class, and, secondly, is it possible to imagine even a tightly-controlled, gradualist development of capitalist accumulation in China that won't inevitably produce a middle class — a development that would obviously be a major rupture with the past and which would thus represent a break not only with the recent Communist revolutionary tradition but also with the earlier Chinese state traditions, as you describe them?

On the class issue, the interesting thing is that my original project of *The Long Twentieth Century* was actually a class-based project. In comparing these three systemic capitalist crises, or depressions, I was starting from a situation where working-class power was market-based, to a situation in the 1930s where the market-based power had been undermined, to one where working-class power was re-emerging in the new conditions of the later twentieth century. This research was published in a book by Samir Amin, Andre Gunder Frank, Immanuel Wallerstein and myself, *Transforming the Revolution* [1990]. A shorter version, showing the

CCTV headquarters building being built in downtown Beijing on August 2, 2008 ahead of the Beijing 2008 Olympic Games. Photo: GOH CHAI HIN/AFP/ Getty Images.

strengths and weaknesses of the Marxist analysis of the end of bourgeois rule, was also published in the *New Left Review* [January–February, 1990], titled 'Marxist Century, American Century: The Making and Remaking of the World Labour Movement'. So an account of how class struggle underlay the transformations in the long twentieth century was centrally embedded in my work.

The problem arises, however, when you discover that this thing we call capitalism has been around 500–600 years, and has been characterized by regular switches from material to financial expansion — in all honesty, there is no way that such switches can be attributed regularly to the class struggle. Where is the evidence for this? When I returned to Italy from Africa in the 1970s I was very workerist and I got involved in the formation of a Gramscian group that was involved with the workers' struggle in the factories. In fact, in the chapter in which I criticize Brenner [see *Adam Smith in Beijing*, Chapter 5], I argue that in the switch of the 1970s, the workers' struggle did play a role, whereas Brenner says it did not. However, the fact that workers played a role in that particular switch does not mean that they did it in all the other earlier switches. In fact there is no evidence that the workers played a role in the earlier switches. So, if you try to put the class struggle everywhere in the long twentieth century, you don't see how class relations have changed over time and have come to influence the more recent cycles much more than they ever did in earlier periods. In her chapter on the social origins of the hegemonic crisis and cycles in *Chaos and Governance in the Modern World System*, Beverly Silver analyses how hegemonic transitions were influenced differently by different kinds of class struggle.

One thing that I took from Braudel is that the chief characteristic of capitalism is its adaptability. Capitalism changes continually. Slavery was absolutely essential for seventeenth- and eighteenth-century capitalism, but capitalism survived, and in some ways even promoted, the abolition of slavery. Then capitalism depended on colonialism and imperialism to a much greater extent than it had done before, and so it seemed to many that capitalism could not survive the abolition of colonialism. But it did survive colonialism; it once again transformed itself. Capitalism continually transforms itself — economically and socially, and so on — and therefore, to go back to your earlier question, I'm pretty agnostic and quite frankly don't care whether people will want to call the system that emerges in the twenty-first century capitalist, socialist, or whatever. The point is that it's going to be more egalitarian than what we've had thus far. One of the problems we have with inequality is how to measure it. There are a lot of disputes about whether inequality has increased or decreased, but two things are for sure: 'between country' inequalities are much greater, twice as great at least, as 'within country' inequalities. Now, if we are for equality, in a cosmopolitan or international sense, it's clear that we have to give priority to at least the reduction, if not the elimination, of 'between country' inequalities. And this leads me to the second point: if there has been any reduction at all over the last twenty-five years in total inequalities in 'between country' inequality in the world, then this has been almost exclusively due to the rapid rise of China. In other words — and this is a key point — China has had a contradictory influence on world inequalities. On the one hand, inequality within China has increased tremendously since the 1980s reforms. That is to say, China has contributed to an increase in 'within country' inequality. However, China has also reduced 'between country' inequality, even though it was and still is a very poor country — that's the other important thing to bear in mind. Statistically, all the evidence suggests that any overall reduction in global inequalities — if there has actually been any — has been due to China. If you take China out of the equation, not to mention if you take India out of it, then the last twenty-five or thirty years have been an absolute disaster in terms of inequality. But, according to the World Bank, 400 million people have been lifted out of poverty in China over that period — that's equivalent to the population of sub-Saharan Africa. Now, I simply do not understand my socialist friends who just ignore this basic fact and look at the undoubtedly huge increase in internal inequalities, in exploitation, and so on. Even if China continues to emerge at a slower rate — and I'm sure it's going to go through a major crisis — the ascent of China — and of India, albeit to a much lesser extent — is nonetheless dramatically changing the global picture from the point of view of inequality. Whether the Chinese future will be called capitalism or socialism, I don't know, but in changing some of the most fundamental and biggest inequalities, the 'between country' ones, then China has had a powerful equalizing effect on the world system.

And then you have, of course, the big dispute about democracy and what does it mean to have democracy in China. Now, for one thing, the Chinese revolutionary tradition had its own form of democracy, which had in many ways continued the best traditions of government in earlier periods. The Chinese Communist Party was not a Leninist vanguard party; it did not see its role as one of giving the line or leading the masses; it claimed it would learn from the masses. This was obviously mere rhetoric in many ways, but there is also an element of truth to it and without that element there was no way that the Communists could have come to power or have then consolidated their power. According to Stiglitz and other World Bank officials, this tradition still exists much more in China than in a democratic country like India. He argues that more consultation takes place between different levels of Chinese society when there is a change in plan, much more so than in a bureaucratically run democracy.

I'm not defending the Chinese here, because being of bourgeois origins, and being what I am, if I were asked if I would prefer to be born in China or in India — which in my view is the greatest democracy that has ever existed, no question about that — my choice would certainly be India. I challenge you to identify any Western state that has a parliamentary democracy functioning as well as it has done in India for such a long time, one with the ethnic diversity and with the enormous poverty of India. No other democracy has matched that level of challenge and survived it. India is the greatest democracy in world history, but it is a poor country. China, clearly, is not a parliamentary democracy and it doesn't have basic freedoms;

to these, indeed, I do get attached. The point I'm trying to make is that I, as a bourgeois attached to bourgeois freedoms, given the choice, would certainly prefer to be born in India. However, I'm quite convinced that if any cosmopolitan peasant, if such a thing exists, were asked the same question, that peasant would say that he or she would prefer to be born in China rather than in India. Indeed, you just have to have any contact with Chinese or Indian peasants of similar conditions to see what I mean. In other words, the Chinese revolution not only secured the peasant's access to land but has also uplifted the peasant masses in terms of literacy, in terms of health, and so on. And that actually is the strength of the Chinese chain — the strength of that chain is not cheap labour, cheap labour may be had all over the world. The strength of the Chinese chain is that it's cheap labour of extremely high quality — quality of health, education, everything. We have our kinds of democracy, ones that come out of Western tradition, but I think it would be madness to think that China should just adopt or emulate these Western forms. It may be true that it has already begun to introduce elections at local level — but those are not very substantial things.

Furthermore, the whole issue of democracy, of what it means, is up for grabs with the emergence of a reality like China. You also mentioned the issues of workers' rights and unions. Quite frankly, I don't see any difference between the US unions and the Chinese unions. If anything, the Chinese unions are probably better. And in any case, I don't think that unions make movements; I think that movements make unions. Isn't this the experience of the US itself? It was not the AFL [American Federation of Labor] that made the big struggles in the US in the thirties, but rather that the big struggles in the thirties made the Congress of Industrial Organizations that then formed the movement. So the unions are made by the struggles and not vice versa. From this point of view, I'm like Bakunin and Kraus — bit of an anarchist, kind of. But the point is that over the last fifteen years very few countries — probably South Africa would be one — have experienced a level of struggle comparable to China's, and I think that in recent years, from the nineties forward, the rate of change has escalated to such an extent and the leadership has so changed its policies— that's where I agree also with you — that if things continue on this path, there will be the formation of a Chinese middle class, and after that, it's very hard to tell what kind of political institutions will emerge.

What about the whole question of Chinese nationalism? Don't both declining hegemonic powers (like Britain in the early twentieth century, or the US currently, if you are right) or emerging hegemonic powers (as you conceive China to be) usually develop very assertive, even aggressive and dangerous forms of nationalism?

We have to draw some kind of distinction between the nationalism of the rich and powerful, on the one side, and the nationalism of the poor and powerless, on the other. Clearly there is a grey area in between. But I live in the United States and the United States is actually one of the countries where nationalism is strongest, taking the form of national chauvinism. Left-wing people like to draw a distinction between nationalism and patriotism, one in which patriotism is good and nationalism is bad. I'm always a bit confused about this: why is one good, the other bad? The problem in any case is that in China there is also a nationalism that they call patriotism. In the US the force of so-called patriotism is such that it is very difficult to say in public very basic truths that would in fact be patriotic and that would help the United States. For example, one cannot say in the US that, in terms of results, the all-powerful US army is actually pretty pathetic. You can't say a thing like this in public. You may say it in a graduate seminar because graduate students are a particular kind of group, but already with undergraduates you are in trouble if you say a thing like this. Or maybe you can say it but only after a lot of careful preliminaries and qualifiers. But it is true: the US has hardly won any wars by itself. In other words, it won the First and Second World Wars because in the First World War the Europeans were shooting each other, and in the Second, the Red Army broke the back of the Wehrmacht. On each occasion the US came in at the last minute and managed to dictate the terms of the peace because it had supplied the warring European states with goods; the biggest increases in US GNP occurred during the First and Second World Wars. Later, the Korean War was a draw, and the Vietnam War was a defeat. Then the US army stopped fighting wars directly and fought wars only by proxy — except, of course, against pathetically weak little countries like Panama and Grenada. The record is ridiculously bad. And now the neo-conservatives under Bush say: 'We have to do something with this army because otherwise we lose credibility'.

Thatcher led the way for Reagan, not only in economic but also in military terms. In the war in the Malvinas, or what they also call the Falklands War, Thatcher showed the US what to do. She basically told them: 'Don't try to go in a room and battle it out. Find an enemy on a barren island or landscape and bomb them out — that's the idea, because we have this advantage, we can just bomb them out'. Since then, US strategy has been based on how to drag some tinpot Third World dictators or whatever onto terrain that suited the US, rather than allowing the US to be dragged onto their terrain. This, in essence, was the basis of the Colin Powell doctrine, one that meant that the US did not press on into Iraq after it had secured Kuwait in the First Gulf War, because you just don't go onto the enemy's terrain. But of course, then the neo-conservatives came along and said: 'Yeah, but if we don't go onto their terrain, we don't have credibility. We have this huge army and we have to show its usefulness'. So, they went into Iraq and straight into another disaster. But US patriotism being what it is, you cannot say this in public; there is no freedom of speech, not because the police will arrest you — in fact, when the police are repressive it's easier, you have more freedom. As Gramsci said, it's when every citizen is a policeman that you cannot say certain things. Yet it would help the United States a lot if these things could be said.

And in China?

In China you have the same kind of patriotic thing. In the same 150 years that the US emerged as a great state — by practising genocide against the Native American Indians and by conquering the continent to the Pacific, and then by going on to become a would-be global state with bases all over the world — China went from being a comparatively wealthy and well-administered society to disaster. After the Opium Wars it suffered a hundred years of true devastation, enduring all kinds of humiliation — warlord anarchy, Japanese invasions, civil war — until the Communist regime was established. But by then China had become the poorest country in the world, much poorer even than Africa. Ever since the Communists took power, the Chinese have tried to pull themselves together, and one needs to understand Chinese nationalism, and its difference to US nationalism, in this context. Personally, I don't like any nation; in fact, I still have my Italian passport and I never became an American citizen for one reason only — namely, because Italy is the only country I know for which one cannot feel patriotic. Italy is a joke of a country; it is certainly not a serious country; that's why it is okay to be Italian, because you are vaccinated and inoculated against patriotism and nationalism and everything else. Therefore, because you cannot be patriotic in Italy, you can be a cosmopolitan and an internationalist. But having said that, and to answer your question, one always has to discriminate between different forms of nationalism and it is very difficult to evaluate Chinese nationalism closely because it is hard to tell how much of our fears of it are really only projections of the dreadful history of Europe's nationalist past onto China's future.

That's a real problem.

How do you think global warming or the worsening ecological crisis will impact upon the future of the world system?

With regards to China? Yes, that's the big question. What is pretty obvious, even though it is not always clear to the Chinese leadership or masses, is that China cannot develop in the same way that the United States did, with that kind of energy, intensity, pollution and so on. The Chinese will simply choke themselves and everybody else to death if they do. The question is, how can this be avoided?

I went to China at the time of the Cultural Revolution [1966–76] and then more recently after the reforms had taken place. The thing that struck me most even during the Cultural Revolution was that there were no birds — the landscape was pretty stark, but at least then there were no cars; instead there were bicycles. I thought that this mode of transport was one of the bases of China's competitive advantage, because bicycles are good for your health and they don't pollute. Later, I started to notice that there were more and more cars and that the bicycles were being squeezed into smaller and smaller traffic-lanes to accommodate them. I've always told my Chinese friends: 'You are crazy. You went to the wrong city to see the modernity you want. You went to Los Angeles; you should have gone to Amsterdam'. But they didn't go to Amsterdam. Now they are beginning to realize that they adopted the wrong kind of modernity and they are beginning to plant trees and so on.

One of the big problems as far as ecology is concerned is that people everywhere think that China is governed by a very controlling dictatorship but, in fact, the top, I think, doesn't control much. They sent a middle cadre into business, and now they don't control them any more. So even when they want to change things, it's a big problem. It's a pretty anarchic kind of situation. Of course, the market may help now that everybody is worried about the end of oil and the escalation of prices in the US. Can you imagine paying $4 for a gallon of gas in the US? There, this is seen as a national tragedy. I'm cheering for gas to go to $10 or $20, because that's the only way people seem to understand that they have to change. Whether such change will come through the market or through planning, or whether it comes at all, is very hard to gauge right now. But certainly the emergence of China and India as economic powers brings into the open and aggravates a contradiction that has been there all the time. The contradiction it highlights, even though China and India are still relatively poor societies, is that development as we have known it in the West was sustainable only as long as a minority of the world's population enjoyed it. *Adam Smith in Beijing* ends with this note: it asks, who sets the rules for this crisis?

LUKE GIBBONS: This *is* a historical question. One of the breakthroughs in world systems theory was that it managed to challenge evolutionary versions of capitalism and modernity and development, particularly versions that arranged everything in history in terms of sequences that ran from pre-capitalist and pre-modern to modernity and then on to postmodernity. The question of what is internal to capitalist modernity or what is outside of or predates such modernity comes up a lot in discussions about Ireland. The question I'm interested in here, though, is the one of slavery. To what extent was slavery, the slave mode of production, integral to modern capitalist development or only a residue of some earlier mode of production? Some historians argue that, far from being an archaic residue from the past, slavery was one of the most efficient, brutal and productive ways of producing wealth that the world has known. They would also argue that it was abolished because some more productive way of producing wealth was discovered. My question, then, goes back to Joe Cleary's question earlier as to whether new forms of capitalism that may emerge in the twenty-first century might not be more regressive than earlier versions of capitalism. Since

capitalism as a system does not guarantee workers' rights, as the role of slavery in capitalism shows, is there a real possibility that capitalism in the future may be more, not less, draconian than what we have already known in the past?

That's a difficult question, with many answers. But, firstly, slavery was definitely inside and integral to the capitalist system, not an anachronism. The textile industry in Manchester could not have prospered as it did without slave-grown cotton in the United States; and plantation-grown cotton in the US displaced many competitors. That's also why I prefer to define capitalism as a mode of accumulation and rule rather than one of production only. Capitalism became a mode of production in the way we understand it now only very late in the day, with the arrival of the Industrial Revolution. But even if we say slavery was internal and integral to capitalism, this does not mean that slavery actually made a full 'return to history', except in relatively marginal forms. Thus, however much I hate the word 'progress', we can still observe some progress. I think that capitalism without slavery is better than capitalism with slavery. I think that capitalism without colonialism is better than capitalism with colonialism. And I think that a version of capitalism that enables the vast majority of humanity to have a living wage is better than the capitalism that we know today that doesn't do that, one that excludes the majority of the world population from a living wage.

Perhaps that's where the class struggle comes into the picture. As the capitalist system has extended itself across the world spatially, and as it has deepened its grip on the world functionally, then the whole global population comes within its compass and has to come up with solutions. I don't just mean everyone sitting down solving intellectual problems in committees or of a world government setting universal policies or whatever; what I am referring to is the global extension of class struggles. It was the rebellions of the slaves that eventually did away with slavery — not everywhere, but as a tendency. Other agencies had to intervene in that process; and the process by which slavery was abolished was not the same in the Caribbean as in Brazil or the US. However, slavery was ended as an overall tendency not so much because it had become inefficient — after all, how efficiency is defined depends on the human subjects who are involved in these processes — but because the anti-slavery struggles made it hard to manage and even unworkable. Likewise, colonialism came to an end not because it was inefficient but because the competition among the Western imperialist powers created an opening for what has been called the 'revolt against the West'; this has constituted a major transformation in the world system. So, these major anti-systemic rebellions of various kinds that occur at different times in history do have real consequences.

There are all kinds of struggles going on today. We don't know yet what will be the defining struggle of the many present struggles. But struggles are the guarantee that change will continue. An ecological disaster remains a real possibility, and even today we observe such disasters all over the world, including China. But I also think that the fundamental unruliness and rebelliousness of the Chinese people is a guarantee — or as near to a guarantee as history offers — that we are not going to have a regression to a more authoritarian version of capitalism. What will emerge in the future? This is up for grabs.

REVIEWS

Smugglers on the Irish Coast (1808), Julius Ceasar Ibbeston, oil on canvas. ©Tate, London, 2009

The Whole People of Ireland?

Ian McBride

Divided Kingdom: Ireland 1630–1800
S. J. Connolly
Oxford: Oxford University Press, 2008
xiv + 519 pages. ISBN 978-0-19-954347-2

Is it possible to write the history of Ireland's Protestant Ascendancy from the bottom up? From the angle of the dispossessed and the disadvantaged, of those sometimes described, in that rich Old Testament phrase, as hewers of wood and drawers of water? Perhaps 60 per cent of the island's population lived at subsistence level in the eighteenth century. They were the subjects of the grotesque computations of Swift's *A Modest Proposal* (1729), the outstanding literary product of the Ascendancy, in which Swift imagined the ragged poor being fattened and slaughtered for the tables of the Irish gentry. In Ascendancy Ireland, of course, differences of wealth and status were entangled with religious and ethnic categories, even if they did not coincide neatly. Protestantism, as embodied by the established church, enjoyed a close relationship with property. In approaching Ascendancy Ireland from the perspective of the excluded, then, I am thinking not just of the lower orders but of the Catholic population in general: those who were affected in some way by the Penal Laws, and whose degradation, Edmund Burke claimed, characterized the 'interior history' of Ireland, a history denied in the propaganda of its Protestant chroniclers.

In the multi-volume, semi-official *New History of Ireland* (1986), the long eighteenth century remained the 'Protestant Century', with four-fifths of the population accorded minor roles. Its seasoned contributors, like their British counterparts, began with the state and its institutions, working through the documents generated by parliamentary debates, magistrates' reports and pamphlet wars. Catholics were often the subject matter of such sources but hardly ever their authors. This 'top-down' direction of Irish historiography was consequently vulnerable to attack, not only by practitioners of 'history from below', but by scholars who regarded the eighteenth-century constitution as a colonial imposition. Why the primacy of high politics and constitutional development should have proved so enduring in Ireland is a question subject to conspiracy theories and canards. The *New History* team, with their claims to impartiality and their 'scientific' research techniques, have sometimes been accused of airbrushing the atrocities of colonialism in order to distance the Dublin establishment from the unfinished business of the IRA in Belfast and Derry. Such allegations rest on frustratingly indiscriminate readings of their work.

More pertinent, perhaps, are the limitations of documentary evidence. It is true, for example, that the legal records blown up in the Four Courts in 1922 are simply irreplaceable. Consequently, W. P. Burke's otherwise outdated classic, *Irish Priests in the Penal Times* (1914), remains the most comprehensive source of information on the local enforcement of anti-Catholic legislation. The recent successes of the Old Bailey Proceedings project, which has made almost 100,000 criminal trials available on the web, remind us of just how much has been irretrievably lost. Even this immense disadvantage can be overstated, however. Irish historians have made creative use of fragmentary legal documents, press reports and gallows speeches to argue, for example, that there was no systematic discrimination against Catholics in the criminal justice system, and that violent crime in Ireland was not in general politically motivated.

Finally, it is sometimes suggested that the persistent imbalance in Irish historiography can be explained by the reluctance or inability of most historians to engage with Gaelic sources. Irish was the language spoken by the majority of the island's inhabitants before the Act of Union (1801), but only a tiny proportion of that majority wrote in the language. Those that did left a substantial amount of verse, often touching on social and political issues, and useful prose tracts. However, the archive has limitations: there are no Irish-language newspapers, pamphlets, or handbills, and almost no memoirs or correspondence, while the diocesan reports of Catholic bishops were written in Latin, Italian or French. One of the many areas in which Sean Connolly's *Divided Kingdom: Ireland 1630–1800* (2008) improves upon all previous accounts is in its regional survey of linguistic change — a central, if neglected feature of this period. Ironically, the erosion of Gaelic was not the conscious achievement of the Protestant state: a failed bill introduced in 1697 to suppress Irish was never repeated. If anything, the determining factor in anglicizing Ireland was the hostility of the Catholic Church towards a culture already regarded as backward. Although the rather mysterious observation recurred that young priests 'forgot' their Irish while training at continental seminaries, they had no problem remembering their English. The key difficulty was the failure to establish a standardized form of Gaelic in print, a telling contrast with Welsh or Breton. In 1768 Bishop John O'Brien's *Focalóir gaoidhilge-sax-bhéarla; or An Irish–English Dictionary* appeared in Paris, sometimes instanced as an example of the commitment of the [Irish] Catholic hierarchy to its mother tongue. But a reading of O'Brien's lengthy introduction and notes (all in English) immediately suggests that the volume was intended as an intervention in the antiquarian debates surrounding Macpherson's *Ossian*, while the words selected confirm his preoccupation with classical 'Iberno-Celtic' rather than colloquial Irish. By the 1760s, in any case, it was too late: the link between literacy and anglicization, reinforced by the massive influence of London as a centre of print culture, was firmly established.

Divided Kingdom, the first major synthesis on this period in two decades since David Dickson's *New Foundations* (1987), stretches all the way from the Wars of the Three Kingdoms to the French Revolution and the 1798 rebellion. The author is almost alone in this field in combining exact archival scholarship with the imagination and audacity necessary to construct large-scale interpretative statements. His previous work demonstrates intellectual curiosity across a range of sub-disciplines, including the sociology of religion, political ideas, social unrest, gender and sexuality. Connolly is probably best known, however, for the *ancien régime* thesis elaborated in his *Religion, Law and Power: The Making of Protestant Ireland 1660–1760* (1992). There he argued that the religious inequalities of Ascendancy Ireland must be viewed within the wider context of a hierarchical, pre-industrial society, dominated by a landed élite and not so very different from its European counterparts. In a polity based on property rather than numbers, the apparent denial of political rights to the majority under the Penal Laws constituted a purely hypothetical disability. Or, to put the matter counterfactually, a Jacobite victory at the Boyne would have made little difference to the political or social position of the Catholic trader or tenant-farmer of the eighteenth century, and none at all to the common people so beloved of nationalist historiography.

Religion, Law and Power drew upon a generation of scholars whose work would nowadays be recognized as 'revisionist' — either in the English sense (it questioned the narratives and certitudes generated by Whig or Marxist positions), in the Irish sense (it rejected the moralizing nationalism that underpinned Irish independence), or both. The key arguments are all reproduced in *Divided Kingdom*: that electoral and parliamentary success demanded not just patronage but skilful diplomacy; that relationships between London and Dublin, like those between borough proprietor and freeholder, were characterized by reciprocity rather than coercion; that landlord–tenant relations were relatively harmonious; that successive waves of agrarian rebels — the Whiteboys and similar oath-bound movements — were defensive reactions to market forces rather than a rejection of the social order rooted in the Cromwellian and Williamite settlements. On this latter point, Connolly now adds demurely that the persistence of agrarian violence over half a century indicates 'a deficiency either in channels of communication or in levels of mutual comprehension between rulers and ruled'.[1] But such misunderstandings are not a major concern of the book, except insofar as they animate the negative stereotype with which Connolly implicitly contends whenever he tells us that something 'is easily overestimated' or 'more complex' than generally acknowledged.

For much of the postwar period, revisionist historians of Ireland directed their energies in concentrated bursts of analytical fire. Their muted iconoclasm was not translated into overarching narratives; in fact, overarching narratives were part of what they were against. One development that helped give Connolly's work its more ambitious, hard-edged qualities was the cultural debate of the late 1980s, dramatically accelerated by the impact of postcolonial theory on Irish studies. While the history professors, often trained at Cambridge or London, stuck to the constitutional framework traditional to the discipline, there was a persistent counter-history, dating back to Daniel Corkery's study of Munster poets, *The Hidden Ireland* (1924), and echoed by Irish-language specialists. (A further complication was that the Catholic Church sponsored its own in-house journals, dedicated to the valuable,

1 S. J. Connolly, *Divided Kingdom: Ireland 1630–1800* (Oxford, 2008), 303.

if pedestrian, translation of records from Rome, Paris and Louvain.) Even the *New History of Ireland* included chapters on Gaelic literature and the arts, appropriately sealed off from the main narrative: if Catholics possessed a 'hidden' culture of their own, they apparently left no imprint on *politics*, formally conceived, or on the conventional periodization adopted by historians.

By the 1990s, however, the postcolonialists were promoting a new, explicit counter-history, one which denied the epistemological premises upon which the whole historiography had been founded. Corkery's picture of two antagonistic Irelands — the world of the Gaelic underclass and the cottier's cabin abruptly juxtaposed against that of the Big House — had long been discredited: rural Ireland possessed an increasingly complex social hierarchy of large and small tenant-farmers, dairymen, artisans, cottiers and labourers. Yet postcolonial readings generally reverted to a flattened-out picture of Irish society, split into monolithic blocs of propertied dominators and peasant resisters. This drastic binarism greatly oversimplifies the range of political commitments and compromises pursued in Ascendancy Ireland, forcing us to discard the many individuals and groups who cannot be neatly stacked into these opposing piles. Connolly makes the point vigorously in his nicely deflationary account of the 1798 rebellion (which slices the number of fatalities to a third of the conventional 30,000): the '98 was a messy, many-sided civil war, in which large numbers of Protestants, Catholics and Dissenters united to *preserve* the English connection.

Connolly's *ancien régime* terminology was predictably characterized in some quarters as an attempt to normalize a warped society, to exonerate the Protestant Ascendancy from well-founded accusations of brutality and exploitation. Like all rich and original works of historical scholarship, it is better viewed as a much more sophisticated product, in which the personality of the historian, inevitably formed by particular intellectual and social experiences, intersects with historiographical traditions and influences (an unholy alliance, in this case, of E. P. Thompson and J. C. D. Clark), with contemporary attitudes to the past, both academic and popular, and with an expanding corpus of primary material. *Religion, Law and Power* is still the most innovative and provocative conceptualization of Irish social relations in the century after Cromwell. There, as in Connolly's latest book, the argument is both tightly forensic and finely textured: every paragraph combines lively accessibility with the sort of freshness and arresting detail that will make the specialist pause. But Connolly also left a number of disconcerting challenges for anyone courageous enough to hazard a new overview of the period. First, could the notion of an Irish *ancien régime* be developed comparatively? Other European societies certainly existed in which rulers and ruled were divided by language or ethnicity; but how far, for example, could the Catholic middle classes usefully be compared to the Utraquists of Bohemia, or the Gaelic peasantry with the Czech underclass? Secondly, if 1798 was not the natural outworking of inbuilt colonial tensions, as Connolly argued, where did all that combustible material come from? And above all, was it possible to reconstruct the world of the Catholic majority with the same subtlety with which Connolly approached the Protestant élite?

Readers turning to *Divided Kingdom* for answers to these questions will be puzzled. Previously a trenchant critic of his peers and predecessors, Connolly has been forced by the customary poise of the Oxford general survey to step back from the historiographical fray, confining his disagreements to a few discreet footnotes. The only overarching theme, flagged briefly in the prologue and epilogue, is that 'of the fluid and contingent, of identities made

W. 3. R. M. 2.

DIEU ET MON DROIT

BY THE

Lords Justices of Ireland,

A PROCLAMATION.

SYDNEY. THO. CONINGSBY.

Whereas several Irish Papists within this Kingdom, notwithstanding the Grace and Favour extended to them by Their Majesties gracious Declaration, and the protection they enjoyed under Their Government, have most ungratefully relapsed into their former Rebellious courses, and whilst they feignedly pretended to pay Allegiance unto Their Majesties, have most Treacherously Aided and Assisted Their Majesties Enemies, not only by giving them intelligence, but also by assembling themselves in great numbers to terrify, plunder and destroy Their Majesties good Protestant Subjects. We do therefore for the prevention of the like evils for the time to come, and for the greater security of their Majesties good Subjects, and the peace of this Kingdom, strictly charge and command all persons of the Popish Religion within this Kingdom, upon pain of Imprisonment That they do not without Special Lycence from Us, or the General of Their Majesties Forces, or from some one of Their Majesties Justices of Peace of this Kingdom, Depart, or Travel out of the Parish where they respectively inhabit or dwell, unless to the Market Town next to such their dwelling, and upon Market-days, except in Cities or great Towns, and there not to go out of the Liberties and Precincts of such Cities and Towns, unless to the next Market as aforesaid. Excepting also that the foresaid Irish Papists may, during the time of this present Harvest, for their lawful and necessary occasions, travel three miles beyond the Parish in which they dwell, and no farther: And if they shall presume to act contrary hereunto, We do hereby strictly Charge and Command all Magistrates, Constables, Petty-Constables, and other Their Majesties good Subjects, to Arrest the Offenders, and to bring them before the next Justice of Peace, who is hereby required to commit them to safe custody, as persons who contemn the Royal Authority, and design the disturbance of the Peace of this Kingdom. And all Justices of Peace are commanded to forbear Bayling any person so committed, until they have given Us an account

'By the Lords Justices of Ireland, a Proclamation, Dublin'. Printed by Andrew Crook, assignee of Benj. Tooke, printer to the King and Queens Most Excellent Majesties, and reprinted at London for him, 1690. Courtesy of Beinecke Rare Book and Manuscript Library. A proclamation confining Irish papists to their own parishes, September 18, 1690

and remade against an uncertain and sometimes dangerous background'.[2] Rather than develop this uncontroversial notion, however, the author is keener to reiterate and defend his previous positions, notably on the Penal Laws. In *Religion, Law and Power* Connolly contended that this clutter of statutes, enacted over several decades, reveals no consistent or coherent strategy for tackling religious division. The combination of a complex procedure for initiating and amending legislation, involving London as well as Dublin, certainly makes it difficult to reconstruct the intentions behind any single bill. It is clear enough that the general intention behind the popery laws (as they were known to contemporaries) was to destroy the military and political threat posed by Catholic Ireland, to eliminate the Catholic hierarchy and eventually the priesthood, and subsequently to destroy the landed base of the Catholic ruling class. Nevertheless, Connolly's theme, once again, is the confused chronology of anti-Catholic legislation and the avowed absence of any coherent policy; and he repeats his view that the penal code was simply the 'by-product' of the constitutional shifts centred on a newly assertive Dublin parliament.

This insistent note, now stripped of its polemical context, may seem perverse to the uninitiated reader. The popery laws were not so much a by-product of parliamentary government in Dublin as its fundamental underpinning: as Connolly himself shows, the bargaining process whereby MPs traded financial co-operation in exchange for anti-Catholic measures was quite explicit. Of course, the legislative onslaught demonstrates confused and impractical attitudes to Catholic resilience. By the 1720s it had even produced a core of disillusioned Anglican bishops who attempted to block penal bills in the House of Lords. Heavyweight Whigs such as Archbishop King of Dublin and Archbishop Synge of Tuam contrasted parliament's ingenuity in squeezing Catholic landowners with its failure, session after session, to back practical measures for promoting clerical residence and improving the maintenance of Anglican curates. Perhaps, King worried, there was something in the complaint that the legal disabilities imposed upon Catholics were designed not so much to convert them as to control a large pool of slave labour. But such principled reservations, highlighted by Connolly, did nothing to halt the dismantling of Catholic estates. No less problematic is Connolly's injunction that we must disaggregate the penal code into its component parts, thus robbing the legislation of its full, distinctly aggregative significance. Individual bills blended restrictions on the inheritance of property with attempts to choke off the supply of priests; the legislation generated its own momentum as each new statute sought to close the loopholes left by the last; and from the 1760s every proposed reform, however modest, was bitterly opposed as the thin edge of a very menacing wedge.

The problem is not that Connolly's characterization of the penal code as a muddle is incorrect; but rather that this overriding focus obscures the gravity of the determined campaign to destroy popery in the decades after 1690. Similarly, few would argue with Connolly's verdict that Catholics, for most of the penal era, were subject to 'multiple petty tyrannies' rather than uniform repression; but he neglects to investigate the cumulative impact of these routine aggravations. From the 1720s the practice of the Catholic religion was seldom disrupted, but always exercised with circumspection. In contrast to the parish churches of the Anglican establishment, situated on principal streets with large graveyards, 'popish' mass-houses were usually tucked away on narrow lanes in overcrowded residential areas. Catholic landed families were able to cheat the law by a variety of strategies, including nominal conversions, reliance on trustees, and the friendly legal action known as the 'collusive discovery' which enabled them to secure landed property against potential predators.

2 Connolly, *Divided Kingdom*, 3

There was an expanding shadow-gentry of substantial Catholic leaseholders and middlemen, whose younger sons made their way as army officers (on the Continent), as wholesale merchants, traders, physicians and priests. But Catholic petitioners in 1739 claimed that two-thirds of the legal business in Dublin consisted of 'discovery' cases: the conditions of life under the Penal Laws, while seldom very oppressive, were nevertheless marked by insecurity.

The collusive discovery and the backstreet chapel are more appropriate emblems of the penal era than the popular image of redcoats surprising a priest at an open-air mass. This was a world in which Catholics were permitted to survive, and increasingly to prosper, so long as there was no overt challenge to Protestant Ascendancy. Despite the impact of confiscation, banishment and legal repression, the continuity of Irish social structures is remarkable. Catholic landed interests were reduced to the level of middlemen and leaseholders, the ranks from which the comfortable gentlemen farmers of the later eighteenth century emerged; or they sought to escape through the traditional cracks and outlets afforded by the continental regiments and the merchant houses of Bordeaux, Nantes, Cadiz and other Irish communities overseas; or they secured estates, legal careers and even public office by means of tactical conformity to the Established Church. The increasing complexity of Irish social structures, anatomized by Connolly in two superb chapters entitled 'Restoration Ireland' and 'Atlantic Island', highlighted the disjunction between the Protestant population's complete monopoly on public life and its narrow demographic base. By the 1670s the integration of the English élite and the Gaelic population into a single economic system was already sufficiently far advanced to make renewed schemes for the expulsion of all Catholics from cities and towns completely impractical. In the following decades a distinctive urban topography emerged, in towns such as Cork and Wexford, where Protestant houses of stone and slate dominated the centre, surrounded by Catholic cabins clustered outside the old walls. Expanding trade fuelled the growth of Dublin from 45,000 inhabitants (1685) to 62,000 (1706) to 92,000 (1725) to 140,000 (1760), but in the process reversed the two-thirds majority that Protestants enjoyed at the beginning of the eighteenth century — a dramatic transformation only dimly understood by historians. The maintenance of the penal code was one way of managing unresolved conflicts in this increasingly stratified, increasingly Catholic society. By keeping the contradictions and anomalies of eighteenth-century Ireland out of public view, the penal code permitted the Ascendancy to admire its own confident self-portrait, undisturbed by the continuing challenge posed by the resilience of the majority faith on the island.

Remarkably, the 'Church of Rome', to which 80 per cent of the population adhered in some way, warrants only five pages of *Divided Kingdom*. That makes half the number devoted to the Established Church; it is also half the number of pages devoted to Catholicism in *Religion, Law and Power* — a book that set out to analyse *Protestant* Ireland on its own terms. Connolly does not examine the erratic factionalism, indiscipline and mud-slinging that marked the Catholic priesthood, or the possibility that these deficiencies were among the products of state hostility. Nor does he investigate the unseemly contests over vacant parishes — a major theme of the extensive Irish material in the Vatican Archives which sometimes involved Catholic priests (or their local Protestant allies) trumping their rivals by threatening to invoke the penalities of the Bishops Banishment Act of 1697. Catholic spokesmen and intellectuals such as Cornelius Nary, the Abbé MacGeoghegan and Archbishop Troy (one of the pre-eminent ecclesiastical statesmen of modern Ireland) are mentioned in passing or not at all. The writings of the celebrated antiquary and pro-Catholic campaigner Charles O'Conor are not explored, although his voluminous correspondence throws light on the predicaments of 'a Roman Catholic in a Protestant country, that of one in a low way, obnoxious to the laws'. In short, Catholics get almost no airtime. An exception is made for Jacobites, and in particular for those Irish-language poets who rejected the Hanoverian dynasty, portrayed here as mired in remarkably tenacious habits of solipsism. If the Jacobites are at last getting their due, however, we have scarcely begun to recover the activities and networks of those Catholics who sought a pragmatic accommodation with Hanoverian rule — a group just as 'hidden' as their disaffected co-religionists. We might begin with the 'Article-Men', those who claimed the protection of the laws under the Treaty of Limerick in return for submitting to William III, or with the diplomatic missions of a number of Irish priests in Paris and Rome who hoped to have the Treaty confirmed in the general peace settlement of 1713, or with the wealthy Catholic and convert lawyers who represented Irish interests at the Inns of Court in London. The significance of the 'convert interest', an amphibious species of conformist Catholic that moved between the worlds of the Anglican élite and the old Catholic gentry, is not explored in *Divided Kingdom*, nor are the interventions of its most distinguished product, Edmund Burke.

It might be seen as something of an embarrassment for advocates of the *ancien régime* thesis that Edmund Burke, the most implacable enemy of the French Revolution and all it stood for, was also the most articulate critic of Protestant Ascendancy in Ireland. After all, Burke's classic treatise, *Reflections on the Revolution in France* (1790), was the most powerful and influential defence of the old European order, based on the twin pillars of aristocratic government and established religion. Yet Burke identified the principle of Protestant Ascendancy not with the *ancien régime* but with its enemies: there was a continuity, he insisted, between the malignity of the Irish penal code, the despotic 'Indianism' of the East India Company and the violence of French Jacobinism, since all of these forces drove a wedge, within their respective societies, between the many and the few. In his *Letter to Sir Hercules Langrishe* (1792), calling for the admission of Roman Catholics to the franchise, Burke described the Protestant Ascendancy as a 'plebeian oligarchy': it was a contradiction in terms or, as Burke put it, 'a monster'. The Protestant community was not sufficiently numerous to form a 'democracy' on its own, but too large to fulfil the function of an aristocracy. The natural relationship between property and authority, he believed, had been contorted by ethnic and religious antagonisms resulting from colonization, so that Protestant tradesmen and servants were regarded as superior to Catholic noblemen, while Catholic landowners, merchants, and even titular bishops were grouped together with 'an oppressed and licentious populace' merely because of their religious allegiance.

Somewhat surprisingly, *Divided Kingdom* presents an Ireland viewed predominantly through the eyes of Dublin Castle officials, parliamentary managers and (Anglican) bishops. It is better on Protestants than Catholics, on the propertied classes than the poor, and on men than women. Ironically, the historian whose first, pioneering monograph explored pre-Famine Catholicism has relatively little to say about the differences between official and popular belief that once fascinated him. He does not consider how far the moral and pastoral laxity generally attributed to the eighteenth-century priesthood resulted from the disruption of ecclesiastical administration by the Bishops Banishment Act. (And the same historian who uncovered the intense, possibly sexual, friendship between Letitia Bushe and Lady Anne Bligh has produced a book without any reference to women's experiences.) We are left wondering how far the sporadic closure of chapels, or attempts to apprehend priests (often reported, revealingly, to have fled from 'their usual place of abode'), served to check Catholic assertion in the face-to-face context of local communities. And yet the story of how individual 'papists' survived, undermined, and even occasionally colluded in the operation of the popery laws, is surely a central, unavoidable feature of Ascendancy Ireland.

It is tempting to conclude that the peculiar top-heaviness of Connolly's synthesis may be partly explained by the paradox of revisionism. That is, in seeking to liberate scholarship from contemporary concerns, revisionists themselves became inadvertently 'present-minded', their own enterprise dependent upon the same master-narrative they aimed to demolish. Perhaps it is Connolly's continuing tendency to resolve all differences of interpretation into a choice between the *ancien régime* and varieties of nationalism that is responsible for closing off further research on Catholic Ireland. There are interesting parallels here with the historiography of Stuart England, traditionally organized around the search for causes of the English Civil War. Peter Lake once remarked that Conrad Russell, arch-revisionist scholar of early Stuart parliaments, was locked into a fatal embrace with his quarry, rather like Sherlock Holmes clutching at Professor Moriarty as they hurtled into the watery depths at Reichenbach. Russell's early essays, collected together under the provocative title *Unrevolutionary England* (1990), had dramatically inverted the Whig interpretation by replacing conflict with consensus. It would be grossly unfair to say that Connolly's *ancien régime* thesis presents only the reverse image of nationalist orthodoxy. It has also served to defamiliarize important political and social aspects of Ascendancy Ireland in many stimulating ways. But it remains true that Irish revisionist writing depends for its integrity and coherence on the continuing plausibility and relevance of crude nationalism. Unless we forge new techniques and categories of analysis we are condemned to conjure up the ghosts of nationalism in order to wave our revisionist swords. *Divided Kingdom* successfully extends and reinforces Connolly's earlier assault on Irish exceptionalism without the hard polemical force of *Religion, Law and Power.* An attentive Dr. Watson might nevertheless discover signs of the sleuth's struggle with his old enemy, as he follows both sets of footprints towards Reichenbach Falls.

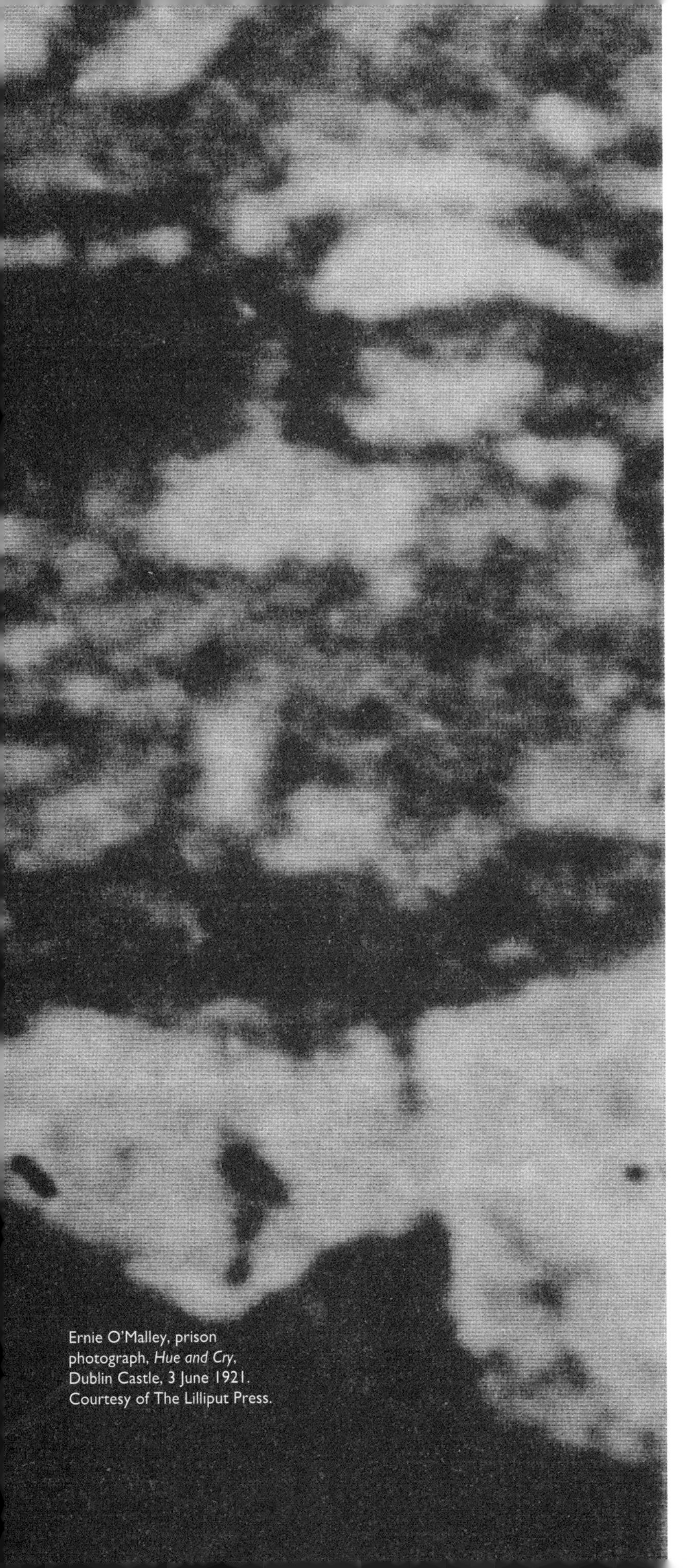

Ernie O'Malley, prison photograph, *Hue and Cry*, Dublin Castle, 3 June 1921. Courtesy of The Lilliput Press.

Shadows of a Gunman

David Lloyd

'No Surrender Here!': The Civil War Papers of Ernie O'Malley, 1922–1924
Cormac K. H. O'Malley and Anne Dolan, eds.
Introduction by J. J. Lee
Dublin: Lilliput Press, 2007
lxxviii + 642 pages. ISBN 978-1-84351-127-4

> ... the whole might be useful, in extract, to any of our literary people who feel inclined to devote attention and proper interpretation of a much unstudied period of our history, which has simply been glossed over by the words: murderers, fanatics, gunmen, wild foolish boys, idlers, looters, impractical idealists.
>
> Ernie O'Malley to Molly Childers.

> This was no academic seminar, consumed with the search for truth. Physical force would decide. It was a reality check for the Irish delegates — as for any account of Irish history with the British gun left out.
>
> J. J. Lee

'No Surrender Here!': The Civil War Papers of Ernie O'Malley, 1922–1924 is an indispensable book for anyone concerned with the history of decolonization in Ireland. It is also a very odd book.

It is indispensable in offering the reader a first-hand, unfiltered set of documents that furnish a glimpse of the Civil War as it was being fought day by day. It is an inside glimpse almost entirely, of course, of the republican struggle against the newly established Free State, and a glimpse from the inevitably restricted perspective of an officer in virtually constant hiding, in virtual seclusion from even those under his direct command, the Eastern and Northern divisions, and seeking from such isolation to organize, strategize and conduct operations against a far superior and better-equipped force. It also gives ample testimony to O'Malley's frustration with his role: his desire to be in active combat, his chafing at the incessant paperwork — the communiqués, requests for reports and assessments of men and supplies, the demand for accounts of activities without which no overall picture of his command could be gleaned — that was an essential requirement of his position (and for which, and for his meticulousness in demanding them in the face of his subalterns' reluctance or inability, he is regarded even by his editor as authoritarian and overbearing). This collection of documents makes available, in the first place, an invaluable source for understanding the causes and the conduct of the Civil War; moreover, its availability helps to make it possible for the non-specialist to assess not only the conflict itself and the persons and ideological positions involved in it, but also the accounts that have been presented to us by the specialist historians. It is not a perfect source for such assessments: not only is it necessarily partial, but by the nature of the documents, which range from interchanges composed in the midst of war between O'Malley and other republican commanders to prison letters written after his capture and mostly sent through unofficial channels, it lacks any larger statement of the goals of republicans or even the personal political vision of O'Malley himself. This is not a body of political writings like Gramsci's *Prison Notebooks*, nor a statement of a utopian political vision. What it offers instead is an intimate and detailed picture of the unfolding of a struggle, of the interaction of principle, improvisation and pragmatism that informs it, and, above all, a sense of the complexity of that interaction, which belies the historian's tendency to view the revolutionary as zealot, anti-modern fanatic, or brutal idealist. It is, indeed, to riff on Ranajit Guha's famous essay, an instance of the 'prose of insurgency', a body of writings produced for the most part in the heat of the moment, lacking by circumstance an overall perspective on the dispersed and fragmentary armed resistance of the republicans to the Free State and the Treaty, which they regarded as a continuation of the war against British domination.[1]

The book's third section, the letters from prison, also furnishes some sense of the broad intellectual curiosity and culture that would come to characterize O'Malley's post-Independence trajectory, his absorbing interest in literature and art and the auto-didacticism that drives his never-institutionalized erudition as it drove his military intelligence. There is no particular reason to believe that O'Malley was alone among republicans in this. Indeed, it is among the peculiarities of a republicanism, which historians generally seek to characterize as narrow, superstitious and backward-looking, that, together with many of the most advanced feminists and most radical socialists in the nationalist movement, it included in its ranks and among its sympathizers most of the important artists and intellectuals of the post-Independence decades: O'Malley himself, Francis Stuart, Frank O'Connor, Liam O'Flaherty, Peadar O'Donnell, Thomas MacGreevy — the list goes on and might extend to include both of O'Malley's later friends, Jack B. Yeats and Samuel Beckett. The paradox is, that while the historical record emphasizes the refusal of the republicans to compromise with the Treaty and the Free State it dragged into being, characterizing them as fanatical idealists, it remains the case that it was to be the Free State that became the organ of a narrow and intolerant nationalism, subservient to the most repressive forms of Catholic morality and to cultural provincialism. It was very largely the republican tradition that, with the often admirable capacity for critical reflection on its own legacy that O'Malley himself everywhere exhibits, gave rise to some of the

1 Ranajit Guha, 'The Prose of Counter-insurgency', in Guha, ed., *Subaltern Studies II: Writings on South Asian History and Society* (Delhi, 1983), 1–42.

most vigorous currents of cultural criticism and cosmopolitanism in the first decades of Irish independence.

It is perhaps this paradox that gives rise to some of the oddness of the collection. Ernie O'Malley was a crucial actor in both the Anglo-Irish War and the Civil War and, as Richard English emphasizes throughout his insidiously ambivalent biography, *Ernie O'Malley: IRA Intellectual*, an indispensable example for understanding both the Irish nationalist struggle and the intellectual and cultural perspectives of Irish republicanism. Deeply and widely read, an art critic and historian, a traveller and a farmer, he was perhaps the most articulate and conventionally 'cultured' of the republicans who survived the Irish revolution, a fine, if not tremendously innovative, writer, whose memoirs of the conflict, *On Another Man's Wound* and *The Singing Flame*, continue to retain compelling literary interest even as they stand as vital documents for understanding the processes and vicissitudes, and the violence, of decolonization — a theoretical term markedly absent from the historians' vocabulary. This conjunction of the cultured intellectual with the man who unrepentantly took up arms in a nationalist struggle clearly sticks in the craw of the contemporary academic historian even as it fascinated the writers and artists O'Malley would meet in his United States sojourn in the late 1920s and early 1930s. It is a strange and remarkable thing that the book's editor, Anne Dolan, who has done invaluable and arduous scholarly service in gathering, together with O'Malley's son, Cormac K. H. O'Malley, these voluminous and varied writings, would commence her introductory essay on the papers by citing no less a rancorous and inveterate anti-republican than journalist Kevin Myers, who accuses O'Malley of being '[t]he literary model for the killer-as-writer', who 'oozed the cant of the artist-killer, flaunting the exquisite sensitivity of the terrorist unflinchingly attending to a regrettable historical necessity: poor creative me'.[2] The self-advertising excess of such invective, which with grand moral self-delusion rehearses the self-evident but comforting fallacy that culture and violence are normatively antithetical, lacks the restraint of Sean O'Faolain's terser judgement of *On Another Man's Wound*, that it was 'a book without pity',[3] with which Dolan opens her essay. But in their conjunction they nicely present the well-worn stereotype of the pitiless gunman and sentimental terrorist, old turves around whose carefully banked embers revisionism has for a long time warmed its hands, fostering its cosy belief in its own moral and intellectual superiority over the 'simplified version of history', which, they claim, justifies 'contemporary brutalities in relation to Northern Ireland'. As Richard English, typical in this respect, sententiously, and rather comfortably, continues: 'Such validating certainties offer some comfort and are frequently used to sanction political violence; historians tend instead to offer complexities which subvert both the comfort and the sanction.'[4] Dolan understands the project of *'No Surrender Here!'* in quite similar terms (indeed, her introduction and prefatory notes for each section are consistently indebted to English's biography). It is to retrieve from both popularly circulated myth and from the 'character' produced by O'Malley's writings themselves a more complicated picture of the man: 'The point of this book, one could argue, is to escape his memoirs. This book is Ernie O'Malley's Civil War in his own words, Ernie O'Malley's Civil War in its own time. There is no artistry, little hindsight; there are perhaps a few more complications.'[5]

Complications there are, indeed, and the papers as a whole belie any simple image of the pitiless, terrorist gunman. Taken alongside the memoirs, and set in critical but informative relation to them, they reveal both continuities and ruptures between the Anglo-Irish War and the Civil War that have equally much to say about the complexities of a decolonizing struggle, its monumental difficulties and its political momentum. In a far more finely grained

2 Myers quoted in Cormac K. H. O'Malley and Anne Dolan, eds., *'No Surrender Here!': The Civil War Papers of Ernie O'Malley, 1922–1924* (Dublin, 2007), xliii.

3 Quoted in O'Malley and Dolan, *'No Surrender Here!'*, xliii.

4 Richard English, *Ernie O'Malley: IRA Intellectual* (Oxford, 1998), 202–03.

5 *'No Surrender Here!'* (hereafter *NSH*), xliii–xliv

way than the theoretical writings of, for example, Frantz Fanon or Amílcar Cabral, and with a considerable degree of tactical realism, O'Malley recounts the almost insuperable tasks of mobilizing a population long accustomed to being ruled by superior force, with only the most sporadic memories of insurrection, without continuous traditions of military organization (though many who fought between 1919 and 1923 had received some training in the British army), and often sceptical as to the possibilities of overthrowing British rule when not openly hostile to the very idea. O'Malley's writings of all kinds are eloquent about the exhaustingly demanding task of organizing the IRA out of the dispersed, ill-trained and inexperienced groups of Irish Volunteers around the country, about the challenge of improvising guerilla strategies, practices, flying columns, literally and figuratively 'on the run'. The officers with whom he worked were rarely promising material for guerilla struggle, as lacking in discipline and experience as they were in weapons, uncomprehending of the need for careful planning, detailed mapping, constant training, and often half-hearted in their commitment to the struggle in ways that were dangerous to those they were elected to command. The essence of guerilla warfare is, as Tom Barry once put it in a phrase echoed later (if not borrowed from him) by both Mao Zedong and Che Guevara, 'discipline, speed, silence and mobility'.[6] None of these was easy to achieve or instill in volunteers accustomed to the rhythms of agrarian labour or to traditions of easy-going conviviality. O'Malley is everywhere clear both about the enormous obstacles that the cultural formations of a long-colonized people present to mobilization and organization and about the degree of earnestness, moral and political as well as military, that the decision to engage in armed struggle demanded. Nothing in O'Malley's writings suggests the casual adventurer, the pathological killer, the fanatical terrorist. He was, however, at a remarkably young age what in a state-sanctioned military force would be called, with some admiration, a professional (and it should be recalled that O'Malley's brother Frank, to whom he remained close, had joined the British army, and that it was British army manuals that Ernie consistently relied on for his tactical education). But he sought always to be a professional against the grain of most of those he worked with and in circumstances, human and military, that made the sustained organizational structures that shape the professional soldier impossible to achieve.

It is this commitment and its frequent frustration that counterpoints, in surprisingly moving ways, the passages of lyrical description of the Irish countryside or the accounts of raids and ambushes for which *On Another Man's Wound* is probably more commonly remembered. In both the encounter with a rural Ireland largely unknown to him before and in the slow and frustrating process of getting to know the people with whom and among whom he worked, O'Malley, indeed, anticipates the dilemmas of the decolonizing intellectual militant whom Fanon so memorably describes in *The Wretched of the Earth* as the inevitable product of a colonial formation. And O'Malley is by no means oblivious to the contradictions his position entails any more than he and other republicans were to the deconstructive *mise-en-abyme* that faces *any* political organization that is obliged to forge the very people in whose name it claims to speak, a dilemma exacerbated by the mentalities of the colonized:

> I was on the outside. I felt it in many ways by a diffidence, by an extra courtesy, by a silence. Some were hostile in their minds; others in speech; often the mother would think I was leading her son astray or the father would not approve of what the boys were doing. We of the Volunteers were talked of at first: 'Musha, God help

6 Tom Barry, *Guerilla Days in Ireland* (Tralee, 1962), 25.

36 Ailesbury Road, Dublin, home of Humphreys/O'Rahilly family (now French Embassy) and scene of O'Malley's capture after shoot-out with Free State troops, November 1922.

them, but they haven't a stim of sinse'. Yet there was a tradition of armed resistence [*sic*], dimly felt; it would flare up when we carried out some small successful raid or made a capture. Around the fire it would be discussed; it would heighten the imagination of those who were hostile. In their minds a simple thing became heroic and epical. Perhaps the sense of glory in the people was stirred, and the legend that had been created about myself, whom they did not know, helped them to accept me as part of it.

> I felt that I should be able to fuse with my material, so that I could make better use of it; yet look at them dispassionately, as if from a distance. My approach to teaching and training of the men was impersonal; they would have to learn to do without me, to depend on themselves and to avoid too much trust in what they considered leadership. This often meant a cold quality creeping in, but few could mingle with them without gaining warmth.[7]

7 *NSH*, 128.

To read O'Malley on the process of forging and waging guerilla war, on the obstacles and the hindrances, on the groping and cumulative lessons of experience and often fatal error, is far from the reading of an adventure story by John Buchan, to whom Dolan in passing compares O'Malley. His writing is far too attuned to the costs and losses, the peculiar mix of instrumentality and human warmth, violence and compassion, that compose both the terrain of guerilla war and the underlying conditions of colonial culture from which it seeks emancipation.

Both the sense of loss and the organizer's frustration infuse the Civil War writings collected in *'No Surrender Here!'*. It is, in the first place, a record of deeply held principle adhered to with an increasing sense of futility and waste, both of lives and of political and military opportunities. As is evident from the central section of the book, which consists of O'Malley's memos from hiding, when, much against his will, he was 'Acting Assistant Chief of Staff' of the Dublin-centred Northern and Eastern sections of the IRA, O'Malley's assessment of the republican military position was at best grimly optimistic. These memos are counterpointed by — and often reply to — numerous memos from Liam Lynch, chief of staff of republican forces operating in the far more sympathetic south-west, and from Con Moloney, adjutant general of the IRA, which give a fuller, and generally far more optimistic picture of the republican situation than any O'Malley could possibly muster. A larger number of memos, to and from O'Malley and his 'staff', generate a continual drumbeat of frustration and failure. Desperately seeking some kind of overview of the situation of his command, O'Malley begs for reports of numerical strength, weaponry, actions and training, often to no avail. Over and again he has to report to Lynch that yet more of his seasoned officers have been arrested, to be replaced, if at all, by even less experienced ones. Mere survival, and occasional sabotage of transport lines, are the best that he seems to be able to envisage for his area of command. He festers and grumbles, mostly between the lines of these largely very professional memos, at his own inability to act, urges his desire to join his former brigade in 'Tipp', and consistently criticizes the lack of proactive republican moves, military and political, that might succeed in seizing the initiative and countering the barrage of official propaganda against the 'Irregulars'.

With hindsight it is easy to cast the republican struggle as the misguided product of inflexible principle and idealism and, worse, as the enactment of a fundamentally anti-democratic and religiose adherence to a cause bound to failure, callously taking with it the lives of many former comrades and Irish non-combatants. This is the politics of blood sacrifice that has become the commonplace of analyses of a later generation of republicans, since Richard Kearney's myth-making essays of the 1970s, 'The IRA's Strategy of Failure' and 'Myth and Terror'. It is a motif that Dolan uncritically repeats in her assessment of O'Malley and of the republicans in general — 'the obstinate man who seemed so desperate to fight', 'a man who always seemed to know that he had failed', a soldier with a 'contempt for electoral politics ... that he shared with many of his republican peers'.[8] But to a reading less predetermined by the conventional myths about republicanism, the memoranda reveal a genuinely complicated picture. They are, of course, documents composed by soldiers already committed to a cause and a campaign, written to record the day-to-day activities of an underground organization, and accordingly lack any general discussion of political principles or utopian hopes.[9] What they provide, through the tantalizing picture they offer of one small segment of the war itself fought from locality to locality, is a sense of the process of the struggle and, more importantly, insight into what at least some of the republican commanders thought they might achieve. Aware that they have no control of the apparatuses of the state or of the media for propaganda, O'Malley remains for some time convinced that, through proactive military engagement with the Free State forces, public opinion might be swung to the anti-Treaty side. His often expressed desire for 'a return to the field, a return to active command in the west'[10] seems less the Buchan-ish man-of-action's intoxication with action for its own sake than part and parcel of his conviction that only by taking the fight to the Free State could the propaganda, as well as the military, victory be won. It is a strategic more than a psychological or quasi-religious conviction and one come to almost certainly in the light of the gradual development of the

8 *NSH*, lii, xlvi.
9 See *NSH*, li, where Dolan comments, somewhat unrealistically: 'Among the leaders, one could be forgiven for expecting a little more consideration, if not a rethinking of the principles of the Republic, whatever they may be, then at least some contemplation of the policy of war in the light of events as they unfolded. Instead there was simply the sheer will to carry on.' Later, however, in the introductory note to section II [37], Dolan cites Michael Hopkinson, *Green against Green: The Irish Civil War* (Dublin, 1988), 174, to the effect that 'Ernie O'Malley frequently asked his Chief of Staff for clarification of the anti-Treaty IRA's political, social and military aims'.
10 *NSH*, li.

IRA's popular support during the Anglo-Irish War, in which O'Malley had just played so active a role.

But the need to portray O'Malley as the callous, fanatical diehard persistently slants the editor's reading of the documents assembled here, and often in interestingly symptomatic ways. There is the peculiarly insensitive response to O'Malley's apparent indifference to his younger brother's death, as compared to his sorrow at the death of a fellow prisoner, Jimmy Mooney: 'There was little sadness at his brother Charles's death ... He had more in common with a fellow prisoner than with a brother he no longer really knew.'[11] Dolan here omits the crucial evidence that O'Malley's writings supply. He writes with considerable cultural as well as personal insight in a long — and invaluable — autobiographical letter from prison to Molly Childers, Erskine Childers's widow, about his middle-class Irish family and its inability to foster loving relations: 'There was very little love in the family. I can honestly say that I never loved my parents, but I respected them.'[12] Home life, he explains, 'was none too congenial as its ties were never strong enough'.[13] The sense of lack of affect is hardly unique to the O'Malley (or Malley) family in the Ireland of the time or for many generations since, and it would be valuable to have further study of the ways in which the intersection of Victorian values and colonial culture may have impacted the 'structures of feeling' in Ireland at the time of the revolution rather than this resort to normative family values that implies that there is something essentially inhumane in O'Malley's lack of grief for a brother whom he had hardly seen during long years on the run. Jimmy Mooney, to the contrary, was not merely 'a fellow prisoner', but a young man who acted as O'Malley's orderly and effective nurse in prison, and with whom O'Malley shared music and probably reading.[14] Indeed, the portrayal of O'Malley as a man with little affective relation to others and limited capacity for friendship, an assumption that Dolan shares with Richard English, is belied in a passage of the letter to Childers that is appalling in its matter-of-fact roll call of dead friends, lost not only in the Irish wars but also in the British military — fifteen in all, including his older and closest brother Frank, who died in the British army in East Africa. It is scarcely an index of his lack of feeling that O'Malley should remark: 'now I am often afraid to make friendships'.[15]

Yet this shadow of unfeelingness constantly haunts the reception of O'Malley in what one can only term counter-insurgency historicism. The convention that a commitment to revolutionary principles goes hand in hand with callousness and indifference to ordinary human affects has a long genealogy, finding its classic expression in Edmund Burke's *Reflections on the Revolution in France* and its invocation of Marie-Antoinette as the repository of humane traditions and right feeling. Not surprisingly, then, it is around O'Malley's relation to the women to whom he writes from prison that the ascription to him of a certain emotional indifference unfolds. Dolan suggests that

> the letters by Ernie O'Malley's mother are particularly telling. Notably changing her name from Malley to O'Malley for her later correspondence, she presents a very different perspective of civil war than that of her son ... By the time of Ernie O'Malley's capture in November 1922, Marion Malley had lost two sons — Frank in East Africa and Charles, aged seventeen, in the Dublin fighting in July 1922. Two more boys were imprisoned and Ernie was reportedly dying with multiple bullet wounds.[16]

This — her 'great heartbreak and worry', writes Dolan — 'was a mother's understanding of war'.[17] To O'Malley's mother, as opposed to Molly Childers and Sighle Humphreys, 'who sang from the same republican hymnal', 'there was nothing more than "those wretched awful Irish affairs", that

11 *NSH*, xlix.
12 *NSH*, 422.
13 *NSH*, 423.
14 *NSH*, 381, 435, 413 and 613 n. 285.
15 *NSH*, 423.
16 *NSH*, xlix–l.
17 *NSH*, l.

Sighle Humphreys (1899–1994) in Cumann na mBán uniform. Courtesy of Magan family.

had in whatever form taken the lives of two of her sons and imprisoned three more'.[18]

The stereotype, quite evidently posed against the Pearsean virago-mother who is willing to sacrifice her sons for the nation, presents Marion Malley as the vessel of feeling, as the grieving, desperate mother, at the same time depriving her of agency or intelligence, political engagement or analysis. We are supposed to receive the response to the Anglo-Irish War and Civil War as 'those wretched Irish affairs' (which can scarcely include Frank's death in British wars to hold on to their other colonial possessions in East Africa) as the index of true maternal feeling, free of ideology or myth. If the stereotype of the sacrificial Mother Ireland has its genealogy in Yeats's Cathleen ni Houlihan and Pearse's poems, this counter-stereotype has an equally distinguished genealogy in O'Casey's melodramas, novels like O'Flaherty's *The Informer*, or films like *Some Mother's Son*. It requires, of course, the consistent denial of women's agency in the republican struggle, even as it seeks to imply the illiberal masculinism, even misogyny and anti-feminism, of the republican struggle — indeed, of anti-colonial struggles in general. Republican women activists and supporters are reduced to automatons, singing from the republican hymnal. And Marion O'Malley (to use the name she chose for herself) has to be effectively censored by selection to produce this image of her. One statement, unsigned but apparently in her handwriting, also on O'Malley's medical condition, presents a quite different sense of her than that 'she thought only of her child in danger and pain'.[19] In it, she records her conversations with the doctor treating O'Malley in prison, Henry Barniville:

> I spoke that day about the shooting of [Erskine] Childers. His remark was — you need not fear — the four men were robbers and Childers was a spy. Well, I spoke up and said I am ashamed of you and his reply was you and I won't agree. I said not on your politics anyhow.[20]

She continues with an entirely political judgement of Barniville:

18 *NSH*, l.
19 *NSH*, 333.
20 *NSH*, 339.

> In my opinion (and a good many Dublin people know it) Dr Barniville acted a real blackleg and did the Free State dirty work well by treating his patient so badly — and he will yet suffer for his lack of attention to that poor wounded boy.[21]

It is hard to square such political statements with the image of Marion O'Malley as the apolitical grieving mother. The tone and contents of this document, which was apparently not written for official consumption, is quite different from those Dolan relies on, written to Free State Minister for External Affairs, Desmond Fitzgerald, and begging for official intervention on Ernie's behalf. Like so many of the documents in this collection, her letters need to be read in their contexts and can be seen clearly to be acutely attuned to them. Ironically, though, the attempt to pose Ernie's callousness against his mother's 'natural' grief ends up, as so often in revisionist interpretative selection, to be itself quite misogynist.

Comparable simplification takes place in the effort to portray O'Malley's class position in relation to the republican movement as a whole. Sometimes it is simply silly, as in Dolan's caricature of one of O'Malley's Civil War safe houses, that of the Humphreys family on Ailesbury Road, during a two-month period that ended in his bloody capture, a period that she describes as being 'like civil war the Jeeves and Wooster way'. As O'Malley explained in *The Singing Flame*, the location was chosen for its very unlikeliness: it was in a 'sedate, leisurely, respectable and imperial' neighbourhood and the house itself 'was so frankly Republican that I thought it would not be suspect'.[22] It would have been difficult, given the necessity of his location in the capital, for him to have hidden out 'in the barns of the simple farmers',[23] and given the house-to-house searches then in progress throughout Dublin, the choice seems a quite logical bluff. The point of such caricatures is, of course, to dispel the myth 'of a united band of comrades fighting for Irish freedom'.[24] But the myth is itself yet another historical myth. No one who studies nationalist movements anywhere is unaware of the peculiarities produced by the fact that what they seek to achieve is what the Indian historian Bipan Chandra has termed the 'vertical integration' of class-stratified colonial societies, rather than the 'deep, horizontal comradeship' by which Benedict Anderson characterizes the dream of the nation. It is the process that Fanon explores in depth in his essays on the role of the intellectual in decolonizing movements, where the acculturated and generally middle-class nationalist intellectual has to overcome a range of prejudices, tastes and distastes, and ideological assumptions in order to even begin to comprehend the 'zone of occult instability where the people dwell', as he puts it.[25] In his memoirs, O'Malley — in rather less poetical and perhaps more self-ironizing and dispassionate terms — explores with some honesty his difficulties in entering into the mores, diet and poverty of rural Ireland while staying among small farming families (whom he never describes as 'simple' nor holds, as Dolan claims, in contempt). When O'Malley admits in his biographical letter to Childers that he 'was hated thoroughly',[26] it is clear in the context Dolan fails to give that he was hated not for his class but for his rigorous discipline and expectations. Indeed, the resentment that O'Malley suffers, and any contempt that he shows, in this volume and elsewhere, is rarely for the ordinary volunteers but directed mostly at the largely middle-class officers who failed to carry through orders and instructions and consequently endangered the men under their command. As he reflected from prison to Liam Lynch in a letter that probably refers to an article on him in *An Phoblacht*: 'Most of all I would have liked to talk about the rank and file where I found much solace when broken hearted with the officers'.[27]

Nor, by any means, is there much evidence that '[e]ven in prison he preferred

21 *NSH*, 339.
22 Ernie O'Malley, *The Singing Flame* (Dublin, 1978), 160.
23 *NSH*, xlvi.
24 *NSH*, xlvii.
25 Bipan Chandra, 'Colonialism, Stages of Colonialism and the Colonial State', *Journal of Contemporary Asia*, 10, 3 (1980), 272–85; Benedict Anderson, *Imagined Communities: Reflections on the Origin and Spread of Nationalism*, Revised Edition (London, 1983), 7; Frantz Fanon, *The Wretched of the Earth*, Preface by Jean-Paul Sartre, trans. Constance Farrington (New York, 1968), 227.
26 *NSH*, 432, xlvii.
27 *NSH*, 355.

the company of the cultured and landed gentry', as Dolan tendentiously suggests.[28] While O'Malley admits at a low moment to missing Robert Barton (who had been crucial in his early prison days in nursing and cheering him), 'because the rest of the lads here, with a few exceptions, are not much good',[29] Dolan omits much else that might have provided some context: the fact that he is also missing Jimmy Mooney; the other letters where, for example, he relates with good humour his project to write a volume entitled 'Irish History Unidealized' with 'a lad here, a quite good fellow, who was one of the few who fought with us in O'Connell Street in recent times';[30] and the simple fact that his energy for convivial association in prison was severely limited by his difficult convalescence from the nine bullet wounds he received at the time of his capture and the remaining fragments that continued to plague him throughout his life. With the possible exception of David Robinson, former British army major, none of the rest of the closer associates who did spend more time with him, including Frank Gallagher, Seoirse Plunkett, and Peadar O'Donnell, could be described as 'the cultured and landed gentry'.

One could enumerate at tedious length numerous other such distortions-by-selection that riddle the prefatory material of each section of the book. They share a single tendency, one they have in common with English's biography, which is to present, under the rubric of historical complexity, a simplified portrait of O'Malley as intransigent republican, as out of touch with the plain people of Ireland, as a romantic committed to violent struggle for its own sake. The portrait is one that it is difficult to sustain in the face of voluminous evidence, much of it presented in this volume, that furnishes material for a genuinely more complex picture of republican militancy and of the contradictions republicans worked with in a war of decolonization. Such a portrait would, of course, require a much broader context for comparison than most academic Irish historians are willing or able to engage in, and a much richer and more critical theoretical framework for doing so. Within such a context, the contradictions O'Malley both confronts and articulates, the difficulties of engaging in a war of decolonization in a country whose population still has, in language he draws from a long tradition of Irish nationalist analysis while anticipating later thinkers like Cabral and Fanon, 'the slave mind',[31] even the relative brevity of the post-Treaty Civil War, would be both illuminated and illuminating. Certainly none of these aspects of the period could be so crassly reduced to the psychological peculiarities of individual participants. We might, indeed, learn to read O'Malley's and others' memoirs as often self-critical theoretical reflections rather than as tissues of '[e]mbellishment, artistry, hindsight, lies'.[32] To give just one example, O'Malley comments in *On Another Man's Wound* that

> [a]reas of the country had a habit of going to sleep. They would wake up after a century or more and step into a gap. This unexpected quality was there in what I knew to be a bad area. It might awaken of itself: the times and situation might start the spark.[33]

Such remarks are richly suggestive as to the peculiar rhythms and temporalities of popular resistance to colonialism. Similarly, there has been little work in Irish historiography to compare with that of, for instance, Rey Ileto on the Philippines, which could illuminate imaginatively what 'spirituality' (understood by both Dolan and English in unhelpfully restrictive terms as Catholicism and romantic nationalism) might actually represent in terms of the ways in which anti-colonial popular movements lay hold of and transform for radical purposes the available religious rhetorics. Governed by the kind of division between the spiritual and the material that Partha Chatterjee has explored as an essential

28 *NSH*, xlvii.
29 *NSH*, 372.
30 *NSH*, 370.
31 *NSH*, 473.
32 *NSH*, xliii.
33 Ernie O'Malley, *On Another Man's Wound* (London, 1936), 129.

— and deeply gender-coded — aspect of nationalism, and that recurs as an essential aspect of the division of spheres in the liberal state, Dolan and English are unable to read as fundamentally political a terminology expressed as spiritual. Consequently, they can only read the recourse of republicans in the prisons to a language of spirituality as a recursion to the institutional Catholicism that would come to dominate the Free State and to which, on the contrary, it may be deeply opposed.[34] Such instances could be multiplied. The intellectual damage suffered by Irish historiography by its leading exponents' casual and usually sparsely informed dismissals of postcolonial theory, not to mention their apparent lack of awareness of the long and voluminous histories of decolonization globally, is nowhere more evident than in the sparse and, frankly, ideologically driven scholarship on the republican movement and on the Irish revolution.

This is hardly surprising, since what underlies the dismissal, out of hand, of colonial contexts for the understanding of Irish history is itself a contest over legitimacy and sovereignty, with all the consistently deferred questions about the normativity of violence or coercion that shadow such debates. Thus Richard English's biography of O'Malley postures about objectivity and complexity and performs a pseudo-ethical fastidiousness about O'Malley's participation in an 'elitist' militarist movement that 'acted in the name of the people while disavowing much that the people actually believed'.[35] Yet it turns out to be little more than a covert legitimation of the establishment of Northern Ireland — that 'Protestant state for a Protestant people' — against the will of the majority of what was then the political unit of Ireland. Similarly, indeed, the very title of '*No Surrender Here!*' seizes on a single outburst of O'Malley's as he was resisting arrest to make it stand metonymically for an intransigence equivalent to that of Ulster Unionists under Sir Edward Carson. In both instances, the traces of the repressed are very close to the surface. What is always at stake in the delegitimation of republicanism is the legitimation of a state forged out of the refusal, backed by the very real threat of force by both an armed minority and the colonial power, to accept what was the will of the electoral majority. That that state had to survive by the virtually perpetual exercise of a state of exception in order to coerce the large minority incorporated into the state (which is what one means by referring to the territorial unit of Northern Ireland as having been artificially constituted) is what brings to the fore over and over again the problem of sovereignty and the roots of *both* post-Independence states in violence. To a historiography a little more theoretically informed, and less driven to hide behind the conventional humanist truisms of academic historicism, this insight would provoke a little less anxiety and make of Ireland a remarkably interesting case study, through which recent debates on violence and sovereignty, which derive from the contemporaneous work of Weimar political theorist Carl Schmitt and of critical theorist Walter Benjamin, could be comparatively addressed.[36]

But to do so would mean relinquishing a cherished belief in the merely curative intervention of state-sanctioned violence, as in the innocence of civil society and the status quo that defends it. It would demand addressing the violence of the colonial state itself, rather than understanding the police work of the state to be directed at a primordial violence that emanates from the colonized. It would mean confronting the fact that non-violent civil disobedience movements in Ireland, from the Repeal Association to the Northern Ireland Civil Rights Association, have been understood and confronted by the British state, just as in other colonial contexts, as if they were violent insurrections and therefore subject to coercion. This is so precisely because, as Benjamin understood, such movements question the legitimacy of the state, challenging its very existence. It would mean understanding that the context for the Irish revolution and for its violent unfolding lies in the consistent reliance of

34 Reynaldo C. Ileto, *Pasyon and Revolution: Popular Movements in the Philippines, 1840–1910* (Quezon City, 1979); Partha Chatterjee, *The Nation and Its Fragments: Colonial and Postcolonial Histories* (Princeton, 1993); one might also invoke, among many others, Shahid Amin's brilliant work on the popular memory of one peculiarly violent moment in Indian nationalism and its connection to religious understandings of Gandhi: *Event, Metaphor, Memory: Chauri Chaura, 1922–1992* (Berkeley, 1995). Irish historiography has proven sadly limited in this respect by the mythic paradigm circulated by Kearney and others.

35 English, *Ernie O'Malley*, 194.

36 See Giorgio Agamben, *State of Exception*, trans. Kevin Attell (Chicago, 2005), 52–64.

the British state itself on the use of force. It is another of the peculiar oddities of '*No Surrender Here!*' that, despite its possibly even unwitting ideological agenda, it should be introduced by a remarkably forthright essay by the eminent historian J. J. Lee that argues precisely this. Lee commences his essay on the background to the Irish revolution by pointing out the simple fact that '[t]he British were by this stage [1898] normally stationing between 25,000 and 30,000 troops in Ireland, and maintaining about 10,000 police, the Royal Irish Constabulary, as an armed force, in contrast to the unarmed police of Britain'.[37] (This presence of an *armed* police force is among the many things that makes colonial Ireland resemble more colonial India or West Africa than Britain itself). The constitutionalist Nationalist Party 'simply assumed this as a fundamental reality'.[38] The fact that that assumption was determining has, however, often been occluded by historians and it is testimony to the efficacy of British self-representation as a 'civil' power that this occlusion has been so consistent. As Lee points out:

> The gun was already there, as the fundamental fact of political power, the bedrock on which British domination was based. That it can be conjured out of existence is either wishful thinking or testimony to the hallucinogenic impact of British mind games. The power of domination derives even more from capturing the minds than the bodies of the dominated — whether in terms of nationality, race, ethnicity, religion, class, gender, age or any other marker of identity. Part of the genius of British domination skills in Ireland was to so skilfully disguise the elementary fact that British gun-power determined the framework within which Irish politics operated. The suffocating skill of British control techniques had ensured that for many, British guns in Ireland were somehow purged of any association with violence. Conquest was not violence. It was only resistance to conquest that was violence.[39]

If, as O'Malley well saw, this context made of the Irish resort to arms 'an exercise in basic political education ... stripping away the beguiling but self-deluding facade of "constitutionalism", behind which the British gun was disguised',[40] the force of British and Unionist guns no less determined the partition of Ireland against the will of the majority of the population. Richard English is typical of revisionist historians and journalists who are accustomed to accuse the republicans of having sought to exclude 'large numbers of Irish people' from the Irish nation[41] in an undemocratic resort to force, but, as Lee points out, '[t]he line of the border stood as irrefutable evidence that far from achieving nothing, [Unionist] command of violence was crucial in determining the outcome of the conflict over partition'.[42]

Along with other republicans, O'Malley 'grasped the terrible simplicity that so many others chose to ignore, the elemental truth that the gun was the basis for British control over Ireland. Getting the British gun out of Irish life was a prerequisite for the creation of a sovereign Irish state'.[43] What republicans understood themselves to be resisting was, in effect, the acceptance by their counterparts of state terrorism, encapsulated in Lloyd George's infamous threat of 'immediate and terrible war'.[44] But fundamentally at issue, if veiled by its expression through the symbolic form of the oath of allegiance, was the question of sovereignty. But sovereignty is not merely a question of 'symbolic supremacy', of 'honour' or 'status', as Lee suggests.[45] 'Sovereign is he', as Carl Schmitt put it, 'who decides on the exception'. Sovereignty is at once the decision over the power of lawmaking itself and over the life and death of the subjects of the state. Or, as Benjamin was to put it in an

37 *NSH*, xi.
38 *NSH*, xi.
39 *NSH*, xv.
40 *NSH*, xxii.
41 English, *Ernie O'Malley*, 202.
42 *NSH*, xxiii.
43 *NSH*, xxxi.
44 *NSH*, xxiv.
45 *NSH*, xxvi.

essay Schmitt much admired, 'Lawmaking is power making, and, to that extent, an immediate manifestation of violence'.[46] That is, the state's sovereignty, its authority or *Gewalt*, rests on its monopoly of violence. For republicanism, the limited sovereignty offered by the Treaty was a contradiction in terms, leaving the monopoly of violence in the hands of the colonial power. Ironically perhaps, the terrible miscalculation of *force majeure* that led O'Malley and others to believe that resistance to the Free State could be a further 'exercise in basic political education' and bring the coerced majority to their side may have concluded by establishing, with British assistance, the monopoly of violence effectively in the hands of that very Free State. For, as Kevin Higgins well knew in ordering the execution of republican prisoners in reprisal for ambushes, 'in the exercise of violence over life and death more than in any other legal act, law reaffirms itself'.[47] The fratricidal violence of the Civil War was as terrible as it was precisely because it was at every level about the state's monopoly of violence. But it would be the merest 'wishful thinking' to believe that the surrender of the republicans removed the shadow of violence from the state, any more than the establishment of Northern Ireland could avoid casting forward the perpetual question of its legitimacy.

It is of course the ruse of the state to persuade its population that what it represents is a normative state of peace and non-coercion, to which violence is the irruptive exception. Essential to that ruse is the division of social spheres. While the state retains the right of resort to force to preserve the law and to protect the citizen, civil society is assumed to operate normally without coercion. Yet at the heart of civil society, and at the core of what the law is established to preserve, is the principle of private property, a principle in its essence predicated upon violence. Historicism, whose means and end is the civil society that sanctions its supposed academic disinterest, offers to legitimate the established state by proposing a critique of violence that always stops short of the critique of state violence. Masquerading as an ethical humanism, pretending to a judicious complexity that its caricatures and its predictability belie, it maintains a posture of moral purity and empirical scruple against the terrible certainties of the idealist, while residing comfortably in the sanctuary of the violence of the state. The challenge that a figure like O'Malley presents to such comfortable assurance lies less in the violence in which he engaged than in the principle of non-violence that he aspired to make possible, one embodied in the republican aspiration for a society predicated on non-domination.[48] While the liberal democratic state has shown itself remarkably accommodating to coercion and domination, whether by transnational corporations or the security apparatus, European political élites or military alliances, the alternative to violence as means and foundation of the political order may yet be found, not in the pieties of revisionist moralizing, but from the perspective of a radical non-violence. Only from such a perspective could the means to which O'Malley resorted, for ends that were their antithesis, finally be adjudicated.

46 Carl Schmitt, *Political Theology: Four Chapters on the Concept of Sovereignty*, trans. and intro., George Schwab, foreword by Tracy B. Strong (Chicago, 2005), 5; Walter Benjamin, 'Critique of Violence,' in *Reflections: Essays, Aphorisms, Autobiographical Writings*, trans. Edmund Jephcott (New York, 1978), 295.

47 Benjamin, 'Critique of Violence,' 286.

48 On freedom as non-domination, see Philip Pettit, *Republicanism: A Theory of Freedom and Government* (Oxford, 1997).

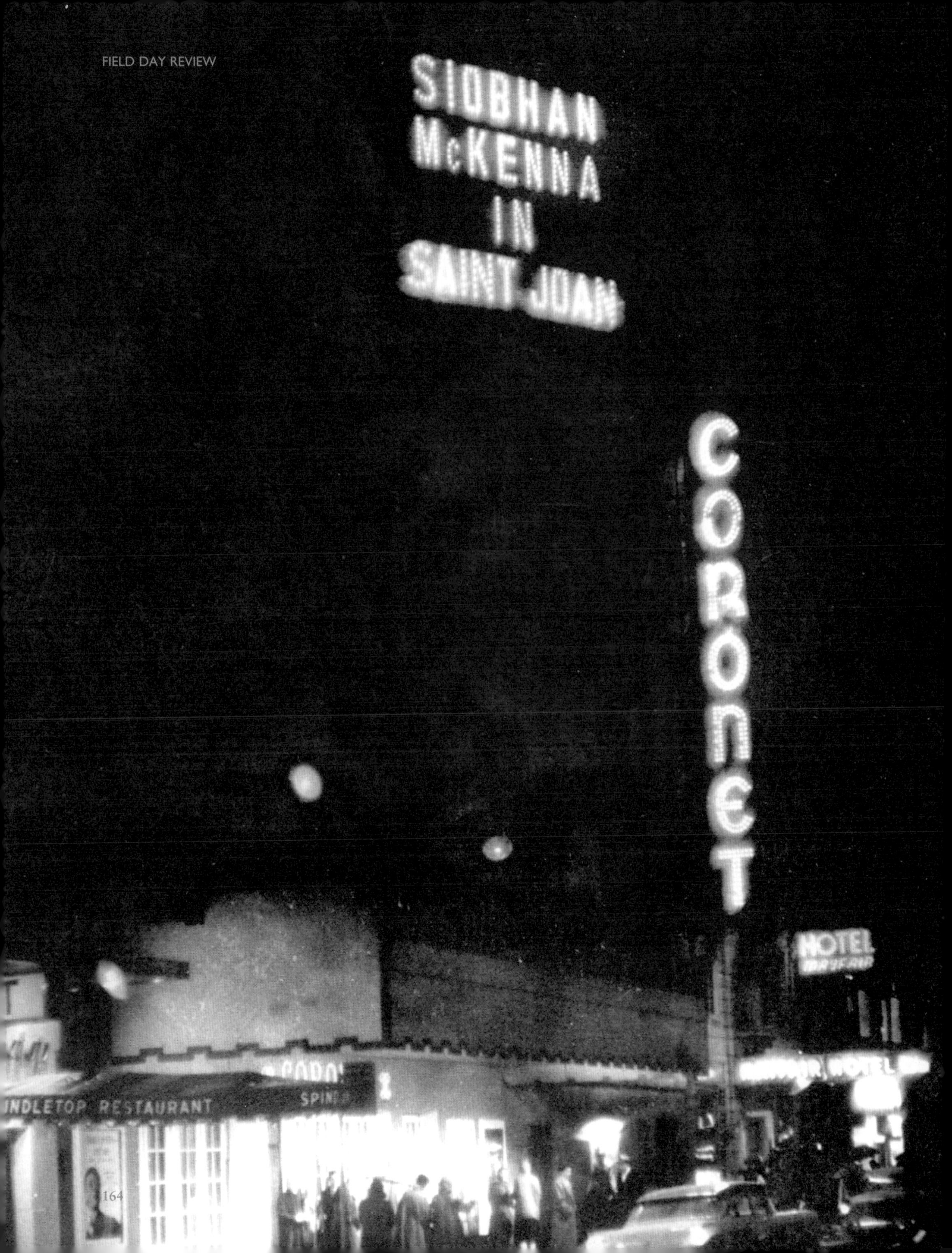
SIOBHAN McKENNA IN SAINT JOAN
CORONET
HOTEL
RESTAURANT

Siobhán McKenna playing Joan in the play *St. Joan*, 1956. Photo: Gjon Mili//Time Life Pictures/ Getty Images.

Theatre, Globalization and Recalcitrant Audiences

Chris Morash

Irish Theater in America: Essays on Irish Theatrical Diaspora
Edited by John P. Harrington
Irish Studies Series, edited by James MacKillop
Syracuse: Syracuse University Press, 2009
xix + 226 pages. ISBN 978-0-8156-3169-9

Theatre and Globalization: Irish Drama in the Celtic Tiger Period
Patrick Lonergan
Houndmills: Palgrave Macmillan, 2009
ix + 248 pages. ISBN 978-0-230-21428-6

Hegemony and Fantasy in Irish Drama, 1899–1949
Paul Murphy
Houndmills: Palgrave Macmillan, 2008
ix + 266 pages. ISBN 978-0-230-53683-8

Modernism, Drama and the Audience for Irish Spectacle
Paige Reynolds
Cambridge: Cambridge University Press, 2007
ix + 257 pages. ISBN 978-0-521-87299-7

Since it first appeared, Benedict Anderson's *Imagined Communities* (1983) has wielded considerable explanatory power in Irish cultural studies. In part, this is due to the importance that Anderson accords to the printed word. Whether in relation to newspapers like the *Northern Star* in the 1790s, the circulation of the *Nation* in the 1840s, or the astonishing flowering of the written word between 1890 and 1922, Anderson's basic model — admittedly with some modifications from Edward Said, Partha Chatterjee and others — mapped neatly onto the Irish context. However, in the very years that this notion of a print-mediated nation was being woven into our conceptual apparatus, print itself has been undergoing the most profound transformation in its five hundred-year history. Digitization, and the consequent acceleration of globalization, has changed utterly the ways in which print circulates, exceeding the space of the nation, and in the process complicating our understanding of how we came to imagine nationhood in the first place. This, in turn, has brought into new focus those recalcitrant elements that never did quite fit into the model of a print-mediated national culture — among which we must include live theatre.

'If digital technology allows globalization to become an "imagined community"', writes Patrick Lonergan, 'theatre can imagine other kinds of community'.[1] This understanding has been percolating through the wider world of theatre theory, at least since, Philip Auslander's book, *Liveness: Performance in a Mediatized Culture,* appeared a decade ago.[2] However, the books considered here mark the point at which similar concerns reach a certain critical mass in Irish cultural studies. Admittedly, the whole area of performance has come to Irish theatre studies somewhat belatedly, partly for institutional reasons (most theatre scholars were trained in literature departments), but also for some of the same reasons that the link between print and national consciousness has taken such a deep hold in Ireland. At around the same time that *Imagined Communities* was first published, Irish theatre critics and practitioners began to ask themselves why Irish theatre had been for so long dominated by writers and the written word, particularly in comparison with other theatre cultures. So, for instance, there is still no authoritative scholarly study of Irish stage design or Irish theatre architecture, no survey of Irish directing, and the emerging scholarship on Irish acting has been concentrated so far in film studies. In other words, Irish theatre studies is only really beginning to come to terms with performance at a moment in history when the place of live performance within culture more generally is undergoing a profound shift. The most comprehensive remapping of this double shift has been Patrick Lonergan's *Theatre and Globalization: Irish Drama in the Celtic Tiger Era*, its title indicative of the author's remarkable ability to put the recent past into a historical perspective. 'What we see', he argues, 'is a transformation between 1991 and 2002 of the conception of a national theatre in an Irish context, whereby the Abbey has moved from the pinnacle of a vertical network of Irish theatres and cultural organizations, to being one hub on an international horizontal network'.[3]

Comparing, for instance, the historical conditions under which Sean O'Casey's *The Plough and the Stars* was first produced in 1926 with Garry Hynes's 1991 production, and later with Ben Barnes's 2002 production, Lonergan posits that 'it may be the case that national theatres are thriving because the concept of the nation is now regarded as largely obsolete, at least insofar as theatre is concerned'.[4] Barnes's production, he argues, staged the play for export in ways that confirmed expected images of Ireland, and thus presented national identity as a 'globalized brand'. On the other hand, Hynes's production, by foregrounding issues of social class in ways that were deeply uncomfortable for many in the audience, suggested the possibility of a different type of national theatre, 'grounded in notions of citizenship — one that assumes that theatre practitioners share experiences and concerns with local audiences, even when these experiences exist only to be rejected or evaluated'.[5]

In this frame, the central dynamic in Irish theatre culture is between theatre as the production (or, more properly, the reproduction) of Irishness as a recognizable global brand and theatre in performance as

1 Patrick Lonergan, *Theatre and Globalization: Irish Drama in the Celtic Tiger Period* (Houndmills, 2009), 220.
2 Philip Auslander, *Liveness: Performance in a Mediatized Culture* (New York, 1999).
3 Lonergan, *Theatre and Globalization*, 74.
4 Lonergan, 78.
5 Lonergan, 78.

a site for civic engagement, creating in the audience a real (if transitory) community (which is something quite different from Anderson's imagined community of the nation). What makes his argument more than a black-and-white snapshot of a recent cultural moment is not only that he manages to historicize the period of economic growth of the recent past, but that he is able to suggest that this dynamic is not new in Irish theatre, but can be extended back well before the term 'globalization' came into use. Arriving in Dublin airport in 1960 after playing for a month in New York, Micheál Mac Liammóir announced that Americans responded to his Irishness in one of three ways: talk of the colour green, references to shamrocks, or simply an indulgent smile. 'Their image of Ireland is not only incorrect but belittling.'[6]

Mac Liammóir's comments are quoted in Joan FitzPatrick Dean's analysis of his American tours of *The Importance of Being Oscar*, in a recent collection of essays edited by John Harrington, titled *Irish Theater in America: Essays on Irish Theatrical Diaspora*.[7] Contributions to the volume include an entertaining account of the role of Irish-Americans in the creation of the American musical (Mick Moloney); a survey of the stage Irishman (Maureen Murphy); and an impressive analysis of Dion Boucicault's American career (Deirdre McFeely), nicely complemented by an essay on Boucicault and the US press (Gwen Orel). Peter Kuch traces the career of George Tallis in Australia and New York; Lucy McDiarmid contributes a detailed essay on the fund-raising culture that sustained the early Abbey; Harrington himself develops his work on Samuel Beckett's reception in America; and Claire Gleitman looks at the ways in which Frank McGuinness's *Someone Who'll Watch Over Me* was transformed by production in a post-9/11 context. Nicholas Grene goes back to the manuscript correspondence surrounding the first production of Brian Friel's *Faith Healer* (at the Longacre Theatre in New York) and what he finds there significantly changes our understanding of that play. And Patrick Lonergan considers *Riverdance* and Brian Friel's *Dancing at Lughnasa* as defining touring phenomena of the 1990s. By shifting his focus from the aesthetic qualities of the two productions to the business of theatre, Lonergan shows us how these very different works are part of the same globalized theatre world.

However, the pieces that best illuminate the shift taking place in Irish culture are Christina Hunt Mahony's interrogation of what constitutes, for American audiences, an 'Irish play', and Christopher Berchild's research into the repertoires of Irish-American theatre companies. Berchild takes as his starting point a concept that Lonergan works out more fully in *Theatre and Globalization*, and which theatre theorists such as Auslander and Peggy Phelan[8] have explored in other contexts: that in an increasingly globalized and mediatized culture, audiences attend live theatre in search of an 'authentic' experience. But given the rapid structural transformations of Irish culture in the past two decades, just what constitutes an 'authentic' Irishness is by no means clear. Hence, Berchild argues, often what appears on American stages for Irish-American audiences is 'an image and a vision' of 'displacement', such as that conveyed in plays by writers like Mark O'Rowe or Enda Walsh, which present glimpses of 'a fundamentally unrecognisable Ireland'.[9] For his part, Berchild identifies three distinct types of Irish-American theatre companies — 'conservative', 'moderate' and 'aggressive' — each in its own way attempting to stage versions of what constitutes an 'authentic' Irishness, whether by trying to conserve a recognizable stage image of Ireland (which will seem real because it is familiar) or, alternatively, by bringing to American audiences cutting-edge Irish theatre. The most interesting moments occur, one suspects, when members of an audience expecting one form of authenticity find themselves facing another.

6 Quoted in Joan FitzPatrick Dean, 'Mac Liammóir's *The Importance of Being Oscar* in America', in John P. Harrington, ed., *Irish Theater in America: Essays on Irish Theatrical Diaspora* (Syracuse, 2009), 108.

7 Harrington's volume is the third publication to result from the Irish Theatrical Diaspora (ITD) project, started by Nicholas Grene in 2002. It brings together the proceedings of an ITD conference in New York 2006; other conferences have been held in Dublin (2004, 2007), London (2005), Lille (2008), and most recently, Galway, in April 2009.

8 Peggy Phelan, *Unmarked: The Politics of Performance* (London and New York, 1993).

9 Christopher Berchild, 'Ireland Rearranged: Contemporary Irish Drama and the Irish American Stage', in Harrington, ed., *Irish Theater in America*, 40.

A scene from an Abbey Theatre production of Sean O'Casey's *The Plough and the Stars*, 1942. Photo: Haywood Magee/Picture Post/Hulton Archive/Getty Images.

In the contributions of Berchild and others to *Irish Theater in America*, it is not only performance that comes back into focus; so too does the audience. In a like manner, Paige Reynolds argues in *Modernism, Drama and the Audience for Irish Spectacle* that if one seeks to reveal the complexity of culture, which can too easily be cut into clean ideologically shaped slices, one must first recover audiences: 'Live audiences could, more accurately than abstract and intangible theories of the nation, exhibit the rich complexities of colonial and postcolonial Ireland to itself and to the world'.[10] In Irish culture, she contends, revivalism and modernism have often been seen as antithetical, yet, on a closer look, it becomes clear that a study of past audience reaction to modernist spectacle causes such neatly drawn distinctions to merge and fold into something messier, and far more interesting. Reynolds focuses on five moments: the riots that accompanied the first week of John Millington Synge's *Playboy of the Western World* in 1907; audience responses to productions of Henrik Ibsen's *Rosmersholm* during what was known as 'Suffrage Week' in December 1913; the funeral of Terence MacSwiney, which attracted huge crowds in Cork in October 1920; the 1924 Tailteann Games; and the disturbances that met the opening of O'Casey's *The Plough and the Stars* in 1926. In the final case, Reynolds argues that the characters in the drama perform for one another (as well as for the audience gathered in the theatre), thus creating a play that is, in some ways, not just performed for an unruly audience, but about unruly audiences. 'As Synge had done years before', she writes, 'O'Casey offered onstage fictive audiences as a critique of real Irish audiences'.[11] Lonergan's reflections on the same play in *Theatre and Globalization* lead him to broadly similar conclusions; however, for Lonergan it is not only the original production that is of interest, but equally the

10 Paige Reynolds, *Modernism, Drama and the Audience for Irish Spectacle* (Cambridge, 2007), 206.

11 Reynolds, *Modernism, Drama and the Audience for Irish Spectacle*, 203.

way in which this critique can be reanimated (or suppressed) in subsequent stagings for new audiences. Clearly, productions of classic Irish plays are not necessarily the reiteration of a global Irish brand: one cannot predict what an audience will do with a play. As Reynolds concludes, 'the continuing recalcitrance of the audience, as demonstrated by our inability to define it concretely and conclusively, may in fact be its supreme attribute'.[12]

Recalcitrance may take many forms. For instance, in 1946 Roger McHugh encountered one particularly recalcitrant audience member while reviewing Frank Carney's controversial play about demonic possession, *The Righteous are Bold*. At a key moment in the action, when a possessed character spits at a priest and smashes a statue of the Virgin Mary, he overheard a voice behind him say: 'It's all right, mother, I have my eyes shut tight; I'm not looking at it at all'.[13] Paul Murphy relays this story in his study of Irish drama in the first half of the twentieth century, *Hegemony and Fantasy in Irish Drama, 1899–1949*. Although less concerned with the politics of production or audiences than Lonergan and Reynolds, Murphy presents complex, theoretically informed studies of plays that only a few years ago were thoroughly forgotten — plays such as Carney's *The Righteous are Bold*, Louis D'Alton's *Lovers' Meeting*, Paul Vincent Carroll's *Shadow and Substance*, and Margaret O'Leary's *The Woman*, as well as slightly more familiar works such as Teresa Deevy's *Katie Roche*. His earlier chapters explore work by Padraic Colum, George Fitzmaurice, George Shiels, William Boyle, as well as Lady Gregory and the figure who is in some ways the foundational figure in his study, Synge.

Murphy opens by establishing the theoretical lens through which he reads these plays, a highly refractive mixture of Jacques Lacan and subaltern studies, arguing that the middle-class hegemonic structures that emerged in Ireland after the Wyndham Land Act of 1903 made it necessary to construct figures against which the newly dominant class might define itself — figures which were, in the Lacanian sense, fantasies. For Murphy, the two iconic figures created by the theatre in the first half of the twentieth century were the Irish peasant and the Irish woman, and he accordingly divides his material between them (although there are, of course, areas of overlap). In some respects, this involves a certain amount of forcing his material into shapes that fit the argument, because as well as a thematic argument, he also organizes his material chronologically. Nevetheless, there are moments of real insight here. For instance, Murphy looks at T. C. Murray's 1917 play, *The Briery Gap*, which the Abbey declined to stage, presumably because it includes a character, Joan, whose pregnancy before marriage transforms her from 'the mould of the ideal Irish Woman to a "fallen woman"'. Her 'candidacy for incarceration in a Magdalen Asylum', writes Murphy, 'is assured'.[14] Reading Murphy's analysis in the wake of the 2009 *Ryan Report*, which makes it possible to see such institutions as, effectively, internment camps for the poor of an Ireland desperately trying to remodel itself as a respectable bourgeois society, it is difficult not to feel that Murphy's relentlessly critical reading of the theatre of this period — including the plays of Synge — might not be justified. At the same time, however, when Murphy's *Hegemony and Fantasy* is read alongside Reynolds's more nuanced reading of audiences (or, indeed, some of the work on differing audiences in Harrington's collection, or the retrospective suggestions of Lonergan's *Theatre and Globalization*), one cannot help but wonder if some of the plays that he finds so coercive might not have yielded meanings for individual audiences that were far more various, contingent, and even playful.

As Irish theatre enters a world in which liveness takes on new valences, and as Irish culture increasingly spills over the rim of the map of Ireland, it will become more difficult to write about plays as if they, at least in ways that are more or less analogous to print, constructed the imagined community of the nation.

12 Reynolds, *Modernism, Drama and the Audience for Irish Spectacle*, 206.
13 Quoted in Paul Murphy, *Hegemony and Fantasy in Irish Drama, 1899–1949* (Houndmills, 2008), 211.
14 Murphy, *Hegemony and Fantasy in Irish Drama*, 165.

Germany c. 1919: *The Cabinet of Dr. Caligari*. Photo: by Buyenlarge/Getty Images.

Modernism at the Movies

Sean Mannion

The Tenth Muse: Writing about Cinema in the Modernist Period
Laura Marcus
Oxford: Oxford University Press, 2007
xv + 562 pages. ISBN 978-0-19-923027-3

Cinema and Modernism
Critical Quarterly Book Series
David Trotter
With a Foreword by Colin MacCabe
Malden: Blackwell Publishing, 2007
xii + 205 pages. ISBN 978-1-4051-5982-1

Early Irish Cinema: 1895–1921
Denis Condon
Dublin: Irish Academic Press, 2008
xiv + 305 pages. ISBN 978-0-7165-2972-9

Cinema and literary modernism have long shared a special kinship, marked as much by mutual admiration as by fractious dissent. Film held a central place in that emergent mass culture against which many modernists reacted. However, it was also foremost amongst those 'technologies of perception' that, as Sara Danius has argued, were 'in a specific sense *constitutive* of high-modernist aesthetics'.[1] Writers of the period frequently commented on this ambivalent relationship, a typical example of which can be found in Ezra Pound's 1916 essay on James Joyce's *Exiles*. The cinema, as Pound pointed out in this piece, offered its viewers a steady diet of 'unfathomable imbecility';[2] in his famous poem *Hugh Selwyn Mauberley*, published four years after this essay, Pound would imply that such fare degraded high art, the public demanding of the poet 'prose kinema' rather than 'the "sculpture" of rhyme'.[3] But Pound also believed that the movies

1 Sara Danius, *The Senses of Modernism: Technology, Perception, and Aesthetics* (Ithaca, 2002), 3. Italics in original.
2 Ezra Pound, 'Mr. James Joyce and the Modern Stage', in Forrest Read, ed., *Pound/Joyce: The Letters of Ezra Pound to James Joyce, with Pound's Essays on Joyce* (London, 1967), 54.
3 Ezra Pound, *Hugh Selwyn Mauberley (Life and Contacts)* [1920], in Lawrence Rainey, ed., *Modernism: An Anthology* (Malden, 2005), 31–32.

possibly promised the mass cultivation of aesthetic taste, granting its audience an opportunity for critical and detached reflection unavailable in the traditional theatre. 'The minute the spectator begins to wonder why Charles Chaplin amuses him,' Pound contends, 'the said spectator is infinitely nearer a conception of art and infinitely more fit to watch creditable drama than when he, or she, is entranced by Mrs. So-and-So's gown or by the colour of Mr. So-and-So's eyes.'[4] And though he does not dwell upon this point, Pound also seems to imply that, by emphasizing motion instead of sculpture's stasis, both the films of Chaplin and film more generally aided this resuscitation of artistic discernment: 'Chaplin is better than X—, Y— and Z—, because he, Chaplin, gets the maximum effect with the minimum effort, minimum expenditure, etc., etc.'[5] The opposed strands of this brief but conflicted treatment of film are immediately familiar to us, inherited by our contemporary critical discourse through the influential writings of Theodor Adorno and Walter Benjamin, respectively.

This special connection has been so long assumed that we can at times evoke it glibly, praising, for instance, Ernest Hemingway's 'cinematic' prose or Joyce's use of montage. But such commentary blithely ignores the vast gulf between writing and film as media, and between film as we now understand it and film as experienced by its first audiences in different countries. Indeed, both the terms 'cinema' and 'modernism' as presently used emerged well after the phenomena that they supposedly delineate.[6] Laura Marcus and David Trotter offer their recent revaluations of this relationship in order to rectify such oversights. Trotter sums up well their shared complaint with earlier studies of the subject: 'There has been a systematic failure in discussions of early cinema and literary modernism to take proper account either of films made before the First World War, or of films made after it for a mass audience.'[7] Both Marcus and Trotter, by differing routes, seek to correct this lack of historical specificity and to reflect upon exactly how a new visual technology can impact an essentially verbal art, enriching in the process our understanding of how the movies shaped modernism.

In *The Tenth Muse: Writing about Cinema in the Modernist Period*, Marcus assesses film's impact on modernist writing by reconstructing with great deftness what primarily British and American critics actually wrote about film at the time. As 'the Cinderella of the arts', 'an unforeseen art ... that is absolutely new', film, from its public debut in 1895, put commentators 'in search of a genre and a language with which to describe the new medium, with its unprecedented powers of movement'.[8] In those days before D. W. Griffith and Orson Welles, thinkers were apt to see film less as a potential art form and more as a new piece of machinery, and they actively questioned 'the extent to which it could be an art form if it were entirely the product of the machine'.[9] The main problem with the 'cinematographical method', as Henri Bergson put it, was that it captured only a series of superficial instants, while completely missing the greater depths of truth and beauty.[10] These first writers adequated both film's novelties and its perceived lack of artistry by comparing it to other technologies — comparisons that, as Marcus's study illustrates, would be repeated and re-formed as film evolved. For instance, they continually evoked trains, responding both to the content of many early films and to film's formal essence as a technology of mechanical motion, one which radically altered perception of time and space; it also reminded them of automata, because of its uncanny ability to reproduce an illusory 'life'. These early film critics expressed a concern, shared with many literary modernists, for the fate of art and culture in an increasingly technologized modernity.[11]

Cinema at this early moment desperately stood in need of apologists who could vouch for its capacities as an art form. In

4 Pound, 'Mr. James Joyce', 55.
5 Pound, 'Mr. James Joyce', 55.
6 Denis Condon, summarizing André Gaudreault, makes this point about 'cinema' in his *Early Irish Cinema: 1895–1921* (Dublin, 2008), 17; (hereafter, Condon). For a concise genealogy of the term 'modernism', see Fredric Jameson, *A Singular Modernity: Essay on the Ontology of the Present* (London, 2002), 228–29.
7 David Trotter, *Cinema and Modernism* (Malden, 2007), 8; (hereafter, Trotter).
8 Laura Marcus, *The Tenth Muse: Writing about Cinema in the Modernist Period* (Oxford, 2007), xiii, 79 (hereafter, Marcus). The first two quotations, from Jean Epstein and Eric Walter White, respectively, come from the wonderful series of epigraphs with which Marcus opens her study, all of which describe initial reactions to film's radical newness (xiii–xv).
9 Marcus, 248.
10 Quoted in Marcus, 139.
11 For a nuanced discussion on the impact of technology in general on modernist art, see again Jameson, *A Singular Modernity*, 141–60.

12 Marcus, 220.
13 Quoted in Marcus, 188.
14 See Friedrich Kittler, *Discourse Networks, 1800/1900*, trans. Michael Metteer, with Chris Cullens (Stanford, 1990), 225.
15 Quoted in Marcus, 209. Italics in original.
16 Quoted in Marcus, 215.

chronicling the early polemicists of the 1910s and 1920s, Marcus traces the growth of film studies as a distinct discipline with its own fixed canons of criticism. Almost all of them returned to a foundational German text of eighteenth-century aesthetics, Gotthold Ephraim Lessing's *Laocoön*, to argue that film fused and transcended the traditional distinction between painting and poetry as arts of space and time, respectively. Film's defenders generally broke into two camps: those who, reversing the terms of Bergson's critique, emphasized the still flashes of beauty, glimpsed in spite of film's constant motion, and those who, embracing the terms of Bergson's critique as an endorsement, stressed film's motility and mechanism. Marcus dwells more extensively upon the former group of critics, because it represents a 'pictorial tradition in film and in film criticism' neglected in '[r]ecent modernist studies, with their tendency to equate film and montage aesthetics'.[12] These critics are also notable for deploying categories and concepts fundamental to modernism in defending film. For instance, the American poet Vachel Lindsay, in calling for an 'Imagist photoplay',[13] brought Pound's call for a poetry of terseness and restraint into the picture palace; his suggestion that film communicated via hieroglyphs — a potent and universal fusion of word and image — additionally recalled Pound's theory of the ideogram and modernism's more general aspirations for a universal language. Hugo Münsterberg, the Harvard perceptual psychologist with whom Gertrude Stein studied,[14] found film's art, in its emphasis upon human subjectivity and perception, '*overcoming the forms of the outer world, namely, space, time, and causality, and ... adjusting the events to the forms of the inner world, namely, attention, memory, imagination, and emotion*'.[15] And Victor Freeburg, one of the first film lecturers at Columbia University, drew upon the new philosophies of time articulated by William James and Edmund Husserl to argue that film achieved beauty by uniting an 'ever originating series of ever vanishing aspects' through careful, highly formal repetition within shots.[16] These critics found their ideal in the 1920 German expressionist film *The Cabinet of Dr. Caligari* [*Das Cabinet des Dr. Caligari*], which concentrated on *mise-en-scène*, symbolism, and visual beauty. The other group of critics, to which Marcus devotes less time, found its ideal in the frenetic movement of Charlie Chaplin. Writers such as Élie Faure and C. A. Lejeune found film's art in its technological and locomotive essence, and in this they agreed with avant-gardists such as Blaise Cendrars and Gertrude Stein.

This work of conceptual explication laid the foundation for film's institutionalization in the 1920s. Marcus sees the avant-garde Film Society, founded in London in 1925 by Ivor Montagu, as central to this story. By screening 'classic' films from countries as diverse as Germany, Russia and India, the society constructed a history and a canon for film; by citing studies of film in its explanatory programme notes, it similarly constructed a canon of film criticism. Perhaps most importantly, the society imported the theories of Soviet cinema into a Britain, where Soviet films were banned. It screened films and hosted lectures by Vsevolod Pudovkin and Sergei Eisenstein, granting to montage the conceptual importance that it still holds in film criticism today. These events led to the first regular columns of film criticism in newspapers, as well as the first periodicals dedicated to the topic, and spurred the creation of archives dedicated to preserving film. Though detractors would continue to doubt its aesthetic merits, film had finally come into its own.

Such a short summary cannot hope to do justice to Marcus's detailed and thorough work, in which she provides countless surprising insights through careful close reading and draws attention to important commentary upon film by

General Mulcahy being photographed by Pathé Gazette movie cameraman, Gordon Lewis. Courtesy of the National Library of Ireland.

unexpected authors such as H. G. Wells. To cite just a few interesting examples, she uncovers in Lindsay's writings an early attempt to rebut Adorno's critique of film. While Adorno believed that the movies and mass culture vitiated the liberal public sphere, 'imped[ing] the development of autonomous, independent individuals who judge and decide consciously for themselves ... [and who] would be the precondition for a democratic society',[17] Lindsay thought that the movies might cultivate a more robust civic spirit, imagining a cinema where, as Marcus summarizes, '[t]he democratic art of photoplay should be open to other forms of democratic process, including control over selection, questions of censorship, and critical responses'.[18] Marcus also points out the implicit nationalism of British film criticism, which sought to clarify the principles of film for the greater glory of an indigenous cinema dwarfed by the output of American studios. Perhaps the most fascinating and sustained reversal of popular critical assumptions, though, comes when Marcus addresses gender and film. Detractors of film at this time negatively identified it with women, following a general tendency, noted by Andreas Huyssen, whereby 'aesthetic discourse around the turn of the century consistently and obsessively genders mass culture and the masses as feminine, while high culture, whether traditional or modern, clearly remains the privileged realm of male activities'.[19] However, Marcus uncovers a simultaneous discourse among female film critics that actively revised and reversed these assumptions. For instance, within the writings of Iris Barry and Lejeune, Marcus finds a feminist reappropriation of film that stressed the importance of women, both as critics and viewers, and that critiqued the failure to create an adequate cinema for women.

This sympathy between film and femininity seems to carry into Marcus's discussion of how film impacted modernism. For example, she dedicates an entire chapter to Virginia Woolf, whose writings on film — phrases from which unexpectedly appear in her novels — betray a familiarity with

17 Theodor W. Adorno, 'Culture Industry Reconsidered', in *The Culture Industry: Selected Essays on Mass Culture*, ed. J. M. Bernstein (London, 2004 [1991]), 106.
18 Marcus, 196.
19 Andreas Huyssen, *After the Great Divide: Modernism, Mass Culture, Postmodernism* (Bloomington, 1987), 47.

its contemporary discussion. While Woolf at times derided film as merely locomotive, 'as a surface vision incapable of suggesting interiority', she ultimately advocated a cinema similar to the one championed by critics of the pictorial tradition, where 'the spectator's facilities ceased to be "detached from use" and [were] moved to seize sense-impressions at the moment of their fleeting unity'.[20] This prescription, as Marcus recognizes, could just as aptly describe Woolf's own experiments with the narration of sensation and consciousness in novels such as *The Waves* (1931). Woolf also admired, along with other film critics of the 1920s and 1930s, film's ability to capture a world of objects from which human subjectivity remained absent — as she puts it in her 1926 essay 'The Cinema': 'We behold them as they are when we are not there. We see life as it is when we have no part in it.'[21] This, Marcus suggests, explains Woolf's abiding preoccupation with light and with the framing of things, perhaps most famously displayed in the 'Time Passes' section of *To the Lighthouse* (1927), in which Woolf traces the fate of the Ramsay house and its furnishings amid the prolonged absence of its occupants. Marcus's reading of Woolf suggests film's centrality to most of those features we consider typical of modernist writing.

The other female modernists considered by Marcus, H. D. (Hilda Doolittle) and Dorothy Richardson, contributed to England's first avant-garde film journal. *Close Up*, founded by Kenneth Macpherson and Bryher (Annie Winifred Ellerman), itself meditated on the relationship between film and literature, soliciting contributions from writers as diverse as Stein, Woolf and Wells. By combining early film criticism's concern for motion and emotion with theories of Eisensteinian montage and psychoanalysis, the journal also began to create the parameters of film theory as currently practised. More importantly, those modernists contributing to the journal were forced to consider how film's unique effects could be rendered in language. Marcus suggests that to do so, these writers adopted a 'dynamic discourse' that performatively captured film's motion stylistically.[22] For instance, film led Richardson to a writing that better approximated inner speech and free association to capture the distinctive modality of film viewing, and which at times resembled a version of *écriture féminine*, 'a form of demotic, unpunctuated speech intended to represent a feminized, mass cultural reception'.[23] For H. D., an intense interest in film translated into a focus on light and vision in her poetry, and to a style of inner speech in her critical film writing. In arguing that film accessed the depths of the unconscious through a language of ideograms, she also expanded upon Lindsay's earlier writings and most clearly connected film and modernist literature in their aspiration for the universal image and word, respectively.[24] Within the pages of *Close Up*, we see modernism and early film achieve their closest alliance — one that would soon end as modernism passed into late modernism, and hieroglyphic silent film disappeared with the advent of sound.[25]

David Trotter similarly seeks to historicize the interaction between cinema and modernism, and his findings generally agree with those of Marcus.[26] However, his study *Cinema and Modernism* reaches these conclusions by a rather different route, examining in detail the films that modernists could have actually viewed in a cinema. In doing so, though, he avoids arguing for the occurrence of specific film techniques within modernist texts, as this would raise questions about how literature can hope to reproduce film's primarily visual effects. Instead, he suggests a parallelism between the form of early cinema and the philosophical questions at the heart of modernism. Specifically, he claims that film evoked for modernists a tension between presence and absence, between an experience of unprecedented vital immediacy and of inescapable

20 Marcus, 103, 113.
21 Quoted in Marcus, 108.
22 Marcus, 343.
23 Marcus, 359.
24 Marcus, 364.
25 On late modernism, see Tyrus Miller, *Late Modernism: Politics, Fiction, and the Arts between the World Wars* (Berkeley, 1999), esp. 105–10, where Miller makes a relevant argument about the impact of the sound film on Wyndham Lewis's late modernist aesthetic.
26 Each, in fact, approvingly cites the other's work on Virginia Woolf and cinema; see Marcus, 109, and Trotter, 170.

mechanical mediation: as he puts it,

> some early film-makers shared with some writers of the period a conviction both that the instrumentality of the new recording media had made it possible for the first time to represent (as well as to record) *existence as such*; and that the superabundant generative power of this instrumentality (the ever-imminent autonomy of the forms and techniques it gave rise to) put in doubt the very idea of existence as such.[27]

Clearly, this tension coincides nicely with those uncovered by Marcus, where film's motion clashed with its potential for depth, and where its mechanism stood in uneasy relation to the glimpses of beauty it also allowed. For Trotter, this tension led modernists into a 'curious' engagement with 'film's neutrality as a medium',[28] provoking them to adopt 'a will-to-automatism, a determination to view the world, for however brief an interval, as a machine would view it'.[29]

Trotter carefully traces this dialectic within early examples of film. He points to how the first actualities — films that lingered for a minute or so upon real life events, such as the gathering of crowds in a city or the arrival of a train — allowed their audiences to analyse with minute precision the contingent details of everyday life, as if one were actually there. However, such presence was enabled by the viewer's ultimate absence, in that the filmed scenes necessarily belonged to a time past, and that the foregrounding of random detail within them attested to 'the constitutive absence of the human observer whose authority and compassion might have mediated the scene: might have made a meaning of it, rather than sense of it'.[30] These actualities, in other words, announced the camera's discovery of what Benjamin called 'the optical unconscious', which 'manages to assure us of a vast and unsuspected field of action' invisible within everyday existence.[31] The stereoscope, an early film technology in which two images viewed through binocular lens created the illusion of depth, offered the same contradiction, as images in the foreground appeared tangible and present while those in the background seemed flat and abstracted, available for detached spectation. Trotter convincingly argues that such 'stereoscopic effects' persisted well into the era of narrative cinema.[32] Even the works of D. W. Griffith, the director who displayed an almost paranoiac concern for integrating each detail of a shot into the overarching story, contain an 'anti-system' of random physical detail and contingency,[33] conveyed through both close-ups and focus upon objects that hold 'a sense generated by or in the photographic image which yet falls short of intelligibility'.[34] Similarly, the lateral tracking shots occasionally used in film epics up to the 1930s disrupted narrative meaning, the camera's movement, which humans could not hope to replicate, focusing attention upon the scene's details and the camera's own status as machine.

It is this tension between sense and intelligibility, between presence and absence, that Trotter discovers throughout modernist writing. For instance, Ireland's most famous and hopeless cinema entrepreneur, James Joyce (who, in 1909, opened a cinema in Dublin, which soon after failed), engaged with film particularly in the 'Wandering Rocks' episode of *Ulysses* (1922) — though not in the ways that we normally assume he did. Trotter disagrees that the episode relies on montage, since the theory of montage available to Joyce when he wrote came not from Eisenstein, but rather from Griffith, whose use of the technique stressed an abstraction from milieu alien to Joyce's Dublin-obsessed novel. For Trotter, 'Wandering Rocks' resembles less the epics of parallel editing and more the actuality films made in Dublin at the turn of the century, as both display the city crowd in all its richness and without any overarching rationale. Consequently,

27 Trotter, 181. Italics in original.
28 Trotter, 10. Italics in original.
29 Trotter, 113–14.
30 Trotter, 182.
31 Walter Benjamin, 'The Work of Art in the Age of Its Technological Reproducibility (Third Version)', trans. Harry Zohn and Edmund Jephcott, in *Selected Writings, Volume 4, 1938–1940*, eds. Howard Eiland and Michael W. Jennings (Cambridge, Mass., 2004), 265–66.
32 Trotter, 49.
33 Trotter, 51.
34 Trotter, 50–51.

the episode breaks from the novel's initial style and assumes a camera-like perspective upon the random objects and individuals that people it, obscuring the novel's two main protagonists amid the city's busyness and vitality.

Film equally impacts the poems of T. S. Eliot, the writer whom, as Trotter acknowledges, most critics see as constitutionally allergic to mass culture, 'the mandarin High Modernist'.[35] However, building upon David Chinitz's ground-breaking research on Eliot and his productive engagements with popular culture,[36] Trotter argues that his poetry addresses, head-on, film's implications for literature and modernity. Trotter admirably displays Eliot's familiarity with film and film technique throughout his letters and essays, discussing at length 'Effie the Waif', a joco-serious Western scenario drafted by Eliot in a letter to his cousin Eleanor Hinkley. References to film appear in both the first and final drafts of *The Waste Land*, and the focus on visuality and flickering illumination throughout Eliot's poems recalls film's essence as a medium of light and shadow. All of these facts lead Trotter to suggest, in a close reading of *The Waste Land*, that the poem's complex use of poetic rhythm owes much to film. As Trotter points out, the poem often suddenly assumes a repetitive, formal metre within scenes where mass society's homogenization is most evident. This deadened metre, Trotter claims, approximated film's resilient focus on the mechanical at the expense of spirit and intuition, and allowed Eliot to express, at the level of poetic form, his critique of modernity. Eliot might have ultimately disdained film, yet he relied upon it to represent the society of which it was a symptom.

Trotter's assessment of Woolf's engagement with cinema generally coincides with that of Marcus's, both suggesting that film's ability to present the world focused Woolf's engagement with everydayness. Trotter additionally argues that Woolf's complex treatment of space and movement also owes a debt to early cinema, just as her thoughts on time were prompted by the film newsreels that she viewed. These newsreels, which vividly reproduced people and events long lost to the past, suggested to her a way to narrate a world vacated of its participants, as in *To the Lighthouse*. Trotter concludes his study with an unexpected modernist — Charlie Chaplin. Chaplin shared with the other three high modernists discussed by Trotter — Joyce, Eliot, Woolf — an interest in film's automatism. By emphasizing rote imitation of others and of machines within his slapstick comedies, Chaplin turns himself into a machine much like the movie camera.

Trotter's study contributes tremendously to our understanding of both the films and literary texts he examines. He displays an enviable literacy in both modernist and film studies, and this knowledge serves him well in bridging their shared concerns. His research confirms a more general point made by Tim Armstrong about modernism's relationship to technology: 'rather than being a reaction against or escape from the forces of modernity, cultural Modernism is implicated in numerous ways with the scientific, technological, and political shifts which characterize the modern era'.[37] Trotter alludes to this broader technological universe to which early film belongs, citing Hugh Kenner's magisterial study of the effects of the second machine age on modernism, *The Mechanic Muse*;[38] his own impressive and insightful study, however, would have benefited from a longer discussion on how film's impact on modernism differed from the impact of other technologies on literature at this time. At times, both Trotter and Marcus are too quick to treat different technologies as metaphors for film — the electric light, for example. There are compelling reasons to do so, of course: after all, film is essentially a medium of light. Marcus homes in on one such example from Woolf's 1922 novel *Jacob's Room*:

35 Trotter, 125.
36 See David Chinitz, *T. S. Eliot and the Cultural Divide* (Chicago, 2003).
37 Tim Armstrong, *Modernism, Technology, and the Body: A Cultural Study* (Cambridge, 1998), 4.
38 For instance, Trotter, 4, quotes Kenner's observation that T. S. Eliot was 'undeniably his time's chief poet of the alarm clock, the furnished flat, the ubiquitous telephone, commuting crowds, the electric underground railway'.

> The light from the arc lamp drenched him from head to toe ... You could see the pattern of his trousers; the old thorns on his stick; his shoe laces; bare hands; and face ... Whether we know what was in his mind is another question.[39]

Trotter cites a similar use of light in Eliot's poetry, where it consistently illumines a world without greater meaning, confirming 'the sheer resilience of the practical intellect'.[40] However, to adapt Freud's famous admonition, let us say here that sometimes a light is just a light. Indeed, the electric light was still a relatively recent invention when Woolf and Eliot were writing, making its first significant public appearance in 1878; books such as Matthew Luckiesh's *Artificial Light: Its Influence upon Civilization*, which lauded the electric light as initiating an unprecedented transformation of human life, were appearing in print as late as 1920. Critics such as David E. Nye have suggested that the city's electric lights crucially inspired modernist aesthetics, providing 'the cultural ground from which modernism sprang', as 'the landscape's chaotic brilliance also expressed an implicit ideology that valued simultaneity, fragmentation, and montage'.[41]

Before turning to film to explain modernist references to light, one should first see whether these references make sense in the technology's own contemporary terms and discourse. In fact, people responded to electric lights in ways that resonate with Woolf's and Eliot's descriptions of them. For instance, the art historian Wilhelm Hausenstein, forced to write by candlelight amid the blackouts of the Second World War, observed that

> in the 'weaker' light of a candle, objects have a different, much more marked profile — it gives them a quality of 'reality'. This is something that is lost in the electric light: objects (seemingly) appear more clearly, but in reality it *flattens* them. Electric light imparts too much brightness and thus things lose body, outline, substance — in short, their essence.[42]

Ernst Bloch agreed, arguing in his 1935 essay 'Technology and Ghostly Apparitions' that the electric light rid the world of spirit and replaced it with pure empiricism and rationality:

> Without exaggeration, it can be said that the electric bulb, having banished the shadows from our dwelling places, has cured attacks of nighttime anxiety more decisively than Voltairean skepticism — for it has driven evil spirits not only from the mind, but from the nooks and crannies of the external darkness as well.[43]

Both thinkers suggest that the electric light, in powerfully illuminating the details of the visible world, robbed that world of any depth or spirit — just as the lights described by Woolf and Eliot do. The electric light, then, reminds us that we should not be so quick to forget the other new technologies that emerged in that era.

Moreover, tensions cited by both Trotter and Marcus as central to film can be found in technologies invented prior to the moment of modernism. Both compare the effects of film with photography, for example. Trotter quotes Stanley Cavell's observation that '[p]hotography ... maintains the presentness of the world by accepting our absence from it', while film intensifies this by offering 'a succession of automatic world projections'.[44] Similarly, Marcus discusses the importance for Woolf's fiction of editing a volume of her great-aunt's photography, prompting reflection upon 'visual representations' beyond film.[45] Furthermore, Trotter's description of early film as marked by both presence and absence, narrative meaning and resistant detail, recalls Roland Barthes's distinction between *studium*

39 Quoted in Marcus, 133.
40 Trotter, 134.
41 David E. Nye, *Narratives and Spaces: Technology and the Construction of American Culture* (New York, 1997), 88.
42 Quoted in Wolfgang Schivelbusch, *Disenchanted Night: The Industrialization of Light in the Nineteenth Century*, trans. Angela Davies (Berkeley, 1995 [1983]), 178. Italics in original.
43 Ernst Bloch, 'Technology and Ghostly Apparitions,' in *Literary Essays*, trans. Andrew Jordan and others (Stanford, 1998), 315–16.
44 Quoted in Trotter, 195.
45 Marcus, 152.

and *punctum*, central to his theory of photography. He defines the former as those intelligible aspects of an image, freighted with symbolism or cultural meaning, which the viewer implicitly interprets as part of the image's 'story'. The latter, however, disrupts this overall message, in the guise of a small object or detail that resolutely refuses explanation.[46] This *punctum* for Barthes calls attention to photography's inevitably belated nature, attesting to its subject's existence within the past and, by extension, its absence in the future, much as film for Trotter stresses the viewer's ultimate separation from the world he or she witnesses on the screen. Given the similar logic shared by both photography and film, one might wonder why the invention of photography did not have an impact comparable to that of film on the literature of its time.

Both Trotter and Marcus answer this question by implying that film functions for modernists as what Fredric Jameson calls (in discussing Benjamin's use of technology) 'an exercise in allegorical meditation, in the locating of some fitting emblem in which to anchor the peculiar and nervous modern state of mind'.[47] Trotter suggests as much when discussing the impact of film on Woolf's aesthetic, noting that movies merely sharpened an emphasis that would have inevitably emerged in her writing. Similarly, film allowed Eliot to articulate an analogous mechanization of modern society. However, Marcus offers the most sustained reflection on this issue, hinting that film functions as an objective correlative for the conditions of industrial modernity, where '[t]he movement that defines cinema (as it comes so often to define modernity itself) is also a more fragile and unstable ephemerality at every level'.[48] She points to an explicit 'connection between cinema and urban modernity' in film writing throughout the period,[49] while also highlighting the connection made by critics between film as machine and the increasing mechanization of labour. Lindsay, for instance, treasured the intimate moments of Chaplin's films for 'giving human measure to mechanized modern time, including the factory-time of a society dominated by Taylorist and Fordist models of "scientific management", with its autonomization of the human body and its energies, and to cinematic time'.[50] Münsterberg, who published on both film and the psychology of industrial efficiency, becomes a key figure in this regard. He studies 'the new forms of mental and physical life demanded by modern industrial society',[51] while also advocating cinematic beauty, suggesting that film succoured the harm inflicted by modern life. In other words, film's ability to offer its audiences an experience of both intense vitality and of dwarfing, inhuman mechanism formally reflected the historical realities of America and England at the turn of the century. German sociologist Georg Simmel, in fact, discovered an analogous tension at the heart of metropolitan modernity in 1903, which offered an individual heightened subjective freedom, while objectively '[t]he individual has become a mere cog in an enormous organization of things and powers which tear from his hands all progress, spirituality, and value in order to transform them from their subjective form into the form of a purely objective life'.[52] Modernists perhaps latched on to these latent tendencies in film and photography, while the Victorians did not, because these intimated the manifest conditions of an emergent modernity.

However, such analogies and analyses seem more apt for the England and America upon which Marcus focuses, rather than for a peripheral country such as Ireland. As Joe Cleary has pointed out, Ireland, with the exception of Belfast, did not experience the same intense industrialization and mechanization endured in parts of Europe and America at this time. Instead, 'across the island as a whole, the economy and workforce were still overwhelmingly rural, artisan, and pre-industrial'.[53] Cleary notes that, consequently, Ireland had nothing resembling a modernist moment in film,

46 Roland Barthes, *Camera Lucida: Reflections on Photography*, trans. Richard Howard (New York, 1982), 25–27.
47 Fredric Jameson, *Marxism and Form: Twentieth-Century Dialectical Theories of Literature* (Princeton, 1971), 76.
48 Marcus, 183.
49 Marcus, 142.
50 Marcus, 199.
51 Marcus, 211.
52 Georg Simmel, 'The Metropolis and Mental Life,' in *The Sociology of Georg Simmel*, trans. and ed. Kurt H. Wolff (London, 1964), 422.
53 Joe Cleary, *Outrageous Fortune: Capital and Culture in Modern Ireland* (Dublin, 2007), 86.

as this technology was 'dependent on rather large scale political and economic institutional supports and constraints'.[54] As a result, cinema is often seen as what Nicholas Andrew Miller calls 'ex-centric', 'external to that comparatively narrow range of discourses conventionally linked with Ireland'.[55] Given this, one might wonder how Marcus would explain the emergence of James Joyce, in some ways the archetypal modernist, within a society where cinema and industrialization played a markedly lesser role. While she interestingly discusses film technologies in both Dublin and Trieste, she generally treats Joyce alongside the Anglo-American modernists of her study, not expanding upon how Joyce's specifically Irish experience of cinema might have differed from that of these other writers.

Luke Gibbons has shown how Ireland's different historical conditions could generate a literary style approximating cinematic innovation. In his brief yet insightful essay 'Montage, Modernism and the City', Gibbons suggests that the violent shocks of colonial history fostered the violent juxtapositions and montage of *Ulysses*. Though Ireland had avoided extensive industrialization, it experienced similar traumas long before: 'the disintegration of experience visited by the city and modern life on Dickens' work was brought about by the antinomies of colonial rule in Ireland'.[56] In addition, the recent work of Denis Condon, which exhaustively tracks the exhibition and (very limited) production of early cinema in Ireland, enables scholars to examine the impact of film on Irish modernism with the historical specificity on display in both Trotter's and Marcus's work. Such an approach would also more generally historicize how technology caused modernist style by highlighting the differential impact of technology on specific national cultures.

The impress of Ireland's colonial history upon film can be seen in the very periodization of Condon's *Early Irish Cinema: 1895–1921*. Marcus's study ends with the dawn of sound film, which destroyed the visual emphasis of early cinema and its criticism. The significant rupture for early cinema in Ireland, however, arose from circumstances external to film as a technology: the partitioning of Ireland and the subsequent violence of the Irish Civil War, which put to an end Ireland's slight indigenous film production. National pressures also transmuted many of those tropes identified by Marcus as central to early film. For instance, the train took on specifically Irish implications in light of films that simulated railroad travel into the Irish countryside. While still significantly connected to film's essence as movement, the train also evoked for an Irish audience questions about the foreign technological reproduction of their country's pastoral countryside, while signalling the growth of an Irish heritage industry. Condon's study, with its tireless and minute reconstruction of the films shown and produced in Ireland at this time, complements well the work of Trotter and Marcus by emphasizing a particularly Irish reception of the international film industry.[57]

Condon's book, like those previously discussed, also focuses upon early cinema's emergence within a context radically different from the genteel one into which it would later settle. 'Because the cinema did not exist as an independent cultural institution at this time', Condon contends that 'cinematograph shows relied on the physical infrastructure and/or the aesthetic language of other cultural practices to reach their audiences'.[58] Thus, long before Dublin had theatres dedicated solely to cinema, short films and actualities were shown at music halls alongside live performance, and alongside celebrations of cultural nationalism at charity bazaars; film was understood along a continuum of other visual technologies such as the X-ray. Though this situation sounds familiar, one fact distinguished this experience of early film from that in England and America:

54 Cleary, *Outrageous Fortune*, 94.

55 Nicholas Andrew Miller, *Modernism, Ireland and the Erotics of Memory* (Cambridge, 2002), 12.

56 Luke Gibbons, 'Montage, Modernism and the City', in *Transformations in Irish Culture* (Notre Dame and Cork, 1996), 168.

57 For a salient and brilliant example of such an approach, see Miller's discussion of *The Birth of a Nation*'s premiere in Dublin on September 18, 1916 in *Modernism, Ireland and the Erotics of Memory*, 97–126.

58 Condon, 16.

its belatedness. These technologies often appeared first in London, and Condon points out that newspaper reports of them did much to prepare Irish audiences discursively for their later arrival. One must consider this belatedness alongside the unique state of Irish film culture, in which, as Condon notes, 'the development of indigenous [film production] was considerably slower than in other countries'.[59] Irish film, then, seems to symbolize the country's colonial modernity, just as film in England and America embodied industrial modernity. Just as '[t]he Irish film industry, by contrast [to other countries], was largely an import, wholesaling and retail business because the "product" was overwhelmingly manufactured elsewhere',[60] Ireland's colonial economy relied upon the importation and consumption of British and foreign goods to compensate for the practical non-existence of indigenous manufacturing.[61]

However, film soon focused more nationalist energies. It is true, as Condon notes, that Irish nationalists were initially wary about film: for instance, as film began to be institutionalized in the 1910s through the erection of picture palaces and the publication of periodicals such as the *Irish Limelight*, the Irish Vigilance Association sought to have censored films regarded as insidiously immoral and, consequently, English. However, its potential for audience participation led to an entente between film and nationalism. Newsreels of the Boer War, for example, sparked nationalist protest in movie theatres; local views not only of Dublin street scenes but of important national events, such as the 1913 Gaelic football finals and the funeral of IRB president Thomas Ashe, moulded the isolated spectators of these films into a national community. Foreign film companies working in Ireland stoked such sentiments by adopting Dion Boucicault's political melodrama to history films that fused fiction and contemporary documentary material, 'showing that the historical process in some sense culminates in the present and emphasizing the relevance of the past to the current project of defining the Irish nation'.[62] If, as Marcus argues, film came to represent the city, then in Ireland it began to represent the nation, a fact given articulation in 1916 with the founding of the Film Company of Ireland, the country's first major production company. Collaborating with actors from the Abbey Theatre such as Fred Donovan, this company adopted Charles Kickham's *Knocknagow* for the screen, striving to create Ireland's *Birth of a Nation*. Indeed, Condon argues that the importance of such participatory nationalist engagement with cinema delayed the adoption of the standards of narrative cinema within Ireland.

These three studies, then, greatly expand our understanding of early cinema and its moment, while also allowing scholars to adopt an approach to the relationship between visual technologies and literary modernism that is 'as "comparative" as possible', as Jean-Michel Rabaté has recently prescribed.[63] Reading Marcus's and Trotter's work in light of Condon's, also opens up rewarding areas of investigation for Irish studies into both the possibilities and contours of a particularly Irish modernism. A combination of Trotter's and Marcus's elucidating comments on Joyce's engagement with film with Condon's work on Irish cinema might provide one potential approach to this issue. Such a constellation would emphasize the colonial modernity through which Joyce filtered both film and modernism.

Marcus offers a concise yet compelling treatment of Joyce's filmic modernism, arguing that 'Joyce's focus on the minutiae of the everyday and the breaking down of gesture into its component parts is shaped by the ways in which the camera frames reality, and by the new relation to the object-world, including the animation of the inanimate, and the mechanization of the human, that it brought into being'.[64] She focuses on the mutoscope, mentioned in the 'Nausicaa' episode of *Ulysses*, and argues

59 Condon, 237.
60 Condon, 235.
61 On this point, see Joseph Lee, *The Modernisation of Irish Society, 1848–1918* (Dublin, 1973), 15.
62 Condon, 202.
63 Jean-Michel Rabaté, *1913: The Cradle of Modernism* (Oxford, 2007), 5.
64 Marcus, 93.

that Joyce actively engages the trope of film as automata by bringing to life in 'Circe' the Venus statue that Bloom ponders outside the National Library in 'Lestrygonians'. As Marcus concludes her comments: 'Bloom's is indeed a dream of the moving statue, and *Ulysses* takes us back to the fantasies generated by the vision-machines of cinema at the medium's very inception.'[65] It is interesting, however, that Marcus finds the height of film's impact upon *Ulysses* within what is, from a psychoanalytic perspective, the novel's most regressive chapter. The chapter is famous for lingering upon sexual taboo and perversion, and for transgressing the boundaries between genders and species. However, as Marcus rightly points out, this 'regression' occurs in an episode in which film as well as other visual and recording technologies proliferate, such as the electric light and the phonograph.[66] Marcus observes that Joyce, while dwelling upon the primal urges of the human, simultaneously deploys within the episode early stop-motion film tricks for bringing objects to life, such as Bella Cohen's fan or Bloom's loquacious bar of soap, 'for his own animations of the object world in *Ulysses*'.[67] In 'Circe', Joyce places the mechanical modernity of cinema into uneasy proximity with atavism and primitive regression.

Such an apparent contradiction, however, makes sense when one remembers the colonial frame for Ireland's reception of film, in which film's modernity simultaneously evoked Ireland's colonial underdevelopment. This colonial reality looms large throughout 'Circe', culminating in an attack upon Stephen by two drunken English soldiers. As David Lloyd has recently observed, the very contiguity of technologies like film alongside a supposedly non-modern focus on the sexual and the body within this episode captures the particular logic of Irish history, 'such that the medieval grotesque becomes the recursive analogue of capitalist and colonial subjection of the human even at what stand as their most technologically advanced moments in any given epoch'.[68] In other words, Joyce's reflections on film might stand in intimate relation to his reflections on Ireland's colonial underdevelopment, recalling the fact that, as Condon argues, film reminded Irish's audiences not only of cutting-edge modern technology, but of the lack of it within their country.

Such a reading might explain the appearance of film and other recording technologies at other points in *Ulysses*. For if 'Circe' represents the 'dream of the moving statue' come true, as Marcus suggests,[69] it is notable that other statues continually fail to materialize within the novel, such as 'the slab where Wolfe Tone's statue was not', depicted in 'Wandering Rocks'.[70] This latter episode, in which Trotter saw film's most evident impact upon Joyce's novel, reveals an additional aspect of Joyce's colonial engagement with film. Trotter points to one example when he notes that Joyce plays on the failure of mutual recognition within actuality films in order to undercut deference to British rule. However, as the reference to Tone's statue hints, there might be a further, melancholic aspect to the episode's cinematic mechanism, given that, as Condon observes, Irish film tapped the medium's participatory potential, exemplified by actualities, to foster a deep sense of national community in its audiences. The episode's repeated failures of recognition might indicate the ultimate failure to form a national community through the cinema, the 'dream of the moving statue' left unrealized.

Joyce's other treatments of reproduction technologies within the novel reiterate this failure. As Condon argues, Irish films cultivated this sense of community by re-creating scenes of the Irish past and placing them alongside contemporary Irish newsreels, thus showing the continuity of Irish history with the present aspirant nation. However, it is just such an attempt at fusing past and present through technology that fails in the 'Hades' episode. Set primarily in Glasnevin Cemetery, Bloom

65 Marcus, 98.
66 See James Joyce, *Ulysses*, ed. Hans Walter Gabler (New York, 1993 [1922]), 15.150–51, 15.2170–73, for respective examples of electric lights and gramophones within the episode (hereafter, *Ulysses*).
67 Marcus, 92–93.
68 David Lloyd, *Irish Times: Temporalities of Modernity* (Dublin, 2008), 93.
69 Marcus, 98.
70 *Ulysses*, 10.379.

71 *Ulysses*, 6.963–64.
72 *Ulysses*, 6.966–68.
73 *Ulysses*, 6.965–66.
74 *Ulysses*, 6.975.
75 *Ulysses*, 6.970.
76 *Ulysses*, 6.977–78.
77 *Ulysses*, 6.923–24.
78 *Ulysses*, 6.926–27.

here reflects on a scheme for remembering the dead by recording their voices and placing gramophones 'in every grave or keep it in the house'.[71] Such ingenuity shares a common project with film, as it would '[r]emind you of the voice like the photograph reminds you of the face. Otherwise you couldn't remember the face after fifteen years, say.'[72] Bloom's imagined example, however, where a family '[p]ut[s] on old greatgrandfather', fails miserably, as the aged record transforms the venerable ancestor's voice into a crackled garble of onomatopoeia: the voice's message, that 'amawfullyglad kraark awfullygladaseeagain ... amawf krpthsth',[73] is patently absurd, as the voice's inaudibility stresses the greatgrandfather's absence. What is important for our purposes, however, is that within Bloom's stream of consciousness, this technological failure is linked to the irrevocable absence of Ireland's historical heroes from the present. When Bloom soon after sees an old rat within a crypt, '[a]n old stager: greatgrandfather',[74] which also communicates via onomatopoeia — 'Rtststr!'[75] — he connects it to the gramophonic greatgrandfather about whom he had just pondered. However, this greatgrandfather moves not to reproduce the past, but to devour it, scampering into a grave of which Bloom asks, 'Who lives here? Are laid the remains of Robert Emery. Robert Emmet was buried here by torchlight, wasn't he?'[76]

Within a page, then, Joyce links technology's failure to recover the past to the failure to recover the heroes of Irish nationalism. For instance, Mr. Power suggests upon seeing Parnell's grave that '[s]ome say he is not in that grave at all. That the coffin was filled with stones. That one day he will come again.'[77] However, Joyce seems to agree with Hyne's assessment of the situation: 'Parnell will never come again ... He's there, all that was mortal of him'.[78] In suggesting that technologies like the gramophone and the film will fail to bring about this resurrection, Joyce expresses doubts about technology's potential to mitigate and redeem Ireland's colonial past, while yet drawing upon its effects in generating his own revolutionary modernist style.

These three studies, then, are necessary reading for any student of modernism. Trotter's and Marcus's careful, meticulous research resituates modernism's relationship to its times, highlighting the myriad ways in which one of the most powerful new technologies of mass culture helped to create arguably the most important moment in twentieth-century literature. Their admirable impulse to attend to and cite copiously from the contemporary discourse on both of these phenomena, whether from avant-garde journals or daily newspapers, additionally relocates particular modernist writers, traditionally regarded as transnational, universal, and aestheticist, within their specific historical and national milieux. Along with Condon's work, these texts begin a remapping of modernist studies, emphasizing the differential impact and experience of many of modernism's long-standing keywords — such as technology, the city, and mass culture — within different national contexts and within cultures at opposite ends of the colonial relationship. Extending the method of these three works to the modernisms of other countries promises a more robust understanding of global modernist style and of how modernity, in its many guises, spurred such innovation.

Breakfast party at Samuel Rogers', 1763–1855, Charles Mottram, c.1823, with Sheridan, Moore, Wordsworth, Southey, Coleridge, Byron, Kemble, Flaxman, Mackintosh, Lansdowne, Smith, Irving and Jeffrey. © The Art Archive.

'A Different Grammar'

Carl Dawson

The Cambridge History of English Romantic Literature
Edited by James Chandler
Cambridge: Cambridge University Press, 2009
xii + 782 pages. ISBN 978-0-521-79007-9

This welcome volume begins with a wide-ranging Introduction by James Chandler and concludes with a probing essay by Jerome McGann. From first to last it offers a wealth of information and sets a high standard in its discussions of 'the new poetries', late eighteenth- and early nineteenth-century publishing, shifting genres and literary tastes, and the ethos and reception of *writing* in the 'Romantic' period. It seems appropriate that the scholarship in this *new* history comes to us in the form of *essais*, Montaigne's legacy to future generations and the favoured prose genre of English Romantic writers. One advantage to a collection of this scope is that the essays overlap, and the result, for this reader, is the sense of a palimpsest, a layered way of seeing and understanding — or, a bit more critically, a volume growing piecemeal to an admirable, if not fully realized, whole.

The subject of the essays, 'Romantic literature', remains as elusive as it has always been. A. O. Lovejoy would chuckle in his grave about the types and names with which scholars have divided and subdivided 'that wide expanse' since his time, and he may have counted how many of his first sightings persist in a volume that sophisticates its material while describing but not defining the nominal subject. Chandler, in his otherwise masterly Introduction, says that English Romantic literature requires 'a different grammar' from, say, 'English Medieval Literature', because '"Romantic Literature" forms a category so powerfully intelligible in itself that it makes more sense to speak of the English variety of that literature than of the "Romantic Age"'. This may result, he says, from the association of the period 'with the concept of a *movement*'.[1] But 'a different grammar' can mean in a limited sense merely a different name, and the name 'Romanticism' itself raises questions, even for a contributor like Susan J. Wolfson, who has doubts about the book's title. 'This present "History of English Romantic Literature"', she writes, 'still likes this old naming-convention for a cultural and a chronological span that does not always spell "Romantic".'[2]

A slippery monster, 'Romanticism' has teased and tested scholars, as it teases these scholars, for good and maybe obvious reasons. Across generations, indeed across two centuries, the discussions of English Romanticism favoured those writers singled out to be the giants of their time, though they were not necessarily the giants *in* their time. William Blake, William Wordsworth, and Samuel Taylor Coleridge, from the first generation; Percy Bysshe Shelley, Byron, and John Keats, from the second, grew in the minds of early nineteenth-century and Victorian critics; fell into minor decline; and enjoyed a new incarnation through the second half of the twentieth century. Until the mid-nineteenth century, the writings of these poets mattered more than fiction, and even novelists like Walter Scott, Jane Austen, or Mary Shelley, hung on the fringes of genius. Writers such as Robert Southey, Thomas Carlyle, T. L. Peacock, William Hazlitt, Charles Lamb, Leigh Hunt, the once popular women poets Letitia Elizabeth Landon and Felicia Hemans, and male poets like John Clare, languished somewhere behind. The canonized Romantic poets, volatile as their reputations often were, remained at the top of the literary hierarchy.

Tacitly at least, the authors of *English Romantic Literature* raze that hierarchy and insist on a kind of flat *democracy* for the period they study, as for their own even-handed but paradoxically restricted scholarship. Gone from most of these pages are qualitative discriminations, biographical studies, the foregrounding of poetry, and textual studies or recoveries. References to literary scholars such as the contributors to the Bollingen-Princeton Coleridge series, the work on Mary Shelley's *Frankenstein* by Charles Robinson, the Keats and Shelley Pforzheimer project, and others central to contemporary research are few or missing. Here 'the new criticism' seems as antiquated as Francis Jeffrey's Wordsworth or Matthew Arnold's Shelley; even the more recent 'close reading' approach plays a diminished role. In their place we find multiple and intertwined analyses of social and philosophical issues, driven indirectly by Marxist or related theory. 'British' or 'English' or international writers from Adam Smith to David Ricardo, Thomas Jefferson to Helen Maria Williams, Immanuel Kant to F. W. J. Schelling, Thomas Malthus to Humphrey Repton, and Thomas Paine to Edmund Burke receive as much critical

1 James Chandler, 'Introduction', in Chandler, ed., *The Cambridge History of English Romantic Literature* (Cambridge, 2009), 7.

2 Susan J. Wolfson, 'The New Poetries', 426

attention as the poets, novelists, and essayists themselves. *Literature* in such a context becomes *writing*, which embraces historical treatises, government records, political broadsides, economic analyses, though not the still-overlooked writers of the time, women writers excepted. Subjects as disparate as the French Revolution and its commentators, the near revolutions in England, the press gangs and the enclosure laws, periodicals and the poor, mechanics of printing and mass reading, associations of literary *genres* with the biological, more than outweigh the matter of 'Romantic literature'.

For good or ill, *English Romantic Literature* reflects the state of contemporary literary studies in Britain, the United States, and elsewhere. Here is one example. Thc index to a 647-page text includes fewer than 25 references to the word 'literature', and those references usually pertain to topics such as 'children's literature' and 'technology'. Itself a reflection of the times, Chandler's collection draws heavily from other disciplines, above all from historiography. Whether historians or students of literature or both, most contributors share an approach to their topics. They differ stylistically and in the ways they think or present their material; some 'theorize' or 'problematize' their subjects (the two are practically inseparable), while others write with an uncluttered clarity that their colleagues may find antiquated; some build and finish their arguments; others prefer a greengrocer's display of historical facts, illustrative examples, comparative statistics, brief biographical reminders, and a plethora of secondary sources. Nearly all work as 'cultural historians', citing other historians as much as literary scholars, and consciously reshaping literary scholarship with vocabularies drawn from sociology, biology, anthropology, or European philosophy. Students of literature have always been engaged in redefining not only their approaches to a subject but the subject itself. That said, what else would a reader expect from a new *Cambridge* ***History*** *of English Romantic Literature* except historical scholarship in a modern guise?

In a dozen years, perhaps, this collection might be seen as a kind of hybrid, a milestone-cum-signpost of an ever-nascent discipline. Chandler's organization of the essays emphasizes the historical (or geographical) impetus behind his four sections, which he titles 'The Ends of Enlightenment'; 'Geographies: The Scenes of Literary Life'; 'Histories: Writing in the New Movements'; and 'The Ends of Romanticism'. The essays in 'The Ends of Enlightenment' section fit nicely together. John Brewer explores the implications of 'the language of feeling, with its key terms of sentiment, sympathy and sensibility' through the second half of the eighteenth-century. 'In its concern for interiority', he writes, the language and literature of sensibility was not only 'central to the discussion of man and society, manners, ethics and aesthetics', it 'rehearsed' the feelings, the shifts in language, the creative imagination we associate with Romanticism.[3] Brewer's excellent essay anticipates a number of later pieces that intersect with his emphasis on late eighteenth-century social and literary issues, and on writers who used to be called precursors of the Romantic period. In fact, the collection addresses 'the age of sensibility' as much as the 'Romantic period'.

Susan Manning offers an equally broad *and* specific overview of 'antiquarianism, balladry and the rehabilitation of romance'; she deals elegantly with complicated figures, groups, and historical conundrums, while pulling together the materials themselves and providing bibliographical routes for other scholars. If not comprehensive, Manning's essay delivers a long, thorough, and readablc study. So too, Catherine Gallagher's. Her 'Romantics and Political Economists'

3 John Brewer, 'Sentiment and Sensibility', 21.

Ruins of Rievaulx Abbey, Yorkshire, watercolour, 1803 Artist: Cotman, John Sell (1782–1842). © The Art Archive / Victoria and Albert Museum London / Sally Chappell.

bridges diverse fields and illustrates the often direct relationships between the (largely) Scottish economists and English 'Lake Poets', especially Coleridge. She moves effortlessly through works by Adam Smith, William Godwin, William Cobbett, Coleridge, Shelley, Malthus, Ricardo, and Thomas De Quincey, who seem almost to converse with each other in this essay. While Gallagher's emphasis seems at times distinct from 'literary' history, she has a persuasive answer. 'Romanticism and political economy,' she writes, 'should be thought of as competing forms of "organicism", flourishing scepticism toward ... unreal faith in unrealized human rationality.'[4] I would not want to argue with her.

4 Catherine Gallagher, 'The Romantics and the Political Economists', 73.

Nor with Clifford Siskin in his dazzling 'The Problem of Periodization', which reaches back to the Enlightenment with the purpose of anticipating the various 'natures' or types of Romanticism. He insists on two versions of Enlightenment thinking, the one an attempt at incorporative systems, the other a movement from systemic to essay writing. Siskin defines this historical shift as a powerful metamorphosis reflected in Romantic writing and the wider culture. His essay (a system-maker itself) weaves easily from Kant to Byron to Bacon to Wordsworth to Malthus to Scott. Its journey is demanding but the thinking, as with the other essays in this section, is clear-headed and persuasive.

We might anticipate that these informally related essays would launch discussions about the effect or interplay of late eighteenth-century elements on the next generation. This happens to a surprisingly limited extent. Part II, the 'Geographies', remains grounded in the eighteenth century and either replicates material from the earlier essays or explores similar topics. John Barrell's erudite 'London in the 1790s' lays out a spatial and temporal examination of London, its growth, its parts, its industries, its statistics, along with its dispositions of wealth and struggles of the poor. Barrell follows Godwin's *Caleb Williams* into the heart of a city of anonymity, or what Wordsworth called 'streets without end'. London was of course a hotbed of British radicals — John Thelwall, Mary Wollstonecraft, Thomas Holcroft, and the many supporters of the French Revolution — and home, at times, to both Wordsworth and Coleridge. Barrell gives a virtual tour through the rich and poor areas of a divided capital, though how it developed, or how it pertains directly to English Romantic literature, seems left to a reader's imagination. Fair enough, perhaps, given the quality of the essay and its implied importance to the coming century.

There are nine entries in the 'Geographies' section, several of them excellent, but in their number and coverage too much of the same thing. Occupying about a third of the book, they may be a consequence of the project itself, which requires an editor to match unexpected detours and disparate voices. I suspect that most readers would have preferred at least half of these essays to be on literary topics, to emphasize the poets and novelists themselves. This is not to say that the 'geographers' fail to link places with people. Ian Duncan on 'Edinburgh and Lowland Scotland', Luke Gibbons on 'Romantic Ireland', Esther Schor on 'The "Warm South"', and W. J. T. Mitchell on 'Country Matters' (at once a play on words and an engaging essay on landscape) are all thoroughly informed about their topics. The issue is balance or distribution of topics. One later essay, out of place in 'The Ends of Romanticism' but well within the parameters of 'Geographies', would have allowed a helpful complement to Romanticism and its international implications. Saree Makdisi's 'Romantic Cultural Imperialism' links English aristocracy with interpretations of 'Oriental' culture in the late eighteenth century.

Part III, 'Histories', proves no less or more historical than the 'Geographies', the topics of which it, too, tends to repeat. Anne Janowitz's 'Rebellion, Revolution, Reform', a clever linking of four contemporaries in the years of the French Revolution — Mary Wollstonecraft, Thomas Paine, Thomas Jefferson, and Helen Maria Williams — as 'intellectual travellers [and] citizens of the world', whose responses to unfolding and sometimes dangerous events emerges in their political and private rhetoric. 'As writers they aimed to write in a way that corresponded to the idea of a citizen rather than the subject ...'[5] Janowitz's weaving together the four writers brings in 'Romantic' poets — Blake, Wordsworth, and Clare — for short mention, but that seems the extent of Romantic 'discourse', unless we accept the implication that her principals themselves are 'Romantics'.

Several essays stand out in this grouping. Adrian Johns's 'Changes in the World of Publishing' provides readers with an important account of publishing in England from the last quarter of the eighteenth century into the first quarter of the nineteenth, when the word 'publishing' in its present meanings first appeared. Though writing about a topic covered earlier in the book, this account is disciplined and comprehensive. 'The New Poetries' by Wolfson is also exceptional, as a synthesis of the new literary voices and new genres of the early nineteenth century. 'Something, anyway, was stirring,' Wolfson writes, and her excellent overview of the 'Lake School', the 'Cockney School', the major poets, the rising critical voices moves quickly and breezily in this essayistic essay. Her essay is in fact the first to pay full attention to poetry and immediately related topics, including 'the annuals and the she-poets'.[6]

Paul Hamilton's 'Romanticism and Poetic Autonomy' presents at once a second half to Wolfson's 'new poetries' and — rare in this book — a critique of and tribute to Meyer Abrams, Marilyn Butler, Harold Bloom, and other predecessors about the roots, the claims, the history of Romantic poetry. Hamilton reaches back to Rousseau, Kant, and Johann Gottfried Herder, and others who inspired Coleridge and his contemporaries to see poetry as an autonomous and elevated and philosophical utterance. 'For our purposes here', Hamilton writes, 'it is obviously very hard to find established interpretations of Romanticism that are not basically situated in relation to Romantic poetry's claims to autonomy'.[7]

Chandler includes two studies of the late eighteenth- and early nineteenth-century novel: Deirdre Lynch's 'Transformations of the Novel — I' and Ina Ferris's 'Transformations of the Novel — II'. Both raise questions about the popularity and public recognition of the newly emergent novel, and, in Ferris's case, the 'British' or national issues stemming from the Act of Union in 1801, the ramifications of which can be seen in Lady Morgan's and Maria Edgeworth's fiction. In each case, however, the treatment of massive numbers of published novels and the diversity of authorship seem daunting, all the more so when two, relatively brief, essays cover so much material. Ferris, for example, can only touch on William Godwin, James Hogg, John Galt, Mary Shelley, to name a few of her authors, and though she discusses Walter Scott, she does not have the space to do him justice. Georg Lukács's master of historical fiction never reaches his full height here, and Lukács himself gets no mention.

Tilottama Rajan's 'The Epigenesis of Genre' (epigenesis being a biological theory that 'the embryo develops in stages, forming structures not originally in the egg') touches on another failing in the now dominant field of cultural studies: the use of scientific terminology serving as literary terminology. Rajan herself admits that 'Biological models for genre have been criticized for projecting the determinism of Darwinian evolution onto literature ... as well as because they confuse the more open system of the history of species with an individual life cycle of growth and decline.' There is, however, a simpler criticism for those not immersed in biology: biological theories apply to biological processes. To whatever extent they *seem* applicable to other fields — history, sociology, literature — they remain metaphors, or what Tilottama

5 Anne Janowitz, 'Rebellion, Revolution, Reform: The Transit of the Intellectuals', 376.
6 Wolfson, 'New Poetries', 403, 420–21.
7 Paul Hamilton, 'Romanticism and Poetic Autonomy', 435.

8 Tilottama Rajan, 'The Epigenesis of Genre: New Forms from Old', 514.
9 Jan Golinski, 'The Literature of the New Sciences', 529.
10 Julie Carlson 'Theatre, Performance and Urban Spectacle', 490.

calls 'etymological links'.[8] I admit my own bias here, not against literary historians borrowing from other disciplines, but their illogical and misleading imitations of those disciplines. Rajan is hardly alone in making tenuous connections with other fields. But to turn things around: would any biologist take the word *genre* and use it to explain *genus*, or speak about *organic* and related topics as if the same words held the same meanings in radically different areas of research? The misuse of metaphor, which amounts to reification, results in a breakdown of careful argument and of *literary*, in the sense of professional, discourse.

On the other side, scientists call their own writings 'literature', as does the historian of science, Jan Golinski, in 'The Literature of the New Sciences'. 'From the crucible of the 1790s', he writes, 'new forms of public science emerged. New institutions extended the size of middle-class audiences'.[9] Golinski describes the politically divisive shift from Enlightenment science through the early nineteenth century and manages to stretch his argument to Victorian scientists such as Charles Lyell. It seems ironic that Golinski introduces more poetry than many of his co-contributors.

Two essays in the miscellaneous 'Histories' section suggest, like Hamilton's, other avenues that might have been explored: Julie Carlson's "Theatre, Performance and Urban Spectacle,' and Katie Trumpener's 'The Making of Child readers.' Carlson offers the only treatment of theatre and 'closet drama' in the collection. It speaks to a new theatricality essential to the Georgian period, which Carlson calls 'phenomenal' and 'extraordinary'. Her enthusiasm runs throughout this personal essay (delivered in the present tense), which moves quickly from contemporary claims for the value of theatres, to descriptions of the Royal (and immense) theatres Drury Lane and Covent Garden (as well as the far more numerous 'minor' theatres), to the legal bases and control of theatres, to an evocative visit to theatres, to types of plays, advertising, the great actors of the day, mechanical and aesthetic stage changes, and the roles and influence of the reviewers. This list does not include her paragraphs on closet theatre (which has a bearing on Hazlitt's and Lamb's critiques), or how theatre 'forms and informs individuals',[10] nor a section called 'Urban Spectacles', which follows the influence of theatre into politics, the diorama, the court, and the street.

Trumpener explores the expanding market for children's books in the late eighteenth century, along with the authors who wrote them and the publishers who profited. She traces the fortunes of the Newbery family, among others, as if she knew them personally, and she writes a packed essay on the multitude of books suddenly available to children. Even better, she details the ways that Coleridge, for example, grew up reading children's books and how Charles Lamb and so many of his contemporaries came to write for children. Trumpener's intersections of reading, advertising, education, and child-raising come together with the formative childhoods of Romantic writers and the vast industry in which they took part.

Part IV, 'The Ends of Romanticism', includes three essays on topics appropriate to earlier sections and a final essay by Jerome McGann. In 'Representation Restructured', Frances Ferguson distils her argument into one short sentence: 'In the Romantic period various writers brought important modern senses of 'representation'— political, epistemological and aesthetic — into relation with one another.' Her complex topic and the slippery word 'representation' may need more pointed guidelines, but otherwise Ferguson writes with her usual innovative authority. Invoking John Stuart Mill's observation that Coleridge and Jeremy Bentham 'were destined to renew a lesson given to mankind by every age, and always disregarded — to show that speculative philosophy ... is in reality the thing on earth that most influences mankind', Ferguson illustrates the modes and implications of Romantic writing, the self-consciousness of writers from De Quincey to Shelley, the claims they made, and what she desribes as their 'acceptance by an audience' adjusting to the 'differences between one use of language and another'.[11]

Religion plays a small part in *English Romantic Literature*, which provides little commentary on British dissenters and other groups crucial to science, literature, and political movements. Enter Kevin Gilmartin. 'Romanticism and Religious Modernity' may be a slightly odd title for Gilmartin's impressive contribution to this collection. Gilmartin ranges across layers of historical, literary, and religious topics, speaks more fully than any contributors except Chandler, Hamilton, and McGann about Romantic scholars in the second half of the twentieth century (including Harold Bloom, Geoffrey Hartman and Alan Liu, and describes the ways in which Romantic poets and essayists used or dealt with the shifting climate of religion in an age of revolution and 'dissent'. His final sentence is typically apt: 'If faith has to some extent been displaced from the centre of critical discussions of Romanticism, its pivotal role in the social and cultural history of the period ensures that it will remain present in any finely grained account of British Romantic literature'.[12]

Chandler must have known that Jerome McGann's essay would surprise — and make a suitably indefinite conclusion to an open-ended book. McGann does surprise. 'Is Romanticism Finished?' — the question Chandler gave him — results in an essay Montaigne himself would have enjoyed, with similar right-angle turns, returns, twists, ironies, and tangents. In two witty pages McGann skips over centuries, raising questions and rejecting his own answers, almost dancing around the one, missing thing: his definition of the Romanticisms he is supposedly considering. He invokes the enemies of the field (or era), T. E. Hulme, Irving Babbitt, F. R. Leavis, T. S. Eliot; and praises the 'heroes', W. J. Bate, Northrop Frye, Meyer Abrams, Carl Woodring, and others, who resurrected Romanticism in the last generation. And in answer to Chandler's question? Well, 'Let's ask J. M. Coetzee'. At this point McGann goes modern. He moves away from the fate of Romanticism to a brilliant critique of Coetzee's 1999 novel, *Disgrace,* which contains its own critique of Romanticism, mainly Byronic Romanticism, in a triad of wounded (and worse) characters playing out Byron's relationships with Teresa Guiccioli and his daughter, Allegra, called 'Lucy' in the novel. Lurie, the central figure, is a modern and deeply troubled South African Romanticist, who writes an opera on Byron. 'The situation,' McGann writes 'is exquisitely Byronic in a full Baudelairean sense'.[13]

With another sharp turn, McGann comes back from Coetzee's 'sceptical view of Romanticism' to 'summarize Romantic ideology' and some of its paradoxes before returning to the original question, 'Is Romanticism finished?' McGann's response ends the book appropriately, as if to say, 'In my beginning is my end, and in my end is my beginning'. I'll quote from his final paragraph and quote his own quotation from Wallace Stevens:

> Something important is gained when we willingly suspend our disbelief in Shakespeare and Rousseau, the Bible and the Upanishads, and consciously enter a sympathetic relation to their weakened and alienated condition. Byron called it an act of 'mobility', Keats called it 'negative capability' — and in each case the move is consciously represented under the sign of what Byron called a 'spoiler's art'. That

11 Ferguson, 'Representation Restructured', 581.
12 Kevin Gilmartin, 'Romanticism and Religious Modernity: From Natural Supernaturalism to Literary Sectarianism', 647.
13 Jerome McGann, 'Is Romanticism Finished?', 649, 655.

kind of sympathy, a latter-day form of Socratic self-questioning, is the unfinished — possibly the unfinishable — business of Romanticism. Perhaps this is a good point to start from again. 'Perhaps that is what I must learn to accept. To start at ground level. With nothing. Not with nothing but. With nothing. Or, as a twentieth-century latter-day Romantic famously put the matter: with 'nothing that is not there and the nothing that is.'

Nothing may well come of nothing, in life or in literary reviews, but I'll conclude with this: it may not matter whether Romanticism is dead or alive, because Romanticism is itself a conflation, an elastic historical age, a list of multiple qualities, a few poets or a few million contemporaries; in short, a virtual entity. It is what contemporaries of every generation wish it or imagine it to be. It is *nothing* without the scholars and readers who continually reinvent it, which is precisely (or not so precisely) what James Chandler's collection has accomplished. How good is this book, written by twenty-eight contributors and the editor? That too is a matter for any and all readers to decide. I find it both flawed and admirable, disorganized and well-presented; but whatever its failings, or its virtues, *English Romantic Literature* will guide a generation of students through perhaps the most demanding, the most engaging period in British literary history.[14]

14 McGann, 'Is Romanticism Finished?', 663–64. McGann quotes in part from Coetzee's *Disgrace* and Wallace Stevens's 'The Snow Man'.

Just Another Country?

Francis Mulhern

Outrageous Fortune:
Capital and Culture in Modern Ireland
Joe Cleary
Field Day Files 1
Dublin: Field Day Publications, 2007
xii + 320. ISBN 978-0-946755-35-6

'Capital and culture in modern Ireland' is the admirably terse, plain subtitle of Joe Cleary's landmark contribution to debates on and about Irish culture. The chronological range of 'modern' here extends from the later nineteenth century, though returns to earlier periods play an important part in the overall historical reasoning of the book and in one case form the substance of a whole essay. 'Culture' is for the greater part literature and drama, above all the novel and short story, but cinema features as well, and Cleary closes his book with a memorable discussion of the Pogues. The Ireland of the subtitle is, for most of the course of the book, the South — the partitioned North gets one chapter to itself and otherwise features intermittently — and its critical constitutive social relation is capital. The eight studies that make up the book are in effect excerpts from a very ambitious undertaking, demanding in scale and in conceptual complexity, and no one can expect uncomplicated results. The complexities of method, focus and address present themselves before the book is even opened, on its cover, which displays three or even four titles altogether, each of them gesturing quite differently at the matters in hand.

The main title, *Outrageous Fortune*, is direct enough in its reference to the hyperbolic contrasts of Ireland's social

John McGahern (1934–2006), 1992. Photo: Steve Pyke/Hulton Archive/Getty Images.

and economic history since the Anglo-Irish Treaty of 1921, and in its silent borrowing from Shakespeare also takes the opportunity to signify one of Cleary's formative interests in literary studies. Yet Hamlet has not often, if ever before, been collocated with Shane MacGowan, who stares from the cover photograph in his youthful capacity as editor of the punk fanzine *Bondage*, which he holds unemphatically but legibly to camera. There is grotesque irony in the reinscription of that title here, thirty-odd years on, a stock feature of English punk style suddenly catching an echo of the high register of Irish literary-nationalist lamentation. And then, as if to mock this, there is the caption that dominates the front page of the magazine: 'Just another country'. Cleary's cover is a theatre in itself, in which high and low, canonical and abjected meanings, and a range of national evaluations, extending from piteous identification through disenchanted realism to throwaway nihilism, are put into play.

'Just another country': where the phrase came from and what it refers to we cannot infer from the photograph alone. But if the claim is good, this cannot matter very much. The point is that it, whatever 'it' may be, is just another country. It is doubtful whether Joe Cleary would say this, just so plainly, about Ireland, but he could do worse. The 'other' in 'another' signifies sameness as well as difference (and difference as well as sameness, to add the balancing counter-emphasis that the word ordinarily includes) and in this regard the phrase serves well enough as a provocative caption for the programme of historical reconstruction and cultural criticism he broaches in this book. Ireland is different, as nationalists of all kinds have always maintained. But to say so is not necessarily to reiterate an article of faith, let alone to reach conclusion. What matters is how that difference is understood, in what it is taken to consist.

Cleary pursues this understanding with considerable theoretical erudition and steady self-awareness and remarkable consistency. The consistency is, in the first place, that of purpose: what he adumbrates is a historical theory of Irish culture. It is remarkable, given the varied beginnings of the essays that make up his book. These are strongly convergent, of course, and have been made more so in the editing. Still, the book remains a collection, not a single composition, and variations of formulation and emphasis remain. These circumstances are reinforced by another — Cleary's writing, combining range and thoroughness of argumentation, is characteristically dense — and suggest the preferable forms of a first response of the kind I offer here: a free generalizing account of Cleary's principal theses rather than forensic attention to textual particulars, and an associative series of counterpoints rather than a singular, linear statement. Given the range of the book, this will inevitably be selective. A further reason for this quasi-conversational mode goes to the heart of the occasion. *Outrageous Fortune*, for all its solidity and boldness of achievement, is dedicated to work in progress, and a broad but non-summary response is more likely to capture its essential features, whether for emulation or for critical appraisal.

I

Two basic concepts underpin Cleary's elucidation of southern Irish society and culture. The first is capitalism. His introductory pages are a striking illustration of how dramatically perspectives have been revised in just a few years. Writing today, towards the end of the first decade of the new century, he would hardly feel the need for such emphatic reminders of the unabated misery attendant upon capitalist accumulation and of the insurmountable precariousness and ultimately illusory character of advanced consumerism. All that is more widely accepted now, and not least in Ireland, where the Tiger's leap has ended in a most unfeline crash-landing. In a longer time frame, these pages are striking also as a reminder of the long-drawn-out resistance among republican-inspired commentators to the idea of an Irish capitalism. It was a politico-cultural reflex. Capitalism was imperialism, in truth — a crucial domesticating trope even where there was good evidence for the identification. Irish capitalism, insofar as it existed, was dependent, comprador, an artificial thing sustained by tax breaks — as if to imply, with considerable casuistical resourcefulness, that one way or another, it really did not matter which, there was a quasi-ontological mismatch between the Irish people and mere capitalism.

There are times when Cleary seems vulnerable to the gravitational pull of that discourse. He is a little too insistent on the dependent character of capitalist development from the end of the 1950s, tacitly setting an unrealistic and perhaps anachronistic standard of autonomy for a small, late-coming economy with few special resources to speak of. He is tempted to overlook his own better judgement concerning the efficacy of 'choice' in the evolution of Irish capitalism, which, insofar as popular agency has been in question, has owed at least as much to inertia and pragmatic adjustment as to anything so momentous as a national decision. Contrary to Ernest Renan's stirring declaration, a nation is not a daily plebiscite. But the general thrust of Cleary's argumentation is unmistakable. Capitalism has been the governing economic reality of Irish life for a long time, and it is within the terms of the international capitalist system that its character and possibilities must be understood. If there is another social world, it lies in a time beyond capitalism, not in an imaginary space outside it where the otherness of the Irish can be accommodated. The difference that is Ireland is a matter, not of otherness, but of specificity. The search for specificity involves the effort to go beyond national nominalism, to clarify the individual configuration of elements that has made the Irish experience of capitalist development both normal and distinctive. The single most critical distinction in that experience was that for centuries it was mediated in a subordinate relation to one of the pioneer capitalist societies of the planet, Britain. The second of Cleary's grounding concepts is colonialism.

Here we are on canonical ground, but not quite. There is no reliance on customary verities in the long study 'Irish Studies, Colonial Questions: Locating Ireland in the Colonial World', which indeed offers one of the most illuminating general discussions in the book. Committed in this, as in his understanding of capitalism to framing Irish historical experience comparatively, in international terms, Cleary returns colonial Ireland to its real conditions of formation in the early modern Atlantic. It is disconcerting, in a wholly positive way, to see England's interventions in Ireland thus classified together with Spain's proto-colonial initiative in the Canaries and Portugal's on the island of Madeira — even if a main effect of the comparison is to underline the unique and weighty military significance of Ireland's location just a handful of miles west of a big power with powerful enemies. The disposition of the country's effective rulers — be they indigenous or colonizing — was by this fact alone crucial for England's domestic security and maritime communications, and remained so until after the mid-point of the twentieth century. It is more disconcerting still to be shown the Irish colony in the company of the various imperial possessions in the Americas, and so to be prompted to ask the unsentimental question, what would — or could — have been the outcome if by some fluke of arms Ireland's creole revolutionaries, the United

Irishmen, had succeeded too? The memory of the sweet equal republic-that-never-was hardly acknowledges the real balance of likelihood in the kind of colony Ireland had by then become.

Cleary proposes a valuable typology of colonial varieties, ranging from the administrative (as in the case of India, where the indigenous population, organized in largely inherited social structures, was the productive force of the colonial economy and the colonizing settlement was small and politically specialized) to cases such as Australia and New Zealand, where a 'pure' settler colonialism displaced the indigenous population and in effect created a substitute society through demographic restocking and expansion on seized lands. In this spectrum (which, Cleary insists, should not be reduced to a simplistic, disjunctive taxonomy) Ireland was one of an assorted class of hybrids, a 'mixed' settlement colony where the indigenous population remained in place but in transformed social relations based on extensive land seizures and a correspondingly substantial colonizing settlement.

This is a very helpful complication of historical understanding, and it is all the odder then that it should quietly omit the most painful complication of them all. Ireland was not simply a mixed settlement colony. It was also one of a subset characterized by strong regional differentiation. (The United States furnished one of the outstanding cases of this: a pure settlement colony in the north coexisting with the southern plantation economy based on imported slave labour.) Ireland's colonial landlord class formed a homogeneous settler bloc of the 'mixed' variety, but the labouring population was crucially differentiated, a largely indigenous tenantry in most of the island with an alien counterpart in the settler population of north-east Ulster. In this corner, the settlement tended towards the 'pure' variety, aim-inhibited by comparison with the genocidal record of North America and the Anglo-Scottish Pacific but recognizable nonetheless in its generic tendencies, including its egalitarian 'frontier' ethos of inter-class bonding, or Orangeism.

II

Cleary's determination to elicit the specificities of Irish history from overweeningly generic accounts of capitalism and colonialism is matched in the critical procedures he adopts in his engagements with his core cultural material, literature. Now, in an essay on 'the national novel' that is the makings of a whole book in itself, received histories and fixed habits of comparison and generalization form the dialogic context of his reflections on the Irish novel and its critics. He challenges the normalizing grand narrative of 'the rise of the novel' for its Anglocentrism and unwarranted centring of realism, which, he maintains, has tended to function either as the standard by which the nineteenth-century Irish novel is found wanting (the missing *Middlemarch*) or as the pole against which the national culture is made to assert its virtuous alterity. This essay is a widely read and resourceful prospectus for an unwritten 'postcolonial history' of the novel in Ireland, whose purpose would be 'to establish both the achievement of the colonial peripheries and the negative consequences that invariably attend such situations'.[1] Another essay goes some way towards implementing that prospectus for the case of Irish modernism. Again, Cleary constructs his study in extended dialogue with the influential grand narratives associated with Georg Lukács and his intellectual posterity, notably Fredric Jameson. Again, his critical point of departure is the observation that these Marxist cultural histories 'cannot easily be transposed onto the Irish situation',[2]

1 Joe Cleary, 'The National Novel in an Imperial Age: Notes on the Historiography of the Nineteenth-Century Novel', in *Outrageous Fortune: Capital and Culture in Modern Ireland* (Dublin, 2007), 47–75, 75.

2 Cleary, 'Capital and Culture in Twentieth-Century Ireland: Changing Configurations', in *Outrageous Fortune*, 76–110, 77.

3 Cleary, 'Capital and Culture in Twentieth-Century Ireland', 93.
4 Cleary, 'Capital and Culture in Twentieth-Century Ireland', 94.

and this for reasons that illuminate the metropolitan narrowness of the intellectual construction rather than Ireland's cultural waywardness. (After all, as a prominent dissenting Communist philosopher once wryly said, history cannot be wrong.) Cleary takes pains to show that the Irish modernist interest in the past was neither as unvaried nor as conservative in general implication, nor, come to that, as unusual in comparative perspective as many have been prone to say. The archaism of the Revival receded over time. The idea of modernity as catastrophe was potent in a culture only decades removed from the Great Hunger; and it surely made a difference to the balance of Irish modernist propensities that the country's most 'modern' region, the industrial enclave in the north-east, was by the early twentieth century locked in political reaction and historical pessimism. Folkish themes were commonplace across the arts in modernism — even in Brecht, it might be added, with his *faux-naïf* parables and sayings. In this too, Ireland occupied a historically intelligible place on a spectrum, not a zone apart.

While defending Irish modernism in such terms, Cleary remains conscious of limitations of range and impact. Lacking the broad formal repertoire that the great centres of European innovation inherited from their royal court cultures, Irish modernism was a relatively private, minority affair. 'In the end,' he writes, 'what distinguishes Irish modernism above all else from its European counterparts was that its literary modernism began so early and still managed to extend itself across several successive stages of modernist literary development, yet without reaching much beyond literature.'[3] An essentially linguistic style of experimentation, prompted by a sense of national cultural alienation and loss, and capable of flourishing without large-scale institutional support systems, produced a brilliant but sequestered strain of modernism lacking the public presence of 'music, architecture, public design or the performing arts'.[4]

Given the substance of this case, the list of authors with which Cleary thinks to support it comes as a surprise: Wilde, Synge, Yeats, O'Casey, Joyce, Beckett and Ó Cadhain. What is unmissable in this 'literary' role call is the salience within it of *theatre*. Of these seven, four owe their reputations above all to their plays; a fifth, Yeats, was a playwright too and a publicly committed man of the theatre. Joyce, likewise, had his aspirations in that quarter, even if they came to little. It is not uncommon for scholars and teachers to assimilate drama, as play-text, to 'literature', but in the present context of argument, with its critical emphasis on the value of public presence and an explicit opposition between 'literature' and 'performing arts', this does not seem an adequate explanation.

It may be that the difficulty lies elsewhere, and closer to the heart of the issues of theory and method that Cleary tackles. It seems possible that this lapse of logic has been induced by the attempt to answer an incorrectly framed question about reach and impact. And it is not, this time, that the Irish case is being held to an exaggerated standard, rather that the general concept of modernism is itself a faulty construction. Cleary has a tendency to assume, if only by default, that the historical schemes he considers are inadequate insofar as they are overgeneralized, but probably sound on their native/metropolitan terrains. But it need not be so, and the Anglo-American category of 'modernism' is a case in point.

It has often been said — and Cleary seems to agree — that the international array of movements and individuals grouped and putatively unified under the heading of 'modernism' had little in common except their negations. There is a great deal of truth in this, and much of what was held in common was not historically distinctive. The great negations

Edna O'Brien at the Paraty International Literary Festival, Brazil, July 4, 2009. Photo: Luciana Whitaker/LatinContent/Getty Images.

themselves — the disruptions of canonical forms, codes and expectations — were distinctive in their intensity, but not in kind. Negation is the constitutive gesture of the modern as such, across a historical range far more extensive than that of 'modernism'. Why bother with the category at all? The devil is in the suffix. Modern-*ism*, once so designated, must have its commonalities — which critics must then find, or not finding them, explain their absence — and the other appurtenances of a full-dress period in cultural history. There is no need for this, and good reason — not least in the empirical record — to look for an alternative construction. It is preferable, arguably, to abandon the notion of modernism, with its singularizing, unifying suggestions, and to refocus its referents as a plural, a proliferation of departures in the special conditions of their time. The time itself — say roughly 1890–1940 — is better not seen as that of a cultural order such as neo-classicism — as Jameson proposed, with his tricyclic schema realism–modernism–postmodernism.

This is the furthest implication of Perry Anderson's theses on modernism, in which Cleary finds his principal interlocutor for his discussion of modernism in Ireland. It is not merely that Anderson is far more closely attuned to the historical concrete, avoiding Jameson's schematism in a 'conjunctural' analysis of the specific conditions that prompted these dramatic European departures: a marmoreal high culture persisting amid the novelties of the second Industrial Revolution and excited or brooding expectations of fundamental social change. It is that his analysis calls into question the equivalence that Jameson assumes in his grand succession. In this alternative reading, we can pursue the idea that 'modernism' is not a historical order on categorically equal terms with its predecessor and putative successor, but, precisely, a conjuncture, however long drawn out, a phase of convulsions marking a transition in some respects, but at any rate a profound disturbance.

Re-viewing those decades of European culture in this modified perspective, we can more easily open up a question that the familiar schemes foreclose. In its broad terms, it is the question of realism in the twentieth century. Modernism and postmodernism are historically notable in the ways that Jameson and others before him have described. But what is less often remarked is the perdurance of a broadly realist narrative ethos, and not as an unsurmounted anachronism but as a vigorous, various tradition with a marked ability to renew its own repertoire by adapting resources from others both old and new. Gabriel García Márquez once observed of his metropolitan readers that they looked at so-called magic realism and saw only the magic. Something similar can be said about the varieties of novelistic realism after about 1930: what we are inclined to look for is the modernism (and post). T. S. Eliot's review of *Ulysses* and Virginia Woolf's essay on Arnold Bennett have long been stock references for literary modernism in English, no small achievement for such spectacular failures of historical expectation. The Joyce who entered the repertoire of the twentieth-century novel was not the contriver of the 'mythic method' but the pioneer of a new phase of big-city narrative. The moderns made their mark, not in a new canon of story-telling such as Woolf envisaged, but as contributors to a more versatile realism, a repertoire to which her own subjectivism now belonged. In this sense, the central modernist novelist was Proust: inheritor and refounder of the whole apparatus of realist narrative, he more than any had the future in his bones. We might say with Jameson, but perhaps with a stronger sense of consequences, that 'modernism' was 'the dominant', but just that, the element that dominates and modifies what it subordinates, not a spirit suffusing the culture of the time. The traces of that moment are everywhere in the writing of later decades. But what has survived more strongly is the modified subordinate, the continuing narrative culture of realism. The same kind of argument can be made for the successor regime of postmodernism, prompting the general thought that the history captured in that and its parent category have been passages in a continuing narrative order of realism. And if that should be so, then Ireland's twentieth-century literary culture is closer to the international norm than Cleary takes it to be.

III

The dominant in Irish writing over the past one hundred or so years has been naturalism. This is Cleary's central cultural-historical thesis, set out in 'This Thing of Darkness', another essay with more than enough range and ambition for a book to itself. The understanding of naturalism he brings to his argument is not at all formalist in the manner of the conventional histories or of Georg Lukács, to whom, nevertheless, he gives full acknowledgement. Naturalism is a variety (or cluster of varieties) in the broad history of realism, but not only of the realist novel and drama, the usual ground of reference: it includes poetry as well, most notably Patrick Kavanagh's *The Great Hunger.* It has its characteristic repertoire and occasions, of course, and like realism in general is socially extended, orientated to the present, and secular (in narrative cosmology if not authorial conviction), but its basic unifying tendency is a disposition and an expectation. Naturalism in this sense is an ethico-ontological habitus not normally aligned with the more doctrinal varieties of high Naturalism (to call it that) but nevertheless quite settled in its vision of an overpowering world against which critical will may not prevail, as a collective undertaking or even as a personal bid for release. Schematically speaking, this is a prolonged rhetorical agon between the great narrative modes of realism and romance, each in its moment invalidating the other, without ever discovering a productive union of criticism and desire. Cleary traces the workings-out of this Irish naturalism from its self-conscious beginnings in the Ibsenites George Bernard Shaw and James Joyce and the Francophile George Moore, through the years of the Free State and the work of Sean O'Casey (the Dublin plays), Sean O'Faolain, Frank O'Connor and Kavanagh; then via the extremist case of Samuel Beckett, into the fifties and onwards, in discussions of John McGahern, Edna O'Brien and Tom Murphy. With this, we reach the present, where, Cleary goes on to argue, the literary lease of naturalism has been renewed even where it may appear to be ending. Ireland's novelistic postmodern, conveyed in the ironies of Robert McLiam Wilson or Patrick McCabe, is perhaps best thought of as 'neo-naturalism'.

Here, more emphatically than elsewhere in *Outrageous Fortune*, Cleary's historical construction operates as a mode of politically charged cultural criticism. Naturalism's historic vocation has been as an art of exposure, in the name of reality or right or the good, and thus as a critical resource for reform. But what it ends by exposing, again and again, and as a part of its preferred kind of truth, is the inadequacy or illusoriness of the right and the good, the preordained failure of reform and the persistence of oppressive social or natural order. The fatalist tendency of the naturalist imagination is a form of conservatism that reinforces the conservatism it affects to expose. This is a novelistic culture whose genius — to borrow a stoic formula from Freud — is the conversion of suffering into pain. It is not a socially innocent culture. In its terms, a literate middle class acknowledges suffering, and with due sympathy, but also due weighing of probabilities, agrees the imaginable forms of redress. And this perhaps goes some way to explain in general terms a feature of Irish naturalism that in one way is not characteristically naturalist at all, a creeping anachronism of temporal range attendant upon a fixation with the Ireland of Eamon de Valera.

There was in truth a lot to write about, but that does not quite deal with Cleary's point. Fifty years after the official exit from national autarky, the concentration of narrative energies in that thirty-year mid-century span and the corresponding paucity of writing about more recent periods seems disproportionate and suspect. The critical construction of 'de Valera's Ireland', Cleary reminds us, was one of the cultural conditions of the emergence of 'Lemass's Ireland' and all that came from that, and, it may be, serves the new order still as a displacement-object accommodating a ritual of critical exposure, while the new oppressions and inequalities of the last forty years pass as the *faux frais* of historical deliverance.

Cleary is unsparing in his insistence on the depressive complicity of Ireland's naturalist tradition. He offers positive acknowledgements and concessions where he believes they are due; he is refreshingly lucid in his estimate of the extremely weak position from which any socialist cultural criticism must begin today; and he has no master-template to hand down, rather urging a bold, fallible elaboration of discoverable forms of a culture of liberation. For all that is discouraging in the present, he declares, 'no cultural moment is ever without either its structural conditions or utopian resources, and a radical Irish culture critically responsive to the demands of the new global conjuncture must always attend to these to discover its own project'.[5]

IV

Cleary's critique of naturalism as the Irish literary dominant is important in the simple sense that it makes a difference, in the politics of culture, whether it is substantially valid or not. And it matters, then, that it should be clearly distinguished from other considerations with which, at times, he associates it. His qualitative evaluation of naturalism as an ethico-ontological narrative disposition is not the same kind of thing as a conventional judgement of literary quality, and certainly not when the pole of comparison is the modernist canon. 'Works of some merit' appear in every current mode of Irish writing, he says, but there is no sign of a project 'charged with ambition sufficient to disturb and reconfigure the whole literary field itself'.[6] Here, a familiar composed retrospect of European (including Irish) modernism is cited as the standard and type of literary achievement. The claim is debatable in both respects, and in any case not obviously relevant to a critique of naturalism as a way of seeing. Cleary makes a strong case, and the critical questions to put to him can be formulated without reference to modernism. They are, in the main, empirical.

The first thing to note is that the novelistic corpus on which he bases his claims is small. Even if it supports them, how representative is it of the archive as a whole? So far as I can tell, it does largely support the claims, though others with far greater knowledge may well find reasons to resist the onward march of the general thesis, as I do in the case of John McGahern's late novels. It seems to me something like a category mistake to assimilate *Amongst Women* and *That They May Face the Rising Sun* to the mainstream of his earlier work, pausing only to allow their '"autumnal" serenity'. The first of these is dominated by retrospect, and ends in release. The second, McGahern's last novel, is an elegy for a way of life that cannot be rejoined. Its title, transplanted from a sentence reporting an old burial custom, undergoes a change of grammatical mode, becoming a benediction, a pagan leave-taking. The

5 Cleary, 'Capital and Culture in Twentieth-Century Ireland', 110.

6 Cleary, 'Capital and Culture in Twentieth-Century Ireland', 101.

point of Dev's Ireland, in all its characters good and bad, is that it has gone.

In one respect, to ask whether Cleary's corpus is representative is to miss a point. He is attempting to elucidate a literary dominant, not to generalize inclusively across the whole range of Irish writing in the twentieth century, whose overall plurality he acknowledges. In another respect, however, the question is necessary. This is also an ageing corpus. No writer born since 1948 receives more than a few sentences of particular attention, and the pattern of selectivity can be telling. Much of Roddy Doyle's work does indeed answer to Cleary's general naturalist thesis, but it is emphatically contemporary in focus, and there is only limited point in criticizing 'Northside realism' for its distance from the contrasting social worlds of the affluent middle class.

Colm Tóibín's *The Blackwater Lightship* presents a more difficult case for Cleary's theses on all these counts and, further, for what it suggests for the kind of radical critical practice Cleary advocates. Set, again with emphasis, in the cultural conditions of Ireland in the 1990s, this is the story of three mutually estranged generations of middle-class women, whose stand-offs are thrown off-balance by the demands of a newly revealed AIDS crisis in the family. As the illness takes its course, friendship and family are tested as contrary versions of personal solidarity, in the one case active but transgressive (the gay friends), in the other conventional but blocked (the mother–daughters). The story closes on the prospect of a possible peace between the protagonist and her mother.

The Blackwater Lightship, an essentially private story, part drama, part comedy, part romance, is not many people's idea of a political novel. But the kind of story it tells and the kind of novel it is belong to the micro-politics of gender and sexuality, which, on a state-wide scale, convulsed Irish society in the eighties and nineties of the last century, and it is in the nature of those orders of social relationship that their politics are always fought out *in parvo* as well as in the grand registers of the political. Such reflections have some bearing on the question of 'impact', which assumes an exaggerated scale in Cleary's criteriology of literary politics. The ripple-effects of reading and reviews and conversations about reading are normally modest, lacking the sublimity of the modernist myth, with its giants and their signs taken for wonders, but they are effects nonetheless. The same reflections bear on the question of selection. Cleary urges critical attention to the 'utopian resources' that are to be found in any 'cultural moment' but confines himself, in the field of recent Irish writing, to a persisting naturalist dominant, with contrastive side-references to high postmodern practitioners such as John Banville and Paul Muldoon. Other kinds of writing, differently accented and surely not less promising, on the face of it, for his critical purposes, flicker on the radar, then disappear. 'Women's writing' and 'gay writing' appear just so, generically and in inverted commas, like two syllabus subheadings, in a non-committal statement beginning 'it might be argued' and ending 'and so forth'. A wholehearted search for utopian resources calls for greater exertion than this — for some of the energizing conviction that Cleary brings to his defence of *céilí*-punk.

V

After all that literary naturalism, Cleary turns to music, and Shane MacGowan's carnivalesque. Perhaps as a feedback effect, the writing here is noticeably warmer, the diction a little freer, as if registering a certain *détente* in the protocols of ordinary dialogue with those various collective subjects whose names end in 'studies' ('postcolonial', 'Irish' and 'feminist' and the rest). It may help, of course, that Shane MacGowan is among the most literate songwriters of his generation, but at any rate this is a welcome and convincing extension of the critical project beyond literature and drama. It is one of the openings on to the material social world of cultural production and circulation, inevitable in writing about popular music but, in reality, no less necessary in the study of literature, where textual reductionism remains the norm, even where a text called 'context' has been brought into play. Among the many strengths of *Outrageous Fortune* is that by its very tenacity in posing the broadest questions, it forces literary studies to look and ideally go beyond familiar boundaries. The elucidation of novelistic naturalism is one conspicuous case, in effect creating the demand for an exploration of the wider culture of Irish narrative, in which audio-visual media — typically in this — have long been systemically dominant: cinema, yes, but more importantly radio and television. How can you have a history of narrative in modern Ireland without *The Riordans*? How, then, considering that remarkable institution, might we characterize and specify the role of narrative forms in all media in the construction and conduct of an Irish public sphere? And what spheres of operation would be least inhospitable to counter-hegemonic initiatives from the left? These are some initial questions; others will have their own. They are the more easily put with the help of Joe Cleary's indispensable book.

The Great Nation and the Evil Empire

Seamus Deane

The Writings of Theobald Wolfe Tone, 1763–98 Edited by T. W. Moody, R. B. McDowell and C. J. Woods
Volume 1, *Tone's Career in Ireland to June 1795*; Volume 2, *America, France and Bantry Bay, August 1795 to December 1796*; Volume 3, *France, the Rhine, Lough Swilly and Death of Tone, January 1797 to November 1798* (Oxford: Clarendon Press, 1998, xl + 540 pages, ISBN 0-19-822383-9; 2001, xviii + 435 pages, ISBN 978-0-19-820879-2; 2007, xxvi + 599 pages, ISBN 978-0-19-820880-8)

[*References to these volumes in the text are in the form of an arabic numeral to indicate the volume number, followed by a period and arabic numeral to indicate the page number.*]

On the morning of 30 April 1795, the United Irish agent William Jackson, who was also a clergyman of the Established Church, faced the chief justice, John Scott, Earl of Clonmel, in the King's Bench court on Merchants' Quay in Dublin to receive the sentence of death by hanging for treason; earlier that day he had been seen vomiting from the window of the coach

Theobald Wolfe Tone (1763–98). Engraving by T. W. Huffam. Photo: Hulton Archive/Getty Images.

that brought him there from Newgate Prison. Now he was slumped against the dock, sweating profusely. He rallied for a moment and whispered to his legal counsel, 'We have deceived the senate'.[1] His hat was removed and 'a dense steam was seen to ascend from his head and temples'; his face twitched, his eyes alternately closed and glared. When ordered to stand before the court, he stood rocking from side to side, his arms crossed over his breast and was asked to say why 'judgement of death and execution thereon should not be awarded against him, according to law'. He made no response. 'Sweat rolled down his face...and he grasped the iron spikes, which encircled the dock, with avidity.'[2] His counsel intervened to ask for an arrest of sentence, the windows of the courtroom were opened to relieve Jackson who, nevertheless, was in his final agony and suddenly 'sunk in the dock'. Clonmel declared: 'If the prisoner is in a state of insensibility, it is impossible that I can pronounce the judgement of the court upon him'. A doctor Thomas Waite and a Thomas Kinsley, who identified himself as 'an apothecary and druggist', offered to examine Jackson. Kinsley was a Quaker and refused to have his opinion of Jackson's condition sworn in to the record on oath. Waite told Clonmel straight away that the prisoner was 'verging to eternity'. Indeed, within moments he was dead; his body remained in the dock in the position of its final collapse until an inquest on the following morning. Jackson was found to have swallowed a large quantity of 'metallic poison', probably arsenic, almost certainly supplied by his wife on her final visit earlier that day, when the jailer had seen him 'much agitated' and vomit 'very violently' after taking some tea.[3] And perhaps Mrs. Jackson had agreed to co-operate with her husband in the shared hope that his suicide would preserve for her any chance of retaining the little money they had left from confiscation by the government —inevitable if he were to be hanged as a traitor. At any rate, after a swift inquest, Jackson was buried the following Sunday 'in all the triumph of treason'.[4]

Apart from the dramatic public suicide, Jackson's trial was significant in other respects. First, the evidence in the case so compromised Tone that he had to make a deal with the government to go into exile in America in order to avoid a charge of treason at home. It also revealed both to government and its opponents that there was a genuine interest in revolutionary France in the possibility of an Irish expedition. Further, it was the first in a series of trials against members of the United Irishmen in which a new departure from English law, peculiar to Ireland, was employed. Henceforth, the evidence of one witness was sufficient to convict a prisoner upon a charge of high treason (two was the minimum in England). The consequence was that a trail of informers issued from Dublin Castle, 'where they had been worked upon, by the fear of death and the hopes of compensation, to give evidence against their fellows';[5] their witness led in almost every instance to execution. This was integral to government strategy at the time: a reign of terror face-masked by the law, the summary character of the proceedings disguised in the public ritual of conformity to ancient rules.

At the heart of it all stood the friend or colleague turned informer, the state's witness. It was in this decade that he began his career, scarcely interrupted since, as the villain in Irish public imagination; infamous, a traitorous and fawning wretch in the secret organization and vengefully powerful in the 'bad eminence' of his sudden new public position; not a villain in law; *au contraire*, and far worse, the villain of and for the law; 'in this wicked country is the informer an object of judicial idolatry'.[6] (And the decade had an abundance of informer-villains, such as Francis Higgins, the Sham Squire, and Tone's brother-in-law, Thomas Reynolds; Leonard McNally's even more shocking and deep-seated treachery was not revealed until his death in 1820.) When the informer came into a courtroom

1 William Henry Curran, *The Life of John Philpot Curran*, 2 vols. (Edinburgh, 1822), vol. 1, 275–84.

2 Candid Observer, *Biographical Anecdotes of the Founders of the Late Irish Rebellion* (London, 1799), 3.

3 Thomas Mac Nevin, *The Lives and Trials of Archibald Hamilton Rowan, The Rev. William Jackson, etc.* (Dublin, 1846), 280.

4 *Biographical Anecdotes*, 15.

5 Curran's own words; Curran, *Life*, vol. 1, 321.

6 Curran, *Life*, vol. 1, 322.

7 Curran, *Life*, vol. 1, 322.
8 Thomas Otway, *Venice Preserv'd*, ed. Malcolm Kelsall (Lincoln, Nebraska, 1969), 95.
9 See John Barrell, *Imagining the King's Death: Figurative Treason, Fantasies of Regicide, 1793–1796* (London, 2000), 567.

under guard, 'Have you not marked, when he entered, how the stormy wave of the multitude retired at his approach?'[7] asked John Philpot Curran — himself gulled all the way by McNally, who had 'entertained' Jackson and some friends within a day or two of his arrival in Dublin in 1794.

Jackson had been betrayed by his friend John Cockayne, to whom he had revealed his mission to collect information about Ireland for the French revolutionary government. It is the fact of the betrayal of friendship in his own calamitous case that gives his whispered last words to one of his assistant counsel (Curran was his chief counsel) such a melancholy resonance. They are from Thomas Otway's *Venice Preserv'd* (1682), in which the hero Pierre asks his friend Jaffeir (who has in fact betrayed him in their conspiracy against the corrupt Venetian senate) to save him from a dishonourable death on the wheel and gallows by stabbing him. The anguished Jaffeir does so and then, in remorse at his own treachery, fatally stabs himself also. Pierre exclaims: 'Now, now — thou hast indeed been faithful! This was done nobly! — We've deceived the senate'.[8]

The play was popular for about 150 years — performed every year but one of the eighteenth century in London, published in scores of editions in London and Dublin, the roles of Pierre and Jaffeir famously and repeatedly filled by David Garrick and Spranger Barry — and was generally taken to be a coded parable about Whigs or Tories or Papists conspiring against the English court or parliament. But for the most part, in popular performance and imagination, it was a play that celebrated male friendship and a male conception of honour as greater than heterosexual love and as the ground of political fidelity to the cause of justice. Equally, the part of the abandoned heroine, Belvidera, who goes mad after the final spectacular double killing on the platform of the gallows, was one of the most sought-after of all tragic roles. Her anguish was, in 'loyalist' versions of the play, taken to represent the brutal effect on human feeling of ideological fanaticism, a counter-revolutionary propagandist theme pursued with especially monotonous vigour in the 1790s. Yet there was a 'plot' by the English radical John Thelwall, as revealed by the spy Taylor at Thelwall's trial in London in 1794, 'to steal [the play] from the loyalist canon' by mounting a campaign against the current production at Covent Garden. According to Thelwall, the play had been written to damage the patriots of its day 'by representing all reformers as conspirators'. Thelwall and his friends had loudly applauded the 'republican passages' at the first night of the Covent Garden production, and the 'civic republicanism' element was further heightened in a new production at Drury Lane by Sheridan and John Philip Kemble; in the light of the Treason Trials of the previous year, the conspirators looked like 'civic martyrs'. But this production closed after only three nights, partly because of the climate engendered by an attack on the king's coach on 29 October 1795 at the state opening of parliament.[9] Still, the exchanges and speeches of Pierre and Jaffeir, or a selection from them, certainly had gained a more decisively republican timbre since Jackson's whispered last words in April. And the final gesture of giving up wife and family in the act of deceiving the corrupt and vicious senate, of refusing to allow the state to impose a criminalizing sentence carried out in public, by choosing an honourable suicide — to control one's own death even while in the jaws of the monster — bore the mark of ancient Roman stoic republican pride, which Jackson, and, three and a half years later, Tone, reasserted for posterity by the manner of their deaths.

If ever I have the power

> Well, for me, ... only one real sentiment exists — friendship between man and man. Pierre and Jaffeir, such a bond as theirs is what I care for most. I know *Venice Preserved* by heart.

The speaker here is the villianous Vautrin in Balzac's *Père Goriot* (1832),[10] exemplifying the later decline of the republican ideal of friendship and honour into a masquerade, as he draws the horrified Eugène de Rastignac into his debt and into his power. Vautrin's was the Paris of the July Monarchy of Louis Philippe, far from the revolutionary city of heroic virtue — although this was now the Paris of the Directory and not of Robespierre — where in 1796 Tone heard the Marseillaise sung every night he went to the Comédie-Française 'and the verse "*Tremblez, Tyrans*" [was] always received with applause' (2. 42). Tone remained entranced by the revolution and by the French, although he acknowledged in a conversation with General Clarke in March 1796 that its initial enthusiasm had subsided (2.121); for the most part he is silent about or unaware of the premonitory indications of corruption that marked the rule of the Directory that had come to power just a few months before he arrived in February 1796. Still, his 'first adventure' there was with a swindler who now appears like a characteristically shabby representative of the public sleaziness that was then rapidly colonizing the newly expanded public sphere. 'The republic of vice seemed to have succeeded the Republic of Virtue.'[11] This was not quite Tone's view; he sensed there was indeed no further appetite for revolution in Paris, after the ending of the Terror and the revolutionary tribunals which he abhorred. Nor did he want to see the Republic threatened, partly because that would further diminish the prospects of a French invasion force for Ireland. Thus, he showed no sympathy for the Babouvist conspirators, arrested on 10 May 1796. In his diary next day, he records working on the *Proclamation to the People of Ireland* for General Hoche, copies of which were to be distributed by the French army after it had landed in Ireland, and responds to the carefully overheated government announcement of the plot to massacre those in authority:

> I would show no mercy to any man, whatever might be his past merits, who would endeavour in the present position of France to subvert the existing government ... the French have at this moment an exceeding good form of government ... It might possibly be better but the advantage which might possibly result from an alteration is not such as to warrant any honest man in hazarding the consequences of another bloody revolution. (2.179)

On Bastille Day in 1796, Tone reports that Carnot told him 'he was satisfied that Babeuf's plot was the work of an Orléans [royalist] faction' (2.236). The leaders of the conspiracy, betrayed by a notorious spy, Grisel, were Babeuf and Darthé. They attempted (but failed), in keeping with their Roman stoic republican beliefs, to commit suicide in court after sentence, by stabbing themselves. They were nevertheless, after a night of great pain, hauled off to public execution on 27 May 1797. (Two years before, the martyrs of Prairial, six Jacobin members of the 'Crest' group in the Convention, had committed mass suicide, again by stabbing one another, on the way to the guillotine. For them too this was a call to action to posterity and an assertion of their freedom to die as republicans. And Robespierre of course had left himself in agony with a shattered jaw after his botched suicide in 1794.) Tone was in Cologne that day, vainly trying to fix a meeting with Hoche, seemingly unaware of the guillotining in Vendôme (outside Paris), but learning, belatedly, from a newspaper of the betrayal and arrest of a number of United Irishmen in the north of Ireland (3.75). All during his years in Paris and in French-dominated Europe, Tone lived in this liquid suspension of slow-floating information and frustration, the increasingly attenuated strains of the revolution yielding to the dark rumbling of the news from Ireland, picked up at second or third hand, the doom-laden sounds of sanctioned slaughter at home and whispered,

10 Honoré de Balzac, *Old Goriot*, trans. Marion Ayton Crawford, Penguin Classics edn. (London, 2002), 183.

11 Colin Jones, *The Great Nation: France from Louis XV to Napoleon* (London, 2002), 508.

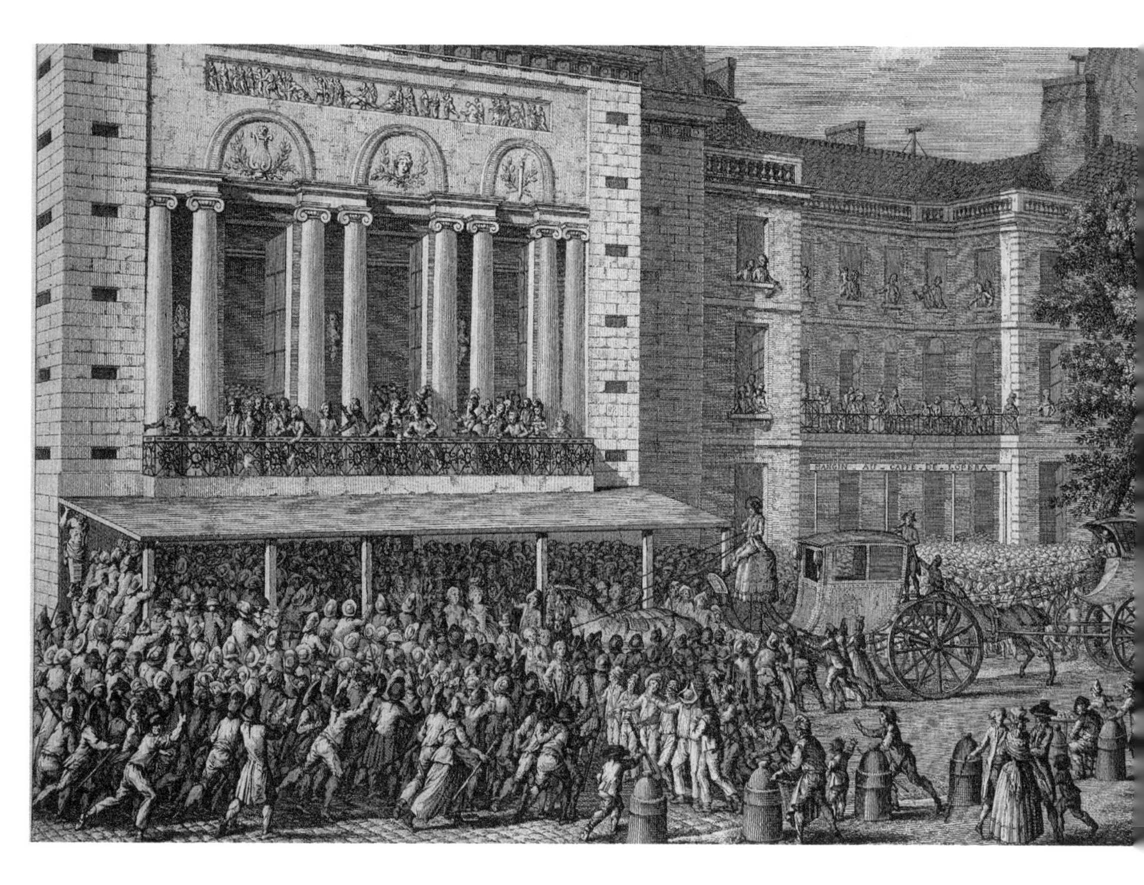

The People closing the Opéra, Paris, France, 12 July 1789 (French Revolution). Engraving by Prieur and Berthault. © The Art Archive / Fondation Thiers Paris / Gianni Dagli Orti.

pervasive betrayal there and in Paris too.

Spies and informers were everywhere — in Paris, in London, in Ireland. *L'or du Pitt*, Pitt's gold, spread out in a giant delta, from the north of Ireland, to Dublin, Scotland, La Vendée, into France's army and political system and into the consciousness of exiles, émigrés and police. It became more attractive as the French currency weakened. 'Pitt is as cunning as Hell, and he has money enough, and we have nothing here but assignats' (2.120). Tone was suspicious that so many 'Americans' were to be found in Paris; even more so, he was suspicious of his own countrymen and their indiscretions or provocations. Tone lived undercover, as Citizen Smith, in a state of justified paranoia, trying to conceal his presence in France from the British authorities who believed him to be still in America. Secrecy was unavoidable, yet the boast of republicanism had always been its open, public stance. As a consequence, since he was without his wife and children (who did not get to France from America until 1797), or his closest friend, Thomas Russell, he spent a lot of time drinking a lot of wine on his own. In February 1796, after a useful meeting with the American ambassador, James Munroe, Tone marvels in his diary at 'so obscure and individual' as himself should be 'thrown into such a situation'. And goes on: 'I hope I may not ruin a noble cause by any weakness or indiscretion of mine; as to my integrity I can answer for myself. What shall I do for want of P.P. [Thomas Russell]? I am in unspeakable difficulties for the want of his advice and consolation' (2.75). And his wife is in effect the person to whom the diary is confided; how often he wishes she could see and hear what he is recording; how much he wants to impress her and make her proud of his achievement! At the Opéra: 'I lose three fourths of the pleasure I would otherwise feel for the want of my dear love, or my friend P.P. to share it with. How they would glory in Paris just now!' (2.54).

Even in those ecstatic moments when he could delight in the democratic celebrations of the revolutionary crowds, at festivals and military displays, his unease and solitude persist. For instance, at the Victory Festival at the Champ de Mars, 29 May 1796, Tone was included with the diplomatic corps, but 'for particular reasons I chose to remain *incognito* ... the tears ran down my cheeks when Carnot presented the wreaths and the standards to the soldiers. It was a spectacle worthy of a great republic and I enjoyed it with transport. *Vive la République!*' (2.192). A couple of months later, while walking through the Tuileries gardens he by chance met an old friend, the British radical John Hartford Stone, whose brother William had been involved in the Jackson trial, and the writer Helen Maria Williams. 'I was fairly caught, for I have avoided Stone ever since my arrival; not that I know anything to his prejudice, but that I guard the incognito' (2.246). Living in such studied anonymity (or pseudonymity),Tone was greatly taken by the powerful reality, as he experienced it, of the alternative public life of the incandescent revolutionary unity in which the mixed elements of one's subjectivity could be, if only temporarily, dissolved. And the delirium of evenings at the Théâtre des Arts was heightened further by the recognition that the National Guardsmen who filled the stage were not actors but the men of the armies that had won such dazzling victories in the Netherlands and on the Rhine (2.50). '*Here*,' Tone writes, '*was no fiction*; and that is what gave it an interest which drew the tears irresistibly to my eyes' (2.52, emphasis in original). Theatre was, in his view, wisely subsidized by the government; it had become an inspirational display of music, heroic gesture, military splendour and public enthusiasm co-ordinated into an official ritual. The political, pedagogical and socially regenerative function of their theatre was one of the features that, he thought, made the contemporary French resemble the Athenians of ancient Greece (2.440).

Yet Tone had other, more frequent, occasions for tears of vexation and frustration. The delays and intricacies of his mission, straining to gain access to key figures such as Carnot, Hoche or Delacroix via (undeservedly) suspect intermediaries such as General Clarke, sapped his patience; besieged by the anxiety that the mediocre contacts he was obliged to rely on and be nice to were putting self-interest before the cause of Ireland and, as ever, the looming fear of betrayal and the empty, imagined revenge — this was deep stress:

> Dined at Ahern's lodgings with Madgett, Sullivan, &c. Choice champagne! Got half tipsy, partly with rage and vexation at the prospect before me. Have I risqued my life, ruined my prospects, left my family and deserted my country to be baffled by a scoundrel at last? If he prove one, woe be to him! (2.156)

There was also the nagging doubt, not only about French government intentions but about his own capacity to fool himself about them; a diary entry for 18 February 1796, on foot of an encouraging conversation about which general should lead the Irish invasion force, asks: 'Am I too sanguine in believing what I so passionately wish — *that the French executive will seriously assist us?*' (2.59, emphasis in original). In similar fashion, regularly hearing of the atrocities in Ireland, often ten days or more after they happened, or of arrests of United Irish or former Catholic Committeee leaders (like John Keogh), he begins to lose his natural gaiety and records the feeling:

> Well! a day will come for all this! If we cannot prevent his [Keogh's] fall, at least I hope we shall be able to revenge it; *and I for one promise if it be in twenty years from this not to forget it.* My heart is hardening hourly, and I satisfy myself now at once on points which would stagger me twelve months ago. The Irish

> aristocracy are putting themselves in a state of nature with the people, and let them take the consequences. They shew no mercy and they deserve none. If ever I have the power I will most heartily concur in making them *a dreadful example* (2.149, emphasis in original).

And as the arrests of United Irishmen leaders and the assaults of the military on the civilian population continued, so the hardening of feeling continued: 'I feel my mind growing every hour more and more savage. Measures appear to me now justified by necessity which six months ago I would have regarded with horror. There is now no medium' (3.221).

A dog's life

When the French Revolution rejected historical precedent of the kind favoured by the *ancien régime* of Europe as a source of political legitimacy, it became necessary to invent or re-create an alternative in classical antiquity, particularly the republican Roman version — austere, heroic, sacrificial, suicidal. Roman, or neo-Roman, ideas about freedom and servitude played a comparable role before the outbreak of civil war in England in 1642.[12] But in France, at least until 1797, the Roman influence pervaded the whole public sphere, so that even the style of dress of the ancient republic was approved, indeed mandatory at times, because of its ivorian simplicity in contrast to the insolent frivolity and artificiality of monarchical fashions. Tone often comments on the 'classical' costumery of the Parisian fêtes and of actors and actresses — more often the latter. Even the opposition to this style took the form of a political fashion statement. The year before he arrived, the anti-Jacobin, royalist vigilante gangs, christened *'la jeunesse dorée'*, or 'Muscadins', appeared on the streets with their 'victim's style', spiked hair, long over the ears, cropped at the back to bare the neck, as for the guillotine. They rioted frequently at theatres and fêtes. Tone mentions that they 'and the *elegant women* of Paris made it a point to stay away' (unsurprisingly) from a fête at the Champ de Mars to celebrate 'the anniversary of the subversion of royalty in France' (2.307, emphasis in original). They remained a threat until the anti-royalist coup of Fructidor, 4 September 1797, which also led to the deportation of two of Tone's favoured candidates to lead the Irish invasion, Carnot and Pichegru — the latter on charges of treason. ('Such treachery,' Tone writes, 'in a man of the situation, character and high reputation of Pichegru is enough to put a man out of humour with human nature' [3.148].) And in the same month General Hoche died of consumption — or possibly, according to Fouché, minister of police, he was poisoned.

Tone recognizes that he is witnessing (and is himself part of) the emergence of a new symbolic order; the old system of representation, political and aesthetic, had begun to weaken, even to disappear; what had previously 'stood for' the people, no longer did. '*Here was no fiction*.' A different form of representation was required because, in both France and Ireland, the relationship between the 'nation' and the 'people' was being reconfigured. Louis XVI was briefly rechristened 'King of the French' rather than 'King of France' in 1793; Louis Philippe in 1830 affected revolutionary credentials when assuming power specifically as 'King of the French'. However, this axiomatic, natural connection between people and nation — according to a condescending logic — had to be rediscovered and reaffirmed after enduring a long period of artificial and coercive separation. To effect this would require a sustained programme of education that would culminate in a recognition like that of Emile in Rousseau's great educational tract: 'I have decided to become what you [have] made me'.[13] That would be the revolutionary decision in which the people and the nation would become one,

12 Quentin Skinner, 'Classical Liberty and the Coming of the English Civil War', in Martin van Gelderen and Quentin Skinner, eds., *Republicanism: A Shared European Heritage*, 2 vols. (Cambridge, 2002), vol. 2, 14.

13 Jean-Jacques Rousseau, *Emile*, trans. Barbara Foxley, Everyman edn. (London, 1993), 522.

where the presiding idiom is one of will but the prevailing experience is one of discovery. And it is individually a discovery of identity as released in and through an indissoluble union with others.

The French had begun to exhibit the transformation they had undergone in the revolutionary drive to create this new (or 'natural', therefore not strictly new, but re-newed) version of the human in their dress, decorations and rituals. The calendar, with the *décadi* replacing Sundays (Sunday, 7 February 1796, 'I was curious to observe how this day would be kept in France' [2.43]), theatre, fêtes, ballets, opera, all manifested this change; public singing in chorus and dancing (the Carmagnole, in particular), the salutation of 'citizen' replacing the titles and the old graded forms of greeting, the wearing of the *bonnet rouge*, the tricolour flag and cockade, the decorative motif of the Phrygian cap, the cult of the *sans-culottes*. Not everything was new. There were still traces in opera of the old musical tradition that Tone disliked — the French mode of professional singing, for instance, which he found did not compare with the more 'natural' Italian syle that had become popular all over Europe. This echoed the famous dispute of the 1750s dominated by Rousseau and Rameau on the more melodic 'democratic' virtues of Italian as opposed to the formal, mannered court music and even language of the French. Rousseau 'won' the dispute. It was an important defeat for the cultural claims and prestige of Versailles.[14] The renewed emphasis in the 1790s on melody, and the consequent highlighting of the words of the dramatic text or song, reduced complicated harmonic and chromatic effects and increased audience participation in the great communal festive events, much enjoyed and frequently attended by Tone, fond of the melodic chorus as an instance of social unity, a political therapy for the sharpness of his solitude. He sided with the Rousseau faction in disliking the 'very heavy music by Rameau' (2.258) and greatly admiring Gluck, the most celebrated composer of Italian opera in Rousseau's day (2.256). He confesses in his diary that he goes to the opera so much (rather than the theatre) because he as yet understands music better than French (2.134). And again, 'Am I not to be pitied? ... I do lead a dog's life here. My sole resource is the Opera' (2.135).

The opera had long been more popular than the theatre in eighteenth-century France and became even more so in the revolutionary epoch. Tone celebrated the abolition of the distinction between the actors and the audience, both now agents in the great enterprise of emancipation from the strait conventions (and licensed privileges) of the past. In accord with that, he welcomed too the abolition of the distinction in uniform between officers and enlisted men; but his rapture was modified in this instance, for Tone loved dashing and elaborate military outfits. The sight of the Grenadier Guards in the garden of the Tuileries, young men conscripted in the *première réquisition* of 1793, reminded him of the Irish Volunteers as he had seen them 'in the days of my youth and innocence', and he duly supplies the details of their blue, white and red uniforms, just as, on the next day, he describes in detail the splendid dress worn by the foreign minister Delacroix at a meeting marked by a very pleasing and encouraging ministerial courtesy and deference (2.55–56). Tone remarked how the erosion of military discipline of the Prussian sort had been replaced by an extraordinary enthusiasm, itself the new kind of discipline that he thought accounted for the astonishing French victories against conventionally trained forces (2.136, 138). Of course, he had already been involved in Ireland in some of those new forms of political organization and activity that had been developed to such a prodigious level in France — the political club, the underground conspiracy, the printing of newspapers, collections of popular songs, pamphlets, flysheets, placards — and he now witnessed the effects of the

14 John T. Scott, 'Rousseau and the Melodious Language of Freedom', in John T. Scott, ed., *Jean-Jacques Rousseau: Political Principles and Institutions* (London and New York, 2006), 370–98.

Cockade said to be worn by Wolfe Tone at his trial. © Jackie Clarke Library and Archive, Ballina.

technological and political advances in the development of prints and engravings, cartoons, and even of the ubiquitous classical busts on all sorts of pedestals — as well as busts of contemporary revolutionary heroes, particularly of the murdered Marat, especially favoured by the *jeunesse dorée* for smashing — of monumental statuary (including the reused plinths of the statues of the dead king) and paintings heroic both in scale and in subject matter. The Louvre impressed him in March 1796 with the range of its collection, the cynosure ambition that was to be so astonishingly realized under Napoleon: 'All France and Flanders have been ransacked to furnish it' (2.100). The revolutionary *journée*, or fête, even more than the opera or theatre, demonstrated 'the powerful effect of public spectacles, properly directed, in the course of a revolution' (2.137).

France had attained a condition that was the product of the peculiar and potent blend of the *dirigiste*, centralizing spirit of its government and the crusading, iconoclastic energies of the people at large. But the condition of Ireland was, in comparison, abysmal; 'Pat' needed a large dose of French *élan* if he were to be successfully remodelled for freedom. The Fête de la Jeunesse on 30 March 1796 prompted Tone to record the need to bring the Irish 'up to the enthusiasm of the French' (2.136) and, two days later, remembering the disputes he and Thomas Russell 'have had on the subject of discipline', to admit that he too would now 'make the French army our model in preference to the Prussian' (2.139). The planting of the tree of liberty, a ritual repeated thousands of times all over France and Europe— Tone attended a planting at a fête in Bonn on Vendémiaire, 22 September 1797 (3.152) — needed an enthused citizenry, the very phenomenon the English government and its lieutenant adminstration in Ireland was determined to eliminate by every imaginable form of coercion.

All these manifestations of a novel freedom that so impressed Tone also made him frequently disconsolate, for they reminded him of that painfully contrasting, increasingly desperate situation in Ireland. They also brought home to him his own humiliating condition of dependence on others, his writing to order of proclamations and analyses of the Irish situation that he could never be sure were either carefully or intelligently read, his endless waiting, the days when his diary records 'Blank!', or when he — most attractively to many of his later readers — registers his darker moods with a certain connoisseurship, but never with a valetudinarian relish. He regularly dismisses his own miseries with a shrug, quoting the phrase *'tis but in vain*' from a popular song — which is followed in one version by the line '*For mortals to wish again*', and in another, '*For soldiers to complain*'. But the note of desperation is clearly audible at times. 'Well, here I am, and here I must remain, and I am as helpless as if I were alone, swimming for my life in the middle of the Atlantic. 'Tis terrible. However, "'Tis but in vain, &c., &c."' (2.203).

Servitude

Yet these moods are not well understood simply as expressions of a 'personality'. They go to the heart of Tone's political experience and the whole concept of dependence and slavery that ramifies so widely through all republican theory. To be dependent on the wish, caprice or undelegated authority of someone else is to lack autonomy and to be a slave. It is corrupt and corrupting, especially when sustained by violence and an endless bombardment of propaganda and threat. This is Ireland's condition and it is also Tone's. But now that he and his colleagues have moved against it for the recovery of that liberty which human dignity requires, their task is to persuade the Irish to internalize this as a demand of *right*, not just reactively to rebel against oppression. This condition of dependence has, in both subtle and gross ways, demoralized the Irish peasantry, who would have to emulate the French by theorizing their situation to effect a revolution in the very conception of autonomy and authority, not simply a rebellion against its local effects. The changes wrought in Ireland by the French Revolution were, Tone believed, already astonishing. The Dissenters, particularly in the North, were the most obvious beneficiaries, but the Catholic peasantry too had been greatly affected, he claimed. At his first meeting with him, he was asked about this by General Clarke, who was worried about the influence

> the Catholic clergy might have over the minds of the people and the apprehension lest they might warp them against France. I assured him, as the fact is, that it was much more likely that France should turn the people against the clergy than that the clergy should turn the people against France; that within these last few years, that is to say since the French Revolution, there had an astonishing change taken place in Ireland with regard to the influence of the priests. (2.112)

Tone's view of both the Catholic Defenders and the Protestant Dissenters and of their hopes and expectations of

French help was optimistic. His *First Memorial* of 1796 compounds this with an overly sanguine view of the 'great majority' of the Catholic Committee as 'sincere republicans' (2.68). Still, these might also have been tactical overstatements to reassure the French — or himself. Tone believed that a great task of political education confronted him and the United Irishmen, but that it had already begun.[15]

A central function of the United Irishmen organization was the stimulation of the consciousness of the people to an awareness that the end had come for the *ancien régime* both as an idea and as a system. The downfall of the French monarchy and of the papacy marked the end of the ancient system of tyranny (3.208–10). In his *Address to the People of Ireland on the Present Important Crisis*, completed just before he set off on his final journey with the French fleet to Ireland, Tone wrote:

> Without being too much of an enthusiastic visionary, I think I may say I see a new order of things commencing in Europe ... the ancient system of tyranny must fall. In many nations it is already extinct, in others it has received its death wound ... its duration is ascertained and its days already numbered. I do not look upon the French revolution as a question subject to the ordinary calculation of politics; *it is a thing which is to be*; and as all human experience has verified that the new doctrine ever finally subverts the old, as the Mosaic law subverted idolatry, as Christianity subverted the Jewish dispensation, as the Reformation subverted popery, so, I am firmly convinced, the doctrine of republicanism will finally subvert that of monarchy and establish a system of just and rational liberty on the ruins of the thrones of the despots of Europe (2.377, emphasis in original).

The Irish must seek independence as an ethical as well as political goal. But could that dimension be realized? Tone's official optimism faded when he addressed the problem of the effect upon the Irish of centuries of alien rule. In the same address, he says that

> we have been reduced to that lowest state of human degradation, we have almost ceased to respect ourselves; we have doubted whether the opinion of our oppressors was not just and whether we were not in fact framed for that submission to which we have been bent by the pressure of so many centuries of hard, unremitting, unrelenting tyranny. (2.376)

And, scoldingly, in the final paragraph: 'if you do not avail yourselves of the present opportunity to free your country and to make your own fortunes, you deserve to remain, as you will remain, in poverty and disgrace for ever!' (2.396). In similar but even harsher terms, he ends his address encouraging Irish sailors serving with the British fleet to rebel, with this accusation — which clearly does not refer only to the sailors: 'If all this does not rouse you, then you are indeed what your enemies have long called you — A BESOTTED PEOPLE!' (2.391).

Degradation and demoralization of the Irish by tyrannical rule were features Tone had already noticed during his sojourn in America. In a letter to Thomas Russell of October 1795, from Princeton, New Jersey, he had written:

> ... of all the people I have met here the Irish are incontestably the most offensive. If you meet a confirmed blackguard, you may be sure he is Irish. You will of course observe that I speak of the lower orders. They are as boorish and ignorant as the Germans, as uncivil and uncouth as the Quakers, and as they have ten times more animal spirits than both, they are much more actively troublesome. After all, I do not wonder at, nor am I angry with

15 Kevin Whelan, *The Tree of Liberty: Radicalism, Catholicism and the Construction of Irish Identity, 1760–1830*, Field Day Critical Conditions series (Cork, 1996); Thomas Bartlett, 'The Burden of the Present: Theobald Wolfe Tone, Republican and Separatist', in David Dickson, Dáire Keogh and Kevin Whelans, eds., *The United Irishmen: Republicanism, Radicalism and Rebellion* (Dublin, 1993), 1–15; Ian McBride, 'The Harp without the Crown: Nationalism and Republicanism in the 1790s', in S. J. Connolly, ed., *Political Ideas in Eighteenth-Century Ireland* (Dublin, 2000), 159–84.

> them. They are corrupted by their own execrable government at home ... (2.32)

The experience of servitude, according to Tone in his more pessimistic vein of thinking, could have lasted so long that servitude itself became a habit, almost a custom, certainly so ingrained that it could be confused with the natural. And the hanging implication is that along with servitude to the English power, there had also been servitude to popery and the rancid connection between the two malodorously evident in the Penal Laws and in sectarian bigotry. It was in such conditions that the animating force of the idea of the self as citizen was so menacing both to those in power and even to those to whom he wished to see power transferred. Slaves can love their enslavement and become immune to the infectious promise of emancipation.

But ultimately, the real slaves were also the real tyrants, the Anglo-Irish Protestant Ascendancy, wholly submissive to London, although given to the very occasional gesture of independence as in 1782–83, fatally weakened by 'the unjust neglect of the claims of their Catholic brethren' (2.302), but generally shameless and hardboiled in their habitual venality and violence towards those subordinated to them by the existing political order. Tone opens the full repertoire of derision and outrage in his description of this bigoted and interbred faction — as Burke too, from a different angle, regarded them:

> it is England who supports and nourishes that rotten and aristocratic faction among you ... a faction which to maintain itself by the power of England is ready to sacrifice, and daily does sacrifice, your dearest rights to her infallible lust of gold and power. (2.378)

Their lack of fellow feeling for the Catholics, their psychotic rage at the prospect of concessions to them in the franchise or in admission to professions, or at their insolence even in canvassing opinion on such issues — 'sedition, tumult, conspiracy, treason' (1.376) — were the signs of a cognitive failure that was, in its practised lockstep of tyranny and servility, the essence of provincialism. They understood perfectly that it was in their own interest to be dependent upon masters and to be ruthless towards the subjugated. They entertained no other possibility. Their horizon was closed. No generous commitment to a universal was possible. The very idea of it aroused hostility and derision. Tone adds this account of the link between the bad conscience of those who choose servility and the violence of their hatred for those who oppose it. It is, in radical enlightenment and republican discourse, a standard analysis of the tormented condition of those who deliberately violate natural basic instincts and take out their shame on those who expose them: it is to be found in Helvétius, La Mettrie, d'Holbach and in novelists by the dozen:

> There is not a man of them that in the bottom of his soul does not feel that he is a degraded being in comparison of the men whom he brands with the name of incendiary and traitor. It is this stinging reflection that, among other powerful motives, is one of the most active in spurring them to revenge ... Who can forgive the man that forces him to confess that he is a voluntary slave, and that he has sold for money everything that should be most precious to an honorable heart; that he has trafficked in the liberties of his children, and his own, and that he is hired and paid to commit a daily parricide on his country? Yet these are charges which not a man of that infamous cast can deny to himself before the sacred tribunal of his own conscience. At least the United Irishmen ... have a grand, a sublime object in view; their enemies have not as yet ventured, in the long catalogue of accusation, to insert

the charge of interested motives; while that is the case, they may be feared and abhorred, but they can never be despised, and I believe that there are few men that do not look upon contempt as the most insufferable of all evils. (3.248–49)

The triumph of Anglo-Irish servility guaranteed that Ireland would be, in every sense, a province or a colony. All its outcries, as earlier with Molyneux or Swift (or later with Flood or even now with Grattan), about its constitutional and/or commercial subordination challenged this condition briefly and shallowly. For all talk of independence that did not address the Catholic question and the need for separatism was prattle.

Thus, claims of the 'Irish nation' by the Patriot party were never more than those of a governing sect that wanted more room to manoeuvre for itself but was still politically and militarily parasitic upon England. Patriot nationalism, Whig-inflected or no, could not but be a sham. Patriots could lament, as Tone himself repeatedly did, Ireland's invisibility as a nation, but they could not, without self-contradiction, object to its servile status as a colony. The Americans had drawn what was at times a fine line between civil war and a war of independence, but they decisively drew it. The Irish Volunteers did not and could not bring themselves to do so, because a policy of separation could not be pursued without inclusion of the Catholics. There was an alternative. Ireland could forgo its colonial status in exchange for incorporation:

> For my part ... if I were to describe a colony, I would picture a country in a situation somewhat similar to that of Ireland at present. I would describe a country, whose Crown was dependent on that of another country, enjoying a local legislature, but without any power entrusted to that Legislature of regulating the succession to that Crown. I would describe it as having an executive power administered by the orders of a non-resident Minister, irresponsible to the colony for his acts or his advice; I would describe it as incapable of passing the most insignificant law without the licence of the Minister of another country; I would describe it as a country unknown to foreign nations, in the quality of an independent state, and as subject to another power with regard to all the questions which concern alliances, the declaration and conduct of war, or the negociations for peace.[16]

That is Lord Castlereagh, arguing for the Irish Union, two years after Tone's death. Irish separatism, so presented, was an old colonial problem for uneasy settlers to be overcome by union, but a new solution for Tone to be realized by republican independence.

Castlereagh stole the language of the government's opponents in order to clarify further how the treaty of union, and the accusation that it was an exercise in a venality remarkable even by Anglo-Irish Protestant standards, could be dealt with by accepting that Ireland had been a colony but would now be upgraded to membership of an empire. Empire was the goal, union the method: 'It is said, Sir, that an Union will reduce Ireland to the abject situation of a colony. Is it, Sir, by making her a constituent part of the greatest and first empire in the world?' But it was to republicans that 'an Union would not act as a bribe':

> I must readily admit, that it is a measure of the most comprehensive bribery that was ever produced: It bribes the whole community of Ireland, by offering to embrace them within the pale of the British Constitution, and to communicate to them all the advantages of British commerce. It is this kind of bribe which is held out to the Protestant, to the Catholic, to the Dissenter; it is this kind of bribe which is held out to the merchant, to the manufacturer, to

16 *The Speech of the Right Honourable Lord Viscount Castlereagh upon Delivering to the House of Commons of Ireland His Excellency the Lord Lieutenant's Message on the Subject of an Incorporating Union with Great Britain* (Dublin, 1800), 13–14.

> the landholder — indeed, I know but of one class in the community to which an Union would not act as a bribe: It is to those who call themselves the lovers of liberty and independence. That liberty, which consists in the abdication of the British Constotution, that independence, which consists in the abandonment of the British Connexion ... I acknowledge that these are bribes which I am not prepared to offer.[17]

That speech is in many respects a direct answer to Tone's *Argument on Behalf of the Catholics of Ireland* (1791). It uses the famous language of reconciliation between the three sects in Ireland to lead to an opposed conclusion. This in itself is not surprising; Castlereagh had once been a supporter of radical/liberal discourse, and handled it with a degree of suavity; in these few lines from his speech, apart from the more obvious stress on the word 'British', or the loaded terms 'abdication' and 'abandonment', note how often he uses words beginning with 'con-' or 'com-' that indicate union, togetherness or completeness: *comprehensive*, *community* (twice), *Constitution* (twice), *commerce*, *communicate*, *consists* (twice), *Connexion*. But it is the sarcasm reserved for the '*lovers of* liberty and independence' that most obviously labours to make a telling distinction between real union and its fake counterpart, between true and false sentiment.

Friendship

The convergence of reactionary and republican language in the later decades of the eighteenth century is most evident in renewed and widespread disputes about human 'feeling' or 'feelings' and who had best claims to it or to them. Those who opposed the French Revolution and its alleged inversion of 'natural' feeling, led by Burke, claimed that the new doctrinal radicalism was characterized by a dangerous, even demonic form of abstract energy. It dissolved the actuality of all historical and traditional bonds, affections and realities and subjected them to a fanatical repudiation in the name of historical necessity, the new age, *the thing that is to be*. But the tempo of republican language also intensified, obviously enough in the revolutionay decade, but had been rising for some time before that, with the astonishing cult of Rousseau, beginning in the sixties with his *La Nouvelle Héloïse* — by which the dominant rhetoric of popular fiction was moulded for the next forty years — and especially with that novel's revitalization of the notion of a 'civil religion' that should supplant prevailing notions of national and confessional identity, reinforced in *Du Contrat Social* by the central republican assertion of the sovereignty of law over men and the concomitant repudiation of the mastery of the law by any faction for the sake of a private or selfish goal. 'Sincerity', 'candour', 'enthusiasm' and a whole lexicon of such interconnected words became the common currency of radical novels and political discourse — perhaps William Godwin is the most exemplary of those who gained renown in both genres with his *Political Justice* (1793) and *Caleb Williams* (1794) and, in the next generation, Mme. de Staël with *Corinne* (1807) and *Considérations sur les principaux événements de la Révolution française* (1818). All of these works are buoyed by concepts of tropical sincerity or enthusiasm, yet shaken too by the tremor of deep, ineradicable betrayal or compelling renunciation.

In his *Autobiography*, Tone written in Paris in August 1796, that makes a distinction between two groups of his closest friends. On the one hand, stand Thomas Russell and Thomas Addis Emmet; on the other, Whitley Stokes, George Knox and Peter Burrowes. Between Tone and the first pair there has been, from the beginning,

> a coincidence of sentiment, a harmony of feeling on points which we all conscientiously consider as of the last

17 *Speech of the Right Honourable Lord Viscount Castlereagh*, 37.

> importance, which binds us in the closest ties to each other. We have unvaryingly been devoted [to] the pursuit of the same object, by the same means, we have had a fellowship in our labours, a society in our dangers; our hopes, our fears, our wishes, our friends and our enemies have been the same. When all this is considered, and the talents and principles of the men taken into the account, it will not be wondered that I esteem Russell and Emmet as the first of my friends. If ever an opportunity offers, as circumstances at present seem likely to bring one forward, I think their country will ratify my choice. (2.292)

That final phrase is telling. 'Their', not 'our', country; Tone is already absenting himself, but not 'his choice'. There may be a premonition of death here; certainly the last sentence is nuanced towards heroism. The whole section is backlit by the sense of danger, as preparations and negotiations proceed for the launch of the invasion force — which began its slow uncoiling a month later.

Of the others, he remembers the loyalty of Burrowes and Knox, both of whom, despite the 'irreconcilable difference of sentiment' between them and Tone, stood by him after the Jackson trial 'when others ... shunned me, as if I had the red spots of the plague out on me' (2.292–93). Whitley Stokes's 'political opinions approach nearer to mine than those of either Knox or Burrowes'. Yet, indignant as Stokes is at Ireland's treatment at the hands of her oppressors, 'the tenderness and humanity of his nature is such that he recoils from any measures to be attempted for her emancipation which may terminate in blood. In this respect I have not the virtue to imitate him' (2.293). In what sense is Tone using the word 'virtue' here? Perhaps he is merely being humble, or ironic, perhaps the word in this context is designed to remind us that the tender virtue attributed to Stokes is not one wished for by Tone himself, although appreciated as a precious trait.

> I must observe that in the choice of my friends I have been all my life extremely fortunate. I hope I am duly sensible of the infinite value of their esteem, and I take the greatest pride in being able to say that I have preserved that esteem, even of those from whom I most materially differed on points of the last importance and on occasions of peculiar difficulty; and this too without any sacrifice of consistency or principle on either side, a circumstance which however redounds still more to their credit than to mine. (2.293)

Stokes and Knox and Burrowes can be given 'still'(!) more credit than Tone, since 'on the points of last importance' they not only differed from him but, being of more tender stuff, must have found it harder to stay friendly with him than he with them. But in republican language there is virtue and there is also 'virtù', in the sense Machiavelli used it, meaning a capacity to act politically and ethically for the sake of the community and not in deference to or for the satisfaction of one's own admirably exquisite feelings. Thus, by sympathizing with and conceding to his friends' plight, Tone is making his own 'tendresse', and the recognition of it in them, even more fastidious while retaining his political virtù, to use violence against a notoriously violent enemy. Still, this is a last salute to those friends. Tone hops up on his plinth to deliver it:

> If it be my lot for me to fall, I leave behind me this small testimony of my regard for them written under circumstances which I think may warrant its sincerity. (2.294)

If Sincerity as an abstraction had a loyal friend it was Serenity. Serenity, of the kind readily found in English republican writers such as Godwin, Holcroft or Bage in the 1790s, enabled those blessed with it to face or rather outface exile or death. But exile or death were usually prefaced by betrayal and, although betrayal provoked the possessor of Serenity to unpardonably long-winded and implacably assured pronouncements, there was always a quaver audible in the voice. For betrayal of a friend was not wholly a personal matter; it was a breach of human solidarity. It was treason to humanity itself, even though the betrayed, in such narratives, often turned out to be an alleged traitor to the king or the law or the state. But then those who acted for the government in such a case were themselves open to the charge that they were traitors to the nation — usually on account of their violence or venality. Yet treason or betrayal implies that there is something that merits loyalty in the first place. The very concept of betrayal had an inbuilt vertigo and that of friendship also had a thrilling instability. When friend and enemy can be the same person, even when a friend can unwittingly act as an enemy (by loose talk, for example, which Tone feared), and when an enemy can play almost perfectly the part of a friend, then the toxic effects of secrecy on a politics grounded in sincerity and friendship became so pervasive that it had to be accepted that this friend/enemy interchange was itself a structural feature of the politics that seemed to be so radically compromised by it. This is a point frequently made about republicanism — not only that it is a political language and not a programme but also that it is *only* that — a rhetoric that affects a great deal of swagger and dramatic gesture but that cannot deal with the actualities of power, that finds its natural antinomy in 'realism'. The charge is further expanded by the claim that republicanism, which favours consensus and discussion as against despotic or tyrannical rule or fiat, is by its own principles transformed into a talking-shop politics, whereas republicans claim that by being driven by oppression into secrecy and conspiracy its public discussive nature was deformed and its occupational hazard became, not logomachy but paranoia.[18] Friendship was patriotism in an individual form; love for the nation was in turn a local form of human solidarity. The gradient of nobility rose with the degree of abstraction. A discourse such as this needed anchorage in the actualities of the world, otherwise its aeronautical tendencies swept it up into the stratosphere.

It is in Tone's friendship with Thomas Russell that we see an outstanding instance of *fraternité*, the heroic Jacobin version of a male bonding that is also a lived version of a public ideal of self-sacrifice and affection. It had long been a republican ideal that the obligations we have to the communal life should form the core of a true friendship. This is what makes friendship a virtue. Although it is easy to suggest that the Tone–Russell friendship is moulded in the 'romantic' model of a later generation, and that it exhibits an inescapably flawed and faked affinity between the private and the public realms, such an account would have to ignore the dynamic of self-consciousness that gave to such friendship its powerful, commemorative, neo-Roman or stoic quality. It was not that Tone and Russell (and Thomas Addis Emmet) tried to align their personal histories with the unfolding of public events — although that sometimes is the case. It is more that for them their friendship forms not just an alternative history *to* but the true history *of* their times, with its dates and places, its idyllic or its tragic moments, its exemplary idea of the sacrifice of the self to something greater, a sacrifice in which the self is not obliterated but discovered:

> my intention ... was to leave my family in America and to set off instantly for Paris, and to apply in the name of my country for the assistance of France to enable us to assert our independence ... this plan met with the warmest approbation and support from both Russell and Emmet; we shook hands and, having repeated our professions of unalterable regard and esteem for each other, we parted, and this was the last

18 Robert Hariman, *Political Style: The Artistry of Power* (Chicago and London, 1995), 47, 96.

> interview which I was so happy as to have with those two invaluable friends together. I remember it was in a little triangular field that this conversation took place, and Emmet remarked to us that it was in one exactly like it in Switzerland where William Tell and his two associates planned the downfal[l] of the tyranny of Austria. (2.331)

The sentiment of a passage such as this — and there are several of them in Tone's writings — is lodged in the particular, relished detail — the triangular field, the mention of William Tell. Simply because it is remembered, it has the elegiac appeal of a time gone by, a memory that delights and saddens at once, that returns '*me ravir at m'attrister*', as Rousseau put it in the account of his recall of his time at Chambéry in Book III of the *Confessions*. In that pleated doubling, time past still retains its utopian promise of a future society. The friendship here celebrated by Tone is an oath of loyalty to that future; it not only will be, but already *is* the basis for it. Thus the time gone past has already been the opening date of the new age, the moment of separation is the new beginning, only recognized as such in retrospect — just as the Convention in Paris had declared in October 1793 that Year I of the new age had begun on the 22 September 1792 when the Republic had been declared. (Thus the declaration that opened the new calendar was already in Year II.)

One can see why Pierre and Jaffeir were so readily recruited into the republican canon. They were obviously republicans *avant la lettre* and *Venice Preserv'd* its earliest melodrama. And William Tell was soon to join them as one of the best-known names among republican heroes with Schiller's play of 1804 on which in turn Rossini's opera of 1829 was based. The melodramatic element is more pronounced than the tragic in these works, for there can be no tragic ruin where virtue triumphs, even when the virtuous die.[19] Melodrama as a theatrical genre is a French revolutionary invention, although it had a long, very long, prequel in French and English fiction. Tone saw all the elements assembled at the revolutionary fêtes he attended; all that declamatory posturing and those choric crescendos presaged the later, brilliant extension of revolutionary melodrama into Italian opera. From Rousseau's *Letter on French Music* (1753), the Italian language, melodic composition and singing styles were linked with the expression of republican sentiment; the alliance achieved its first great operatic triumph with Rossini's *Tancredi* (1813); its famous patriotic tune 'Di tanti palpiti' became so popular in Italy that it was performed often and spontaneously by crowds attending the law courts to object to Austrian injustice. (Even the wonderful trumpet call indicating the moment of freedom in Beethoven's sole opera, *Fidelio* (1814), is recognizably a gesture that belongs in the genre of French revolutionary drama.) Republicanism had been aspiring since mid-century to the condition of an Italian music that still had to be born, although the conditions for it were assidulously pioneered by the revolutionary fête in France and by the republican apotheosis of friendship.

Tone is for the most part resolutely pragmatic, concentrating much of his attention, as he had to, on matters of political and military policy and prospects. He can sound quite Burkean on occasion: 'It is not by syllogisms that men are argued into liberty; nor by sophistry, as I trust, that they can be argued out of it. I confess I dislike abstract reasoning on practical subjects. I am buried in matter' (1.174). But what most memorably finds its sanction in the 'matter' that he supplies is the hyperbole of his feelings of hatred or of love. By hyperbole, I do not mean an exaggeration. Rather, the hyperbole, whether of friendship or of hatred, is always an indication of a failure to be adequate to reality. It is an aspiration or a stress; it can never really grasp what it reaches for. Friendship or

19 See Peter Brooks, *The Melodramatic Imagination: Balzac, Henry James, Melodrama and the Mode of Excess* (New York, 1976), 19–21; Lynn Hunt, *The Family Romance of the French Revolution* (Berkeley, Los Angeles, 1993), 181–91.

hatred unto death is always hyperbolic, even when someone actually dies for one or the other. Suicide or martyrdom extends and enriches the hyperbolic dimension; it does not close it. It strengthens the claim that love or friendship, hatred or hostility, have an ontological status. But the claim has to remain at a high pitch of intensity if it is to survive as a living belief. Friendship is too rare and precious just to be given to a friend. What friendship is based on is something greater than any friend can be, something of which friendship is the historical, lived correlate. There are obvious similarities here with religious conviction. A Pauline eloquence and hyperbole is the mark of such friendship; it is a belief in something beyond friendship that makes love between people possible.[20]

And thus what is dearest, 'the first object of his heart' has to be, not a person or persons, but a political ideal, 'the independence of his country' (3.416). In his address to the court martial which sentenced him, Tone admitted that his whole adult life had been devoted to this goal:

> For this he relinquished the dearest ties of wife & children, had suffered exile, prison & want, had braved the dangers of the sea and the fire of the enemy. Success in this life was everything, — he had failed. He attempted that in which Washington succeeded and Kosciusko failed. (3.416)

While urging the court to hasten his execution, according to the account given by an Anglican clergyman, he asked to be shot by firing squad, not hanged: 'He begged not to die on a gibbet. To him, after the failure of the great object of his heart, life had nothing to make it valuable ...' (3.417).

Such language in these terminal conditions, attested to by an enemy, is indistinguishable from the traditional language of love. There is indeed, throughout both his *Diary* and his *Autobiography*, although more so in the first, a combat between Tone's devotion to his country and his devotion to his wife and children. The surrender of domestic to national affection is offered as proof of the power and the priority of the public weal over private sentiment. But the battle between them is a close-run thing and only Matilda Tone's complete agreement and support for him in this permits the public interest to prevail. In this, she too is a republican; but she is also a character, or an agent, in Tone's own dramatization of the conflict. The to-and-fro in the *Diary* between Tone's love for her and for Ireland produces an attractive ripple effect when we accept that the *Diary* is, as part of its rhetorical structure, imagined as addressed to her.[21] 'When I get into this track of witty and facetious soliloquy,' he says, 'I know not how to leave off, for I always think I am chatting to my dearest life and love, and the light of my eyes' (2.123). This studied 'chatting', as well as the reporting of 'the most important part of the business', the mixture of formality and informality, is structural; the self-consciousness is that of someone whose subjectivity is being displayed as a historical phenomenon. It is loving so that in return it may be loved for its affectionate nature, admiring so that it may be admired for being so gifted and genial in bestowing admiration. This is an intricate and self-consciously winsome politics of republican patriotism.

> *I hope* (but I am not sure) my country is my *first object*; at least, she is *my second*. If there be one before her (*as I rather believe there is*) it is my dearest Life and Love, and the light of my eyes and the spirit of my existence ... She is my first object but would I sacrifice the interests of Ireland to her elevation? No, that I would not; and if I would, she would despise me, and if she were to despise me, I would go hang myself, like Judas ... Well, I do love my wife dearly ... she is a thousand times too good for me ... but then she is so infinitely better that it throws my

20 See Jacques Derrida, *Politics of Friendship*, trans. George Collins (London and New York, 1997), 75–170.

21 Cf. Declan Kiberd, 'Republican Self-fashioning: The Journal of Wolfe Tone', in *Irish Classics* (London, 2000), 221–42.

great merit into the shade. For all that I have said of her and myself here, I will be judged by Whitley Stokes and Peter Burrowes and P.P., who are three fair men; and I have now done this day's journal ... (2.133–34, emphasis in original).

And about a year later, in April 1797, he again makes a distinction between a friend whom he 'loves dearly', like George Knox, and 'my wife and Russell, [who] make, I may say, a part of my existence' (3.45). The *Diary* enacts that incandescent relationship between himself and the two people to whom it is primarily addressed. It has as a consequence both the intimacy of an autobiography and a confession, in which the distance between the author and his specific chosen audience is always under pressure to dissolve. So the most casual asides function as something said or whispered under breath, audible only to those two whose identity is merging with his own, more than can that of the other close friends whom he loves. It is his solitude that stimulates this envisioned intimacy most vividly, as in that moment in April on his way to Cologne when he feels he 'is quite alone, without a soul to speak to that I care one farthing about or that cares one farthing about me'. Equally, when he senses the political situation slide away from him, he turns towards Matilda and begs her and his friends to assure him he is overreacting. So, in early August 1797, on board ship on the Texel in Holland, 'locked up by the wind' (3.105), enraged and frustrated by the weather delays, he writes to Matilda at some length about the possibility of their going into exile, since a peace deal between France and England that would exclude Ireland was beginning to seem more likely. There is no chance of their again bending their necks to the yoke of English tyranny; nor can he imagine Irish patriots likewise would not rather emigrate than stay; and 'if they are not capable of that exertion, they have deceived themselves exceedingly in the idea that they had the energy which makes revolutions' (3.137–38). But he is sure that there is 'among us enough of virtue and of resolution to embrace even banishment rather than slavery; we have at least the energy of despair' (3.138). Then he continues:

> My dear friends [Lewines and McNeven] and you, the dearest of my friends, and that I love a thousand times more than my existence, where is the country that with the society of those we love and esteem we could not be happy in? Exile I know is terrible, but so is slavery ... no situation that could be offered me would buy me to return to Ireland while she remains at the mercy of her tyrant ...
>
> Let me beg of you, all three, to answer this letter as speedily as possible and if you think me a wrongheaded enthusiast, do not scruple to tell me so, for I in some degree suspect it myself. (3.140–41)

The skills exhibited in the *Diary* in particular remind us of the fact that Tone was one of the authors of an epistolary novel, *Belmont Castle* (1790), miserably represented here by a single extract, although thankfully available in a modern edition.[22] One of the striking features of Tone's contributions to this 'parody of the sentimental novel' is his humorous and satiric attitude towards excessive, stylized heroic gesture.[23] This humour remained with him; it allows him to see the comic, bravura elements of his own habitual striking of a posture. But the novel has a curious after-effect now on the later writings. The stagy suicides within it — that of the character Scudamore in particular — are not just echoes of young Werther; their farce now sounds as a tragic premonition of his own death. Additionally, the libertinage of the cast of characters is presented as a form of egoism. The novel as a middle-class genre inclined to exhibit libertinage as typically aristocratic, whereas sexual virtue (especially female chastity) was not only a middle-class and piously Christian trait, it was also an assertion of individual integrity and of human solidarity. This

22 Theobald Wolfe Tone and divers hands, *Belmont Castle; or, Suffering Sensibility*, ed. Marion Deane (Dublin, 1998).

23 Marion Deane, Introduction, in Tone, *Belmont Castle*, 24.

alloy is evident in Tone's representations of his love for his wife and for his country. In libertinage, there is no important distinction between lovers; but in a passion such as Tone's, one person or country only embodies perfection and remains the stable object of desire unto death.

Hatred

Tone's hatred of England, repeated in letters, pamphlets, *Autobiography, Diary*, in English and in French (3.165), is rooted in his belief in the baneful and corrupting effects of its dominion on Ireland, more pronounced after the conclusion of the Seven Years War in 1763, when England's imperial control was redefined, more shamefully evident after the success of the American War of Independence had given Ireland an example, feebly echoed, and England a warning, firmly acknowledged. English global violence (Scotland, America, India) and greed, forever soldered to its propaganda on liberty, contrasted remarkably with the programme of the French Revolution, its trumpeted extension to humankind at large with the benefits of its more provincial, but still resonant, American precedent. Inevitably, the chief opponent of revolutionary France was England, the natural leader of Reaction. The release of Ireland from this monstrous global blight would be a good in itself. It would give Ireland autonomy. It would be potentially a release too for the world at large, since the loss of Ireland, a strategic possession, would cripple the marauding seaborne empire and French help might be decisive in Ireland as it had been in America. ('France would most probably assist from the pride of giving freedom to one kingdom more' [1.136].) This view of England, especially its role in harnessing continental allies, local élites and counter-revolutionary peasants to protect its dominion, was not at all peculiar to Tone. It was a staple view of British radicals into the next generation, with Shelley and Hazlitt perhaps the best known (both of them had a particular hatred of Castlereagh, for his role in Ireland in the Rebellion and Union years and in the foreign policy that produced the reactionary Holy Alliance in Europe).

Tone's realization of England's deathly role in Ireland is recorded in a famous passage in his *Autobiography* when, after a brief experience as a Whig pamphleteer and a subsequent spell of unemployment under the eye of the political grandee George Ponsonby, Tone, regarding himself now 'as a sort of political character', plunged into a study of the affairs of his country and

> made speedily what was to me a grand discovery, tho' I might have found it in Swift or Molyneux, that the influence of England was the radical vice of our Government, and consequently that Ireland would never be either free, prosperous or happy until she was independent, and that independence was unattainable while the connexion with England existed. In forming this theory, which has ever since unvaryingly directed my political conduct, to which I have sacrificed everything, and am ready to sacrifice my life if necessary ... (2.284)

Later, in early July 1791, on finding that the United Irish Committee would not accept a resolution that would include the Catholics in a motion for parliamentary reform, Tone reacted by forming his 'theory' (by which he means a policy or programme):

> To subvert the tyranny of our execrable government, to break the connexion with England, the never failing source of all our political evils, and to assert the independence of my country — these were my objects. To unite the whole people of Ireland, to abolish the memory of all past dissensions, and to substitute the common name of Irishman in place of the denominations of Protestant, Catholic and Dissenter — these were my means. (2.301)

But he saw the difficulties, the Anglicans chief among them: 'The Protestants I despaired of from the outset ...'

All of this is well known. The most notable aspect of this overquoted passage, and of Tone's pamphlet writing and memoranda in general, is the conventionality of the language. The allusion to Swift's fourth of *Drapier's Letters* in the phrase 'the whole people of Ireland' (not at all original to Swift but canonized by his readers) is the most effective move in the passage, because on this occasion, and significantly, even shockingly, Tone includes the Catholics in it. Otherwise, 'tyranny of our execrable government',[24] 'assert the independence of [my] country', [25] 'never failing source' and even 'the common name of Irishman' (which echoes Defoe's 'An Englishman's the common name for all'), are worn locutions in a recognizable eighteenth-century republican accent. The explosive element, partly muffled by the recycled language, is the double policy — independence *and* the end of confessional identity. Singly, these are scandalous; but conjoined, especially as he argues they *necessarily* are, they reconfigure the Irish political landscape, simply in virtue of having been written as the axioms of a new logic that the French Revolution had introduced and that had now become the logic of world history. Tone's general position makes forgoing confessional identity a political act that in itself constitutes a departure from the British system, which maintains privilege, sows division and stimulates chauvinist feeling by assiduously nursing it, most especially and maliciously in Ireland. Yet the surrender of confessional identity is in effect the demand that the English Revolution of a century earlier admit (in contrast to The French Revolution) its sectarian and provincial basis at the very moment when Protestantism was being refashioned from being the religion of the British nation to the religion of the Empire — available at the dawn of the new century to the Irish through the Union. This changed the numbers game entirely, so that the overwhelming Irish Catholic majority in Ireland (expanding at an alarming rate) would be instantly transformed into an insignificant minority in a Protestant world-system. (This is central to Castlereagh's argument for Union). The democratic implications of all three revolutions of 1688–1789 — English, American and French — meant that numbers mattered more than ever in securing legitimacy. Tone never tired of citing the figure of three million for the disenfranchised Catholic majority and generally of citing how few Protestants there were and how much of everything they owned or controlled.

Within the British system — although rhetorically it had to be located 'outside' it, as the ultimate foreign element — the Enemy was Roman Catholicism. Hatred for Catholicism and love of liberty were a single seam in British national character or history, one regarded as entailing the other. Catholicism had a criminal, British liberty a heroic history. Tone's programme did not just challenge this politico-religious formation, moulded by centuries of suasion and propaganda. It actually transposed the positions of Catholicism and England in its schematic. England assumed the position of the Enemy of Ireland, of human advancement. Revolutionary France now assumed the role of Liberty, the world-historical cause that Ireland, with French help, could join by achieving independence through emancipation (or at least enfranchisement) of the Catholics and by liberation of the Protestants from their anti-Catholicism, the most virulent form of their slavery.

It is reasonable to hate an institution, community or system because it has a record of persecution and oppression, but to hate it by instinct is even better, the mark of a gratifyingly spontaneous personal alert system; if others have the same instinct, then it can be regarded as a definitively human and national trait.

24 For example, *A Letter from Earl Stanhope, to the Right Honourable Edmund Burke: Containing a Short Answer to His Late Sspeech on the French Revolution* (London, 1790), 12: 'Events are NOT to be attributed to the form of their [revolutionaries'] *new* Constitution... they are to be ascribed solely to their *old* wretched and execrable Government, which had been, for ages, the cause of the People's oppression, of their indigence, misery, and consequent despair. It was that execrable and wicked Government that provoked the violent insurrections that have happened in France.'

25 As in James L. Granger, *A Biographical History of England*, 4 vols. (London, 1779), vol. 1, 58, where, under 'Class VII. Men of the Sword', William Wallace, 'at the head of a few fugitives and desperadoes dared to assert the independence of his country, and took every opportunity of attacking the English'.

So anti-Catholicism can be historically and ontologically grounded in human experience and in human nature. Tone dramatizes the development of his hatred of England across a similar polemical range. Its growth fascinates him.The hyperbolic note is again crucial, as the crisis of individual hatred transmutes into anathema of the great enemy at a moment of historical crisis. Burke has a similar structure of hyperbole in his hatred for various groups or individuals — Jacobins, regicides, Anglo-Irish Ascendancy, atheists, Rousseau. The rhetoric of such feeling actually depends on its power to persuade us that no excess of condemnation is possible given the radically evil nature of the target; instinctive recoil from it is the source and the consequence of the polemical attack. The wince of disgust both precedes, as an instinct, and succeeds, as an argued or catalogued culmination, the assault. Like Hazlitt, the politicized citizen needs to be 'a good hater' — that is, in Jon Cook's words, 'not just being good at hating but hating for the good'.[26]

Tone's reasons for hating are clear. England exiled him, imprisoned and executed his friends: 'Judge of my feeling as an individual when Emmet and Russell are in prison and in imminent peril of a violent and ignominious death! What revenge can satisfy me for the loss of the two men I most esteem on earth?' (3.221). It massacred Irish Catholics in the previous century like game, so members of the Catholic Committee are, Tone avers, as 'Irishmen and as Catholics doubly bound to detest the tyranny and domination of England, which has so often deluged their country with their best blood' (2.68). It is doing it again now, it is opposing the French-led emancipation of the world, it is dishonourably involved in international intrigue — the list is long, yet the most grievous part is that England has always been so: 'England will desolate what she cannot subdue. It is a most infernal policy, but no new one for her to adopt' (3.246–47). Finally, the inversion takes place. Reasoning is not abandoned, it is confirmed by instinct. Yet the confirmation provided by the historical record is, in effect, redundant. For the instinct was prior. Writing his *Autobiography* in August–September 1796, he can say: 'My object was to secure the independence of my country under any form of government, to which I was led by a hatred of England so deeply rooted in my nature that it was rather an instinct than a principle' (2.304). In November 1796, he writes in his *Diary* of the proposed razing of Bristol in a French invasion: 'And I will never blame the French for any degree of misery which they may inflict on the people of England ... The truth is *I hate* the very name of England; I hated her before my exile; I hate her since, and I will hate her always!' (2.399, emphasis in original).

Is this Tone's dramatic/melodramatic version of his own development or is it an unwittingly dramatic exposure of Tone being overwhelmed by events and feelings? The elements are incrementally there at one level: a steady hardening of the heart; increasing resolve and courage in facing the monster from which no quarter can be expected and to which, in return, no quarter will be given; all-out vengeance. But there are two perspectives on this; one, already cited, the perspective of 'instinct', which is both originating and conclusive; the second, is the perspective of the noble cause, which has the defiance of failure as well as the 'energy of despair' at its core. He writes to Matilda in July 1797:

> Dear Love, I know not what may be the issue of this great enterprise in which we are embarked; if we fail, we fail in a great cause; we are not embarked to conquer a sugar island or a cotton-factory, but to emancipate a nation, and to change the destiny of Europe ... (3.112)

Debt of honour

This edition is to be welcomed for its achievement in establishing Tone's text, for

26 Jon Cook, in William Hazlitt, *Selected Writings*, ed. Jon Cook (Oxford, 1991), 12–13.

bringing together so much useful material that has a direct bearing on his career and on his death and for the excellent indexes, which make the negotiating of the three volumes so relatively simple. The idea was conceived, we are told, in 1963; T. W. Moody died in 1984, although his editorial decisions seem to have remained engraved here; the volumes themselves have been appearing over a ten-year period in a not very handsome set from the Clarendon Press. Now, apparently, the hardback volumes have been pulped and a paperback edition has appeared. It was always a good idea to create this edition, but the marks of too long a process are clearly evident. The annotations, for instance, were obviously begun before the databases now and recently available on the Internet were up and running. So there are many instances where the footnotes tell us that a particular item has not been identified; but it is now traceable on Google Book Search, on Eighteenth Century Collections, on a number of other databases, particularly those that, like ECCO, concentrate on the eighteenth century. Sometimes an item not identified in one place is identified in another; sometimes in the useful list of the sources for Tone's quotations, a source appears that was not identified in the footnotes. So the level of scholarship is generally very high but it has an unevenness that is clearly the consequence of having been in the drawer too long while the revolution in editorial sourcing was taking place. But there is a larger problem.

Tone's *Diary*, written for his wife and family, and Thomas Russell, not for general consumption, is his most remarkable work. The editors of this edition have not, however, published it *en bloc*; following a 'strictly chronological' arrangement, they have inserted 'letters and other documents whose dates fall within those of a diary sequence ... in their appropriate places within the diary sequence'(1.v). Similarly, the *Autobiography*, written in August–September 1796, has its sections separated from one another by a variety of documents that pursue and maintain strict chronological order. This is quite startling editorial practice. It is clearly based on the idea that 'appropriate'='chronological'. Moreover, this is a chronology based on the order in which Tone (or others!) wrote these documents; so that we can move from the frustrations recorded in the *Diary* in the early days of August, in Paris, 1796 to an account, in the opening of the *Autobiography*, of, for example, how his grandfather was killed when he fell off 'a stack of his own corn' (2.261) thirty years earlier. Or later that year on 7, 8 and 12 October, as Tone describes how he is devoured by ennui and anxiety while waiting for the expedition to Ireland to be undertaken, we are given a letter of the 9th, from Matilda Tone to Thomas Russell, which, interesting as it is, about her homesickness for Ireland in her lonely exile in America, dissipates the tension of Tone's waiting, endlessly waiting, that is generated in the *Diary*. Thus the *Autobiography* and the *Diary* are not considered distinct works, but rather as moments in a narrative that is coherent only in the sense that it begins with one date, the record of Tone's baptism of June or July 1763 and ends with another, the last item in Volume 3 (before the 'Addenda and Corrigenda'), the Orange song about Tone's capture, dated November 1798. Or, if one prefers to take the title *The **Writings** of Theobald Wolfe Tone 1763–1798* in a strict sense, then *that* narrative begins with the selected chapter from his co-authored novel *Belmont Castle* (1790) — although it is not the first chapter he contributed to that work — and ends either with his will or his last letter to his wife, 10–11 November 1798. That is the span of his writings, lightly framed at the outset by the official records of his early life and education and more heavily marked at the end by comments, letters, reminiscences and the like, but quite often interlarded with letters and other material from other people. And the running heads on facing pages sometimes have to do a lot of work to distinguish between time of writing and the time written about, especially with the *Autobiography*. It is not so much a clear as a simple-minded editorial procedure, which produces confusion. No rationale for not treating the *Diary* and *Autobiography* as autonomous works is provided because it seems the thought never occurred, although the *Autobiography* has generally been treated as one. The *Diary*, or the diaries, was/were not published in full until R. Barry O'Brien's edition, *The Autobiography of Wolfe Tone* of 1893; even then they were treated as supplemental to the *Autobiography*. The practice of publishing the *Diary* in extracts was established by Tone's son, William, in his foundational *The Life of Theobald Wolfe Tone* (1826), a mélange of 'memoirs, journals and political writings' that has been the matrix for all versions of Tone's text and reputation. It has generally been the case in the organization of Tone's writings that generic considerations are null compared to the chronological imperative. As a result, since 1826 to the present, their presentation has been both straightforward and warped, warped by various efforts to make their sequence plainer and in particular by the assumption that a 'private' diary is too nonchalant and happenstance a creation to have any claim to literary form.

The general editor of a series called *Autobiography. A Collection of the Most Instructive and Amusing Lives ever Published. Written by the Parties Themselves*, which published an abridged version of William Tone's *Life* in London in 1828 (*Memoirs of William Sampson* was another, in 1833), claimed that it 'abounded in matter which could scarcely be very interesting to anyone else' than Tone's wife. Then he promptly produced one of the inaugural versions of Tone's appeal as a person and links it to his own rationale for deleting the less important parts of the text that Tone's son, inclined to tinkering on 'private' issues too, had published:

> To a steadiness of object which is scarcely a characteristic of his countrymen, Wolfe Tone united the mercurial vivacity and *gaieté de coeur* which most decidely belong to them. These occasionally evaporate in mere fire-side joke and colloquial flippancy, which never being intended for the public eye, nothing but filial partiality could deem fit for it.[27]

According to this editor, who claims that Tone's story has particular interest during the contemporary uproar over Catholic emancipation, the personal details could be excised and the important matters, the political issues, thereby highlighted. Yet even with (maybe even out of) that defence of editorial interference there begins to emerge this personality, characteristically 'Irish' (although not in his resolve), whose appeal depends on the separation of his private relationships and habits from the 'serious' political matters that cost him and so many others their lives. Even the political 'moral' of Tone's narrative, which shows, writes the editor, 'what designs vicious and partial government may secretly engender amidst a disordered and irritated population', unwittingly enhances the profile of Tone as an exemplary figure victimized by a baneful political regime and envisions him and his colleagues as 'archangels ruined'[28] rather than slain revolutionaries. So the vivacious and the tragic versions of Tone are produced as a diptych, even though much of the detail from which they derive is omitted, such as 'fire-side joke and colloquial flippancy'. Thus, the confused and rather amateur 'arrangements' of Tone's writings have actually helped to mobilize the regularly suppressed 'unimportant' elements of his text — their casual, personal quality — to support the allure he has had for so many supporters and opponents of his political principles or indeed those who query, or nurture the query, if there is any need for having any political principles at all. To

27 Anon. ed., *Autobiography: The Life of Theobald Wolfe Tone* (London, 1828), ix.
28 Anon. ed., *Autobiography: Life of Tone*, vi.

them in particular Tone is a telling example of a charming, heavy-drinking and sociable hedonist misled into the abstract world of wild and farouche doctrinal conviction. When editorial policy, which depended for so long on the separation of the political from the private Tone, has so influenced interpretive approach or even capacity, it is more the pity that this new edition, textually so authoritative and thorough far beyond any other, should not have taken the opportunity at least to raise the issue.

It is deeply embedded. Tone's language and demeanour are 'gentlemanly', much given to sensitivity about his honour, his upright conduct, bravery, military status and ornament, his chivalry. These supposedly aristocratic preoccupations contrast with his avowedly democratic principles. ('I was a *Democrat* from the very commencement [of the French Revolution]' 2.295, emphasis in original). He seems much closer to Henry Grattan than to Thomas Paine in his social bearing, although the reverse is true in point of writing style, where Tone had absorbed much of the 'plain' style the republican tradition boasted of in contrast to the elaborate, even baroque, style of its opponents. Even so, his endlessly allusive writing — much Shakespeare and eighteenth-century theatre and fiction, very few references to the Bible — is tiring. It is no surprise to learn that finding apt quotations for a given situation was a game he and Russell played as one of their charade-like friendship devices. William Tone, obviously impressed by his father's code of honour, further reinforces it in his interleaved comments in the *Life*. Tone's mix of advanced opinion and anachronistic manners can be seen at large in the survival of other coterie honour codes — duelling, for example — well after they ceased to be legal, or even in, say, the wearing of a powdered wig as opposed to the cropped hair of the rebel or Jacobin. The dissonance is peculiarly important in the slanting of Tone's reputation, because its source is generally taken to be a conflict between a personality deeply moulded by the conventions of *politesse* and outlandish beliefs. For instance, Tone did not affect, like so many, to dress fashionably down, like a *sans-culottes*. He spent twenty-three assignats on a pair of cashmere breeches soon after arriving in Paris, and when he went to the west wing of the Tuileries to see the Conseil des Cinq-Cents, the 'French House of Commons' in action, he found the members very disorderly and in appearance 'extremely plain. Nobody was what I would call *dressed*, many without powder, in pantaloons and boots'. He thought the General Committee of United Irishmen who used meet in the Tailors' Hall in Back Lane in Dublin 'looked more like gentlemen' and as for any comparison with the Roman senators 'in their ivory chairs'! Yet he immediately adds: 'But it is very little matter what they look like. They have humbled all Europe thus far with their blue pantaloons and unpowdered locks, and that is the main point. The rest is of little consequence' (2.139).

But it *does* matter that he remarked on what they looked like and then contrasted that with what they had achieved. This conflict and contrast was, especially at that time, neither a mirage nor a minor issue:

> For honour's fight for personal independence is not bravery defending the common weal and the call of justice ... or of rectitude in the sphere of private life; on the contrary, honour's struggle is only for the recognition and the abstract inviolability of the individual person.[29]

This is Hegel attacking the hypertrophy of the aristocratic ethos and preparing his analysis of the bourgeois individuality and enterprise that had begun to replace it. The law or the state would take over from duelling the function it claimed to serve; 'in monopolizing the protection of caste honour, the State was actually expediting the liquidation of the concept of honour itself'.[30] For Hegel, in Carl Schmitt's words,

29 Georg Friedrich Hegel, *Aesthetics: Lectures on Fine Art*, 2 vols., trans. T. M. Knox (Oxford, 1975), vol. 2, 550; see the whole chapter titled 'Chivalry'.

30 Cited in Heinz Schlaffer, *The Bourgeois as Hero* (Savage, MD, 189), 84.

> the bourgeois is an individual who does not want to leave the apolitical riskless private sphere. He rests in the possession of his private properrty, and under the justification of his possessive individualism he acts as an individual against the totality. He is a man who finds his compensation for his political nullity in the fruits of freedom and enrichment and above all in the total security of its use. Consequently he wants to be spared bravey and exempted from the danger of a violent death.[31]

Tone and his United Irish colleagues inhabited, some of them even negotiated, that Hegelian 'aristocratic' to 'bourgeois' transition. Tone's career is, in one view, impeccably that of a man of honour, a patriot, a man in a uniform, of the kind the young Sean O'Faolain remembered as part of his own republican imaginary in the 1920s:

> I had heard of people fighting and dying for Ireland, but those had been people in cocked hats with plumed feathers, wearing swords like Lord Edward Fitzgerald or Robert Emmet — which in my view — or rather in the view I had hitherto held — was the only proper and decent way for anyone to die for anything.

Such figures contrasted strongly with the 'scruffy, angry' old Fenians he had actually met; yet they both shared 'these same noble, gallant, hopeless ideas'.[32]

Yet Tone is also a professional revolutionary in exile, an adviser to the French government, badly paid, with a poor incognito, isolated, politically thwarted, sidelined time and again by incompetents:

> This is most intolerably provoking! Here is the liberty of Ireland shuffled back and forth between two French *commis*, one of whom is under gross prejudices and the other absolutely ignorant. What is to be done? As to me, how shall I satisfy Clarke that I am not the dupe of my own enthusiasm in the cause, supposing he is gracious enough to give me credit for being sincere? The more earnestness I shew to convince him, the more enthusiasm I manifest, so here I am in an unfortunate circle! (2.153)

On top of all of which he is desperately unlucky, assailed by boredom as he waits for something to happen, takes to drinking heavily, falls into rages of frustration and humiliation, and in the end, when captured, his final claim to being an officer and a gentleman is dismissed with brutal glee. He was sorely in want of money when he was finally made *chef de brigade* (2.243–49) in July 1796; he had been seeking compensation from the French government 'for what I have suffered in their cause' but feeling ill-rewarded by them — although he still has that commission! — for which he had also petitioned.

> Went out with Madgett and drank punch — told him of my commission, having first sworn him to secresy. What shall I do with my rations? Tomorrow I will see Clarke and learn what report he makes on my letter to Carnot. If they would pay me that £150 it would set me at my ease, but I doubt it very much. I want money sadly. (2.246–47)

The drinking in Paris, a bottle of burgundy a day at one stage (2.98), is also part of the youthful, cavalierish clubbing that Tone and Russell indulged, although in Russell particularly the constant promises to reform his libertine behaviour and reduce his alcohol consumption is typical of a guilt and unease that haunted men whose republican ideals also included the concept of moderation and balance in the private life. But the male drinking club and the libertinage associated with it did find its proper literary memorial in the early work of Thomas Moore and finally found an expression of its guilt in relation

31 Cited in Derrida, *Politics of Friendship*, 140.

32 Sean O'Faolain, *Vive Moi* (Boston, 1964), 111.

to the displaced politics of Ireland in the *Irish Melodies* and in Moore's career as a political satirist and Whig insider. But in the short term, drink, without the politics, but with much singing and good fellowship, was preferred:

> ... better, wiser, far
> To fall in banquet than in war.[33]

Tone certainly fell in banquet often enough, and was hung over quite consistently—three mornings in a row in Belfast on 11, 12 and 13 July, 1792, which helps in part explain his reaction to the harpers at the Belfast Harp Festival—'Strum Strum and be hang'd' (1.213)—although that has been made much of by those who have a quite frantic anxiety to insist this shows that Tone had no sympathy for the early intimations of a 'national' music that was in any case soon to march to a different strummer on Moore's pianoforte. It is perhaps of as much or less moment as Tone's declaring 'In general, I detest the sound of a bell' and wishing himself 'in Turkey, or some peaceable Mahometan country, where bells are forbidden' rather than in London during his sojourn at the Temple when he was near several churches, although he did listen 'with the greatest pleasure' to the bells of the State House in Amsterdam which seemed to him an ideally austere republican city, with clean streets and clean, functional music (3.61). Still, however unfairly, the choice between the hedonistic and the martial life has been taken to contrast a vapid Moore with the dedicated patriots Tone and Robert Emmet. It has helped enhance Tone's (and Emmet's) tragic lives as those of young men of unswerving honour, not of sycophantic and determined careerists.

Specifically in this case of Tone's salary and his commission, the money exchange — or more exactly the wage (in two failing currencies) supplemented by a ration of bread and beef — overshadows the glamorous award of an officer's brevet, about which he is ecstatic. Carnot signs the brevet, but thinks a month's pay in advance is a good offer; Tone does not. So his solution is, 'I will put it to Carnot as a debt of honour, and let him pay it or not, as he please' (2.247). But money is not really convertible into honour. His formal letter via General Clarke to Carnot again argues that it was while he was in France, 'in a situation approaching to an *official character*', that he spent money out of his 'shattered property' and that, whatever proportion is paid, 'I humbly conceive as a debt of honor on the part of the French government', in the discharge of which Carnot should 'consult his own feelings, as a gentleman, and the honor of the Republic, on whose good faith I have come thus far' (2. 248).

Politically, Tone had by this time travelled far indeed, but socially he still spoke in an idiom that seems increasingly quaint. A business contract was being negotiated as a gentleman's agreement; the only stable currency for him was that of honour, trust, faith, and feelings that only needed to be consulted for the decisive answer to be given. Right to the end, his petitions were cast in this form. His only request to the court martial 'was that the mode of his death might not degrade the honour of a soldier' (3.423), '... he trusted that men susceptible of the nice feelings of a soldier's honour would not refuse his request' (3.390). But the response was, of course, that he would be hanged 'in the most public manner for the sake of a striking example' (3.391). And before that, his arrest at Buncrana, his transfer in chains to Derry, his four-day journey from there to Dublin, after being 'taken *through the city of Derry* with his legs ironed under his horse's belly ... and dressed in his uniform as chef de brigade' (as described in John Mitchel's well-known letter of 1845 to Thomas Davis [3.363], emphasis in original), provides the image of proud honour brutally dishonoured, for which the closing ignominy was to be the public execution. But Tone, like Jackson, 'deceived

33 Thomas Moore, *Odes of Anacreon, Translated into English Verse* (London, 1800), Ode xlviii.

the senate'.

Sean O'Faolain, introducing an edition of the *Autobiography* in 1937, said, somewhat fatuously, of Tone: 'His personality, the man himself, is a definition of Irish Republicanism. It is the only sensible definition that exists.'[34] It is, nevertheless, interesting that the creed had by then become a function of the personality, a crossover that was always potentially there, in the editorial construction of Tone's texts, in the *Autobiography*'s plain and programmatic appeal and in the gravitational pull of the disconsolately dispersed *Diary*, the first literary work in Ireland in which we witness what Mark Phillips calls 'the historicisation of daily life',[35] not perhaps emulated until Mitchel's *Jail Journal* (1854). In addition, O'Faolain's observations remind us that it is an *Irish* republicanism that he presides over from the grave at Bodenstown. There were republicans who were Irish before Tone, but there were no Irish republicans before him. Yet it is by looking at the earlier British variation of the republican tradition that Tone's particular extension of that politics can be better appreciated.

Jerusalem in Ireland's green and pleasant land

The greatest of English republican philosophers, James Harrington, in the Introduction to his famous utopia, *Oceana* (1656), described Ireland, which he styled 'Panopea' (England was 'Oceana' and Scotland 'Marpesia'), as

> the soft mother of a slothful and pusillanimous people ... antiently subjected by the Arms of *Oceana*; since almost depopulated for shaking the Yoke, and at length replanted with a new Race. But (thro' what virtues of the Soil, or vice of the Air soever it be) they come still to degenerate.

What would have been 'best in relation to her Purse', he claimed, '(if it had been thought upon in time)', would have been for Oceana to have planted the country with Jews, given them their religious freedom and military protection, for an annual fee. This would have brought Jews 'suddenly from all parts of the world'. Although they 'be now altogether for Merchandize', the Bible tells us 'they were [once] altogether for Agriculture'. They would have been the ideal planters. Otherwise inadmissible into a commonwealth, they would have supplied the English purse; and if Ireland had been so disposed of, 'that Knapsack', as he calls it, would have become an 'inestimable Treasure' rather than the burden it was for the expansion and development of Oceana.[36] This was a very English utopia — the Irish problem, after the vain trial yet again of massacre and plantation, solved — and it's still only the Introduction.

The first scholarly editor of *Oceana* was John Toland, born an Irish-speaking Catholic in Donegal in 1670 and a controversial and combative figure in English republican and deist circles from the 1690s until his death in 1722. The edition of *Oceana* was one of a series of works edited (up to the point of being extensively rewritten) by Toland that was aimed at establishing in the crucial years 1697–1700 'the Whig canon of ideas about political liberty'.[37] The quartet of republican 'heroes' was Milton, Harrington, Sidney and Ludlow. The edition was published in London in 1700 and reissued in Dublin in 1737, with a Dedication, Preface and a forty-four page 'Life of James Harrington' by Toland. In the Preface, Toland declares that Harrington 'far outdoes all that went before him in his exquisite knowledge of the Politics' and that '*Oceana* is, in my opinion, the most perfect Form of Popular Government that ever was'.[38] Part of his enterprise here is to assert the loyalty of republicans to the new monarchy of William of Orange and to relieve those known as 'Common-wealthsmen' of the heavy accusation of being anti-regal. He

34 Sean O'Faolain, in his Introduction, *Autobiography of Theobald Wolfe Tone*, ed. Sean O'Faolain (London, 1937), xix.

35 Mark Salber Phillips, *Society and Sentiment: Genres of Historical Writing in Britain, 1740–1820* (Princeton, NJ, 2000), 310.

36 John Toland, ed., *The Oceana of James Harrington, esq; and His Other Works* (Dublin, 1737), 36.

37 Quentin Skinner, 'The Principles and Practice of Opposition: The Case of Bolingbroke versus Walpole', in Neil McKendrick, ed., *Historical Perspectives: Studies in English Thought and Society* (London, 1974), 114.

38 Toland, Preface, *Oceana*, viii, ix.

Frontispiece representing 'republican liberty' from John Toland's edition of *The Oceana of James Harrington, esq; and His Other Works* (London, 1700).

derides the belief of some people 'that there is a pernicious design on foot of speedily introducing a Republican Form of Government into the *Britannick* Islands'; it was the republicans, he claimed, who rescued 'our antient government from the jaws of Arbitrary Power... [and agreed to fix] the Imperial Crown of *England* on the most deserving head in the Universe [William III]'.[39] Still, England, even under a monarchy, was a genuine commonwealth 'if a Common-wealth be a Government of Laws, enacted for the common Good of all the People, not without their own Consent or Approbation'.[40] In the 'Life' he claims the English people were duped

39 Preface, *Oceana*, vii.
40 Preface, *Oceana*, viii.

into believing Cromwell's rule was that 'of a Commonwealth and came to hate the name', but 'they never had a Commonwealth, but were interchangeably under Anarchy, Tyranny, and Oligarchy, to which Commonwealths have ever bin the greatest enemy ... Thus the People of *England* came to hate the name of a Commonwealth, without loving their Liberty the less.'[41]

Although republicans were inclined to favour a mixed government rather than any one of the standard classical triad of monarchy, aristocracy and democracy, in England republicans were associated with regicide and with hostility to regal display and frippery. In his *Life of John Milton* (1698), Toland tells us that Milton, when asked, 'what made him side with the *Republicans*? ... answered, among other Reasons, because theirs was the most frugal Government; for that the Trappings of a Monarchy might set up an ordinary commonwealth'.[42] In *Anglia Libera* (1701), Toland's anxiety to reassure the political establishment that republicans and royalists can live happily together has become almost painful to watch; royalists have their king and liberty and the republicans 'enjoy Liberty under a King tho they once thought them Things dissociable and scarce to be reconcil'd'. [43] Still, now they are at one: 'I mean by a commonwealth an independent community ... let the form be what it will. I fancy all considering men will agree that the royalists and republicans have always meant the same thing ... ready to pay all good kings not only obedience but double honour'.[44] But republicans in England, from the era of the Glorious Revolution in 1688 until after Toland's death in 1722, found it expedient to proclaim not only their allegiance to the monarchy and especially at the turn of the century to William of Orange who had guaranteed the Protestant Succession, but also to the national religion, the Anglican establishment. Toland sidles along in his arguments in favour of it, the shadow of reluctance never entirely dispelled. 'The greatest part of the People give themselves up to the public Leading in divine Things as well as in other matters', he says in *Vindicius Liberius* (1702), whether or no the opinions involved are true or false; much as one would wish them to be true, '[y]et *Religion* it self is not more natural to Man, than it is for every Government to have a *national Religion*; or from public and orderly way of worshipping GOD, under the Allowance, Indowment, and Inspection of the Civil Magistrat'.[45] Heaven has granted 'this Iland ... to be delivered from the intolerable Yoke of *Popish* Superstition' and, although Protestants are 'in general unhappily divided among themselves about som Articles of more or less Importance', they have so much in common — especially not being Catholics — that 'the *National Religion* ought not to oppress the *Dissenters* from it' on the ground that 'where there is no *Liberty of Conscience* there can be no *Civil Liberty*'. But '*Papists* ought not to be tolerated in any free State'[46] on the usual grounds that Tone, almost ninety years later, had to rehearse all over again — they don't keep oaths, they obey a foreign prince, et cetera; 'wherefore I hope I need not spend many Words to persuade *Englishmen* that *Popery* in general is an Extract of whatever is ridiculous, knavish, or impious in all Religions; that it is Priestcraft arrived at the highest Perfection ...'. He uses this passage at least three times; it is openly recycled in three different pamphlets within a year.[47]

'Priestcraft' is a term coined by Harrington and one used with relish by Toland. It is integral as a concept to Toland's early and once-notorious work *Christianity not Mysterious* (1696) through to his posthumously published collection of tracts *A Specimen of the Critical History of the Celts* (1726). Although it is possible to argue that the 1696 tract brought such furious condemnation from the Irish parliament because its subversion of confessional identity exposed the unjustifiable nature of the Anglican

41 'The Life of James Harrington', in *Oceana*, xxx.

42 *The Life of John Milton* (London, 1698),139.

43 *Anglia Libera; or, The Limitations and Succession of the Crown of England Explain'd and Asserted ...* (London, 1701), 83.

44 *Anglia Libera*, 92.

45 *Vindicius Liberius; or, Mr. Toland's Defence of Himself ...* (London, 1702), 108. He quotes this passage from *Anglia Libera*, 95–96.

46 *Vindicius Liberius*, 108, 112, 111, 113.

47 First used in *The Art of Governing by Partys* (London, 1701), 145; then in *Anglia Libera*, 103–04, and in *Vindicius Liberius*, 114.

48 *A Complete History of the Druids* (London, 1810), 28–29.
49 *History of the Druids*, 47.
50 See Justin Champion, *Republican Learning: John Toland and the Crisis of Christian Culture, 1696–1722* (Manchester and New York, 2003).
51 See Mark Goldie, 'The Civil Religion of James Harrington', in Anthony Pagden, ed., *The Languages of Political Theory in Early Modern Europe* (Cambridge, 1987), 197–224.
52 *Nazarenus; or, Jewish, Gentile, and Mahometan Christianity* (London, 1718), ch. xii, 40.
53 *Tetradymus* (London, 1720), Preface, vii.
54 See Toland, *Clidophorus; or, Of the Exoteric and Esoteric Philosophy; that is, Of the* External and Internal Doctrine *of the Ancients*, in *Tetradymus*, 61–100.

Church's sectarian claim to power, it is much more likely that Toland's target was not so dangerously specific as that. More plausibly, especially in the light of his paraded, tactical support of the 'national Religion', his target was priestcraft as a general phenomenon, whereby a clerical faction made Christianity appear mysterious to the laity so that it could manipulate through superstition and coerce through menace in the whole politico-spiritual realm. Roman Catholicism was the single most extravagant and threatening historical expression of priestcraft, but the phenomenon is and has been recurrent in all religious systems, such as the pagan Druidic one, though it does take on a rather Popish cast in Toland's account: 'The primate of these Druid Priests, was a sort of Pontiff ... Religion not only afforded them a pretence to interfere in the government, but ... to intermeddle in private affairs ... they claimed a power of excommunication.'[48]. There was also the heathen-derived sacrifice of human beings, in 'the human hecatomb they offered under the shape of a man',[49] burning people alive for misdemeanours, crimes, errant beliefs and sometimes just for the fun of it. So there was a distinction between priestcraft and Popery, but it did tend to dissolve in the heat of polemic. Nor did Toland's antiquarianism and his scholarship, neither of which he wore lightly, lack polemical energy, although his disputatious tone may be in part explained by the fact that some of his writings, circulated in manuscript, were part of an exchange or conversation between members of a select group and were designed to elicit pointed response.[50]

There is, nevertheless, legible within the English republican support for the Anglican, national religion, the idea of a civic religion that is sanctioned (to a degree) by the principle of civic liberty, however exclusively Protestant or English that liberty might be — not just for Toland and other republican writers but, for instance, for John Locke as well.[51] Debates about religious toleration circle around this topic. In effect, Toland's position in these debates is at first sight clear. He is for toleration — Papists excepted: '*Toleration* also (in *Scripture*, among other names, called *Long-suffering* and *Forbearance*) is no less plainly a duty of the Gospel, than it is self-evident according to the Law of Nature.'[52] He is a republican, indifferent to particular forms of government just so long as the form is governed by the 'empire of laws' and not arbitrary and damaging to the public interest. In those circumstances it can be said that a commonwealth exists and the function of a national religion is to bind the citizens to it. Toleration is necessary as a civic and politically unifying principle because there is so much disagreement between sects on religious matters. But what then was the basic religion, the spirit of which was once shared by all humans, but the form of which has become so disputed and various?

> [W]hat tale-bearing, what insinuations, what pumping, what wresting, what straining of words or actions both among Church-men and Dissenters, on the account or pretense of religion? ... frequently on the score of metaphysical abstractions, or chimeras that never had any existence out of the hollow noddles of waking dreamers.[53]

In brutal summary, Toland's answer was 'pantheism', a word he coined in English, and a concept that, as a version of 'natural' religion, had been developed in the sophisticated but scandalously materialist philosophy of Spinoza. This philosophy was for the few, an esoteric doctrine, whereas the current version of Christianity in England, so politically useful, was for the many, an exoteric doctrine.[54] It is typical of Toland that he should claim in one of his protestations against those 'certain Mungrel Divines' who accuse him of infidelity, that they 'study *Macchiavel* more than the Bible'. Machiavelli was, of course, a republican

The Wicker Image, illustration from 1810 edition of John Toland's *A Complete History of the Druids* (London).

hero, especially for Harrington, but was regarded as a diabolic figure by most of the clergy and certainly by the unfortunate chaplain who had in this case the temerity to attack Toland.[55]Most of the attacks on Toland were from clergy who would have agreed with (Rev.) John Leland's view of 1757 that Toland, 'although he called himself a Christian, made it very much the business of his life to serve the cause of Infidelity'.[56]

But, although this distinction was vital for the consolidation of a secret brotherhood of advanced (and politically powerful) figures, like his compatriot Robert Molesworth, the republican theorist and friend of Toland, there was no question that the great political issue of the day, at least until 1714, was the global conflict between England, Liberty and Protestantism against France, Absolutism and Roman Catholicism. Louis XIV's attempt at 'universal monarchy' had to be resisted, the cause of Protestantism in Europe saved and the Anglo-Dutch alliance, embodied in William of Orange, given every possible means of support by republicans. Two maxims, Toland claimed in 1701, should govern English foreign policy: one, 'that France *must never be suffer'd to grow too great*', and two, 'to keep *England* the head of the Protestant Interest all over the World'.[57] Toland's polemics against France intensified as the negotiations towards the Treaty of Utrecht opened:

> the *French* Nation, who are the ancient, the avow'd, the natural, and the perpetual enemies of *Great Britain*: enemies of that peculiar stamp, as ever to do us more hurt in time of Peace than in time of War; their Friendship being infinitely more fatal than their Hatred, and their Compliments more dangerous than their Blows ... They are now as much *French*, and therefore as little *English* as ever; they are bigotted *Papists*, and therefore little enclin'd to be *Protestants*; they are much more powerfull, and therefore much more dangerous than heretofore.[58]

To the republican beliefs that we should be subject only to laws and not enslaved at the discretion of others, and that religious tolerance would expand and enrich the operation and concept of a civic religion, Toland adds and re-emphasizes the need to exclude Roman Catholics and the related need to control or defeat France for the sake of the survival of Protestantism in the European world. Apart from the vexed questions of his materialism, Spinozism, or deism, there is another great cause that Toland espoused and that created around him the customary hubbub of controversy — it was, in the phrase that he coined, 'the emancipation of the Jews'. The engraving that forms the frontispiece of Toland's edition of *Oceana* contains among its republican heroes, in a Roman architectural setting, portraits of Brutus, William III, Moses, Solon, Lycurgus, Numa and Confucius. All of these are the great founding legislators of their respective territories, Rome, Britain, Israel, Athens, Sparta, Rome again and China. Moses is very appropriately included here, since Harrington claimed that Israel was a *polis*, like Athens or Rome, and that the Mosaic system operated successfully until the Levite priesthood became corrupt and 'papistical' and the arcane mysteries of the Talmud replaced the simple Word of Scripture.[59] Toland's *Origines Judaicae* was published in Latin at The Hague in 1709 and had on that account a fairly limited audience. His extension of Harrington's elevation of the Mosaic Republic to the level of the pagan, classical systems includes an argument that Judaism and Christianity are part of one original plan of Christianity, that the persecution of the Jews is not only scandalous in itself but also has the effect of divesting Christianity of the great charism that it initially had when it worked in concert with Judaism, including that '*of the Immortality of a Government*',[60] an idea not originally Harrington's about Venice

55 *Mangoneutes*, in *Tetradymus*, 144.
56 John Leland, *A View of the Principal Deistical Writers*, 2 vols. (London, 1757), vol. 1, 43.
57 *Art of Governing by Partys*, 143–45.
58 *Dunkirk or Dover; or, The Queen's Honour, the Nation's Safety, the Liberties of Europe, and the Peace of the World, All at Stake ...*, 2nd edn. (London, 1713), 3–5.
59 Goldie, 'Civil Religion of James Harrington', 218.
60 *Two Problems, Historical, Political and Theological, Concerning the Jewish Nation and Religion*, Appendix to *Nazarenus*, 6.

but in fact Cicero's, and now Toland's own 'whimsical absurdity', as one of his enemies had called it, about the Mosaic Republic.[61] Finally, the Jewish commonwealth, he says, should be renewed and refounded, preferably in Palestine — although Harrington, as we saw, had already suggested Ireland. Since the Jews, dispersed all over the world, were as numerous as the Spaniards or French,

> if they ever happen to be resettl'd in Palestine upon their original foundation, which is not at all impossible; they will then, by reason of their excellent constitution, be much more populous, rich and powerful than any other nation now in the world. I wou'd have you consider, whether it be not both the interest and duty of Christians to assist them in regaining their country.[62]

Toland construed Ireland too as the site of an original Christianity before it was defaced by priestcraft. It is difficult to trace any strong effect of his eclectic and ingenious scholarship on Celtic civilization in the antiquarian researches of the later eighteenth century in Ireland (though it had arrived, so to speak, by the early nineteenth). But it is probably the mark of a more generally republican influence on theories of civilization that Irish antiquaries were so anxious to find an Irish lawgiver, an Ollamh Fódhla, who, like Moses or Solon, gave to the civilization a body of law that made it unique and coherent until it was overtaken either by corruption or by catastrophe, such as military, diplomatic or intellectual invasion, like Christianity, either in its original or, even worse, in its Reformed version. Sylvester O'Halloran famously remarked: 'The reception of Christianity was a mortal blow to the greatness of Ireland.'[63] Toland would very likely have preferred pagan Ireland too, although he did admire the early Irish Christian learned culture and its resistance to papal domination.

The emancipation of the Jews was part of Toland's philosophical, heterodox materialist critique of religious systems; the emancipation of the Protestant Dissenters was part of his devious political programme in England, to defeat what he called in *State Anatomy*, 'protestant popery'[64] or the adamantine refusal of the higher Anglican clergy to concede to the Dissenters full admission to civil society. The tactical obeisance to monarchy and the established religion failed to gain for the republicans in general and Toland in particular the impetus they wanted for their exploration of the ways in which the decisive but limited gains of 1688 could be extended. Priestcraft, in this instance a form of internal Protestant sectarianism, blighted the hopes of his radical generation.[65]

Death of a Pagan

This double emancipation sought by Toland, for Jews and Dissenters, in the aftermath of the English Revolution and during a titanic war with France, was meant both to confirm and to widen the Protestant ideology of Liberty which English republicanism burnished to a high gloss to reflect, dimly at times, figures such as Aristotle, Cicero, Machiavelli, Livy, Sallust, Moses, Lycurgus, Cato and Brutus. Tone and the United Irishmen recognized themselves as belonging to that tradition. But the situation in Ireland, especially after the French Revolution, brought that Protestant ideology to a republican reappraisal that it could not survive. Thus, with Tone taking the lead, it too sought emancipation for a disenfranchised community — the enemy community of Popish believers. In this campaign, the emancipation of the Catholics became central to the inquiry into the relationship between England and Ireland and a switch from the English claim of Protestant Liberty for French universal Liberté. This was, in Irish circumstances in the 1790s, in keeping with the logic of

61 *Two Problems*, 6–7.
62 *Two Problems*, 8.
63 Sylvester O'Halloran, *An Introduction to the Study of the History and Antiquities of Ireland* (Dublin, 1772), 220.
64 *The State Anatomy of Great Britain* (London, 1717), 34–35.
65 See Simone Zurbuchen, 'Republicanism and Toleration', in van Gelderen and Skinner, eds., *Republicanism*, vol. 2, 47–72; Justin Champion, 'Toleration and Citizenship in Enlightenment England', in Ole Peter Grell and Roy Porter, eds., *Toleration in Enlightenment Europe* (New York 2000), 133–56.

66 Alexander Knox, *Essays on the Political Circumstances of Ireland, Written during the Administration of Earl Camden* (London, 1799), 163. For the comment on Catholic dominion, see 187.

republicanism, although intolerable to the practitioners of 'priestcraft'. In comparison to Toland's emancipatory campaigns, those of the United Irishmen are not part of a philosophical critique of religion (although that is implied), nor (at first) of an effort to stimulate a gradual evolution of the principles of 1688, but are instead a revolutionary attempt to replace 1688 with 1789, to replace religious furies and theories of limited toleration — with all the discretionary power that word assumes — with a rights-based form of separatist democracy. Castlereagh's one-time secretary Alexander Knox, who believed (or at least wrote) that the Irish Catholics had been granted 'everything but dominion' by the Irish parliament in 1793, wondered at those like Fox and Grattan who could not see that a reform movement, a kind of civil rights campaign, had always had hidden within it a deeper and more sinister purpose: 'Are we to suppose that these good natured politicians [Grattan and Fox] were caught, in the simplicity of their hearts, by that verbal bait of Reform with which the United Irishmen have covered their barbed hook of revolutionary Democracy?'[66] The inevitable answer is a yes, and the familiar conclusion is that Reform should not be conceded at all, since this is to get the hook in one's mouth. But the not very well-hidden principle in Knox is that it is as much a right as a power of government to persecute as to reform. In *Vindication of the Catholics of Ireland* (1793) the question of toleration was addressed by Tone, as spokesman for the Catholics, in terms that were later to be applied to the concept of liberty. But essentially, it is the same question: 'With regard to toleration, persecution may be negative as well as positive. The deprivation of political rights, because of the exercise of any religion, is for so much a persecution of that religion' (1.387). In 1792, Tone wrote but did not publish a reply to a pamphlet that defended Catholic exclusion: 'The whole of this argument depends on this: that it is impossible for the two sects to co-exist in a state other than that of tyrant and slave, and that all alteration is subversion' (1.181). This is at the heart of his objection to the system's principle; its operation only expresses its inner flaw. A system that is based on an unflinching Protestant bigotry will be undermined by Protestant bigotry; if the 1688 revolution is to become operative in Ireland, it must extend and refine its initial terms of settlement. Toland had asked this of it for the Dissenters. Tone asked it for the Catholics. Liberty is not dependent on confessional allegiance:

> The Protestant religion is not the essence of our constitution, for that was ascertained before the other had existence. The indefeasible liberty of the subject, and of that, the animating soul and spirit, the elective franchise, is co-existent with the constitution; it is a vital and inseparable part of it; it is the substance of liberty — religion but the accident. Freedom may be found where Protestantism is not; but shew me where it exists without the elective franchise. I say, in disfranchising the Catholics, the *Parliament* which did so were guilty of a subversion of the constitution, and not the descendants of those Catholics who now, after a patient suffering of one hundred years, come humbly to demand a remnant of a remnant of their birth right (1.181, emphasis in original).

It may be that Tone believed in the need for separation from England as early as 1791, although he denied this in the letter of 1793 *To the Editor of Faulkner's Dublin Journal,* which was not published, in response to a speech by Lord Fitzgibbon in the Irish House of Lords — which was published by the *Journal* — in which he was charged with being 'an advocate for separation'. He can at this stage feel Fitzgibbon's breath on the back of his neck; therefore he denied being treasonably in favour of separation (1.454–55). In his speech, Fitzgibbon had quoted from a letter sent by Tone to Thomas Russell in 1791, in which he had said:

> My unalterable opinion is that the Bane of Irish prosperity in [*sic*] the influence of England. I believe that influence will ever be exerted while the connexion between the Countries continues. Nevertheless, as I know that opinion is, *for the present*, too hardy, tho' a very little time may establish it universally, I have not made it part of the resolutions [for the Committee of the United Irishmen] (1.104, emphasis in original).

Tone's experience of exile in America seems to have confirmed his conviction that separation should be united Irish policy. That, along with full admission of the Catholics (and aided by the French to effect these aims and destroy thereby the British Empire), was the fully-opened programme.

In *An Argument on Behalf of the Catholics of Ireland* (1791), Tone does not, of course, advocate separation. The primary goal is to end Catholic slavery and Protestant tyranny; thence will come union and 'Ireland is free, independent and happy' (1.128). It was his combination of this vision, along with the separation from England and from the discursive as well as the geographical empire it commanded, that gave distinction to his contribution to the republican tradition. The structure of his thought is recognisably that of Toland—indeed recognisably that of republicanism in general—but with the key polarised terms of dominion and enslavement transposed: France for England, *Liberté* and *Fraternité* for Liberty, Roman Catholics for Jews. He recognized that when exclusion is a principle of the state, then *any* form of inclusion, however wise it might be in a given set of circumstances, can be construed as a threat to the whole system. The purity of this position was always anathema to Burke, who regarded it as an early version of a peculiarly modern fanaticism.

Even before Catholic emancipation was finally achieved in 1829, Francis Jeffrey, the editor of the powerful Whig journal the *Edinburgh Review* was warning of 'an independent state' being formed in Ireland with 'foreign assistance'. It could be that 'by the help of a French army and an American fleet ... an Irish Catholic republic [could be] installed with due ceremony in Dublin'. This could happen, he forecast, unless Ireland was 'delivered from the domination of an Orange faction' by the British government's withholding of support from that 'miserable' group.[67] Tone had not been seeking an Irish *Catholic* republic, although the new form of Protestant Orange tyranny and government support for it had already appeared in the anti-Catholic pogroms in Armagh in 1796. The sectarian policy that had manacled Ireland in the name of liberty had not been weakened but adjusted to stifle revolutionary republicanism, whatever its origins in England or in France.

Yet for all his efforts on behalf of the Irish Catholics, Tone alienated himself from a particularly powerful cohort of them when he made the error of deceiving the senate and dying a republican death:

> Truth compels us to say he died the death of a Pagan; but it was a Pagan of the noblest and finest type of Grecian and Roman times. Had it occurred in ancient days, beyond the Christian era, it would have been a death, every way admirable; as it was, that fatal final act must always stand between Wolfe Tone and the Christian people for whom he suffered, sternly forbidding them to invoke him in their prayers, or to uphold him an example for the young men of their country.[68]

67 Francis Jeffrey, *Contributions to the Edinburgh Review*, 4 vols. in one (New York, 1844), 613–14.

68 Thomas D'Arcy Magee, *A Popular History of Ireland*, 2 vols. (New York, 1863), vol. 2, 313.

John Toland. Only known portrait, as it appeared in volume 3 of U. G. Torschmid's *Versuch einer Vollständige Engländische Freydenker-Bibliothek* (1766). Courtesy of the Sterling Memorial Library, Yale University.

Contributors

Juliana Adelman of Trinity College, and a member of the Royal Irish Academy Committee for the History of Irish Science is working on a book provisionally titled *Science and Society in Nineteenth-Century Ireland.*

Joe Cleary lectures in English at the National University of Ireland at Maynooth. He is co-editor of *The Cambridge Companion to Modern Irish Culture* (2005) and is author of *Literature, Partition and the Nation-State: Culture and Conflict in Ireland, Israel and Palestine* (2002), and *Outrageous Fortune*: *Capital and Culture in Modern Ireland* (2008), reviewed in this issue.

Carl Dawson has recently retired from the Department of English at the University of Delaware. Among his many publications are *His Fine Wit: A Study of Thomas Love Peacock* (1970); *Victorian Noon: English Literature in 1850* (1979), *Prophets of Past Time* (1988), *Lafcadio Hearn and the Vision of Japan* (1992), *Living Backwards: A Transatlantic Memoir* (1995) and with Susan Goodman, *William Dean Howells: A Writer's Life* (2005).

Ciarán Deane is co-editor of the *Field Day Review*, author of *The Guinness Book of Irish Facts and Feats* (1994).

Seamus Deane is the editor of *The Field Day Anthology of Irish Writing*, 3 vols. (1991) and author of numerous books in literary history, including *Strange Country: Modernity and Nationhood in Irish Writing since 1790* (1997) and *Foreign Affections: Essays on Edmund Burke* (2005). He was the inaugural Keough Chair of Irish Studies at the University of Notre Dame.

Catríona Kennedy is a lecturer in the history department and a member of the Centre for Eighteenth Century Studies at the University of York. She has a forthcoming book, *Writing War: Britain and Ireland, 1793–1815.*

David Lloyd teaches at the University of Southern California. Among his publications are *Nationalism and Minor Literature* (1992), *Anomalous States* (1995), *Ireland After History* (1999) and *Irish Times: Temporalities of Modernity* (2008).

Ian McBride is Senior Lecturer in Early Modern and Irish History at King's College, London. He is the author of *The Siege of Derry in Ulster Protestant Mythology* (1997), *Scripture Politics: Ulster Presbyterians and Irish Radicals in Late Eighteenth-Century Ireland* (1998), editor of *History and Memory in Modern Ireland* (2001) and has recently published *Eighteenth-Century Ireland: The Long Peace* (2009).

Barry McCrea teaches Comparative Literature at Yale University. His novel *The First Verse* appeared in 2005. His book *Family and the Modern Novel* is forthcoming.

Sean Mannion is a graduate student in the English Department at the University of Notre Dame and was the Field Day Fellow for 2008 at the Keough–Naughton Centre for Irish Studies.

Christopher Morash is Head of the School of English, Drama and Media Studies at the National University of Ireland, Maynooth. He has published *Writing the Irish Famine* (1995), *A History of Irish Theatre 1601–2000* (2002) and has a book on the history of the Irish media from the 1550s to the present day, forthcoming from Cambridge University Press.

Francis Mulhern teaches English Literature and intellectual history at Middlesex University where since 1992 he has been Professor of Critical Studies. For many years editor of *New Left Review* to which he is still a regular contributor, he has also been Visiting Professor at the Universities of Bergamo, Milan, São Paulo and Johns Hopkins. His publications include *The Moment of 'Scrutiny'* (1979), *The Present Lasts a Long Time: Essays in Cultural Politics* (1998), and *Culture/metaculture* (2000); he was also editor of *Contemporary Marxist Literary Criticism* (1992).

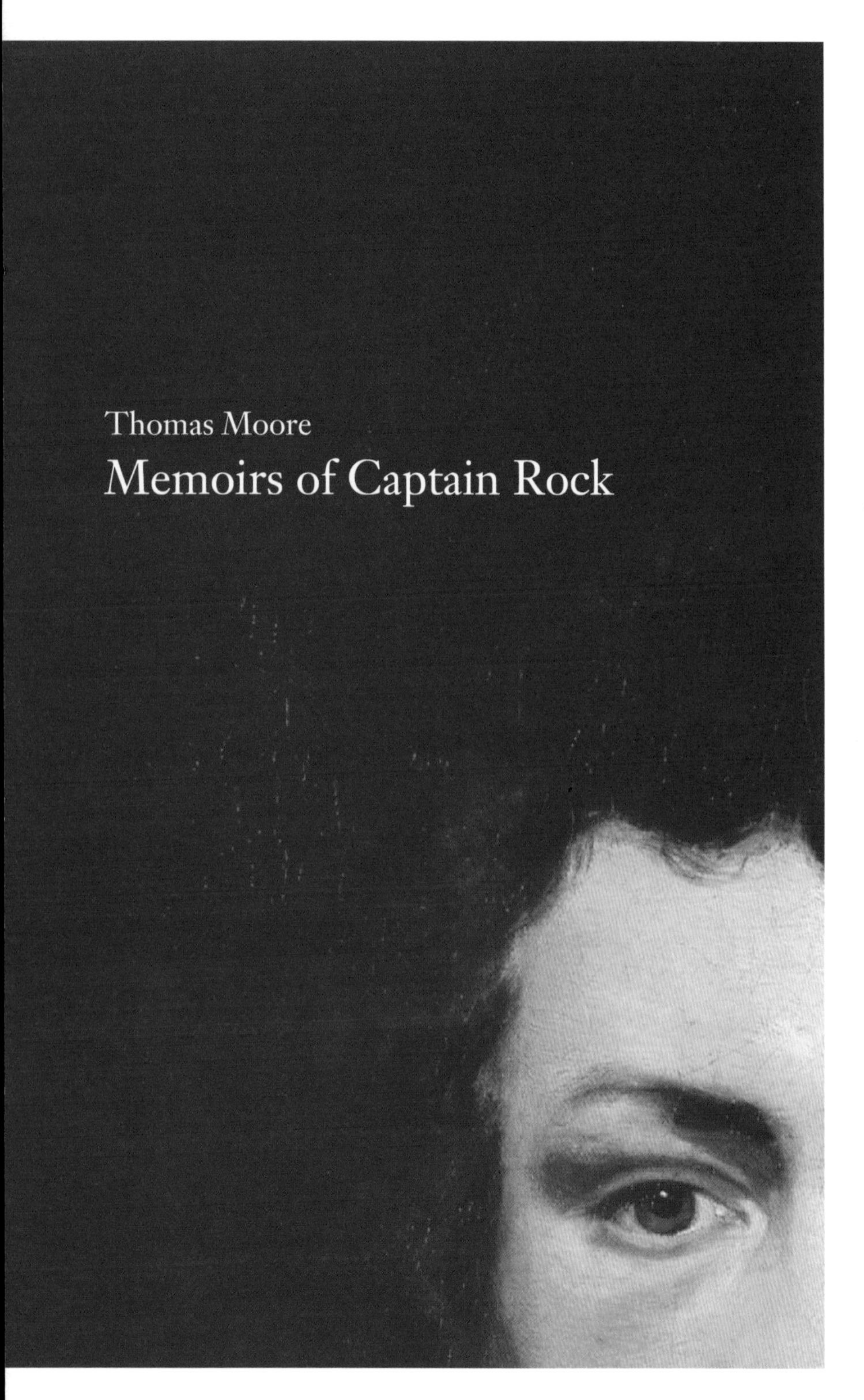

Thomas Moore's **MEMOIRS OF CAPTAIN ROCK** gives Irish rebellion one of its most memorable representations in fiction. Its blend of literary and historical elements secured it a place among the innovatory hybrid works of the Romantic age such as the national tale and the historical novel. This eye-opening edition — enhanced by learned editing, a perspicuous introduction and shrewd notes — will win new readers for what was, in its time, a phenomenally successful publication.
James Chandler, University of Chicago

THOMAS MOORE (1779–1852) was Ireland's 'national poet' in the century before Yeats. His *Irish Melodies* (1808-34), composed and performed for an English audience, 'to sweeten Ireland's wrong' secured him worldwide fame. But **MEMOIRS OF CAPTAIN ROCK** (1824) was a sudden and brilliant variation on 'the-smile-and-the-tear' rhetoric of the *Melodies*. Its attribution of Irish violence to the British state's support for a rapacious Protestant minority and its savage military and legal repression of a Catholic majority inverted Tory platitudes and helped to make the brutal realities of Irish life a subject of serious public debate. Six editions were printed in London in 1824 alone; other editions appeared in Paris, Berlin, New York and Philadelphia. This annotated edition, edited and introduced by **Emer Nolan** of the National University of Ireland, Maynooth, is the first to be published in Ireland. It is available in paperback and hardback from all good bookstores and from **www.fielddaybooks.com**.